MOUNT MARY
Milwaukee,

P9-ASL-071

The Making of the South Australian Landscape a study in the historical geography of Australia

MOUNT MARY COLLEGE LIBRARY
Milwaukee, Wisconsin 53222

The Making of the South Australian Landscape a study in the historical geography of Australia

MICHAEL WILLIAMS

Department of Human Geography,
University of Adelaide, Adelaide,
South Australia

1974

ACADEMIC PRESS · London and New York
A Subsidiary of Harcourt Brace Jovanovich, Publishers

74-1847

ACADEMIC PRESS LTD.
24/28 Oval Road
London NW1

U.S. Edition published by
ACADEMIC PRESS INC.
111 Fifth Avenue
New York, New York 10003
Copyright © 1974 By ACADEMIC PRESS LTD.

All Rights Reserved
No part of this book may be reproduced in any form by photo-
stat, microfilm, or any other means without written permission
from the publishers.

Library of Congress Catalog Card Number: 73–9483
ISBN: 0–12–785955–1

Printed in Great Britain by
W & J Mackay Limited, Chatham

919.42

W67

For Loré

Preface

From my office on the ninth floor of a building in the University I enjoy a broad and varied view across the Adelaide Plain. As I look from the busy thoroughfares and massive blocks of buildings of the central business district in the foreground to the endless miles of gridded streets, and their suburban houses and gardens and then to the quarry gashes and vegetation cover on the distant face of the Mount Lofty Ranges, I am conscious, as a geographer, of one thing—all have either been created or changed in some way since the onset of European settlement less than 140 years ago. It is these processes of creation and change in the visual scene, as man has made—and is still making—the landscape, that are the subject of this book.

Such an investigation is inevitably historical in its method but it is eminently geographical in its result. One cannot understand the landscape of the present without going back to the history that lies behind it, a process which also lends both perspective and insight into current modifications which are occurring with ever-increasing speed and impact. It is geographical because its emphasis is on man's relationship with his environment, on the creation of patterns in the landscape, and on the development of regional contrasts; the maps in this book are a special product of this approach. However, this investigation is not a catalogue of land-scape features, it is, amongst other things, a study of people who, singly or collectively, consciously or unconsciously, rapidly or gradually, made the landscape. Such a study, therefore, cannot stop short of the landscape features themselves, but where necessary must explore the minds of the men who made the decisions which affected the landscape. Their motives, attitudes, prejudices and preferences must be looked at. Having said that, however, it is necessary to stress that this is not a 'history' of South Australia;

the book is subtitled 'a study in historical geography'—a composite term which best describes the emphasis of the work.

What follows is an avowedly detailed study of a sizeable portion of the earth's surface for which evidence exists of nearly every locational decision made by officials and settlers alike. In this respect, the story of the making of the South Australian landscape may be unusual, even unique, but, hopefully, it may also be typical.

When South Australia was being settled so was the remainder of Australia and other parts of the 'Neo-European' world; in North America, New Zealand, southern Africa and even South America and eastern Russia. This study, then, may be illustrative of themes of formation and change in a wider context, as large influxes of people colonized the lightly settled lands of the world during the last few centuries.

M. WILLIAMS
Adelaide, 1973

Acknowledgements

Grateful thanks are made to the following authorities for permission to reproduce the illustrations listed below.

Australian and New Zealand Association for the Advancement of Science, and D. Darian Smith: Figs 35, 67, 89, 97, 98, 113.
British Museum: Fig. 99
CSIRO Department of Nutritional Biochemistry: Figs 75A and B, photographs by Mr H. J. Lee.
Department of National Mapping, Canberra: Fig. 111.
Longmans Green, Australia: Fig. 105.
Oxford University Press: Fig. 100.
South Australian Archives: Figs 7, 9, 11, 12, 17, 37, 42, 45, 46, 47, 48, 49, 69, 70, 78, 90, 96A, 96B, 101, 102, 103, 110.
South Australian Department of Agriculture: Figs 6, 76, 80, 81.
South Australian Department of Lands: Figs 26, 27, 28, 29, 32, 33, 34, 91B, 92B, 95.
South East Drainage Board: Figs 50, 51, 63, 65.

The ideas behind this book began many years ago, and some portions of it have been published previously in geographical journals and books. Thanks are therefore made to the editors of the following journals for permission to reproduce portions of articles previously published: the *Australian Geographer*, *Australian Geographical Studies and Australian Planning Institute Journal*; to Oxford University Press for material in Chapter 2 which first appeared in *Settlement and Encounter*; and to William Heinemann Ltd for material in Chapter 9 which first appeared in *Studies in Australian Geography*.

I was able to expedite the research needed to complete this work through support from the Australian Research Grants Commission (Grant No. A69/17227).

To Helen Connell who collected and calculated much of the material in Chapter 3, I am most grateful; to Elizabeth Steveson who helped in so many ways, but particularly in Chapters 4, 6 and 7, I owe a very great debt. The fine cartography of the maps is mostly due to the skill of Max Foale, and the now unseen, but crucial task of typing the drafts and final copy of this manuscript were performed patiently by Sandra Evans. Mr W. A. Cowan, ex-librarian of the Barr-Smith Library of the University of Adelaide read the manuscript and made many valuable suggestions. I thank them all most sincerely. Staff and Officials at the South Australian Department of Lands and the South Australian Archives were always helpful.

Finally, my thanks to Loré; her judgement and her encouragement made it all possible.

M. WILLIAMS
Adelaide, 1973.

Contents

List of Illustrations

Figure page

List of Tables

Abbreviations

Act	*South Australian Act.*
CLO	Correspondence of the Crown Lands Office.
CSO	Correspondence of the Local Colonial Secretary's Office, Adelaide.
EAO	Correspondence of the Engineers and Architects Office.
H.A.	House of Assembly.
L.C.	Legislative Council.
S.A.	South Australia.
S.A.A.	South Australian Archives.
SAPP	*South Australian Parliamentary Paper.*
SAJA	*South Australian Journal of Agriculture*, Vol. I, 1897/8, Vols. I–VII issued as the *Journal of Agriculture and Industry of South Australia.*
SAPD	*South Australian Parliamentary Debates.*
SAVP	*South Australian Votes and Proceedings.*
SGO	Correspondence of the Surveyor General's Office.
Stat. Reg.	*Statistical Register of South Australia.* (Annually with *SAPP*).

A Note on Metrication

All maps and diagrams have metric equivalents on axes and scales. On graphs the metric equivalents are usually on the inner side of the axes in italic numerals. In tables the nearest convenient equivalent is given in brackets after the title.

Because so much of the discussion in this book is based upon primary sources which quote acreage figures no attempt has been made to provide equivalents in the text. However, common conversions based upon fractions of a square mile, and rounded figures of acres and length are given below.

acres	ha	acres	ha
32	13·355	1	·405
64	25·900	10	4·047
80	32·375	100	40·469
160	64·750	1,000	404·686
320	129·499	10,000	4046·86
640 (1 sq. mile)	258·999	100,000	40468·6
1280 (2 sq. miles)	517·998	1,000,000	404686·0

1 foot   0·305 m.
1 mile   1·609 km.
10 miles   16·093 km.
100 miles   160·934 km.
1000 miles   1609·344 km.

1
Setting: Aims, Areas, Attitudes

Aims

'When, as geographers, we gaze around one question forces itself upon our attention; it takes a variety of form; "Why does this countryside look as it does? What has given the land its present character?" The moment we ask this question, that moment we are committed to historical geography in one form or another.' H. C. Darby, 'On the relations of geography and history', *Trans. Instit. Brit. Geogr.*, XIX (1953), 9.

'Australia is, perhaps, the country from which we have a right to expect the fullest elucidation of these difficult and disputable problems . . . Here . . . exist greater facilities and stronger motives for the careful study of the topics in question than have ever been found combined in any other theatre of European colonization.' G. P. Marsh, *Man and Nature* (1864), 51.

No book exists in Australia which adequately describes the way in which man has moulded and changed the landscape by creating a pattern of fields and roads, by changing the soils and the natural vegetation, and by building settlements, ranging in size from individual farmsteads, to towns to major cities. With very few exceptions, the systematic study of creation and change in the landscape has received little attention except by implication in accounts of the pioneer fringe.[1] No one has written *The invasion of Australia by people, plants, and animals*, as A. H. Clark has for New Zealand; no one has written about *The changing Australian landscape*, or *The making of the Australian landscape* as have H. C. Darby and W. G. Hoskins for England.[2] Most major historical-geographical works in Australia have been concerned with land legislation and the ever expanding edge of settlement,[3] while other authors have been more concerned with official and popular appraisals of the environment and their effect upon land settlement.[4] A notable exception has been the very relevant chapter 'Domesticating the land' in D. W. Meinig's *On the margins of the good earth*. Geologists have written about what lies behind the visual scene, but however good their analysis, it is about the bones of the landscape, and that structural skeleton needs to be padded out with the flesh of man's activities for us to fully appreciate what we see.

The idea that the landscape is made by man should not be new in a world that is growing conscious of the ecological implications of the increasing numbers of mankind and of the environmental consequences of his actions.[5] But for long the idea has persisted that such creation was to be found in urban areas only, an idea that has deep roots in the traditional Western thinking concerning the virtues of country life and the evils of town life. In the early seventeenth century William Penn wrote, 'the country life is to be preferred for there we see the works of God, but in the cities little else but the works of man'. He should have known better, for all around him pioneers were hacking out a new landscape from the woodland. Similarly, Cowper, an English poet, well over a hundred years later wrote, 'God made the country and man made the town', which again was strange as the open fields of Olney, Buckinghamshire, where he lived and wrote those lines had been enclosed a few years before, and a new landscape created.[6]

For anyone living in a 'new' country like Australia the agency of man in making the landscape is abundantly evident, although it is so taken for granted and so commonplace that it is usually overlooked. Spectacular development schemes to 'open-up' new areas of the continent are regarded more as interesting new geographical arrangements than the continuation of processes begun in the past.

The landscape of Australia has all too often been dismissed as so recent in origin and so simple in its patterns to be barely worth serious investigation. It is hoped that this book on South Australia will correct this view and lead to a greater appreciation, by the geographer, historian and interested reader alike, of the richness and variety of the local scene.

This book falls into two unequal parts; its design is depicted schematically in Fig. 1. The first chapter sets the scene by outlining some of the important physical and biotic characteristics of the areas which the pioneers had to contend with, and also by analysing some of the underlying assumptions and attitudes which have

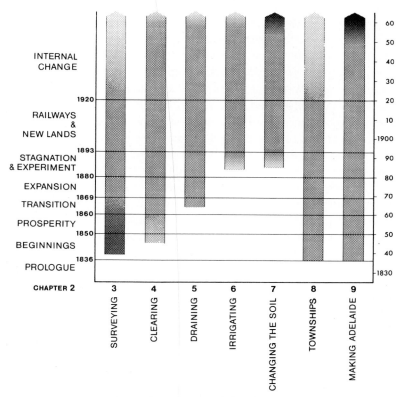

F I G. 1. Schematic diagram of the plan of the book.

coloured the process of colonization and the relationships between man and nature. Chapter 2 deals with the sequence of colonization within the 'settled' part of South Australia,[7] the pastoral areas of the Interior are not dealt with because the impact of man here has been slight compared with the coastal littoral. This geographical over-view provides a framework into which are fitted the chapters of the second part of the book, which are concerned with the ways in which man has created and altered the landscape through time.

First comes the chapter on the survey of the landscape, a process which gave the pattern of roads, sections and farms and also the interior morphology of towns. Then, in roughly chronological order, chapters are presented on four activities of purposive rural change : the clearing of the woodland, the draining of the swamps, the irrigation of the desert, and the changing of the soil, the last including a discussion of the inseparable topic of cultivation. Following these chapters on the activities which changed the rural landscape there are two on urban developments; one on the building of the country townships[8] and the other on the making of Adelaide, a city that covers only a fraction of the land surface of the state but contained, in 1971, 69·1 per cent of its population. These are the themes which are essential to the understanding of the landscapes of the settled areas. The increasing complexity of events as one moves towards the present suggests a convenient cut-off point somewhere in the mid-1960s. The tenth and final chapter attempts to bring together the details of these activities of change and to synthesize their elements.

Inevitably, such a plan has some overlaps, but these have been left so that the individual chapters on landscape change can be related to the larger whole outlined in the second chapter. It is possible that this integrated approach rather than a strictly chronological account of significant phases of landscape change, is feasible only in areas of the world such as South Australia, with a short history of deliberate action to change the landscape, and a wealth of documentary material on nearly every locational decision made. Be that as it may, the plan is attempted here for the opportunity it affords not only of explaining the evolution and transformation of individual landscapes, but also of presenting a synthesis of life and land in South Australia, for this is a book about the landscape as made by man, and his attitudes, ideas, institutions and actions are at the very core of this study.[9]

Areas

'It is sometimes said that Australian scenery is monotonous . . . In South Australia there certainly is a vast amount of dreary-looking country, but there is a very great extent that is pleasant to travel over.' J. P. Stow *South Australia* (1884), 183.

As our aim is to trace the main changes over the face of the South Australian landscape that were produced by the agency of man it is convenient to start with a description of the various areas of the land which constituted the natural setting for change. This suggests a fairly static view of the state of nature, which during the short time span of a century and a half of European colonization is reasonably accurate. These stable conditions might not have existed if our enquiry had ranged backwards into the pre-European centuries, for aboriginal man has an antiquity that is great, and which is constantly being extended by new archaeological work. During his evolution conditions of equilibrium in the environment cannot have existed; climates, vegetational cover, soils and fauna must have changed. However, there is little evidence that aboriginal man altered the landscape; he had not achieved the material culture of Neolithic man with its associated agriculture, domestication of animals, and development of arts and skills. His one effect on the landscape was the burning of the natural vegetation, possibly to drive game to slaughter, and of course, accidentally. Nevertheless, his nomadic life of hunting and gathering was ingenious in its adaptation to a harsh environment, and it was intricately interwoven with the conditions and rhythms of nature. Into that harmonious relationship of man and nature there burst Western man whose purpose was to change all he saw, to re-create in one blow an economy and society that had taken at least 2,000 years to evolve on the other side of the world. A new landscape was going to be made with startling rapidity.

The first settlers in South Australia found a land which, although locally varied, was broadly simple in the features of its physique, rainfall, soils, original vegetation cover and water supply. Despite a great deal of governmental control of the pace and direction of settlement, it still remained for the practically minded immigrant farmer to appraise the country and assess its potentiality for pioneering. In the initial situation the new settler would choose the location that required the least expenditure of his very limited resources of money and labour, and in his eyes, some localities 'appeared' or were 'actually' initially favourable for immediate settlement, while other localities were not. Ultimately, of course, many of the unfavourable localities were only as forbidding as the level of technology permitted, and clearing, draining, irrigation, and fertilizing, together with the provision of railways and water supply, were all factors which led to a revaluation of, and change in the initially unfavourable areas.

The Favourable Areas

Particularly attractive to the pioneer farmer was the upraised block of land that extends northwards through the centre of South Australia like a spine. This was where the first settlement took place (Fig. 2). From the Fleurieu Peninsula, the Mount Lofty Ranges rise to over 1,500 feet, but many broad upper-valley

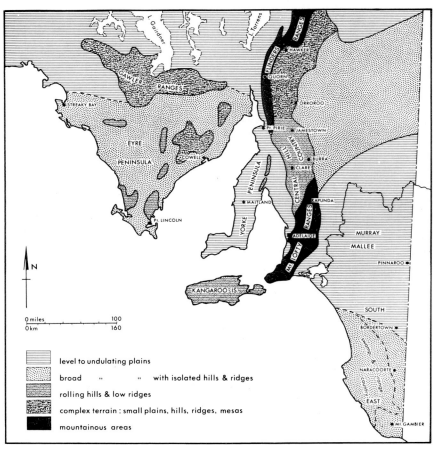

FIG. 2. Generalized terrain regions of South Australia. (After C. Fenner, 1931; A. K. Lobeck *et al.*, 1951; Meinig, 1962.)

reaches and some fault-formed coastal basins and plains provided suitable locations for settlement. Beyond the Barossa Valley is the Central Hill Country where the general highland relief diminishes and is replaced by a series of longitudinal ridges which separate wide alluvial plains and rolling hills. North of this zone and extending into the arid interior is the high ground and truly mountainous relief of the Flinders Ranges, which have an abrupt western scarp but a broken eastern margin of isolated hills, basins and plains.

Relief has a marked effect on the rainfall (Fig. 3) which is over 15 inches per annum throughout the greater part of this

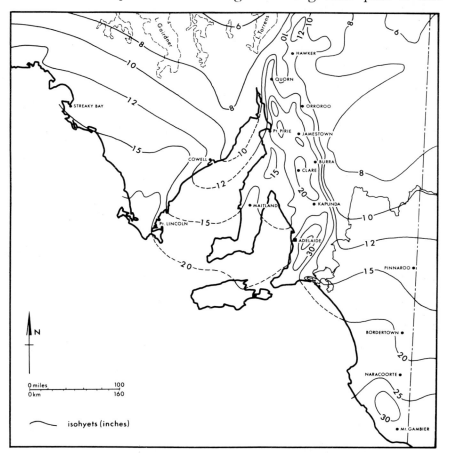

FIG. 3. Average annual rainfall in South Australia.

upland zone, and over 25 inches in the southern core of the Mount Lofty Ranges. The 'Mediterranean' winter maximum rainfall, separated by dry and sometimes searingly hot summers, was an aspect of the environment which took the British immigrant farmers a few years to become accustomed to, and reinforced their preference for the high rainfall areas of the upland block.

Broadly speaking, the soils are moderately fertile, crusty and hard setting loams with a predominantly red or brown subsoil which in the higher rainfall of the southern Mount Lofty Ranges tends towards greater podzolization and lower fertility (Fig. 4). The vegetative cover of the red-brown earths is savannah wood-

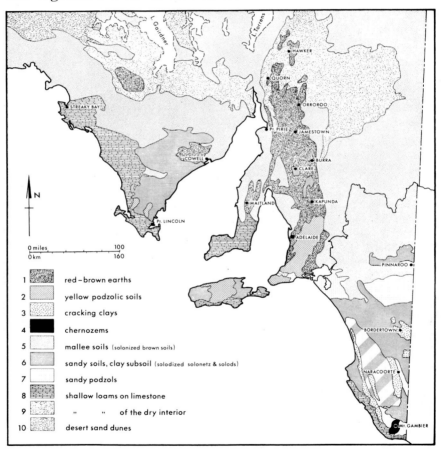

1	red–brown earths
2	yellow podzolic soils
3	cracking clays
4	chernozems
5	mallee soils (solonized brown soils)
6	sandy soils, clay subsoil (solodized solonetz & solods)
7	sandy podzols
8	shallow loams on limestone
9	" " of the dry interior
10	desert sand dunes

FIG. 4. Soil landscapes of South Australia. (After K. H. Northcote, 1960.)

land of blue gum (*Eucalyptus leucoxylon*) and peppermint gum (*Eucalyptus odorata*); the latter degenerates to a mallee habit as the rainfall declines northwards beyond the Central Hill Country, and woodland is gradually replaced by open grassland on the drier eastern side of the hills near Burra (Fig. 5). In the higher rainfall zone (over 25 inches per annum) of the Mount Lofty Ranges and Kangaroo Island the savannah woodland is replaced by a dense and almost impenetrable stringybark forest of *Eucalyptus obliqua*, *E. baxteri* and *E. cosmophylla*, which was largely avoided by the colonist. A fairly similar but smaller zone of eucalypt forest and

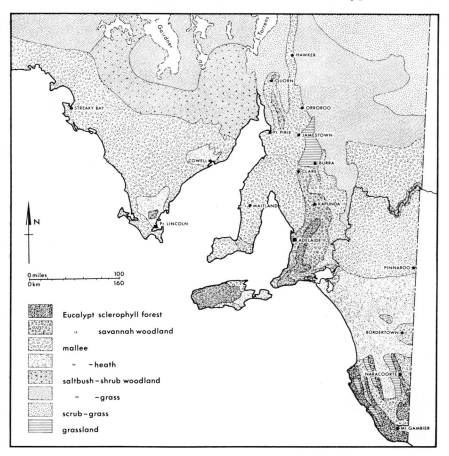

FIG. 5. Dominant vegetation types in South Australia. (After R. T. Williams, 1955; J. G. Wood, 1937.)

woodland on podzolic soils and some sandier soils exists on the high rainfall tip of Eyre Peninsula. The savannah woodland, wherever it occurred, with its herbaceous and grassy ground cover, provided good grazing for sheep in its natural state, and was relatively easy to clear when cultivation was attempted. It is in these woodlands that some of the early episodes of colonization were enacted.[10]

Equally favourable, but in many ways different in character, were parts of the Lower South-East district. Here, a complex topography of low northwest–southeast trending sandy and calcareous ranges separate wide level plains or 'flats', each flat being at a higher level than the one adjoining to the west, the easternmost flat near Naracoorte levelling out to a gently un-dulating plain of about 200 feet above sea level. Until the present, these flats have been subject to prolonged and extensive flooding because of high rainfall, the obstruction of natural drainage by the low ranges, and excessive ground water, which gravitates from Victoria and rises to the surface in the winter months. But at the southern and eastern margins of this uninviting zone of flooded flats and infertile ridges are the black loamy, almost chernozem, soils developed on the volcanic deposits near Mt Gambier, and the sandier, though moderately fertile, soils of the border upland, both areas carrying a savannah woodland vegetation, which merges into open grasslands on the flats in the centre of the region. Both of these areas were of outstanding attraction to early settlers.

Another group of soils favourable for early settlement were the black to dark grey clays of the Bordertown district, which were subject to excessive cracking in summer and to swelling in winter and which produced the typical 'crab-hole' country of the wheat lands of the Wimmera in Victoria, of which this district forms but a small western extension. The potential fertility of these soils when ploughed was not appreciated until the late 1860s. Some of the larger grass-covered flats in the Lower South-East, such as the Mosquito Plains west of Naracoorte, possess similar soils, but periodic flooding makes them far less suitable for cultivation.

The Less Favourable Areas

In contrast, there were the areas less favourable for initial settlement which occupied the remainder of South Australia.

Some of these areas, such as the dense eucalypt forests of the Mount Lofty Ranges and the swamps of the Lower South-East, have been mentioned already, but the remainder were of a different character and consisted mainly of the flat to gently undulating plains that stretched through Yorke Peninsula, the Murray Mallee, the Upper South-East and the greater part of Eyre Peninsula. The soils of these plains consist of a great variety of sands and loams, the most widespread being the highly calcareous loamy earths (solonized brown soils) which stretch across Eyre Peninsula, and occupy most of the north of Yorke Peninsula and the eastern fringes of St Vincent and Spencer Gulfs and nearly the whole of the Murray Mallee. These 'mallee' soils, as they are sometimes called because of their characteristic vegetation, have many north-west to south-east trending dunes which give local relief, and once the vegetation is removed the soil tends to drift easily. Immediately below the loamy surface there often occur nodules of limestone, which, along the west coast of Eyre Peninsula and the foot of Yorke Peninsula, constitute a solid sheet of lime-stone, that hinders cultivation. All these sandy and shallow soils are not naturally fertile; they are deficient in phosphorus and low in organic matter. There is also a lack of surface water in these areas.

An even greater obstacle to the initial utilization of these soils was the dense cover of mallee woodland or scrub, which formed an all but impenetrable barrier and extended 'almost like a blue and level sea towards the horizon'.[11] Mallee is a term which covers a large number of vegetational types including an endless variety of grasses and shrubs, and also trees such as she-oaks (*Casuarina spp.*) and Murray Pine (*E. callistris*) which often occur in localized situations. But the characteristic feature of the mallee is the way in which the dominant eucalypts (*E. dumosa, E. uncinata, E. incrassata*) grow in stunted fashion, the branches splaying out from a thick, shallow root in an umbrella-like cluster of stems and canopy. The trees vary in height from 5 to 35 feet, and in density from impenetrable thicket to a more open scrub with an under-storey of bushes and grass.[12] There was no way of clearing this scrub vegetation except by hand until the process of rolling down its slender stems was discovered in 1868. To the pioneer settler, therefore, the mallee represented a major obstacle. However, the invention of the mallee roller aided settlement, and with conclusive proof, after about 1890, that superphosphate fertilizer could materially alter the basic fertility of the soils, great inroads of settlement were made into the mallee lands.

The seemingly endless expanse of mallee soils and vegetation was relieved in a few places by patches of better soils, for example, the red loams near Cowell in Eyre Peninsula, and around Maitland in Yorke Peninsula. Both these places proved more attractive than the surrounding land to the agricultural pioneers during the period of rapid settlement from 1869 to 1880.

Even more difficult and repelling than the mallee lands to the pioneer settler were the areas of sandy soils (solodized-solonetz and solods) of the eastern parts of Eyre Peninsula, and the highly podsolized soils of Kangaroo Island and Fleurieu Peninsula. High rainfall and prolific vegetation of eucalypt mallee woodland with an undergrowth of low heath-like vegetation in Kangaroo Island and the two peninsulas masked their basic infertility which is due to trace-element deficiencies of copper, zinc and molybdenum. Fleurieu Peninsula, in particular, was the scene of early abortive attempts at settlement. The mallee-heath vegetation associated with the lower rainfall of the Upper South-East was quite clearly repelling, its local regional name, the Ninety-Mile Desert, being indicative of what the pioneers thought of the region. Not until after the Second World War was the trace-element problem of these areas solved—then agricultural settlement took place. Northwards, and beyond all these difficult areas, lay the semi-desert with an annual rainfall of below 10 inches, with amorphous sandy and sometimes loamy soils, and with a varied vegetational cover of grasses, saltbush, scrub and stunted mallee, only the better portions of which were used for purely pastoral purposes. These areas merge eventually into the true desert sand-dunes.

From this review of the physical and biotic setting it is apparent that an important feature of early South Australian settlement was the isolation of the initially attractive core areas of the Mount Lofty Ranges and plains, and the Port Lincoln district of Eyre Peninsula by dry mallee covered plains, and of the Lower South-East District by flooded swamps and the trace-element deficient Ninety-Mile Desert. Consequently, once these core areas had become fairly well settled, or at least the land bought up, the feeling of isolation was accompanied by one of confinement. Therefore, much of South Australian historical geography is concerned with the breaking down of these constricting barriers of difficult lands and existing techniques were applied to new circumstances, or inventions and discoveries were made specifically to meet the needs of the pioneers. It is these activities of changing the land that are the particular concern of this book.

Attitudes

'The goodness of God and the progressive nature of man are unquestionable.' E. G. Wakefield, Letter to Colonization Commissioners, 1835. *British Parliamentary Paper.* Second Report of Colonization Commissioners (1841), App. 35.

The initial appraisal of the landscape was coloured by the attitudes of the settlers and officials who had some marked preferences for a particular type of scene. The attitudes can best be summarized as belonging to man's age-old determination to conquer nature, subdue the wilderness and create a new, improved landscape. The South Australian farmer, like his counterpart in other lands in the 'Neo-European' world, had to gain a foothold in his strange and untried continent so that he could provide himself with shelter and food. Unlike many pioneers he was encouraged in this task by the inspiration provided by the utopian ideals of the Colony's founders, the ideals of 'civil liberty, social opportunity and equality for all religions'.[13] He was conscious that he was 'ushering into existence a new nation' and creating a 'busy civilization' where there had been 'a blank on the great map of the world'.[14]

The ideal new settlement was based upon a triad of linked themes, 'christianizing', 'civilizing', and 'colonizing', which were repeated constantly by the founders in London and by many of the colonists in South Australia. The links between these themes are seen clearly in the relationships between the early colonists and the aborigines. The aborigines did not look like the noble savages of some Polynesian paradise, such as Tahiti, who lived in harmony with nature;[15] rather they were depraved and ignoble, their 'general indifference to whatever is valued by civilized man' was puzzling, even annoying; it was a challenge that could be met only by the 'simple and sublime doctrines of Christianity'.[16]

As with the aborigines so with the land; the heathen un-civilized aborigine was but the human manifestation, even product, some would have suggested, of an undomesticated and wild landscape. The 'tracts of wilderness' in South Australia possessed 'not actual but only potential value' and would remain in that state of waste until labour, capital and enterprise were applied to them, a cardinal point in Wakefield's scheme of 'systematic colonization'. It is significant that the unused lands of the United States were called the 'Public Lands', but that in Australia they were called the 'Waste Lands'. The necessity to clear, fence, make roads, cultivate, and build townships was associated with the civilizing of the aborigines, an association underlined in 1847 by George French Angas, who wrote in the preface of his book on South Australia and New Zealand:

'My aim has been to describe faithfully impressions of savage life as seen in countries only now emerging from a primitive state of barbarism; but which the energy and enterprise of British colonists, and the benign influence of Christianity com-bined will eventually render the peaceful abode of civilized and prosperous communities.'[17]

The same sentiments were still echoed many years later; in 1862 Jessop climbed Mount Remarkable and looked over the settled areas of the mid-North:

'I reflect that within its shadow and within the compass of thirty years, the lowest degradation of barbarism had been changed for the highest refinement of civilization.'[18]

'The highest refinement of civilization' was a beautiful domesticated environment, the product of toil and technology in altering and improving the landscape from its state of waste, mainly by cultivation, a point that was emphasized constantly. In 1849, F. S. Dutton commented on the view from the Mount Lofty Ranges across the Adelaide plain:

'. . . as far as you can see, you observe how extensively the land has been enclosed and cultivated and the former arid surface of the plains changed into waving cornfields . . .'

and he could think only of the words of the English poet, Southey, to describe the emerging, familiar, domesticated, and to his eyes, English-looking landscape :

'Man's wonder working hand had everywhere
subdued all circumstances of stubborn soil
of fen and moor reclaimed, rich gardens smiled.
And prosperous hamlets rose amidst the wild.'[19]

A more detailed and intimate observation was that of Bennett, who visited South Australia in 1838 and again in 1843 ;

'I have seen the plains and forests around Adelaide changed from their original desolation into a continuous mass of farms—some thousands of acres bearing their crops of wheat, maize and barley—while in the more distant parts in which no track or trace of human being could be found when I first rode through them I ultimately saw spotted with sheep and cattle stations, with an occasional field of corn . . . I can scarcely imagine a more interesting scene than to observe a country in the course of being rescued from a state of nature.'[20]

'Rescued from a state of nature'! Like the aborigines the land had to be saved from being raw, untamed and natural; it had to be civilized, subdued and made. This attitude is not altogether surprising—the environment was unfamiliar, uncomfortable, stark in its largeness, and not a little frightening—it was a hard land to love. There are many disparaging references to the Mount Lofty Ranges where the forests were 'dreary', 'sombre', 'gloomy' and 'by no means cheering'; the mallee scrub was 'horrid', 'valueless' and 'barren'; and the open grasslands in the high country near Burra 'an abomination of desolation'.[21] The interior areas were generally regarded as repulsive and monotonous. Nearly everything in nature that was not of immediate and practical use was rejected.

Such views of the environment go a long way to explain the preference for the savannah woodland of the Adelaide Plains and similar areas. It was not only easy to occupy without clearing but seemed to display the artifice 'of land in the possession of persons of property rather than left to the course of nature alone', and having 'a degree of landscape arrangement, not to be exceeded by art'.[22] As Shepard suggests in his study of the early reactions of migrants to the landscape of New Zealand, the parkland type of landscape was not only a sign of gentility, evoking an attitude deeply rooted in the tradition of English landscape aesthetics, but it lent to a raw country the romantic notion of artistic achievement suggesting a previous civilization.[23]

And yet, there was confusion in this idea. A traveller to the woodlands to the east of the Barossa Valley described the district as 'almost fresh from its Maker's hands, man had scarcely interfered with it'. He could think of nowhere in England that rivalled its beauty, fertility or natural grandeur except Chatsworth, which, in the traditional British manner, he did not realise was one of the most artificial landscapes in Britain, honed to its appearance by centuries of effort.[24]

Thus, with few exceptions, the South Australian pioneer's preference was for 'cultured scenes' and 'smiling landscapes' (Fig. 6). But, in order to achieve what he liked he had to do something about it; before the view could be obtained the work had to be done, and a preference for the domesticated scene and a sense of duty in making it were hard to separate. This meant making the new landscape, first by laying out roads and farm sections which were the skeleton of any civilized scene; then by cultivation and the inevitable introduction of plants, animals and pests, and the destruction of the native vegetation. In this activity of clearing the land for the purposes of cultivation, perhaps more than any other, lay the key to so much of the South Australian landscape and the attitudes towards it. To G. F. Angas the sound of the woodman's axe achoing through the solitude of the Mount Lofty forests 'proclaimed the dawn of civilization and industry'.[25] In the mallee lands it was hoped 'to change the face of large areas of country from hopeless scrub to smiling fertility', something which the farmers did with such vigour that it was said later that it seemed as though the scrub farmer thought it his 'mission to destroy everything that grows above two feet' and that he had an 'irresistable desire to hack down everything'.[26]

In the late nineteenth century, christianizing, civilizing and colonizing lost much of their appeal; the aborigines had been swept under the carpet of the Reserves and were 'protected' from civilization, but in the rural areas something of the previous attitude was preserved in the aims of 'development', 'progress' and the population of the Australian continent, all stimulated by the new concept of Social Darwinism and the belief in the continuous perfectibility of man.[27] These aims continued to enshrine the Hebraic-Christian concept of man's dominance over the non-human world, a concept of 'exploitation and pride' rather than one of 'care and circumspection'.[28] These attitudes have persisted and redemption has been replaced by 'progress' as a force in shaping the landscape through this present century.

And yet, a curious paradox existed. By the end of the nineteenth century man's greatest achievement in Australia, in terms of labour, capital investment, the visual transformation and domestication of the landscape was the capital city in each colony. For many, however, the city did not represent the ultimate in civilization; in an increasingly urbanized, and by any standards remarkably centralized society, the capital cities came to be regarded as Australia's 'teeming sores',[29] as parasites which lived on the rural areas, so strenuously won and shaped from the waste, sapping them of their vitality. As in the United States,[30] so in Australia the increasing urbanization of the continent, together with the depression and unrest of the 1890s saw the rise of the cult of rural life, the love of the country, and the search for national identity, all enshrined in bush ballads, stories about bushrangers, and the whole evocation of the pastoral outback life which appeared more romantic, more ideal and more wholesome than city life, and, incidentally, than the harsh realities and grinding poverty that were the lot of many a rural smallholder (Fig. 7). It became the 'Australian Legend'[31] which was largely created as McCarty wryly observes, 'by Henry Lawson and his friends, most of whom could be removed only forcibly from the Sydney bars they loved so well to the great outback about which they wrote so well'.[32] The city was rejected, but it cannot be omitted from this book, for it is the most significant feature of the geography of South Australia today.

The urge for 'development' and the tidying-up of a naturally untidy countryside has not abated. One satirical writer has recently said:

'We live in a country which is so over-eager to make a point so enthusiastic that one can never control it, or work with it in a

FIG. 6. The rural ideal. 'A cultured scene', the landscape made by man; improved pastures, orderly hedges and fenced fields, sheep grazing, orchards, exotic trees and individual farmhouses, all within the cleared stringybark forest of the Mount Lofty Ranges.

FIG. 7. The rural reality. A pioneer family, c. 1890, at Hahndorf, near the same locality as Fig. 6. The stringybark has been cleared and the farmhouse is built of split logs, mud, a galvanized iron roof and stone chimney.

Milwaukee, Wisconsin 53222

reasonable manner. People feel temporary, impermanant; and to establish an acquisitive, puritanical, petty bourgeoise society with a mini lower-middle-class background is to create an ironic marriage in which one partner can only feel happy with the other if he can gag her . . . and beat her into submission before having his way with her.'[33]

The quest for tidyness and control is particularly evident in suburbia where people keep their gardens—their miniature piece of the country—in a state of discipline by snipping, manicuring, and polishing; 'it is as if some Sophoclean curse has come upon the district, as if the land were being punished for some unknown crime'—for being natural, perhaps.

1. Notes

1. M. Williams, 'Periods, places and themes, a review and prospect of Australian historical geography', *Aust. Geog.*, IV (1971), 403;
   R. L. Heathcote and M. McCaskill, 'Historical geography in Australia and New Zealand' in *Progress in Historical Geography*, ed. A. L. Baker (1973).
2. A. H. Clark, *The invasion of New Zealand by people, plants and animals* (1949);
   H. C. Darby, 'The changing English landscape', *Geogr. Journ.*, CXVII (1951), 377–98;
   W. G. Hoskins, *The making of the English landscape* (1955).
3. *Inter alia*, T. M. Perry, *Australia's first frontier: the spread of settlement in New South Wales, 1788–1829* (1963);
   S. H. Roberts, *The history of Australian land settlement, 1788–1920* (1924);
   P. Burroughs, *Britain and Australia, 1831–1855: A study in Imperial relations and Crown Lands administration* (1967);
   G. L. Buxton, *The Riverina, 1861–1891: an Australian regional study* (1967);
   D. B. Waterson, *Squatter, selector and store-keeper: A history of the Darling Downs, 1859–1893* (1968).
4. R. L. Heathcote, *Back of Bourke: A study of land appraisal and settlement* (1965);
   J. M. Powell, *The public lands of Australia Felix, Settlement and land appraisal in Victoria, 1834–91, with special reference to the Western Plains* (1970).

74-1847

5. One important and early work on Man's effect on the landscape which still stands out prominently from the great mass of literature that has subsequently been produced is *Man's role in changing the face of the earth*, ed. William L. Thomas, Jr., with the collaboration of Carl O. Sauer, Marston Bates, and Lewis Mumford (1956).

6. W. Penn, *Some fruits of solitude* Pt. 1, No. 220 (1663) and W. Cowper, *The Task*, Bk. 1, quoted in H. C. Darby, 'On the relations of geography and history', *Trans. Instit. Brit. Geogr.*, XIX (1953), 6, respectively.

7. Throughout, the term 'settled areas' is given its South Australian connotation, that is, the area within the outer boundary of the proclaimed hundreds. It is the basic study area of this book.

8. 'Township' is used throughout in its South Australian sense and means an urban centre. The North American usage of 'township' meaning a survey unit of 36 square miles, has no counterpart in South Australia.

9. See C. Harris, 'Theory and synthesis in historical geography', *Canadian Geog.*, XV (1971), 157–72, for a cogent discussion on the reinstatement of synthesis in geographical research and writing. See also H. C. Prince, 'The real, imagined and abstract worlds of the past' in *Progress in Geography* No. 3 (1972), 3–86 for a comprehensive review of aims and practices in historical geography.

10. For accounts of South Australian vegetation see :
J. G. Wood, *The vegetation of South Australia* (1937) ;
R. T. Williams, 'Vegetation regions', map and commentary in *Atlas of Australian resources* (1955) ;
G. W. Leeper (ed.), *The Australian environment* (4th Edit.), (1970), 44–67.
In this work 'woodland' is used as a generic term for all tree and scrub cover.

11. G. F. Angas, *Savage life and scenes in South Australia and New Zealand; being an artist's impression of countries and people at the Antipodes* Vol. I, (1847), 49.

12. J. G. Wood, 'The floristics and ecology of the Mallee', *Trans. Roy. Soc. S.A.*, LIII (1929), 359.

13. D. Pike, *Paradise of dissent: South Australia, 1829–1857* (1957), 1.

14. J. Stephens, *The land of promise* . . . (1839), 100.

15. B. Smith, *The European vision and the South Pacific, 1768–1850* (1960), 6–7.

16. *British Parliamentary Paper*. Second report of the select committee on South Australia (1841), App. 2.

17. G. F. Angas, op. cit., vii–viii.

18. W. H. R. Jessop, *Flindersland and Sturtland: or the inside and the outside of Australia* (1862), 261.

19. F. S. Dutton, *South Australia and its mines* (1849), 151.
20. J. F. Bennett, *An historical and descriptive account of South Australia founded on the experience of three years' residence in that colony* (1843), 43.
21. W. Mann, *Six years' residence in the Australian provinces, ending in 1839 . . .* (1839), 252;
South Australian Register (7 July 1851).
22. W. Light, *A brief journal of the Proceedings of William Light* (1839), 24;
F. S. Dutton, op. cit., 83.
23. P. Shephard, 'English reaction to the New Zealand landscape before 1850', *Pacific Viewpoint Monograph*, IV (1971), 3.
24. W. S. Chauncey, *A guide to South Australia* (1849), 19.
25. G. F. Angas, op. cit., 44.
26. SGO, 463/1866 (out);
Garden and the Field, VI (1880–81), 134 and VII (1881–82), 66–7.
27. R. Hofstadter, *Social Darwinism in American thought* (1955).
28. Yi-Fu Tuan, 'Man and nature', *Landscape*, XV (1966), 30–6.
29. A. D. Hope, *Australia*
'And her five cities, like five teeming sores,
Each drains her : a vast parasite robber-state
Where second-hand Europeans pullulate
Timidly on the edge of alien shores.'
30. H. N. Smith, *The virgin land: The American West as symbol and myth* (1950).
31. R. Ward, *The Australian Legend* (1958).
32. J. W. McCarty, 'Australian capital cities in the nineteenth century', in 'Urbanization in Australia,' *Aust. Econ. Hist. Rev.*, X (1970), 107.
33. M. Boddy, 'All neat, tidy and fixated', *The Bulletin*, XCIV (18 March 1972), 10.

2
The Sequence of Settlement

'The face of the country is changing for the better and it is being proved that what has been accounted waste land is in truth an unrealized asset'. H. T. Burgess, *The cyclopedia of South Australia*, Vol. II (1903), 943.

An expansionist, outward-looking view has coloured South Australia's settlement geography from the very beginning in 1836 until about the mid-1920s. The emphasis has always been on the new emerging frontier of settlement, and this characteristic assists the task of analysing the broad patterns of primary movement in the state, and the selection or avoidance of the favourable or unfavourable areas. This is not to say that developments were not taking place in the older areas of settlement, but these are more or less ignored here, so that the formative outward thrusts can be described. This chapter, then, not only describes the stages in the social, political and economic forces at work behind the patterns of landscape change, but, in a sense, synthesizes some of the regional identities which emerged within South Australia as a whole.

The sequence of settlement is depicted in Figs. 8, 10, 13–16 and 18, which are based on the evidence of the proclamation of cadastral units known as hundreds and the survey of township sites. The reasons for the choice of these two criteria have been looked at elsewhere.[1] It is probably sufficient to say that in most cases the hundreds had to be proclaimed and the rural sections surveyed before any permanent alienation of the land and hence settlement could take place. Because of this the hundreds tend to give an exaggerated picture of the absolute amount of land settled at any one time, but a good indication of the relative sequence of settlement. The distribution of township sites adds precision to the picture by suggesting the presence of a core of well-settled land. Railways also have been included on the maps because they indicate the main patterns of circulation that evolved in the newly colonized areas, and in the later phases of settlement to 1920, they were also the spearheads of new expansion. After 1920, however, other criteria must be used to indicate geographical change as internal re-organization becomes more dominant than the extension of frontier settlement.

It should be stressed that a thin veneer of pastoral settlement had been laid over much of the landscape before hundred proclamation and land alienation occurred. This veneer consisted of stations, and out-stations, wells, tracks and a few townships and ports which were soon obliterated or incorporated with the impact of the agriculturist. Undoubtedly the main contribution of the pastoralist to the landscape was that he was the empirical tester of the environment, the person who found the outer climatically defined limits of settlement and the inner variations of a vegetational, soil and water supply nature.

Prologue to Settlement

The conditions which led to the founding of South Australia and the principles of colonization which were adopted had an undeniable effect upon the course of settlement, both in its pattern and its mode.[2]

The early nineteenth century was a period of economic and social discontent in Britain. Internally the Industrial Revolution was under way : overseas, the American colonies had been lost, leaving bitter memories, and other colonial enterprises such as the Cape Colony, Swan River and New South Wales had failed or were only an indifferent success. Others were bordering on revolt, the Canadian uprisings finally erupting in 1837. It seemed to some economic and political theorists that both the internal and the external problems could be resolved and rationalized by a scheme of orderly colonization which absorbed the poor and unemployed at home, and established a new and stable colonial society overseas.

Of the many people involved in the planning of South Australia,

E. G. Wakefield must be singled out as the one person who did more than any other to weld the many theories together into a plan of 'systematic colonization'. The main principles of his eclectic system of colonization were firstly, that land should be sold at a minimum price and that the revenue obtained should be used to assist the emigration of new settlers. Secondly, the minimum or 'sufficient price' theory, coupled with the device of selling land mainly in sections of about 80 acres for cash down at auctions, ensured that the new migrants would work for established capitalist farmers until such time as they saved enough money to become independent proprietors. The high price of land was designed to discourage pastoralism and encourage more intensive forms of land use. Thirdly, the volume and pace of colonization should be regulated by the amount of land available, and settlement should expand in contigous blocks. Implicit in these proposals were the idea of the survey of the land prior to its alienation and an emphasis on family colonization, although large, capitalist landowners were also encouraged. These principles were aimed primarily against the transportation of convicts and bonded servants, and against the problems of squatter occupation, both of which had bedevilled the early years of settlement in all other parts of Australia. Land, and its survey and disposal, was the key-stone of the new experiment which aimed at producing a soberly industrious, middle-class society of agriculturists. The discovery of the southern coast of Australia and the exploration of the River Murray down to its mouth provided the theorists with a locale for their experiment, and in 1836 the first colonists landed on the coast near what is now Adelaide.

In this summary statement of the origins of South Australia two points need emphasis and elaboration. First, the colonization itself was late, and it was a symbol of the technological superiority and population growth of Europe generally, but particularly, at this time, of Britain. The colonists came from a society which had welded science and technology together to produce the beginnings of modern industrialized society. After a few halting years of semi-subsistence, South Australia adopted the tools, methods and machinery and moved rapidly to become a specialized grain, wool, and also mineral producing region linked to a world-wide economic system, centred on the British 'metropolis'.

Secondly, the idea of the colony was being formulated in the minds of its originators at a time of social and democratic change which asserted the independence of the individual and the desirability of individual holdings. Nevertheless, it was recognized that, in order to achieve an ideal society, planning was essential, first from afar, and later, when the colony became self-governing in 1857, from within South Australia. The whole of Australia was remarkably bureaucratic during the nineteenth century but South Australia was probably more so than most other parts.[3] Settlement was controlled carefully and there was always an underlying and conscious plan for most of the actions taken. It is this curious blend of the theoretical and the practical that characterizes so much of South Australian historical geography.

Beginnings, 1836–49

After the colonists landed near Adelaide in 1837, their most pressing need was to cultivate the land so that they might become self-supporting in food. But because of the delays in the survey of the rural sections and some initial mismanagement of affairs, the colonists remained in Adelaide, and it was not until early 1840 that they started farming in earnest and were said to be 'going into the interior in shoals'. The direction of movement from the Adelaide nucleus was twofold : first there was a thrust southwards into the coastal plains and basins of Noarlunga and Willunga, and secondly a move across to the eastern side of the Mount Lofty Ranges, and then south towards the mouth of the River Murray (Fig. 8). The central Mount Lofty Ranges were avoided because of the steep slopes, podzolized soils and cover of dense stringy-bark forest.

The coastal plains and basins were covered with alluvial and colluvial soils, and were well watered by streams draining the Mount Lofty Ranges. Their savannah woodland vegetation required little clearing for cultivation, and the depasturing of stock was easy. The coastal plains north of Port Adelaide were not settled, however, because of the widely-held view that the rainfall was insufficient for cultivation. Throughout the area, some 13,513 acres of land were enclosed, of which 1,977 were under cultivation, and a great number of small agricultural settlements, or 'villages',

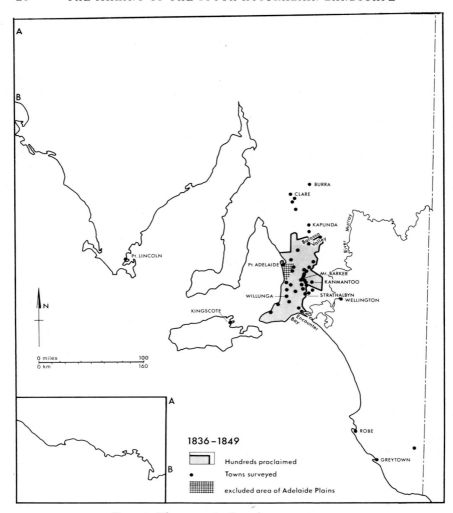

FIG. 8. The spread of settlement, 1836–49.

grew up on the plains around Adelaide. A few of these villages, such as Hindmarsh, Bowden and Thebarton, were large, with populations of between 100 and 600. They were really industrial accretions around Adelaide, and Port Adelaide, which had gathered all the ancillary trades, crafts and professions that benefited the main town and port of the colony.

In the coastal basins to the south, the villages were more

scattered and larger than their counterparts on the Adelaide plain, and the size and the range of the services of Willunga, Noarlunga, McLaren Vale and Morphett Vale were a good measure of the intensity and success of settlement in this area.

The second concentration of settlement, on the eastern side of the Ranges, was in a broadly similar environment. By 1840, a string of small settlements had been established between Mount Barker and Strathalbyn, and 2,036 acres of land enclosed, of which 646 were under cultivation. Although little land was taken up for agriculture between Strathalbyn and the Murray mouth at this time, the possibility of river navigation and trade was a constant lure to settlers in the eastern foothills. The area near where the River Murray broke through the barrier of coastal dunes was particularly enticing because of predictions that a port of transhipment was almost bound to be located somewhere in the vicinity. Already two small settlements existed around the shores of Encounter Bay and Lake Alexandrina.

Beyond the main core of settlement on either side of the Ranges, there were a number of isolated communities such as Wellington, a crossing point on the River Murray, Port Lincoln, at the tip of Eyre Peninsula (an alternative but rejected site for the capital) and Kingscote, a whaling station, on Kangaroo Island.

The later years of the 1840s saw the consolidation of agriculture in the original core of settlement around Adelaide and the establishment of new sub-centres in other places, for example, in the Barossa Valley, about thirty miles north-east of Adelaide, near Clare in the Central Hill Country, and at Robe and Greytown in the Lower South-East where the pastoral estates needed shipping points. But of greater significance than all these were the discovery and mining of copper at Kapunda in 1843 and at Burra in 1844, and at Kanmantoo, east of Mount Barker in 1846. The mines at Burra and Kapunda were the most important and focused attention on the Central Hill Country. They brought about a major influx of capital and people into the colony. By the end of the period in 1849, minerals constituted about 67 per cent of the value of exports of the infant colony compared with 29 per cent for wool and 4 per cent for wheat and breadstuffs, which was a good measure of the importance of mining in the economy at that time. Yet all this should not lead one to underestimate the progress that was being made in agriculture. Once the initial period of experimentation was over and the predominantly British population had acclimatized itself to its new 'Mediterranean' environment, the amount of arable land was expanded. In 1845 there were 1,267 farmers and 26,218 acres of cultivated land, and by 1848 the number of farmers had risen to 1,846 and the acreage had nearly doubled to 48,912. The local invention of Ridley's 'stripper', a small-scale harvesting machine admirably suited to the small 80-acre sections that predominated at this time, was a factor in the expansion of agriculture, and a portent of the ability of the South Australian pioneer to adapt himself to, and to overcome some of the difficulties of his new environment (Fig. 9).

The original Wakefieldian ideal of a self-supporting society of agriculturalists on freehold farms, worked by a sturdy middle-class yeomanry, was all but achieved in these early years. The newly domesticated landscape of the coastal plains and basins,

FIG. 9. Farming in the lightly timbered lands near Mt Gambier, c. 1880. The four-horse teams are pulling large Clark 'strippers'. In the background is a wire sheaf-binder.

and of the eastern slopes of the Mount Lofty Ranges, south to
Encounter Bay, was subdivided into 80-acre sections, nearly every
section a property in itself, with its house and barn. It was the
cause of some pride and sober self-congratulation, for the South
Australian pioneer was well aware of the solid success he had made
of his colonization venture, which was in marked contrast to the
beginnings in other colonies.

Prosperity, 1850–59

The gradual and comfortable progress of the colony in the
previous years was shattered by the gold discoveries in Victoria in
1851, which caused an increase in the population of that colony by
nearly half a million during the next ten years and so acted as a
stimulus to the wheat growers of South Australia by opening up
a new market for their produce. With a rush of optimism new
hundreds were proclaimed eastwards towards the River Murray
but more particularly northwards in the Central Hill Country
which had a vegetation cover and soils similar to those of the
already well-tried and well-known areas on the flanks of the
Mount Lofty Ranges. Moreover, it was an area to which attention
had already been directed by the copper mines of Kapunda and
Burra (Fig. 10).

Developments, 1850–54

The new hundreds created through the optimism generated by the
gold rush were not needed immediately for settlement, so land in
them was not taken up because there was still plenty available in
the old nucleus of hundreds near Adelaide. Therefore, wheat
acreages increased markedly in the Adelaide plains during the
first half of the decade. The land was well farmed and well fenced,
and 'reaping and winnowing machines were everywhere'. Viewed
from the adjacent upland slopes the plain and basins with 'their
square enclosures of varied crops had a map-like effect'.[4] The
prosperity of these coastal areas was reflected as much in the
towns as in the land itself, and the four existing large centres of the
Southern basins were augmented by Reynella and Aldinga.
    The new demand for food succeeded in lessening the prejudice
that existed about the plains immediately north of Adelaide into

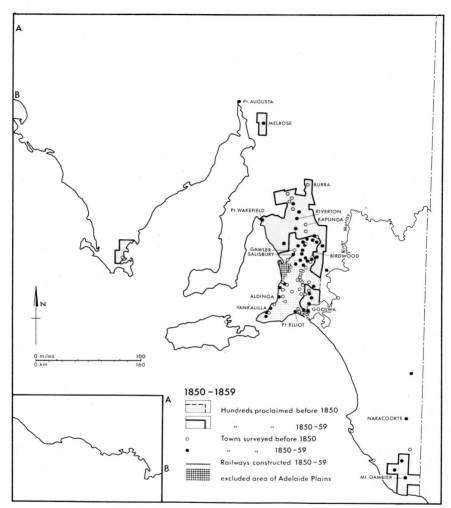

FIG. 10. The spread of settlement, 1850–59.

which settlement was extending; Salisbury was in this new area of colonization and was said to have 'sprung up like a mushroom'. But farther north the 'amazing extent' of the Gawler Scrub, which covered the coastal plains to Port Wakefield, was still regarded as an unfavourable area. It was not cleared and settled for another twenty years (despite the fact that it was blocked out in hundreds as early as 1856) as the lack of townships testifies (Fig. 10).

On the eastern side of the Mount Lofty Ranges the greatest expansion of settlement had occurred in the upper valleys of the Rivers Torrens and Onkaparinga where the extent of cultivation, the number of townships and the capacity and number of flour mills rivalled those of the earlier settled and prosperous southern coastal basins. But the great need of this area was an outlet for produce, and from 1856 onwards farmers throughout the whole of the eastern plains and foothills agitated strongly for a tramway to Goolwa to join the existing line that carried the river cargoes landed at Goolwa to the ocean-going ships docked at Port Elliot.[5]

Away from the main core of settlement, agriculture was beginning in a new and separate nucleus, in the fertile, volcanically derived soils near Mount Gambier in the Lower South-East district. Expansion was limited by the extensive swamps to the west and north, but attention was being paid to the well drained savannah woodland that flanked the swamps in the east and extended along the border with Victoria towards Naracoorte. Like their counterparts in the eastern foothills of the Mount Lofty Ranges, the farmers of Mount Gambier were agitating for cheap transport to the coast, and investigations into a variety of tramway routes to various ports were carried out in 1858. This was a measure of the success and promise of this new settlement.[6]

New isolated townships arose at Melrose near the Mt Remarkable copper mine in the southern Flinders Ranges and at Port Augusta, which was a major wool outport for the extensive pastoral estates that stretched northwards along the line of the Flinders Ranges and southwards towards the main body of agricultural settlement. Port Wakefield, at the head of St Vincent Gulf, was created mainly for the export of Burra copper, and later it imported coal for the mines and smelters.

Developments, 1855–59

During the second half of the 1850s there was a marked change in the locale of colonization. Up till 1855 the modest expansion of townships and agricultural settlement had occurred within the hundreds proclaimed before 1850. But after 1856 a new and distinctive sub-region of colonization began to emerge in the western part of the Central Hill Country in those hundreds proclaimed in 1851 and lying between Kapunda and Clare. Between 1856 and 1859, 56,000 acres of wheat land were added to the South Australian total, of which more than half was new land taken up in the hundreds north of the Barossa Valley in County Light, where there had been only 4,000 acres in crop in 1855. Undoubtedly settlers were encouraged by the construction by 1860 of South Australia's first major railway, through the wheat fields of the plains north of Adelaide to Kapunda, which provided a new outlet for the produce of the emerging region.

To sum up, between 1850 and 1859 the number of acres of land under cultivation had risen from 64,949 to 361,884, the number of farmers had risen from about 2,500 to about 7,000, and the population had nearly doubled from 63,700 to reach 122,735 by the end of the decade. South Australia was riding high on a new prosperity based on the export of three products, copper, wool and wheat, to Britain and the other colonies of Australia (Fig. 11). Wheat and breadstuffs now accounted for 43 per cent of exports by value, compared with 31 per cent for wool. South Australia was now pre-eminent amongst Australian colonies in the amount of land under cultivation, a position which she maintained until 1895. The attainment of self-government in 1856 was one obvious manifestation of this new scale of sufficiency and prosperity. With the early struggles to gain a foothold in this new and strange land successfully overcome and behind them, the colonists were soon to take a closer look at the problems of colonizing the less attractive lands of the immense domain that they had inherited, the forests of mallee, the flooded swamps and the areas of coast disease. Not only did their relationship with their own land need organizing, but also their relationship with the wider world and its markets upon which their prosperity depended.

Transition, 1860–68

The northward probing agricultural frontier hastened the development of the new sub-region as 'an industrious body of farmers' colonized the upper valleys of the Gilbert and Light Rivers and the low, rolling hills between, adding about another 100,000 acres of wheat to the colony's total by 1867. The townships of Riverton, Saddleworth, Stockport and Clare had all been established during the preceding period and by 1860 were flourishing rural centres. They were now joined by a new set of townships: Rhynie (1860), Hamilton (1863), Marrabel (1864), Manoora (1864), Allendale (1864) and Tarlee (1868). A typical example of their growth was Rhynie which was described in 1866 as being a 'rapidly improving place' with the full array of mechanics' shops, tradesmen's shops, a hotel and a flour mill, whereas there had not been a dwelling home 'within miles' some five years before. Similarly, Marrabel was 'only about two and a half years old but in a flourishing and promising state' with ninety inhabitants, a flour mill, two general stores, two black-smiths and a wheelwright.[7] The new area of colonization was not served by a railway because the Kapunda line was not extended to Tarlee until 1869; instead wheat hauling to the ports was done by bullock drays (Fig. 12).

Difficulties and Decline

However, the success of this sub-region of colonization during the early 1860s was not followed up by further expansion north, despite the proclamation after 1863 of a new tier of hundreds with an obvious extension through the mallee to the top of Yorke Peninsula where the three copper mining townships of Wallaroo, Kadina and Moonta had been established. Almost without exception the naturally open grasslands of these new northern hundreds from Clare to beyond Burra fell into the hands of pastoralists who had been established in this area since the early 1850s. They were not prepared to be ousted by the advancing frontier of farms and were able to outbid the small-scale selector at the auctions and so establish themselves on large freehold estates created out of their old runs. The five government townships of Euromina, Canowie, Davies, Anama and Hilltown, east and south of Clare, surveyed to encourage agricultural settlement in this area were extinguished from the landscape by similar purchasing, and a 'cordon of pastoral country' locked up settlement expansion in the north (see pp. 344–46).

As a result colonists were cautiously edging out into the thin soils and mallee scrub in the coastal plains west of the Central Hill Country, and by laborious hand-felling cleared nearly 76,000 acres between 1860 and 1867, and created the new

Fɪɢ. 11. A devastating impact on the landscape. The Kapunda copper mines, dumps and refineries, c. 1870. Kapunda township is in the right background.

Fɪɢ. 12. Carting the first harvest of wheat from Cowell, Eyre Peninsula, to the coast, c. 1880.

townships of Redbanks and Mallala to serve their new farmlands (Fig. 13). No such complementary move occurred in the mallee lands to the east of the Ranges despite the proclamation of a belt of twenty-four new hundreds on either side of the River Murray from the great North West Bend to the mouth (see pp. 78–82).

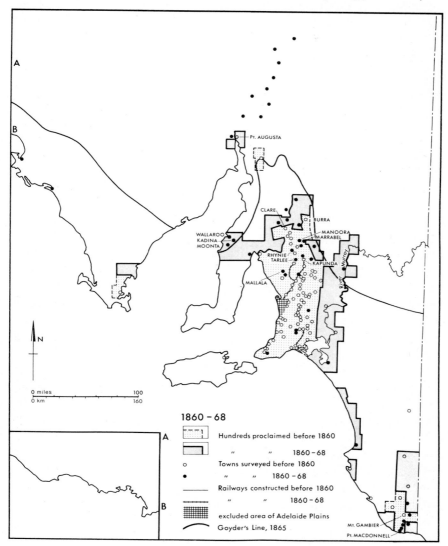

FIG. 13. The spread of settlement, 1860–68.

Away from the main body of settlement two new wool ports were established on the west coast of Eyre Peninsula and new pastoral staging posts and mining centres were scattered over the Flinders Ranges, beyond Port Augusta. In the South-East a large block of hundreds was proclaimed in anticipation of agricultural settlement in the woodlands around Mount Gambier and along the border with Victoria. Settlers were eager to get on the land and were impatient for the survey to begin; 'we are ready not only with our *purses* but our ploughs to develop this fine country' wrote a settler to the Surveyor-General,[8] but like the hundreds to the north of Clare the bulk of this country was bought out by the pastoralists and only a small, isolated but thriving nucleus of cultivation of approximately 26,000 acres was in existence in the vicinity of Mount Gambier by 1867.

The pace of expansion began to slow down after 1866, and for the first time the total acreage of land under wheat fell, from 550,456 acres in 1867 to 533,035 acres in 1868. The decline in acreage was regarded with alarm because wheat was the basis of prosperity, accounting for exactly half of South Australia's export earnings at this time. There were many reasons for this hiatus in the progress of settlement, the most specific being drought in 1865–66 and the heavy incidence of disease in wheat in 1867–68. It was also realized that farmers were leaving South Australia to settle on the grey and black clays of the Wimmera district of Victoria. But the primary cause of this migration, exaggeratedly described as 'an exodus', lay not in the drought and disease but in the difficulty of obtaining new land in South Australia in comparison with the ease of obtaining land in Victoria. The migration was but an obvious symptom of a more deeply rooted malaise that had set in many years before in the process of expansion of colonization.

The problem of the late 1860s was basically one of the availability of land. The new settlers could not get land, while existing settlers could not expand their holdings either to combat declining wheat yields resulting from drought and disease or to profit from greater mechanization. The pastoralist with his 'long purse' and massive purchases had blocked the northward moving frontier in the Central Hill Country and had 'clapped his paw on the whole of the waste land remaining near Mount Gambier'.[9] The farmers in the main body of settlement felt hemmed in by the pastoralists in the north and by the dense mallee vegetation on the dry sandy plains to the west and the east, which extended like 'an uninterrupted waving prairie' and was so thick that if a road was cut through it the mass of trees stood up 'like high walls on each side'.[10] To leap beyond the pastoralist was not really possible because of the Government's control of settlement expansion and because of the isolation and the resultant costs of transporting out the wheat. To go into the mallee land was possible, but hardly a paying proposition under existing conditions of tenure. The mallee had to be cleared laboriously by hand and the stumps grubbed out, water for stock was totally absent, and the minimum offering price of £1 per acre was not attractive to the would-be clearer of scrub.

Hence agitation arose to open up the scrub lands that touched upon the fringe of the well-settled lands, by granting easy and liberal terms to those who were disposed to clear the land. In 1866 the Scrub Lands Act was passed, which set aside Scrub Districts in which land was offered on what amounted to credit, provided a certain proportion was cleared annually. But the initial contact with the mallee was not a success, and with the passing of Strangways Act which became effective early in 1869, the Scrub Districts almost faded from memory (See pp. 138–142).

Changes

The difficult years of the late 1860s marked a transition from one distinctive phase of land settlement, land appraisal and Government involvement to another. The concepts of land settlement laid down in another country, half way round the world, had worked fairly well in the beginning, but were becoming more inappropriate for a rapidly expanding colonization by pioneers who had acquired the experience and the knowledge of the realities of their new environment, as the movement into the Central Hill Country had shown. The ideal of a self-supporting yeomanry was gone and in its place there had emerged the reality of a foot-loose population engaged in a business-like approach to agriculture, specializing in wheat growing for a world-wide competitive market. The settler needed more than honest toil to succeed; new land and large areas of it were necessary for this new kind of agriculture, and the principle of concentration receded in the face of rapid expansion.

The experiment of the Scrub Lands Act in 1866 demolished at last the assumption that all land was equally useful, and a more realistic appraisal of the colony's agricultural resources became possible. Moreover, the Scrub Lands Act introduced what was virtually a system of credit sales, and this chipped away another few stones from the base of the Wakefieldian edifice. Not only did the system and mode of land disposal undergo modification but so did the units of land disposal. There was a formal recognition at last that the system of surveying in grids of 80-acre sections was too restrictive and too rigid; increased mechanization and larger farms in less favourable country necessitated larger sections, as did the varied topography of the Central Hill Country (see pp. 103–109).

But the innovation and change did not end there. After 1865 Governments intervened in new ways in the life of the colony. It was stipulated that at least one township was to be provided in each hundred, and so thoroughly was this policy pursued that there was little opportunity for private town creations. This policy explains the fairly even and dense cover of township sites in Figs. 14, 15, 16 and 18 (see pp. 347–349). As with towns so with railways: after a financially unsatisfactory attempt to sell its interest in the Port Adelaide and Kapunda lines, the Government realized the fundamental value of the railway as a pioneer tool in developing new farming regions and in getting the harvest to the ports, and it made railway construction and operation its sole prerogative.[11]

The Government's role in all these activities was rarely questioned; first because it was perfectly in keeping with Wakefieldian ideas, and secondly because, in what was a basically underdeveloped economy, it was the only body capable of providing the capital and of organizing the works needed for expansion. Yet from 1857 the Government was a democratic body elected by manhood suffrage and, if it wanted to maintain the ideals of stability and order in the colonization process, experience was proving that it had to be more flexible; it needed to abandon old ideas and adapt to new ones which were more in accord with the realities of a more mobile, more commercially oriented and more politically vocal society. So, during the late 1860s governments tended to be less authoritarian than before and guided more by popular demands and therefore they stood back a little and let the pioneer initiate moves. All this is not to say that there were no preconceived ideas of what was needed, but, unlike the rigid adherence to Wakefieldian principles in the past, there was constant modification of the ideas according to circumstances. Pragmatism took place of theory.

Expansion, 1869–79

The expansion of colonization during the next eleven years was spectacular. The legislation responsible for this 'unreasoning boom'[12] was the Waste Lands Amendment Act of 1869, or Strangways Act as it was popularly known, which allowed land to be bought on credit for the first time in specially selected localities considered suitable for cultivation and called 'Agricultural Areas'. Born out of the difficulties of the depression of 1867–68 and the limited experiment of the Scrub Lands Act, Strangways Act substituted credit sales of large blocks of land up to 320 acres in extent—the successful bidder paying 20 per cent down and the balance in four years—for the old system of purchasing 80-acre sections for cash. Certain safeguards were taken to preclude the speculative land agent and the pastoralist by making the settler prove his *bone fides* by occupying his land within six months and residing on it until his purchase was completed.

Armed with this new promise for success the practically-minded and experienced South Australian farmers of the old settled areas, who had been struggling to gain a living from small sections and small farms, stepped over the constricting belt of sheepwalks and moved into the Northern Areas, looked south to the promised land of the Mount Gambier district, and cast a hesitant glance at the little known and isolated tip of Eyre Peninsula. A new phase in the colonization of South Australia had begun.[13]

The Agricultural Areas, 1869–72

The aggregate mass of hundreds proclaimed and townships surveyed during this remarkable phase (shown in Fig. 14) masks

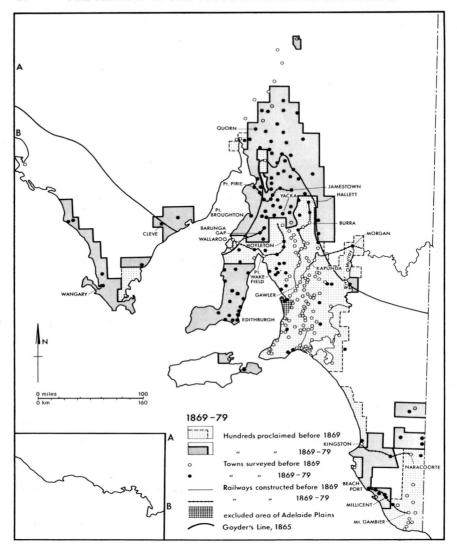

FIG. 14. The spread of settlement, 1869–79.

many locally important sub-movements. Obviously the first
expansion occurred in and near the Agricultural Areas. In the
Northern Areas, the immediate and main locale of colonization
activity was in a zone bounded approximately by the townships
of Port Pirie, Port Broughton, Yacka and Jamestown (the

Broughton, Gulnare, Narridy, Yarcowie and Mannanarie Agricultural Areas for example). The initial progress was slow, but with an excellent harvest in 1870–71 with some yields of between twenty-three and thirty bushels to the acre, the settlement of this zone was accelerated and land was bought eagerly. A second frontier of colonization was located on the edges of the mallee covered plains between Gawler and Port Wakefield and settlers moving north from Adelaide and westwards from the Ranges were undoubtedly encouraged by the credit lands of the Dublin Agricultural Area and by the Port Wakefield-Hoyleton horse-drawn tramway completed in 1870. In the heel of Yorke Peninsula in the vicinity of Edithburgh, the Troughbridge and Penton Vale Agricultural Areas stimulated similar development, while the Kalkabury Agricultural Area in the centre of the Peninsula was another nucleus of cultivation.

In the South-East, completely different circumstances prevailed. It was felt that the delays in draining the coastal swamps would be overcome by proclaiming them Agricultural Areas and two were created, the Mount Muirhead and the Mayurra Areas. But by doing this the Government had committed itself unwittingly to extensive and immediate draining activity because of the wording of Strangways Act; the land was withheld from sale and sixty-seven miles of drains were cut in the flats, and gaps cut through the coastal dunes and ranges that impeded the egress of flood water. By 1872 the land was opened for credit selection, though still not thoroughly drained (see pp. 190–92). Near the Victorian border four Agricultural Areas were created around Naracoorte and the new hundreds to the north. Settlers, particularly from the eastern foothills of the Mount Lofty Ranges, came to these Agricultural Areas only to find that some of the land was under water during the winter and that the regulations about *bona fide* settlers had been flouted by local pastoralists who had bought up the land to protect their leasehold estates. Many settlers 'trekked' into Victoria where free selection was available.

Goyder's Line and Beyond, 1872–79

Although the wheat acreage had increased by about 43 per cent between 1869 and 1872 from 499,937 acres to 715,776 acres the corresponding increase in the wheat production was a mere 29 per cent because of the low yield associated with the poor season of 1872. The farmers were disgruntled about the progress of colonization. In the South-East the demand was for more draining, more and bigger Agricultural Areas, and a more rigorous suppression of bogus selectors. In the Northern Areas the farmers complained of the Government's restriction of credit sales to the Agricultural Areas only and demanded that all land south of Goyder's Line, the line demarcating the northward limit of 'safe' agriculture, be opened to them[14] (Fig. 14). This was approved in 1872, along with a reduction of the deposit to 10 per cent, the extension of credit to six years and the enactment of provisions about cultivation to dissuade speculators and pastoralists.

With good rains and reasonable yields during the next two years (Fig. 74A) settlement surged northward again. Townships blossomed in and around the Agricultural Areas and another quarter of a million acres of land were in cultivation by 1874. This undoubted success was like a heady wine and the farmers, intoxicated with the prospect of even greater prosperity, demanded that 'Mr Goyder's rainfall [line] be shifted out of the colony' and that all land in South Australia be opened to credit sales. Eventually the Government came to accept their view, and in a debate in the Assembly, Blythe, the Chief Secretary, spoke in favour of the farmers' desire to burst the artificial barriers to settlement.

'It was a little singular that the question of what was pastoral and what was agricultural land had been gradually extending year after year. He was old enough a colonist to know the time when it was asserted that land north of the Para River was not fit for cultivation, and could not be ploughed. Subsequently agricultural settlement was extended to Gawler, and they had gone on step by step until a feeling was entertained two years ago that the line of rainfall laid down by the Surveyor-General for defining the classes amongst the pastoral lessees, might be fairly taken as the limit of agricultural land . . . It was generally admitted that this line of rainfall was one which should not be allowed to continue to exist as an obstacle to further settlement. As an obstacle it needed to be removed'.[15]

Thus, between 1874 and 1879 a whole new sub-region of colonization came into being in the northern and eastern edges of the main body of settlement around the Agricultural Areas as settlers moved into the inter-range basins and plains of the Flinders Ranges and reached the far northern mining and pastoral outposts established twenty years before; and to the east reached the edges of the seemingly endless saltbush plains that stretched away into the interior. As Goyder's Line was passed and agriculture safely established beyond, the old idea that 'the rain follows the plough' was invoked to explain the undoubted 'change of season'. Local optimism ran high, probably nowhere more so than in the many new townships surveyed on the advancing northern frontier; the competition for allotments was intense, people giving as much as £150 for a quarter of an acre. A country correspondents' description of one township, Quorn, must suffice for the description of other successful settlements. and the unfulfilled aspirations of many more.

'This township has now commenced in earnest and, instead of kangaroos, we have now masons, carpenters, stone carrier and labourers hard at work. It will be a race between Mr. Greenslades' hotel and Mr. Armstrong's which will be up first. We have two stores already in active operation and one boarding house, one butcher and baker and temperance dining rooms in course of erection, and five or six private homes and two flour mills'.[16]

At the same time, the difficult mallee covered plains of Yorke Peninsula and the eastern side of St Vincent Gulf were the scene of active clearing and colonization which now progressed with a new vigour with the advent of two important inventions: the mallee roller for breaking down the slender but numerous mallee stems, and the stump-jump plough, which, as its name implies, had shares that rode over the mallee stumps. The 'despised' scrub lands now became attractive; the old Scrub Lands Act was revived in 1877 and nearly one million acres of scrub land were taken up in the next four years (see pp. 143–51).

The mallee scrub, one of the greatest obstacles to the spread of settlement, had been overcome by the experimental ingenuity of practical farmers. This was not without a wider significance, for these inventions and later innovations and discoveries were to show that the practical farmer often had the answer to successful colonization, rather than the Government which merely laid down the framework for settlement. The success of the pioneer farmer in assessing and overcoming an adverse environment goes a long way towards explaining why the Government voluntarily abandoned its role as arbiter in land matters during the 1870s. In many instances theoretical planning could not achieve as good a result as practical experiment.

Communications

All these solid achievements in land settlement were not made without improved means of communication. The success of the 1872–74 thrust northward had emphasized the inadequacy of transport facilities from farm to port and of the ports themselves to handle the abundant harvest. Communications became a matter of great concern. The extensive and indented coastline of South Australia encouraged the establishment of a multitude of small ports, and nearly all entertained hopes of becoming the focus of a regional railway system : clearly only a few were going to succeed. The success at Port Wakefield with its short line to Hoyleton, was repeated at Wallaroo with its twin lines, one towards Barunga Gap (constructed 1878–79) and one to Port Wakefield itself. Ultimately, the superiority of facilities at Wallaroo robbed Port Wakefield of much of its trade. Port Pirie's inland line tapped what was perhaps the richest wheat growing land of all, and by 1878 the line had been laid to Jamestown. Adelaide, although far away, was not left out of this race for trade. It was growing with great rapidity and its population jumped from 51,000 to 92,000 between 1871 and 1881, to constitute 59 per cent of the total of the colony. Metropolitan dominance and the trend towards centralization were beginning, and the groping tentacles of the extension of the Kapunda line to Hallett by 1878, tapping the trade of the eastern fringes of the newly settled Northern Area, were a portent of the threat of trade diversion from the locally emerging ports. The threat was to grow greater in later decades. The line to Morgan on the River Murray was not built in anticipation of any rural settlement, but rather to capture the river traffic from Victoria and New South Wales and direct it to Port Adelaide. This dealt a cruel blow to the ports around the Murray Mouth.

In the South-Eastern district, events had not gone so well

between 1872 and 1878 and the region had lost in the race of improvement compared with the Northern Area. The construction of the railway from the coast to Kingston (1876) to the Agricultural Areas near Naracoorte was premature because of the failure to establish a thriving agricultural community in the border lands. Perhaps worse than this was the fact that the construction of the line encouraged the opening up, between 1876 and 1878, of a compact block of six hundreds on the western side of the badly flooded inland swamps. Initially more successful was the Beachport–Mt Gambier line (1879) which linked the rising Millicent area and the well established agricultural zone of Mt Gambier with the coast.

The third region of colonization activity was on Eyre Peninsula, but the Lake Wangary and Warrow Agricultural Areas were near failures. Elsewhere in the Peninsula lack of rail communication tied settlement to within ten or fifteen miles of the coast, consequently the potentially better soils inland were not touched. Except for the nucleus of settlement on the isolated patch of relatively fertile red-brown loams near Cleve and Cowell, the sparse population of the region was confined mainly to the high rainfall western coast of the Peninsula, and it is significant that the whole region was for long to be known as 'The West Coast' and not Eyre Peninsula.

Stagnation and Experiment, 1880–92

The opening of the 1880 season showed all the signs of promise that the previous year had led the settlers to expect, and a whole new tier of townships and hundreds was surveyed and proclaimed on the eastern and northern fringes of the settled area (Fig. 15). But the promise did not hold; by the end of the season drought conditions were widespread, yields dropped to below 2 bushels per acre in those very hundreds created in the previous year, and the total South Australian yield fell from 14·2 million bushels in 1879–80 to 8·6 million bushels, to fall yet again by another million bushels during the next two years. The situation in the Quorn district was perhaps typical of the persistent optimism in the face of adversity that characterized the northward thrusting settlers. In the local newspaper, the editor wrote of the growing prosperity

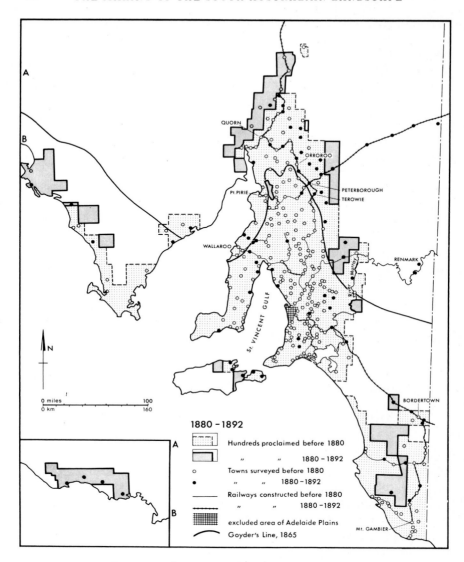

FIG. 15. The spread of settlement, 1880–92.

of the town, and its shops which made the main street look like a 'miniature Rundle Street' (the main retail thoroughfare in Adelaide), and yet in the same article commented that 'every week brings news of disappointed hopes . . . as to the late harvest. The farmers are lamenting the past and dreading the future. In some cases there is some absolute starvation, it is a case of the Irish famine localized.'[17]

One bad season should not have been so disastrous, but as Meinig points out, the general success of the previous years had obscured the grim fact that only marginal crops were being obtained on this frontier, and the 1880–81 drought was not as elsewhere, an abrupt set-back, it was a harsh prolongation of defeat. The next year, settlers' attention shifted towards land near the railway that was being constructed from Terowie to Orroroo and Quorn, and which promised reduced marketing costs. The mallee lands too, north of Wallaroo, neglected as yet in spite of their high rainfall, were looked at with new respect, and a group of towns was surveyed in this new area of colonization (Fig. 15).

At the same time, many pioneers stayed on in the fringes of settlement in the hope of recouping some of their investment in land and labour, but the continuing drought caused them to despair finally and to ask the Government for some relief, either in the form of seed for the next season or the revision of credit re-payments. But the Government refused. It was a strange situation and one that had its roots firmly in the past heritage of theory and planning. The Government had always set itself up as the arbiter in land settlement matters, but had gradually relinquished control at the behest of the farmers themselves, who, in the past ten years, claimed that they were a better judge of what was good for them than was the Government. Yet who was to blame? The farmers who wanted to break down the preconceived theories of colonization, or the Government which let them? It was a nice argument; but like similar arguments over the draining of the swamps in the Lower South-East, the Government realized that the sooner something was done to alleviate the situation, the easier and cheaper it might be. Thus relief was provided for those drought-stricken settlers who got an average yield of only 6 bushels per acre or less during the preceding season, together with a right to surrender their holdings and re-select their land. After a continuation of the drought in 1882–3 these relief provisions were extended to allow settlers to convert their credit purchases into long term leases.

Stagnation

The droughts of 1880–83 were a set-back to settlement that finally proscribed the approximate limits of agriculture in the northern and eastern parts of the state. Many of the townships surveyed during this time never progressed beyond a pattern of surveyor's stakes in the ground, or at best, they were permanently stunted communities, parodies of the grandiose plans from which they started. Even with better seasons after 1884 there was little desire to move out into the salt bush plains again. Consolidation occurred in the areas 'safe' for agriculture, the population immediately north and east of Port Pirie increasing by over 4,000 between 1881 and 1891. But settlers rarely ventured again beyond the reassuring touch of the northward looping line that, like an outer Goyder's Line, marked the margin of the salt bush country and the probable limit of successful cultivation.

The South-East was largely untouched by the drought, but any spectacular increase in agricultural settlement was strangled by the 'cold embrace' of the pastoralists. The only successful agricultural endeavour was on the deep clays of the Bordertown district through which the Melbourne to Adelaide railway had been constructed between 1881 and 1887. By 1883 the acreage under wheat surpassed that of the Mt Gambier district, but the wheat production of the whole of the South-East was trifling compared with that of the Northern Area, which was less humid and climatically more suitable. Plantings of wheat in the South-East fell from a peak of 36,238 acres in 1890 to 21,571 acres in 1892. The only advance made in the settlement of the Lower South-East was the partial drainage of the inland swamps, which is reflected in the distribution of new hundreds (Fig. 15).

Elsewhere, tentative advances were made in the eastern end of Kangaroo Island, and the peripheral settlement of Eyre Peninsula was augmented in the far west by the creation of some townships and the opening up of new land when pastoral leases expired during 1889 and 1900. Eyre Peninsula more than doubled its wheat acreage between 1880 and 1892 when it reached 46,154 acres, while the population increased by 1,800 during the same time. Optimism now ran high and one member of the Assembly had visions of the west coast of the Peninsula as 'the California of

Australia', capable of supporting 'hundreds of thousands of families'.[18]

But, all in all, the droughts of 1881–83 had set the tone for the rest of the decade and South Australia entered a prolonged period of depression and agricultural stagnation, almost ten years ahead of the rest of Australia; as one newspaper editor said there was no doubt that South Australia had 'been living fast' and was now going to pay for its carelessness.[19] The slow down was reflected in many ways; the amount of land cultivated declined from 2·8 million to 2·6 million acres between 1883 and 1892 (Fig. 79), the average wheat yield dropped from 7·94 to 4·15 bushels per acre during the same years (Fig. 74), and the rate of increase in the population of Adelaide was only 28,630 between 1881 and 1891 compared with an increase of 42,581 during the previous decade. Government finances and the balance of trade were in deficit until 1888. Surprisingly enough the rural areas with the greatest change during these years were not on the fringes of settlement, but in the core of the old settled areas in the Central Hill Country where the population fell by 4,300 and the wheat acreage by 164,000 acres. Many migrated to Adelaide which continued to grow steadily during the decade to about 117,000.

Experiment

A few lights pierced the economic gloom. There was the successful establishment of an irrigation settlement at Renmark on the River Murray by the Chaffey brothers of California in 1888, which pointed the way to developments in the future (see pp. 235–236). Secondly, the discovery in 1884 of the Broken Hill silver-lead–zinc mine stimulated the building of the railway from the inner edge of the wheat lands at Peterborough to Broken Hill, and the establishment of smelters at Port Pirie. Less obvious at the time, but far more important for South Australia and, indeed for the whole continent in the future, were four discoveries and experiments that were to lead to the successful colonization of some of South Australia's difficult lands.

First, there was the growing realization that the old methods of rapacious cultivation were reducing yields, and that super-phosphate manure was needed to counteract the downtrend in yields. Secondly, South Australian farmers were experimenting with fallowing as a means of conserving moisture, controlling weed infestation and preparing the seed-bed (see pp. 287–295). Thirdly, from 1880 onwards, experiments with varieties of wheat like Steinwedel and Early Gluyas, resistant to drought and disease, were developed by farmers from Dalkey and Port Germein, and these varieties, widely used, contributed to the extension of wheat growing into drier areas. They preceded the cross-bred varieties of Farrer.[20] Finally, there was the discovery in 1889 by A. W. Howard, a Mt Barker nurseryman, of the potential value of the introduced subterranean clover, which was to be found occasionally in the Adelaide Hills, but which previously had been ignored.

It was indeed a period of folk experiment and innovation that began first and was elaborated in South Australia. If to these four methods and techniques for colonizing new lands and, for raising fertility and yields in existing settled land are added the earlier developments made in machinery to cope with the mallee lands, then the South Australian contribution to agriculture in Australia is conspicuous.

Railways and New Lands, 1893–1920

The depression of the 1880s continued into the next decade and was accelerated by severe droughts in 1896 and 1901. There was a virtual halt to all expansion, attention being turned primarily towards the Central Hill Country; only 70 miles of new railway were constructed and six new townships created between 1893 and 1902 and Adelaide's population increased by only 30,000. In fact, a definite contraction of settlement was under way as the droughts were sharp reminders to those settlers who had ventured to the very fringes of the northern wheat land between 1880 and 1892 (Fig. 15) that their livelihood was precarious and about 3,000 persons left the northern and eastern fringes by 1902. Everywhere, continual cropping without fertilizing was taking its toll and the average wheat yield which had been steadily decreasing over the last twenty years plunged to 1·66 bushels per acre in 1896–97, the lowest it had ever been, thence to rise again only with the increasing application of superphosphate fertilizer and the practice of fallowing (Fig. 74).

Meanwhile, the attractiveness of other states was increasing.

The West Australian Gold Fields at Kalgoorlie opened in 1897, and in the years that followed, that state's very liberal land laws, which were tantamount to free selection, attracted many struggling South Australian farmers. In Victoria, settlers were edging successfully into the fringes of the mallee country at the beginning of the 1890s, and similarly this had caused a marked migration of farmers across the border from South Australia.[21]

With the turn of the century, however, the demand arose for the Government to open up new land in order to promote expansion. Confidence was being gently raised by the good results of superphosphates, better strains of wheat, and the use of fallowing, all of which coincided with a slight increase in seasonal rainfall. The only land left was in the two new regions of Eyre Peninsula and the Murray Mallee, both difficult areas with light, sandy soils, a dense cover of mallee and located well away from the coast. For settlement to be successful in these areas the farmer needed to be primarily a wheat grower and not a wheat carter, and in order to promote settlement the Government re-asserted its authority by building an extensive network of 'developmental railways' so initiating a second great movement of pioneers comparable in scale, and sometimes in substance, with the 1869–1880 surge into the Northern Areas (Fig. 16).

With understandable caution, considering the past experience, it was decided to concentrate attention on the 'Pinnaroo Lands' an area of sandy soils overlaying a clay subsoil, in the south east corner of the Murray Mallee (Fig. 4). A Commission of Enquiry in 1902 thought that the provisions of a railway would 'offer a prospect for a new, large and successful farming settlement', particularly as water could be obtained from the Murray artesian basin by boring down 150 to 200 feet. Some members of the Commission dissented from the findings, pointing out that in their view the land was near, and some of it beyond Goyder's Line with all that that implied. But the Pinnaroo Railways Act was passed in the next year and teams of surveyors preceding the railway, had marked out land. The pulse of settlement was quickening so that when the railway between Tailem Bend and Pinnaroo was opened in 1906 settlement was said to be occurring 'at a very rapid rate', 40,000 to 50,000 acres were under cultivation, and Lameroo and Pinnaroo were emerging as thriving

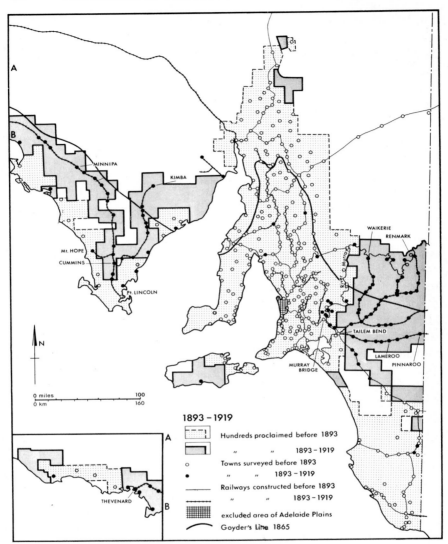

FIG. 16. The spread of settlement, 1893–1919.

towns to serve the new area of colonization. By 1908 all land within ten miles of the railway was taken up and the success of the settlement 'had been almost phenomenal'.

The success of the Pinnaroo venture focussed attention on the whole of the mallee lands as a possible locality for colonization.

Indeed from 1906 onwards, settlers had been moving from the irrigation settlements along the River Murray south and east into the Mallee, particularly in the vicinity of the Big or Pyap Bend, north of Loxton (Fig. 17). The 'second settlement' in Eyre Peninsula was a similar success and the land which formerly had 'hardly a hoof on it' became a flourishing wheat region. For years

FIG. 17. A River Murray paddle steamer bringing up bagged wheat to the Renmark irrigation settlement and bundles of cut timber for making fruit cases. The barge has been loaded with firewood for the down journey. *c.* 1900.

the Peninsula had been looked upon as 'being tied up for the squatter and it was only recently discovered that there was practically a province for South Australia to settle her people'.[22] With the construction of the Port Lincoln to Cummins railway in 1907, the whole of the southern part of the Peninsula was blocked out into hundreds and alienated, so that by 1910, 367,000 acres of wheat were under cultivation. Many of the new farmers here, as in the Murray Mallee, came from the northern and eastern fringes of the Upper North, which lost about 5,300 people through migration during the first decade of the century.

The northern advance in both of the new areas of colonization continued. Over-confidence, fertilizers, and fallows to conserve moisture, all produced a recklessness that was shared by settlers and government officials alike. Between 1910 and 1916 the survey teams could barely keep pace with the farmers' demands; Goyder's Line had long since been passed in the Murray Mallee and it was fast being approached in Eyre Peninsula, even if anybody knew or cared where it was. Certainly the results of the new colonization were impressive, and, whereas there were only three settlers between the River Murray and the Victorian border in 1904, in 1911 there were

> 'two large towns, and six or seven smaller ones, whilst settlers' homes (the population is approximately 3,900), bores and other improvements are visible in all directions throughout the district and the clearing of the land is constantly being extended'.[23]

In language strongly reminiscent of about forty years before, the Premier told Parliament in 1912 that 'A new chapter in the history of South Australia was opening out, and they were glad to know that their country was being regarded as a bigger State than they had ever previously imagined it to be'.[24] The opening of the Tailem Bend to Renmark railway in 1913 and the two other branches of the railway line to Loxton and Waikerie in the Mallee in the next year, together with the extension of the Eyre Peninsula lines to Kimba, Minnipa and Mount Hope in 1913, seemed to be practical confirmation that the State was bigger than ever before.

The declared policy of leaving no wheat farm more than fifteen miles from a railway, the coast, or the River Murray was pursued methodically and does much to explain the digitate pattern of railways. The provision of a siding at approximately five mile intervals also gave a distribution of potential township sites that was as distinctive as it was generous. Not all could grow for in these wheat areas the potential hinterland population of any one township was not much beyond ten or twenty families; time was going to have its effect in sorting out the most rewarding sites, something which can be observed at the present time (see pp. 375–383).

But the unthinking expansion in the Mallee and Eyre Peninsula beyond the well tried limits of Goyder's Line was bound to come to grief one day, and the drought of 1914 told with melancholy effect on the new areas. In the Mallee no area recorded a yield of more than half a bushel per acre and 'absolute failure' was common. The position in the northern half of Eyre Peninsula was the same. But unlike the great reversals of the 1880s one bad season was not enough to absorb the vapour of optimism, and with the assistance provided by the Government in the form of seed, manure and fodder, it was expected that 'a very much larger area of land will be planted for cereals than has been cultivated for that purpose in the past'. But the next two seasons did nothing really to improve matters, and, although over 1,000,000 acres were given over to wheat in the Mallee and Eyre Peninsula, those who had remained on the land from two years before were now in 'a hopeless condition'. Had it not been for government assistance, there would have been 'a wholesale abandonment of the country'.[25] Indeed, retreat was in evidence, and with the Surveyor-General's admission that perhaps the Murray Mallee was 'one of the least favoured portions of the agricultural areas', debts mounted, rents were reduced, and it was declared in 1920 that 'the state had erred in the past in regard to the land settlement policy in the outside country'.[26]

There was a limit to what superphosphate, new wheat varieties, fallowing and new railways could do; these developments could not surmount the basic limitations of the sandy wheat land soils. Drought assistance and the exigencies of war had pushed settlement too far. Instead of becoming stabilized, the position had worsened. In every way the optimism of twenty years before was checked.

Internal Change

The years since 1920 constitute the lengthiest, most complex, and perhaps the most difficult of all the periods of settlement to analyse. With very few exceptions, the outer limits of settlement had been reached and recognized, and from now on there were only blanks to fill in the existing pattern of hundreds and townships. When they were filled the simplicity of geographical change based upon an ever expanding frontier was gone; in its place there emerged a complex set of processes leading to internal re-organization and change. This is not to say that internal re-organization was not already in evidence in South Australia before 1920; the Workingmen's Blocks in 1885 and the break-up of the large freehold estates with Closer Settlement after 1895 had all been examples of radical change in the existing patterns of settlement. After about 1920, however, it becomes an increasingly dominant theme, and since the Second World War it has occurred with ever-increasing acceleration.

Not only has this period since 1920 been characterized by processes of internal re-organization, but the locale and emphasis of change have undergone a profound shift from the rural areas to the urban. The Depression of the 1930s revealed with un-precedented severity how dependent the economy was on rural production and overseas prices, the fluctuations in which probably affected South Australia more than any other State in Australia. In the longstanding tradition of South Australia, a conscious plan to decrease the dependence of the economy on primary production and to expand industrial activity was begun in 1935 and pursued with great resolution.[27] With a few exceptions, such as the steel-making facilities at Whyalla, electricity production at Port Augusta and the pulp and wood industries associated with pine plantations in Millicent and Mt Gambier, this industrial expansion has occurred in Adelaide. Ever since 1911 the population of Adelaide had been growing rapidly as trends to metropolitan concentration, both economically and politically induced, became more marked. The population rose from 199,183 to 312,619 between 1911 and 1933 and its proportion of the State's population rose from 47·5 per cent to 53·8 per cent. But in every way it was during the years since the Second World War that the greatest changes in population took place; the effects of war time de-centralization of industry, the policy of attracting industries, immigration sponsored by the Federal Government, and the changed social and industrial patterns made possible by cars and trucks, all helped to boost the metropolitan population from 382,454 in 1947 to 727,916 in 1966, a rise from 54·2 per cent to 66·7 per cent of the state total. At the same time, the rural component of the population dropped from 30·3 per cent in 1947 to 17·3 in 1966. Therefore, a concluding review of the sequence of settlement can best be made by examining the changes occurring in rural areas and their associated townships and in the Adelaide metropolitan area.

The Rural Areas

Except for the extension of the 'Wanbi-Yinkanie line in the Mallee in 1925 and the Wandana-Penong and Kimba-Buckleboo lines in Eyre Peninsula in 1924 and 1926 respectively there has been no new outward movement of settlement (Fig. 18). The only really new settlement has been in the last of the difficult lands; in particular in the trace-element deficient soils between Coonalpyn and Keith in the Upper South-East, the ranges in the Lower South-East, in Kangaroo Island, and in the tips of the Fleurieu, Yorke and Eyre Peninsulas where a total of about 2,000,000 acres of land have been cleared of scrub and settled since about 1945. The single or multiple deficiencies of micro-nutrients have been corrected by adding minute quantities of the trace elements to superphosphate fertilizers applied in these areas (see pp. 321–324). No new hundreds have been proclaimed except in the Upper South-East and the western end of Kangaroo Island, and few new townships created, with the notable exception of Parndana in Kangaroo Island as sufficient urban centres exist in the surrounding areas.

The chemical basis of this expansion has been reinforced by the biological change in the form of the widespread adoption of pasture legumes, particularly subterranean clover. These have not only helped to upgrade the trace element-deficient soils, but have been used in cereal growing areas to combat erosion and to raise yields. The nitrogen-fixing properties of legumes have made possible a rotation of crops and stock which has halted the decline in soil fertility. In the Lower South-East, further land draining has promoted a more intensive occupation of the flats, and the subdivision of old pastoral holdings in Soldier Settlement schemes. There has also been some intensification of irrigation near Loxton, on the Upper Murray.

None of these changes could have been achieved so quickly or so thoroughly without increased mechanization. Of all the equipment available to the farmer, the tractor best epitomises the 'power' revolution. The number of tractors has risen steadily from a few hundred in 1925 to 7,064 in 1944, then climbed rapidly

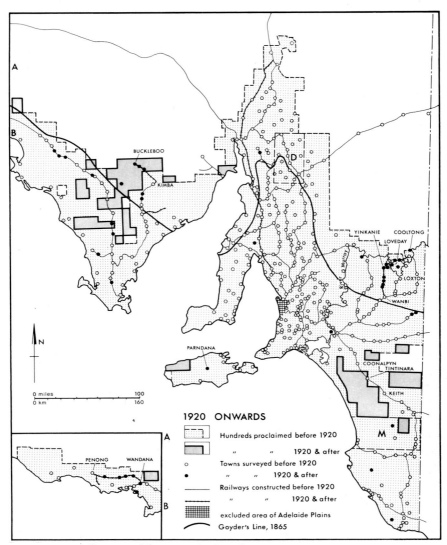

FIG. 18. The spread of settlement, 1920 onwards.

at an average annual rate of about 1,200 to reach 33,998 in 1965. At the same time the number of permanent rural workers has dropped from an all time peak of 45,551 in 1950 to 33,106 in 1965. There are now more tractors than permanent agricultural workers in South Australia.

The chemical, biological and mechanical changes have all had their effect upon the landscape in promoting changes in the patterns of land use and of settlement. But the patterns have not all been towards intensification. The extremes of demographic, social and economic change are typified by two sample areas, firstly County Dalhousie which is in the wheat–sheep zone area in the north eastern marginal portions of the state, and secondly County MacDonnell, a mainly pastoral area in the Lower South-East (Fig. 18). In a sense the changes in both localities are voluntary—a response to changing social and economic patterns and better farming practices, but they have also both been governmentally induced since 1945 when Dalhousie came under the operation of the Marginal Lands scheme (whereby the number of holdings on the fringes of cultivation was reduced and properties amalgamated) while MacDonnell has been the scene of swamp draining, and Soldier Settlement and land development schemes.

Evidence of these changes can be seen in Fig. 19. In Dalhousie the area of land in holdings rose from 780,960 acres in 1945 to 1,088,814 in 1965, but at the same time machinery enabled the individual farmer to work a much larger acreage than formerly and he was encouraged and he attempted, to increase the size of his holding. The number of holdings dropped with accelerating rapidity from 680 in 1925 to 334 in 1945. The number of permanent agricultural workers showed a similarly sharp decline. Because of the drop in the number of holdings, however, the average size has increased from 1,118 acres in 1925, to 2,476 acres in 1951 and then climbed with extraordinary rapidity to 3,250 acres in 1965. The result was a decrease in the farm population, a litter of abandoned houses and a disastrous decline in patronage of the small towns which serve these country areas. The requisite threshold population necessary for the provision of goods and services is now not being reached, and the greater mobility given to the country dweller by his car and the provision of good roads is sufficient to enable him to by-pass his small local centre and seek the attraction of a wider range of goods and services in either the larger country town or the Adelaide metropolitan area.

The opposite situation is shown by the graph of County

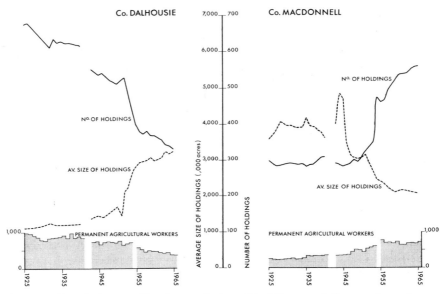

FIG. 19. Rural change. Number and size of holdings and the number of permanent farm workers in two sample counties, Dalhousie and MacDonnell, 1925–65.

MacDonnell which is fairly typical of those areas which have experienced a marked increase of production through new settlement and intensification of land use since the Second World War. In 1925 the number of holdings in the county was 296, a total which barely changed during the next twenty years. After 1945, however, the number of holdings increased rapidly to reach 561 by 1965. The average size of the holdings, on the other hand, showed a remarkable decline as the large under-utilized pastoral estates of the 1920s of about 4,000 acres were reduced to an average size of 2,087 acres in 1965. As agricultural workers have been attracted to these areas and new farmsteads have been established the fortunes of some of the surrounding urban centres such as Kingston, Lucindale, Naracoorte and Bordertown have shown an upswing. The fact that this population increase occurred at a time when rural mobility was becoming greater through the widespread ownership of cars meant that there was no opportunity for a new centre to be established in the newly settled areas and compete with existing centres.[28]

The Adelaide Urban Area

The growth of the Adelaide urban area has gone on unabated since the beginning of settlement, but its size, appearance and functions have undergone revolutionary changes during the last few decades when the population increased from 382,000 in 1947 to about 726,000 in 1966 and is predicted to continue to grow to 1,400,000 by 1990. In terms of the area occupied by urban development Adelaide more than trebled from about 55 square miles in 1947 to 197 square miles in 1966, and the growth is likely to continue at an even greater rate to consume well over 400 square miles by 1990. Some of the reasons for this growth have been outlined already, but suffice it to say here that by 1965 about three-quarters of all the factories, factory employees and value added by manufacturing were located in the Adelaide area, the industries showing a marked emphasis on motor-cars, home appliances and industrial machinery.

South Australia is now essentially a manufacturing industrial society rather than the primary producing one that she has been throughout the greatest part of her history. This change in emphasis is displayed in many ways but is probably summarized as well as any by Table I which shows the net value of production

Table I

Net Value of Production in South Australia for Selected Years, 1925/6–1967/8 (to nearest $ million)

Year	All rural		Mining and Quarrying		Factories		Total
	$ mill.	%	$ mill.	%	$ mill.	%	$ mill.
1925/6	36	56·2	3	4·8	25	39·0	64
1935/6	29	50·9	5	8·8	23	40·3	57
1945/6	56	50·0	5	4·5	51	45·5	112
1955/6	215	43·5	37	7·5	242	49·0	494
1965/6	273	31·6	63	7·3	527	61·1	863
1967/8	230	24·9	63	6·8	631	68·3	924

Source: S.A. Year Book (1971).

of rural industries, factory industries and mining and quarrying for selected years between 1925 and 1967. It seems that South Australia's plan to change the basis of its prosperity and livelihood has been a success.

The emphasis of settlement has changed since 1920 from the problems of the selector in his hut on the edge of the sunburnt plains or the mallee scrub on the frontier, to the problems of the factory and office worker in his house on the waste land of a new subdivision on the edge of an enormous and expanding urban area. Once more, the Government has a plan; this time to alleviate some of the inevitable economic and social strains of excessive urban and industrial expansion by decentralizing growth. Recently, land has been acquired near Murray Bridge for the creation of what, after the Federal capital of Canberra, will probably be Australia's largest new town, capable of housing and supporting 250,000 people. Viewed against the state's history in the last century and a half, the plan comes as no surprise; it is perfectly in accord with all that has gone before in South Australia. As Professor Douglas Pike has said:

'Other parts of Australia may muddle through in the best British tradition: South Australians zealously attach themselves to some conscious theoretical purpose. Goals vary, individuals falter, details go awry, but South Australia sticks to its current plan.'[29]

Summary

The concept of initially favourable and unfavourable areas for settlement goes a long way to explain the broad primary movements of colonists in South Australia and the emergence of regions in the State. But these environmental stimuli and barriers are only a beginning to our understanding of the emerging geography of the new areas. Initial assessments of the environment changed with the development of new methods of farming, new machines, new economic conditions and new political situations, so that the less attractive areas of South Australia certainly did not remain so for long.

In review, one such period of re-assessment occurred during the mid-1860s, before the great surge forward into the northern areas, when the stump-jump plough and the mallee roller were perfected, draining was begun, coast disease investigated and town creation and railway construction taken over by the Government. The decades of the 1880s and 1890s were another period of reassessment, and of experiment with fertilizers, new wheat varieties and fallowing which preceded the thrust into the mallee lands. Another major period of reassessment seems to have occurred during the period of the mid-1930s to early 1950s, when new pasture legumes, new settlement policies and a new knowledge of the soil led to the current rural situation, while a deliberate policy of changing the economic basis of the State with the encouragement of industrialization led to an even greater concentration of the population and economic activity of the State in the Adelaide metropolitan area than ever before.

This sequence of pause, reassessment and thrust seems to have been a recurrent pattern in the spread of settlement in South Australia, and it is a theme which runs through the following chapters.

2. Notes

1. M. Williams, 'Delimiting the spread of settlement; an examination of evidence in South Australia', *Econ. Geog.*, XLII (1966), 336–55.
2. Two excellent studies of the origins and early years of the colony are :
   A. G. Price, *The foundation and settlement of South Australia, 1829–1845* (1924);
   D. Pike, *Paradise of dissent: South Australia, 1829–1857* (1957).
3. See P. Burroughs, *Britain and Australia, 1831–1855: a study in Imperial relations and Crown Lands administration* (1967);
   W. P. Reeves, *State experiments in Australia and New Zealand*, 2 vols (1908).
4. *S.A. Register* (3 and 10 March 1851).
5. *SAPP*, 205 (1855–6); 20 (1857–8); 17 (1859); 75 (1865–6).
   In 1856, a line had been constructed between Adelaide and Port Adelaide, whilst a horse-drawn tramway existed between Goolwa on Lake Alexandrina to Port Elliot for the trans-shipment of cargoes from the River Murray steamers to ocean going vessels. It was probably the first public railway in Australia.

6. *SAPP*, 38 (1859).

7. R. P. Whitworth, *Bailliere's South Australian Gazetteer and Road Guide* (1866), 130, 139 and 192.

8. SGO, 631/1856 (in).

9. *Border Watch* (19 September 1866).

10. R. P. Whitworth, op. cit. 134.

11. *SAPP*, 22 (1865); 98 (1865); 20, 20A, 20B and 141 (1865–6).

12. S. H. Roberts, 'The history of the pioneer fringes in Australia', in *Pioneer settlement*, ed. J. L. G. Joerg (1932), 398.

13. Except where specific quotations indicate otherwise, or where reference is made to the colonization of Eyre Peninsula, or of the South-East District, this section is based on D. W. Meinig. *On the margins of the good earth: the South Australian wheat frontier, 1869–1884.* (1962), 28–77.

14. D. W. Meinig, 'Goyder's Line of rainfall: The role of a geographical concept in South Australian land policy and agricultural settlement', *Agric. Hist.*, XXXV (1961), 202–14.

15. *SAPD*, (H.A.) (1874), col. 905–906.

16. *S.A. Register* (13 June 1878) and *Port Augusta Dispatch* (17 July 1878).

17. *Port Augusta Dispatch*, (7 Jan. 1881).

18. *SAPD*, (H.A.) (1887), col. 1815.

19. *Border Watch* (5 May 1886).

20. Callaghan and Millington, *The wheat industry in Australia* (1956), Chs XVI and XVII;
E. Dunsdorfs, *Australian wheat-growing industry* (1956), 189–192.

21. S. H. Roberts, *The history of Australian land settlement, 1788–1920* (1924), 320; 298.
See also *Victorian Parliamentary Paper*, 1 (1891).

22. *SAPD*, (H.A.) (1905), p. 108.

23. *SAPP*, 10 (1912).

24. *SAPD*, (H.A.) (1912), p. 1325.

25. *SAPP*, 10 (1915); 10 (1916); 19 (1917).

26. S. H. Roberts, *History of Australian Land Settlement, 1788–1920* (1924), 314.

27. *Inter alia.*, T. J. Mitchell, 'J. W. Wainwright: the industrialisation of South Australia', *Aust. Journ. Polit. Hist.*, VIII (1962), 27–40;
R. F. L. Smith, 'The Butler Government in South Australia, 1933–38', unpublished M.A. thesis, University of Adelaide (1964).

28. For greater details see M. Williams (ed.) *South Australia from the air* (1969), 1–17.

29. D. Pike, *Paradise of dissent: South Australia, 1829–1857* (1957), v.

3
Survey and the Landscape

'And there was given unto these wise men chains and measures and staves and little flags . . ., and they went forth into the wilderness rejoicing greatly, and they measured the four quarters of the earth and all the surface thereof; but in straight lines only did they exercise their skill so that the earth became like unto a chess board. And the Governor saw that it was good.' *Border Watch* (18 April 1864).

The theoretical planning of South Australia has nowhere been more clearly seen and actively pursued than in the survey and disposal of the land. These complimentary and evidently inseparable processes of land survey and land sales were the basis on which was built the whole edifice of the Wakefieldian ideal of a new colonial settlement and society. But the survey system, besides being the conscious embodiment of and vehicle for the implementation of the ideals of the new society, also had a definite geographical expression. On the face of the land there was imposed a deliberately created design; an intricate pattern of roads, fences, paddocks, towns and, eventually, farm boundaries and administrative areas, which formed the framework for all subsequent geographical activity. The distribution of the dominant patterns of survey is shown in Fig. 20, and they are made from the major units of survey; 49 counties, 526 hundreds and 92,845 rural sections, to which can be added another 23,691 suburban lots, the majority of which have never been used for anything other than rural purposes.[1] There are, in addition, a multitude of town lots, which probably exceed a quarter of a million. All these units or groups of units are separated by roads. The whole exhibits a fascinating set of patterns of sizes and shapes which

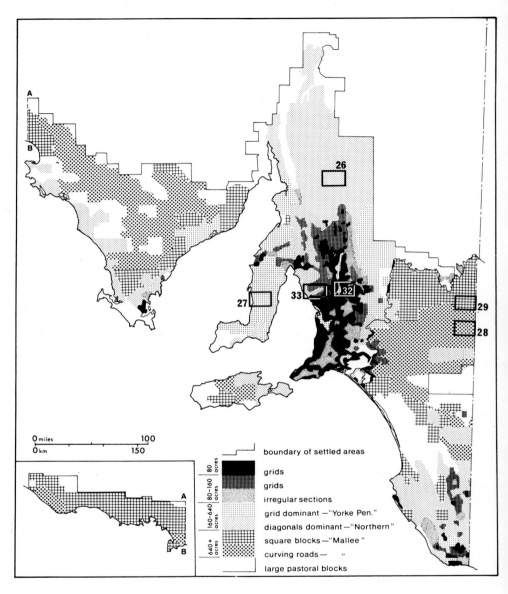

FIG. 20. Dominant survey systems, showing the outlines of the 6 map extracts of Figs. 26, 27, 28, 29, 32 and 33.

immediately stimulate curiosity because of the way in which they vary over space and time. The fact that nearly all the answers to the patterns can be found heightens the interest, for this places one aspect of the South Australian landscape in a unique position compared with other areas of comparable size in the world. In short, survey was the first, the greatest, and probably the most enduring imprint of man on the land in South Australia.[2]

The origins of the newly created landscape were not simple; the survey system constantly evolved in response to new economic, social and political needs, which were influenced by technological developments in farming and the requirements of the new and different types of land that were colonized. In time these developments slowly overrode the idealized norm that had been in the minds of the founders of South Australia. After an initial period of experimentation up to about 1840, during which various schemes of survey were attempted in order to encourage settlement, survey became more formalized and consisted of three major units; the county, the hundred and the section. The county was of relatively little importance compared with the hundred and the section, and in the evolution of these last two units three major phases of change can be distinguished. First there was a period up to about 1860 when there was a great deal of experiment with the form and the function of the hundred, but a fairly rigid policy on sections. After 1860 the roles of the hundred and the section were reversed; the hundred became a fairly formalized unit, the section a more flexible unit. After about 1885, both hundred and section underwent further modification in response to new conditions of farming and new lands. Each phase of change is reflected in the landscape by a distinctive set of survey lines that are the fundamentals of geographical patterns.

The Theory and Practice of Survey to 1840

Nearly five years of difficult negotiations preceded the settlement of South Australia. Finally, extensive regulations were published during February 1836, which specified clearly that surveys should always precede sales, that surveyed rural land was, as far as possible, to be divided into 80-acre (32·375 ha) sections, that it should not be sold for less than £1 per acre, and that the purchase of more than one section was to be made in contiguous blocks.[3] In the light of practical experience, however, three modifications were made to these theoretical ideas in order to stimulate preliminary land sales in Britain so that certain financial guarantees requested in advance by the British Government could be met. First, the price of land was reduced to 12 shillings an acre, which resulted in the holders of the Preliminary Land Orders, who had already paid £81 for 80-acre rural sections plus one town acre in the new capital of Adelaide, receiving sections of 134 acres instead. Secondly, 'Special Surveys' could be requested by anyone who deposited with the Company £4,000 either in London or in South Australia (Fig. 21), and thirdly, as an additional bait, purchasers of every 80 acres of land were entitled to 2 square miles of commonage at a rental of 10 shillings per square mile, and to additional commonage at 20 shillings per square mile if they needed it. Such were the regulations in force when the first landing was made in July 1836, and theory gave way to practice as settlement began.

Colonel Light's decision to establish Adelaide on the east coast of St Vincent Gulf was the crucial geographical decision in the settlement of South Australia. After the town was laid out, Light started the survey of the surrounding sections. He was instructed to survey the 437 Preliminary Land Orders bought at the reduced price of 12 shillings per acre and giving 134-acre blocks 'in a form convenient for occupation and fencing with a reserve road adjoining each section', and then he was directed to survey the residue of the land into 80-acre sections, 'in the best manner you can'.

The two section sizes can be clearly distinguished on Light's map of 1839 (Fig. 22). It shows how the 134-acre sections were surveyed mainly to the east and the south of the City of Adelaide, along the River Torrens (where variations in the size were caused by the irregularities of the river course), and along the two main roads running diagonally across the plain, one north-west to Port Adelaide, and one south-west to Glenelg. The supply of water from the River Torrens and from the numerous creeks running off the scarp edge of the Mount Lofty Ranges, and the prospects of commercial activity along the roads were all significant reasons for this pattern. Most of the remaining area of the plain was divided into 80-acre sections, again some variation in size occurring where there were topographical irregularities, as along the coast.

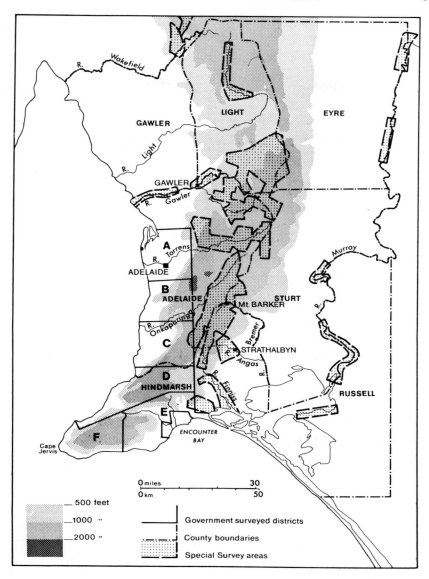

FIG. 21. Preliminary districts, counties and special surveys. Based on material in the S.A. Lands Dept.

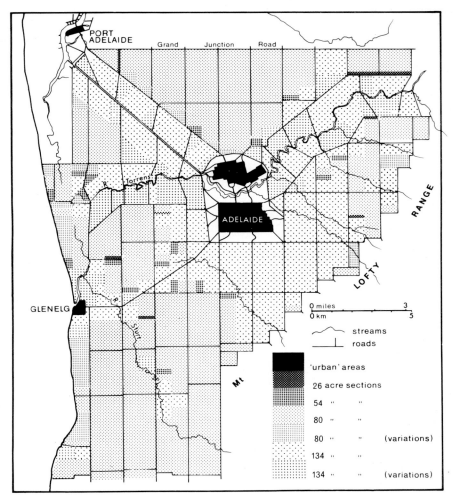

FIG. 22. Survey on the Adelaide Plain (after William Light, 1837).

Sometimes those who held Preliminary Land Orders for 134 acres selected them from two 80-acre sections leaving a residue of 26 acres, which remnants gained the name 'Green Slips' from the way in which they were so coloured on the sale maps. Some of the original 437 purchasers did not take up their options immediately, and when the price of the land was later raised to its old level of £1 an acre they were forced to take only 80 acres out of some of the existing 134-acre blocks, which left a residue of 54 acres. Thus, the simple expedient of dropping the price of land to 12 shillings per acre and then restoring it to £1 an acre, gave sections ranging in size from 26 to 54, 80 and 134 acres. These patterns have had an important effect in the subsequent growth of the urban area of Adelaide, and are fossilized in the landscape by the pattern of main roads and subdivisions (see pp. 445–447).

The tightly knit colonization theory of Wakefield had provided the guidelines from which land survey and disposal were not supposed to stray. Nevertheless, in the face of the practical difficulties of starting the new settlement experiments had been carried out within the general theoretical framework, and *ad hoc* arrangements had been made. The same spirit of cautious experiment within acknowledged limits characterized the next twenty years of survey from 1840 to 1860. Little thought had been given to the wider issues of settlement that were likely to arise as population moved farther away from the core of the Adelaide Plains. Among the questions and problems which needed an answer were the relationship between freeholders and leaseholders, the need for grazing land, the registration of the title of the land, and the systematizing of survey units.

Therefore, step by step, the administrators groped towards a system of survey which was orderly and which would serve the whole colony. One by one, pieces of legislation were enacted which provided the framework for further survey developments. At the present time it is easy to look back and to interpret these as the progressive formulation of a comprehensive survey policy creating a hierarchy of survey units—counties, hundreds, townships, reserves and sections—but nothing seems more unlikely. However, it does seem that the various elements of legislation fortuitously complemented one another, so that during the early fifties they became welded into a fairly rigid survey policy which served as the norm from then on, and which left an indelible imprint on the landscape.

The County

The instructions given to Light for the survey of the rural sections suggested that he lay them out in 'townships and counties' using natural features for boundaries wherever possible.[4] But he did not adopt either these or any other units, and in fact the first large-scale subdivisions were the Preliminary Districts, A to G, which were designated by the Resident Commissioner purely in order to allow the Preliminary Purchasers to select land (Fig. 21).

It is doubtful if the exact phrasing of Light's instructions meant very much, as they were probably no more than the unthinking repetition of an old formula applied to countries of British expansion elsewhere, beginning in East Florida in 1763 and applied to New South Wales.[5] It was not until June, 1842, that the counties of Adelaide, Hindmarsh, Gawler, Light, Stanley, Russell, Sturt, Eyre, and Flinders were proclaimed, initially for the purposes of registering births and deaths, but later as units in which survey had to proceed.[6] The area of each of these nine early counties varied between 1,574 square miles for Flinders in Eyre Peninsula and 928 square miles for Gawler, which was generally less than for the forty counties which were proclaimed in later years and which averaged exactly 1,900 square miles in size. In most cases the boundaries of the earliest counties followed the coast and main drainage courses, such as the Rivers Murray, Gawler, Wakefield and Bremer, and also followed marked topographical features such as the crest of the Mt Lofty Ranges (Fig. 21). Elsewhere, and certainly in later county proclamations, straight geometric boundaries were projected across the mallee-covered plains, a reasonable solution in areas devoid of any marked topographical features, and difficult to cross on foot and therefore to survey.

Imperceptibly, the counties acquired a survey function. By 1855, Freeling, the Surveyor-General, recommended to the Commissioner of Crown Lands that the remaining portions of County Gawler should be divided into hundreds for the purposes of survey, as if this was a common procedure; and it was done.[7] The role of the county in survey procedure was clarified beyond doubt in the 1860s. In 1868 an application for the survey of land in the hundreds of Dalrymple and Melville in the southern portion of Yorke Peninsula was rejected because they were not within a county. After designing new hundreds, Goyder wrote to the Commissioner of Crown Lands:

'The site of the proposed new hundreds . . . not being situated within any county, I have therefore forwarded the usual plan in order that the Commissioner's attention may be directed to the subject and the county named.' County Fergusson was proclaimed two months later. It is an arrangement which has lasted until the present.

In all, forty-nine counties were proclaimed between 1842 and 1920, but because of their size and their infrequent proclamation they do not occupy a prominent part in the total survey system. They were soon superseded as data-collecting districts by the smaller survey units of the hundreds, and later by the local district councils, the boundaries of which were often, but not always, co-terminous with those of the hundreds. In every way the hundred has supplanted the county.

One incidental but interesting point in connection with the counties is their names. Nineteen out of forty-nine are named after State Governors or Acting-Governors. The practice was well established by 1857 when Goyder forwarded to Sir James Mac-Donnell for his approval the tracings and particulars of Counties MacDonnell and Freeling named after the Governor and the Surveyor-General respectively. The Chief Secretary replied :

> 'I am instructed to inform you H.E. has no personal predilection in the matter, but that if it has been the custom to name counties after *all* his predecessors in the Govt. it may be as well to follow the precedent in the present case.'[8]

The necessity of resorting to other names occurred only when the rate of county proclamation exceeded the turnover of Governors, and then the Governors paid proper deference to British Colonial Secretaries (12) or Royalty (5) or their own relatives (2). Explorers accounted for three county names, Surveyors-General for two, aboriginal place names for one, and of the three others, one was named after Lord Lytton the Viceroy of India; one after Lord Hopetoun, the first Governor-General of the Commonwealth, and one after Lord Dufferin, Pro-Consul.

The Hundred

The hundred was the second unit in the survey hierarchy. Its origin and evolution as a land-disposal, as a land-survey and then as a planning unit was perhaps even more haphazard than that of the county, which had, at least, a firm precedent both in Britain and in the overseas territories settled by the British, e.g. the United States. The origin and meaning of the ancient English territorial unit of the hundred were obscure; it was 'an administrative unit of unknown origin and purpose, but of great antiquity', well entrenched as a subdivision of the Shire by the eleventh century.[9] In South Australia, however, the hundred became the name for a subdivision of a county and was commonly supposed to be 100 square miles in size. Its adoption as the secondary unit in the survey system indicated the rejection of the idea of having townships, in the North American sense of the word.

Origin

The origin of the South Australian hundred, like that of its English ancestor, is obscure, but it probably lay in the promise of commonage at the rate of 2 square miles for every 80-acre section purchased. When only a small area of land was surveyed on the Adelaide Plains the implementation of this promise was easy enough, but it became increasingly difficult with the expansion of occupation on land surveyed in contiguous blocks. A compromise arrangement was arrived at by the Commissioner of Crown Lands, Charles Bonney, who suggested that every purchaser should have commonage within 3 miles of his sections, the number of stock pastured being in proportion to the number of 80-acre sections held. This, too, proved unworkable in time because it meant that, to create this commonage, surrounding pastoral properties had to be cut up.[10] After 1845, a second modification was thought of: it was to utilize what Bonney called (later in an inquiry into the hundred system in 1860) 'a territorial division *then existing*, namely, the division of a County into hundreds', and to restrict the right of commonage to the unsold land within the hundred in which the 80-acre sections were surveyed.[11] The only other information Bonney supplied in his recollections in 1860 was that the hundred was a permanent division which was 'to consist of 100 square miles, one-third more or one-third less'; and that it was usually declared after a substantial population had settled, but, if the land was very good there was no reason why the Government should not declare it in advance, which would 'help to bring land up to full price'.[12] Bonney could never cite the legislation that had led to the creation of the hundreds but it is probable that his interpretation of events is correct.

Land Disposal

The 1846 arrangements for commonage implied that all land, either sold, or in the process of being sold, had to be enclosed within a hundred in order to qualify for commonage, and it was not long before it became widely accepted that hundreds had to be proclaimed before land could be surveyed and sold. In time, therefore, the hundred became a device for regulating both the pace and the direction of settlement, a function which was to harmonize well with the Wakefieldian idea of an orderly progression of settlement. This change in the function of the hundred was not formalized until 1860 and there are many examples where land was surveyed and sold outside of hundreds; nevertheless, the years from 1846 to 1860 show a steady strengthening of the idea.

The transformation of attitudes can be traced from requests for survey that came to the Surveyor-General. For example, in 1855, applications were lodged for the survey of 5,280 acres near the River Light in County Gawler, 'some distance north of the hundreds of Port Gawler and Mudla Wirra', and it was suggested that the land 'be proclaimed into Hds. and country surveyed as rapidly as possible', and there were many more.[13] By the end of the decade, the situation became clear. In January 1860, the Commissioner of Crown Lands wrote to the Surveyor-General, Freeling, concerning the plan for survey in the northern and western parts of the hundreds of Clare and Upper Wakefield where they impinged upon the mallee scrub:

> 'I understand you do not include in your scheme any land outside a Hundred except in the proposed work of Mr. Smith . . . Being of opinion that this is the correct system under which the operation of the Survey Dept. should be prosecuted, and that unless in very special and exceptional cases, the declaration of a Hundred should precede the sale of land in any locality, I should be very sorry to see Surveyor Smith's work an exception.'

Therefore the Surveyor-General decided to extend the existing hundred boundaries into the scrub in order to include Smith's work.[14] Within a few weeks the matter had gone before the Cabinet and the Commissioner could inform the Surveyor-General that, 'The Govt. have determined that for the future (except in special cases only authorized) no sales of land of any magnitude shall take place in any locality until the surrounding district is proclaimed a hundred.' A number of cases in later years confirm that this decision was put into effect.[15]

Land Survey

In 1840, Frome had advised his surveyors to familiarize themselves with the areas to be surveyed into sections so that they could identify the best and most direct lines for main roads, and to get a good general view of the problems and requirements of a new block of land before it was surveyed.[16] But the evidence is that such an over-view was rarely achieved by the surveyors in the field who surveyed sections or blocks of sections and their associated roads in a piecemeal fashion, particularly where requests for survey took them away from the main body of surveyed land and beyond the range of constant supervision. In some cases survey groups lacked discipline. For example, the Deputy Surveyor-General, Goyder, went to inspect a camp near Port Elliot, but could not find any of the survey party :

> 'The men were out shooting and the cook informed me that he had only seen Mr. Lindsay (the Surveyor-in-Charge) once during the last fortnight . . . six days of the last two months had been occupied in re-surveying a deviation near Port Elliot; I also discovered that the men had been engaged reaping for Mr. Theodore Hull, at a pound an acre . . ., they slept during the day and reaped in the moonlight.'[17]

At best, in the absence of a precise trigonometrical survey which did not take place until after 1860, the grid of 80-acre sections served merely as a guide for further work. As a result re-surveys were common.[18]

The problems of poor pre-survey planning, inaccuracy, and poor supervision of the surveyors in the field were obviously in Goyder's mind during the winter of 1855 when he was in the field near Kooringa. There he found that two independent survey meshes overlapped rather than abutted each other. When wet weather stopped the corrections being carried out, Goyder, with characteristic energy, rode over the country thinking about ways of overcoming such situations, and later sent the following suggestions to improve accuracy and discipline to the Surveyor-General:

'a competent person should be sent to a locality proposed to be surveyed in sections—and that before the detailed survey is commenced he should run around a block of land, say about 10 miles long and five wide: thus

sketching in the features of the country and chaining the distances to particular objects—such as creeks, gullies and closing the line with the utmost care—and forwarding the result for your examination; one of your assistants should then be instructed to examine this block—marking out what he considers the best lines of road, and other reserves necessary to be made—keeping in view the direction traffic is likely to take— This report would then enable you to decide correctly how the detailed survey should be conducted—and a tracing of this survey placed over the general plans would at once show if the roads had been lost sight of or reserved.

It would also render the persons in charge of parties more careful in chaining—as a constant check would be kept upon them by the original distances of the person who defined the block—it would introduce the features of the country so accurately that a stranger might at once discover any particular locality—and it would save much time in supervision.'[19]

Goyder's recommendations, and particularly his sketch, suggest that he was thinking of the hundred, or at least of a unit very like it, as the basic pre-survey planning unit. Although these suggestions were not adopted in full for some years, a new booklet of instructions for the use of officers in charge of field parties was issued a little while later, and by 1859 Goyder's suggestion that 'a competent person' should go into the field before survey in order to plan the general strategy of survey was an established practice. The procedure was as follows:

'Prior to the survey of fresh lands for sale the locality is visited by the Assistant Surveyor-General when the natural features of the country are carefully examined and the probable direction of the traffic ascertained and the necessary lines of roads to be reserved and method of subdivision which varies according to the character of the soil, pointed out to the surveyor who is generally present during the investigation. The sites of other reserves, as those for water and stone, are also indicated and a rough sketch of the whole forwarded to the Surveyor-General for his information and approval, after which a copy is sent to the Surveyor to guide him in his operations, the original being retained in the office, showing the extent of the work to be performed and affording by comparison with the field diagrams of the Surveyor, a satisfactory proof that the instructions issued to him are adhered to, and that no deviation in the prescribed manner of carrying out the work takes place without special authority. To explain this more fully, a rough sketch of the country under survey is forwarded with the books.'[20]

Revision, 1859–60

The function of the hundred, whether as a unit for the regulation of commonage, for land disposal or for land survey, underwent considerable discussion and alteration during 1859 and 1860. The discussion arose from the proclamation by Governor Young, in 1853, of the Murray hundred, which extended for two miles around the shores of Lakes Albert and Alexandrina and along either side of the River Murray, as far as the state border with Victoria (Fig. 23). The motive of the Governor in this action was not explained, but possibly he thought that the proclamation of the hundred would help to encourage the settlement which it was hoped would occur with the beginning of river navigation and trade with the interior of Victoria and New South Wales. The 4-mile wide and approximately 250-mile long hundred was considered 'objectionable' by many. The Administration, from the Commissioner of Crown Lands down to the local ranger, disliked its shape and extent because of the impossibility of policing the trespass of stock over the whole hundred. It was bitterly opposed by the pastoralists who thought that the land alongside the Murray was totally unsuited to cultivation, and whose leases had been

FIG. 23. The hundred of the Murray, 1853, and Milne's Murray hundreds, 1860. Based on *SAPP* 90 (1860).

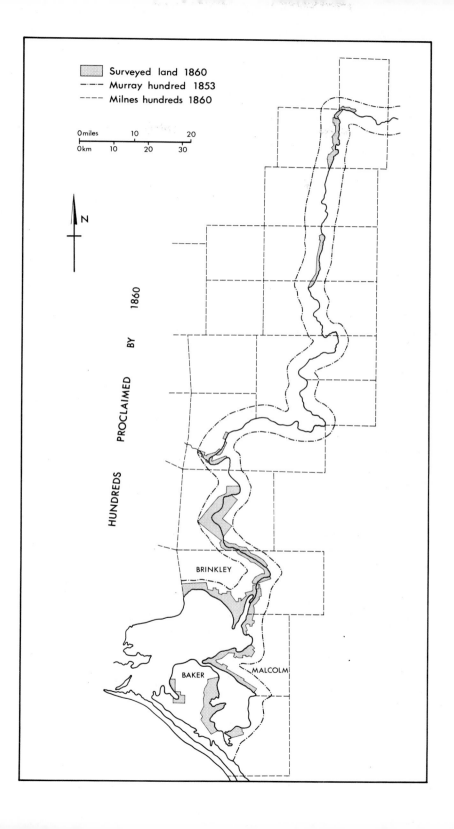

Surveyed land 1860
Murray hundred 1853
Milnes hundreds 1860

0 miles   10   20
0 km   10   20   30

N

HUNDREDS   PROCLAIMED   BY   1860

BRINKLEY

BAKER   MALCOLM

reduced from their original fourteen-year term to an annual tenure.

It is probable that the Murray hundred might have remained unaltered had it not been that Sir Edward Eyre—one-time resident of South Australia and purchaser of land alongside the Murray at Blanchetown, but now Governor of Antigua in the Caribbean— wrote to Milne, the Commissioner of Crown Lands, in November 1859, suggesting that the elongated Murray hundred did not encourage people to settle because they were denied commonage inland from their holdings (Fig. 23). The letter was passed on to Freeling, the Surveyor-General, who saw in it the opportunity to break up the old hundred in favourable localities and thus he suggested three new hundreds around the Murray mouth, later to be called Baker, Brinkley and Malcolm. Milne, obviously with the Government's approval, then recommended the proclamation of twenty-four new hundreds, encompassing all the land on either side of the River, south of the North West Bend (Fig. 13). Milne's action was construed by the squatters as one of personal vin-dictiveness against individual pastoralists who leased land along-side the River Murray. A more simple and probable explanation is that Milne was merely exerting his authority as Commissioner of Crown Lands and not referring the matter to the Surveyor-General, whose rising importance he resented. A few months earlier he had written to Freeling.

'All other responsibilities connected with the Office of Com-missioner of Crown Lands sink into insignificance compared with those which attach to me as the Head of the Department under your management in as much as the carrying out of its operations must involve considerations of Government policy and effect to a large extent the Revenue of the Colony. Under the present system, the Government survey parties are moved about without any information to this Office, no proposed plan of operations is forwarded either for information or approval, the sites of Government townships are fixed, surveyed, and sold without sanction being asked or given—indeed the Commissioner of Crown Lands continues in ignorance of everything which takes place in the Survey Department until the Land is Gazetted for Sale. This state of things is unparalleled in any other of the Responsible Departments of the Government and it is obviously quite unconstitutional . . . [therefore I want] a general knowledge of the operations of your department so as to enable me to judge of the propriety of the system pursued and recommend any modifications, which after consulting with my colleagues, may occur to me to be desirable'.[21]

Whatever Milne's motives, it must be admitted that the declaration of all the twenty-four hundreds at once was premature, and his action gave rise to a special Parliamentary enquiry, which came to nothing. By September, 1860, Sir Samuel Davenport, a spokesman in the Legislative Council for the pastoral interest, asked the Government to specify its power to declare hundreds, a request which was taken up with greater vigour by Mr Lindsay in the House of Assembly.[22] The Commissioner could only reply that

'any authority under which hundreds were proclaimed prior to the assent of our Constitution Act was vested in the Governor as representative of Her Majesty. The Governor, as such representative, still possesses powers of declaring that certain geographical limits of the Crown Lands shall be known by a distinguishing name.'

This vague answer was the best that the Commissioner could do, for there was no entry in the Colony's statute book about the Government's ability to proclaim hundreds. Thus, the very legality of existing hundreds was in doubt and that of new ones suspect, a state of affairs which a new enquiry did nothing to dispel.[23] During the next session a Bill was brought in to declare 'past proclamations valid' and to give the Government 'power to declare hundreds in the future', with the proviso that all proposals for hundreds should be laid before Parliament fourteen days before they were declared. Parliament, in theory at least, now had control over the declaration of hundreds.[24]

Thus, by a complicated process of parliamentary inquiry and debate, the hundred became embodied in new legislation, and the first printed descriptions were laid on the table of the House for approval during the next month, followed by more lists of proposed hundreds, giving their size and brief locality description, which became fuller in time and were later accompanied with maps.[25] The debate over the Murray hundreds had resulted in the forging of an improved and potentially effective implement which could be used for the control of the pace and direction of survey and settlement.

Social and Resource Planning

From the beginning of self government in 1856 to the end of the decade there had been four ministries and six Commissioners of Crown Lands. During the 1860s the situation was worse, with sixteen ministries and seventeen Commissioners in the space of ten years. Because of the rapid changes in office after 1860, the Commissioners relied heavily on the advice of the permanent staff. As Milne had feared, it was the Surveyor-General who exercised his judgement increasingly over survey and land settlement matters, the Commissioner sometimes taking the initiative by suggesting improvements but rarely taking any decision in detail.[26] This whole trend in the shift of responsibility from the politician to the public servant is of great significance in the changing role of the hundred, and it intensified with the retirement of Freeling in 1861 and the promotion of Goyder from the office of Deputy Surveyor-General to that of Surveyor-General, a position which he held without a break until 1890. Increasingly Goyder's judgement was relied upon as Commissioners changed office with startling rapidity. In fact, the story of South Australian land settlement and survey between 1861 and 1894 is the story of Goyder. It was the beginning of the period when it was said that 'Goyder was King'.[27]

Goyder's integrity and efficiency, coupled with his increased influence and responsibility, soon made themselves manifest in the running of the Lands Department, and it was little wonder that he sought to bring order out of the muddle of the hundred system. His suggestion of 1855 for the survey of land in blocks of approximately 100 square miles was now adopted. He also had definite ideas about the necessity for providing for social needs. These are illustrated by the comments in the report which he wrote after inspecting the workings of the new land legislation in Victoria. Obviously comparing its outcome with the ideal he felt existed in South Australia, he concluded that there could be little doubt that the settlement of a region in a scattered manner had 'a tendency to place the selectors beyond the better influences of society. A difficulty is also entailed upon parents in sending their children to school, as, with them, labour is of the first importance, and the distance and expense of schooling is a sufficient excuse, in many cases, for education being dispensed with altogether. Hardy men and women, brought up to a practical and laborious life, are the result; but it is a development of muscle without a proportionate expanse of mind.'[28]

Few in South Australia would have quarrelled with this point of view, it fitted too well into the tradition of method and theory, even 'idealism', that had characterized the first years of settlement in South Australia. Therefore the hundred became not only the means of achieving survey accuracy and supervision, but also the means of planning an adequate system of roads and of locating urban centres in which there could be provided educational, social and religious facilities for the frontier families.

Throughout the late 1860s and early 1870s, the new role of the hundred was generally accepted with little question, but the Government still had to tread cautiously for fear of antagonizing the squatters unnecessarily. The conflict between interests in the creation of hundreds was underlined anew in 1875 when the Government wanted to create seven new hundreds in the agriculturally indifferent lands on the lower west coast of Eyre Peninsula (Fig. 24a). This move was opposed as being premature and unrealistic, for to declare hundreds where the land was not fit for agriculture was 'to destroy one interest without raising another in its place.'[29] The outcome of this controversy was the decision that a surveyor of the Lands Department be sent to examine a stretch of country, fifteen miles deep, along the coast and to furnish a report giving a detailed description of the land and its fitness for agricultural purposes or otherwise'. The plan and report were returned two months later and showed the area divided into eleven blocks 'for ease of description' (Fig. 24b). Armed with this information, the Commissioner of Crown Lands recommended that the best blocks (4, 5, 6 and 7) should be resumed from runs; but Cabinet wanted the blocks reduced in size to be more in accord with the conventionally sized hundreds of 100–120 square miles, and therefore approved of the resumption

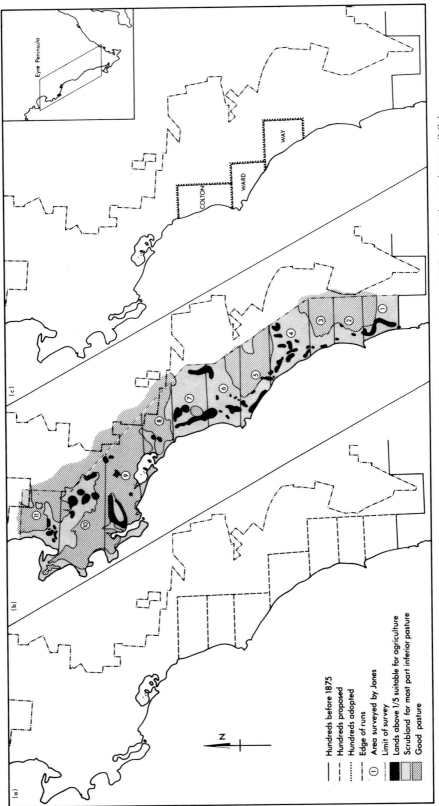

Fig. 24. Eyre Peninsula hundreds. Based on SGO 2742/75 (in); *SAPP* 84 (175); 17 (1875, S.S.).

of the western portions only and proclaimed Way, Ward and Colton[30] (Fig. 24c). A careful reconnaissance survey of resources in all new hundreds was recommended the next year, and, from then on, the description of hundreds to be declared, which was laid before the House, contained estimates of the amount of suitable land, of the natural vegetation and of the reliability of the rainfall.[31] The surveyors' drawings in the Diagram Books of the sections they surveyed, increasingly contained basic information about soil and vegetation. Thus, as in the case of the Murray hundreds, the defensive action of the pastoralists led to more care in the proclamation of hundreds; but even more important, it led ultimately to the bestowing of new functions on the hundred which made it an even more useful unit than ever before in the planning and making of the landscape.

Models and Variations

At the very time when Parliamentary pressure was being applied to the Survey Deparment to provide soil and vegetation reconnaissance surveys of hundreds, the mad scramble for land south of Goyder's Line had begun, and ninety-two hundreds were proclaimed between 1874 and 1879. It does seem that the surveyors had less time for experiment, and therefore, in order to combine efficiency of hundred design with the rapid spread of settlement, they resorted to a stereotyped model, which could be followed without fear of criticism. An examination of the hundreds proclaimed from about 1870 onwards suggests that a basic model was being adopted, modified here and there according to local conditions and perhaps according to the predilections of the individual surveyor. This regularity has been examined by Meinig,[32] but the formalization of the basic pattern is placed beyond doubt by the directions and diagrams which were included in the *Handbook for government surveyors*, first issued in 1887 and reaching its fourth edition in 1914 almost unchanged. First, a preliminary survey was to be undertaken of the likely direction of traffic and of suitable sites for townships in relation to water supplies, building-stone, drainage, roads and access to the sea. This information was forwarded to either the Deputy Surveyor-General or the Chief Surveyor in the Lands Department in Adelaide, who prepared sketches of the direction of the leading lines of roads, sites of townships, reserves for stone and water, and natural features; the sketches were then 'supplied to each surveyor upon his entrance within a new hundred'.[33] The surveyor was to transform the spirit of the sketch into survey lines, the subdivision

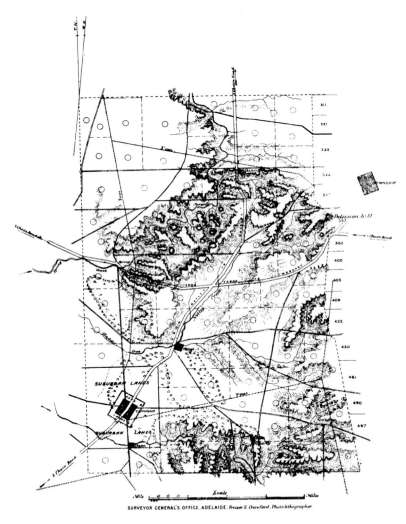

FIG. 25. The model hundred. (From 'sketch of a new hundred', in *Handbook for Government Surveyors*, 1884).

of sections and minor access roads being left largely to his discretion. In case this task proved difficult, the surveyor had a diagram of a 'New Hundred' included in his *Handbook* for guidance (Fig. 25). Most of the hundreds in the Northern Areas, and many of those along the coast of Eyre Peninsula and in the South-East declared between 1870 and 1890 are almost exactly the same in the pattern of their fundamental survey lines as the sketch (compare Fig. 25 and 26). It was almost 'Any Hundred' and served as a theoretical model for land apportionment. A major variation in the model was evident in most of Yorke Peninsula, the Cowell area of the east coast of Eyre Peninsula, and the hundreds on the plains east of the Mount Lofty Ranges. Here

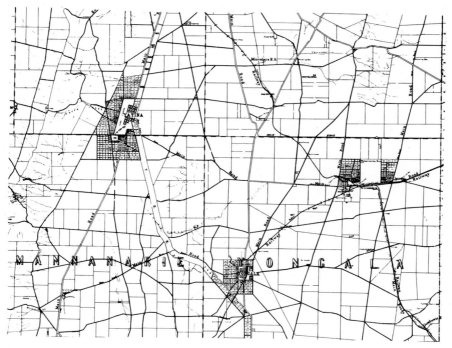

FIG. 26. Typical Northern Areas survey pattern. The roads criss-cross the area and the sections are mostly between 250 and 640 acres. Yatina, with its large area of 1400 acres of parkland, 388 acres of suburban land and 189 acres of townland, was surveyed in 1880 and was one of the largest townships surveyed outside Adelaide. At present it is a loose agglomeration of six farmhouses, two churches and a public house which closed about six years ago.
(S.A. Lands Dept. 1:126,720. By courtesy of Director of Lands: S.A.)

a grid of large sections dominated the pattern with occasional diagonal roads linking major urban centres (Fig. 27).

When the great rush to occupy the North subsided and the rate of proclaiming hundreds slackened after the mid-part of the 1880s and during the next decade, time was available again for more detailed reconnaissance surveys of soils and vegetation. The Diagram Books during these years are amongst the best executed and most informative of all.

During and after the mid-1890s the spread of settlement eventually took the surveyors into the more distant areas of the Murray Mallee and Eyre Peninsula, and later into portions of the Upper South-East. While the method of arriving at a pattern of survey lines by determining the main road lines did not change, there were subtle differences in the configuration of the pattern. The

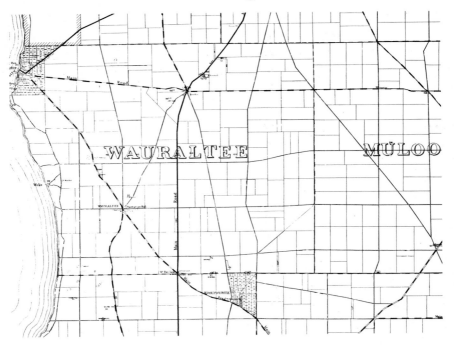

FIG. 27. Typical Yorke Peninsula survey pattern. Here, grids of sections of about 640 acres predominate, with a few diagonals linking up major towns and ports such as Port Victoria on the coast, Koolywurtie to the south and Maitland, just to the north of the map extract. (S.A. Land Dept. 1 : 126, 720. By courtesy of Director of Lands, S.A.)

previous dominance in the Northern Areas of the north–south
pattern of straight roads with some diagonals, dictated by the
characteristic alternating high ridge and broad valley topography,
gave way to an irregular but largely diagonal pattern of roads,
influenced by the orientation of east–west sand-ridges and intervening swales. In addition, the roads were no longer straight, but
'wiggled' through breaks in the dunes (Fig. 28). This new
pattern became so widespread in the hundreds surveyed in the
twentieth century that it came to be regarded as the norm and
was incorporated in a booklet on the survey, valuation and tenure
of land in South Australia, first published in 1958.[34] It illustrates
the delimitation of the hundred area, the most desirable pattern

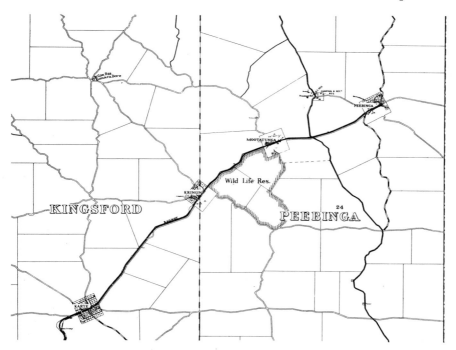

FIG. 28. Typical curved Mallee survey pattern. This map section of Kingsford
and Peebinga hundreds is in the eastern portion of the Murray Mallee region
and it shows the way in which the roads 'wiggle' through the dunes. The
sections are in excess of 4 square miles. The townships post-date the railway
line and most have not succeeded as viable units and only small areas of suburban lands have been surveyed around them. (S.A. Lands Dept. 1 : 126, 720.
By courtesy of Director of Lands : S.A.)

FIG. 29. Typical square Mallee survey pattern. The hundred of Bookpurnong is due north of the area in Fig. 28. The sections are mainly square and made up of subdivided pastoral blocks. The townships are still railway-oriented. (S.A. Lands Dept. 1 : 126, 720. By courtesy of Director of Lands : S.A.)

of roads, the design of the first leading lines of road, and the division of the hundred into sections, the size and shape of the section depending upon what was considered at the time, in a particular place, to be 'a reasonable home maintenance area'. Approximately 100 hundreds proclaimed between 1900 and 1970 incorporate the basic elements of this design. If the landscape was topographically indifferentiated then it had straight roads and square sections (see Fig. 29).

Both the Northern Areas' pattern of survey, with its Yorke Peninsula variation, and the Murray Mallee pattern of survey, with its square variation, were hundred-controlled survey systems.

Boundaries, Shapes and Sizes

For most of the years between 1846 and 1860, the main function of the hundred boundary was to delimit the extent of commonage available to section-holders. Therefore, as the boundaries evolved almost haphazardly around the surveyed sections, there was a marked preference for following the line of easily distinguishable features, such as water courses and prominent crest and ridge lines, which could be used to help in restricting and controlling common grazing. As the commonage function declined, the selection of clearly defined natural boundary features (and hence the shape of the hundreds) appears to have become of less importance to the Lands Department than did the size of the hundred unit. In 1855, a landowner wrote to Freeling complaining that the boundary between Light and Gilbert hundreds did not follow the River Light or any other topographical feature. Freeling replied that, although agreeing that the boundary suggested would 'not only be natural, but distinguishable', the hundred enclosed by it would be only 45 square miles, which was 'insufficient for Hundred purposes; the regulation requiring that each Hundred should approximate as nearly as possible to 100 square miles'.[35] Another example of the same concern for size arose in 1860 when it was debated whether or not the scrub-covered plains west of the hundreds of Clare and Upper Wakefield should be included within those two hundreds. If that was done, then the hundreds would have been 'considerably above the usual size (100 square miles) and will be more or less unmanageable . . .'.[36]

Problems of the boundaries, shape and size of hundreds were all combined in decisions taken in 1852 on the best method of dividing into hundreds the area now occupied by Waterloo and Julia Creek hundreds on the eastern edge of the Central Hill Country. Dutton, a successful pastoralist, who held the land on lease, wanted the area divided by an east–west line to give two roughly square hundreds. This would probably have resulted in the southernmost half of his run being resumed and declared a hundred first, which would have allowed him to concentrate on buying land there, secure in the knowledge that the northernmost half of his run would not be declared a hundred for a few years and therefore be safe from the depradations of purchasers and their commonage demands. The Surveyor-General, however, decided against such a scheme and selected the crest of an intermediate prominent north–south trending range as the hundred boundary, but which gave two elongated hundreds, the shape of which would

now be 'far removed from the square and consequently concentrated shape supposed to be so desirable in all divisions of
land for local purposes'.[37]

After the passing of the legislation of 1860 which required that
a description and the plans of prospective hundreds should be
laid before Parliament for fourteen days before their declaration,
the Survey Department sometimes found itself in a difficult
position since the scheduled line of a hundred boundary was not
necessarily the most convenient one when it came to practical
survey in the field. For example, in 1869, Goyder requested the
permission of the Commissioner of Crown Lands to alter the
western boundary of the Mount Muirhead Agricultural Area
(co-terminus with the hundred of the same name) in the South-
East swamps in order to 'enable me to lay out the land to much
greater advantage for the purposes of drainage and settlement
than can be done if an arbitrary and inconvenient line is adopted'.
Obviously, it was not an isolated request, for he concluded, 'I
would point out that in surveying Hundred boundaries, similar
licence has not infrequently been taken'.[38] In later years, the Commissioner of Crown Lands became more wary of altering existing
hundred boundaries particularly after the Attorney-General
warned him, in 1875, that any such alterations were illegal. Thereafter, any boundary changes were treated as new proclamations
and were laid before Parliament for its approval, for example,
additions to Hynam, Hallett, Joyce, and Wirrega and Tatiara
hundreds.[39]

The complications which arose from the multiple aims of
surveying hundreds which were to be roughly square in shape,
approximately 100 square miles in size, and yet with boundaries
following distinguishable natural features were resolved to a
certain extent, when settlement moved into the mallee-covered
plains either side of the Mount Lofty Ranges and Central Hill
Country. In 1855, when County Gawler was being divided into
hundreds, Goyder reported that 'the country does not present any
natural features to aid description, scrub and plain being the only
characteristics', and therefore suggested a pattern of division
for six hundreds, Inkerman, Balaklava, Alma, Dalkey, Dublin
and Grace, in which all internal boundaries were strictly geometrical lines corresponding to lines of longitude and latitude,

except for one between Alma and Dalkey which was oriented north-west to south-east.[40]

However, the lack of prominent natural features in the new areas of survey did not mean that the question of the visibility of hundred boundaries was forgotten, and it arose again as part of the general debate on the role of the hundred in 1860. As a result of complaints of trespass on pastoral runs abutting declared hundreds, the Government produced a return of the way in which existing hundred boundaries were marked, either by pegs, mounds, trenches, the edges of sections or lines of survey, or not at all.[41] One member of the House of Assembly doubted if 'any one resident in a hundred could tell where the boundaries are'. In the Legislative Council, Sir Samuel Davenport, for long the champion of the pastoral interests in their fight against hundreds, said that he knew of some hundreds which were 'no credit to the country; some were simply absurd', particularly those in which there was a 'division of tracts of country by imaginary lines of latitude and longitude', which, because of the undefined nature of the boundary, allowed trespassing and 'deprived lessees of the power to defend themselves by law'.[42] The Government was urged to adopt a plan, and it was decided to have hundred boundaries carefully surveyed and marked on the ground by posts and mounds.

Looking at South Australia as a whole there are 14,100 miles of hundred boundaries, of which 15·8 per cent follow the coastline, 4·6 per cent topographical features of relief, 5·4 per cent follow rivers (mainly the River Murray) and 74·2 per cent are straight surveyed lines. If this total is analysed by regions it is evident that the older the area of settlement the greater the proportion of natural features utilized as hundred boundaries (see Table II).

Besides the ease of surveying straight lines and right-angles, the practice of defining hundred boundaries along true meridians and parallels ensured considerable accuracy once the starting point had been fixed by reference to the trigonometrical framework. Although modern survey methods have revealed slight inaccuracies between some hundreds, South Australia averted the worst problems of the use of magnetic North which gave the confusing and bizarre orientation of survey lines of parishes in the Western District of Victoria.[43] But, for whatever reason, straight lines and right-angles dominated the rural landscapes, and, if the unusually indented coast of South Australia is excluded from the calculations in Table II, then straight lines accounted for 88 per cent of all hundred boundaries. Geometry was triumphant over geography.

The size of hundreds varied from 30 square miles in Darling in the southern Flinders Ranges to 304 square miles in Bookpurnong in the Murray Mallee. But these were extremes; 26 corresponded

Table II

Types of Hundred Boundary (in miles)

(100 miles = 160·934 km)

Area	Coast	Ranges	Rivers	Survey Lines	Total
Central	493	432	354	864	2,143
Northern	448	155	11	2,806	3,420
Eyre Peninsula	990	32	—	3,597	4,619
Murray Mallee	101	—	398	1,438	1,937
South-East	218	40	—	1,723	1,981
TOTAL	2,250	659	763	10,428	14,100
% of total	15·8	4·6	5·4	74·2	

Source: S.A. Lands Dept. Maps.

exactly to one hundred square miles, and 187, or 35·5 per cent of the total were within 10 square miles of the ideal. In all, 362 hundreds, or 70·8 per cent, were within Bonney's stated 'one hundred square miles, one-third more or one-third less'. Generally speaking there is a tendency for the size of hundreds to increase with the passing of the years, a trend confirmed by the mean values for five-year periods since 1845. For the years 1845–49, the average size was 101·3 square miles, which increased fairly steadily to a peak of 151·3 square miles during 1920–24. This increase in size is reasonable as settlement was progressively penetrating the less humid and less productive parts of the State. After 1925, a decrease in size is apparent as the last remaining vestiges of land in the high rainfall areas were subdivided, particularly in the Upper South-East. It is interesting to note that the instructions of 1887 and 1914 to surveyors make no reference

3 SURVEY AND THE LANDSCAPE

to size, yet the fiction that the unit consists of a hundred square miles still persists. For example, in 1957, Martin said, 'The hundreds throughout the state are roughly equal in size which incidentally would average about one hundred square miles in area'.[44]

The Section

From about 1860 onwards, the hundreds and their design of roads largely controlled the pattern of survey, although the size of sections, which increased steadily, also played a part in determining that pattern. But before 1860, it was the section, the smallest survey unit, that was the basis of survey; and in a sense, we must retrace our steps to the situation after 1840 to fully understand its significance.

In order to examine the importance of the section it is best to look first at the size of sections over time (Figs. 30 and 31). These two graphs are based on the number of sections contained in hundreds proclaimed every year. Figure 30 shows the cumulative percentage of sections of different sizes in the hundreds; Fig. 31 shows the total number of sections eventually surveyed in the hundreds, and has a logarithmically-scaled axis to accommodate the variation of numbers, which ranges from 10 to nearly 10,000. These graphs of section numbers and sizes, together with the map of their distribution, constitute a framework for the discussion of the changing size of sections in South Australia. First, there is the period up to about 1860 when the small sections of below 100 acres (usually about 80 acres) predominated. Secondly, there is the period after the early 1860s when larger sections up to 640 acres became common. Finally, there is the period after 1885 when the very large section of one to two square miles, and sometimes larger, became the norm.

Order and Regularity, 1840–60

In the years before 1860, the number of sections smaller than 100 acres (usually of about 80 acres) was about three-quarters of all sections surveyed (79 per cent of nearly 10,000 sections in 1846), but the number dropped gradually to about half of all sections surveyed in 1860. At the same time, the number of larger sections, ranging from 100 to 320 acres, rose from about a quarter

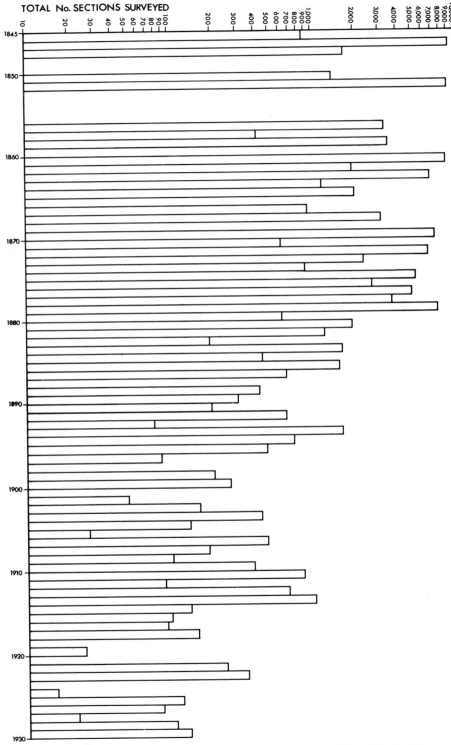

TOTAL No. SECTIONS SURVEYED

FIG. 30. The number of sections surveyed, 1836–1930. (S.A. Lands Dept. records.)

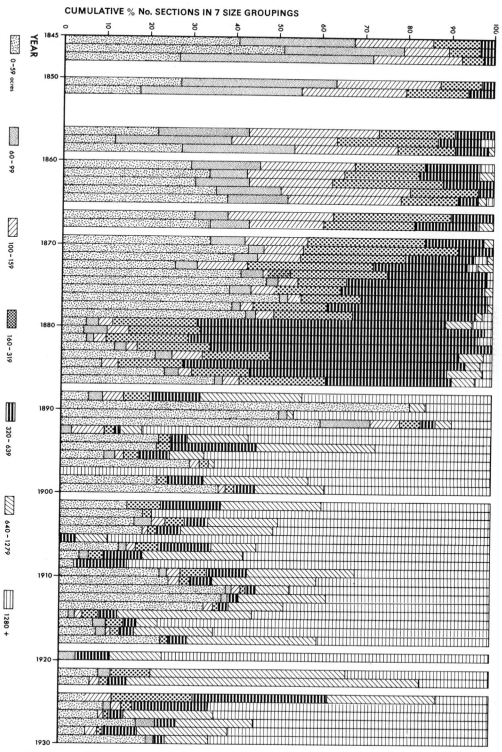

CUMULATIVE % No. SECTIONS IN 7 SIZE GROUPINGS

YEAR

0-59 acres

60-99

100-159

160-319

320-639

640-1279

1280 +

FIG. 31. The sizes of sections surveyed, 1836–1930. (S.A. Lands Dept. records.)

to nearly a half of all sections, while sections of between 320 and 640 acres in size rose from 3 per cent to over 10 per cent of the total (Fig. 31).

The reason for the adoption of the 80-acre module for the division of rural land in South Australia has never been explained satisfactorily. It features in the earliest plans; for example 'lots of not less than 80 acres each' were mentioned in the proposals for the founding of a Colony which were put forward to the British Government in 1831 by the South Australian Land Company, and Wakefield repeated the phrase the next year.[45]

It is often assumed that 80 acres is the logical result of sub-dividing a square mile, the latter being a unit which would have been easy to survey and which had precedents in the U.S.A., Canada and even in New South Wales.[46] But this is not so, since the division of the square mile into four equal portions gives 160 acres (such as the North American Quarter Section) and a further division would have produced 40-acre sections, or one-sixteenth of a square mile. To produce 80-acre blocks out of a square mile would have meant the survey of eight rectangular blocks of 20 by 40 chains, as was suggested at one point for the Adelaide Plains.[47] The only survey logic that one can see in the adoption of 80-acre blocks is that four of them contain 320 acres, or half a square mile, which was an interesting variation on the standard practice elsewhere (Fig. 32). There are two other possible explanations. First, as the survey regulations were drawn up in Britain, perhaps 80 acres was considered an ideal size for a holding there. Yet, what evidence there is suggests that while there were many farms below 100 acres in size in Britain during the early nineteenth century, they would have been re-garded as small and that the average farm was between 100 and 300 acres.[48] The second, and more probable, reason lies in the social values which were woven inextricably into the South Australian system of land sales and survey. With the price of land set at a minimum of £1 per acre, and the land surveyed into 80-acre sections, the farm-labourer had to save at least £80 before he could become an owner, as there were no facilities for credit purchases. In fact the sum needed to establish oneself was put higher than a bare £80 and was placed at about £150 for every 80 acres purchased and this could take at least five years to

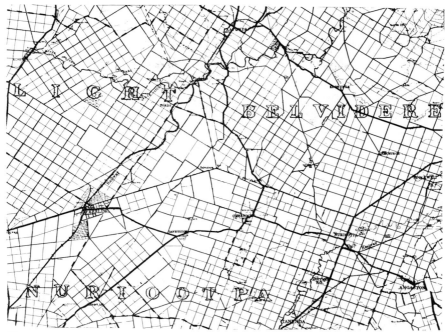

FIG. 32. Typical 80-acre survey pattern. The Barossa Valley, County Light, between Freeling and Angaston. The 80-acre grids are orientated in varying directions according to the lie of the land. Difficult to subdivide hill ranges were left in larger sections. (S.A. Lands Dept. 1 : 126, 720. By courtesy of Director of Lands : S.A.)

save. In this way a constant supply of labour for existing farmers was ensured and the labourer wage-earner did not get premature ideas about associating 'wealth and station with property in land'. Confirmation of this intricate link between section size and labour supply was given in 1838 when the surveyors were given the opportunity of increasing section sizes if labour became scarce.[49] Thus, an ordered hierarchical society could be ensured, consisting of capitalist farmers employing those who were labouring to accumulate capital. However one may view the philosophy implicit in this arrangement, the result was initially successful and in marked contrast with the systems prevailing elsewhere in Australia.

The earliest known instructions to field surveyors in 1839 said little about the size and shape of sections except that they should 'adopt the square form', but a year later, comprehensive instructions were drawn up by the Surveyor-General, Lt. E. C. Frome, with the purpose of ensuring 'regularity and a conformity of system' which became necessary after the hurried and sometimes disorganized survey carried on after 1836, and the confusion which arose from the temporary expedient of lowering the price of land to 12 shillings per acre, thereby producing a variety of section sizes.[50] This part of Frome's *Instructions* on 'Duties in the Field' is worthy of some detailed comment because it is the clearest statement of survey practice during the early years of settlement.

1. 'The primary objects in view . . . are—the division of all land available for the purposes of agriculture into sections containing eighty acres and the determining and marking out the best main lines of communication through the Province, upon which the direction of the boundaries of sections will in great measure depend.'
2. If the terrain permitted, sections were to be square with a 'reserve occupation road surrounding each four sections'. But near the coast, main roads and rivers, the frontages of sections should be halved 'to give as many as possible a participation in this advantage'.
3. In particularly hilly country, sections did not need to be exactly 80 acres, 'but they should not be laid out in blocks of less extent, land not being sold in smaller quantities'.
4. In similarly hilly situations, a strictly geometrical grid of occupation roads half to one chain wide might not be practical, and larger sections could be surveyed (up to three acres) in order to allow occupiers to make their own roads at the most convenient places.

So widespread and distinctive is the pattern of the 80-acre sections surveyed during the ensuing ten years that they can be mapped with comparative ease and they are shown in Fig. 20, with a detailed example, in Fig. 32, of a part of County Light, in the Central Hill Country.

But section sizes were increasing slowly during the 1850s, and this trend is placed beyond doubt by Goyder's analysis of the sizes of sections sold and the number of acres involved for every year between 1850 and 1857 (Table III). Whereas in 1850, 79

Table III

Number and Size of Sections Sold and Open to Application, 1850–57

Year (From 1st June)	Sections containing 80 acres and under (32·422 ha)		Sections containing 80–160 acres (32·422–64·75 ha)		Sections containing 160–640 acres (64·75–259·0 ha)		Total sections	
	No.	Area	No.	Area	No.	Area	No.	Area
1850	821	41,752	212	20,691	5	2,451	1,038	64,894
1851	732	46,483	279	27,593	26	8,510	1,037	82,586
1852	738	53,858	281	26,400	16	6,396	1,035	86,654
1853	1,479	104,675	603	61,052	144	47,513	2,226	213,240
1854	1,050	60,125	686	69,108	299	84,614	2,035	213,847
1855	705	42,976	627	65,312	201	63,282	1,533	171,570
1856	565	34,869	750	78,381	232	74,179	1,547	187,429
1857 (6 months only)	99	6,733	139	15,274	106	37,709	344	59,716
Total Open to application	6,189	391,471	3,577	363,811	1,029	324,654	10,795	1,079,936
	579	41,116	579	60,930	215	57,150	1,373	159,196
TOTAL	6,768	432,587	4,156	424,741	1,244	381,804	12,168	1,239,132

Source: SGO, 869/1857 (out).

per cent of all sections were 80 acres or less, 20·4 per cent between 80 and 160 acres, and only 0·6 per cent over 160 acres, the proportions changed progressively each succeeding year, so that by 1856 only 36·5 per cent of all sections were 80 acres or less, but 48·5 per cent were between 80 and 160 acres, and 15·0 per cent were above 160 acres. The acreage of land encompassed within sections of different sizes also changed so that by 1856 only 18·6 per cent of land sold was in sections of 80 acres, compared with 64·3 per cent in 1850.[51] Nevertheless, despite the increased size of sections many of them were laid out in a grid fashion (Fig. 33).

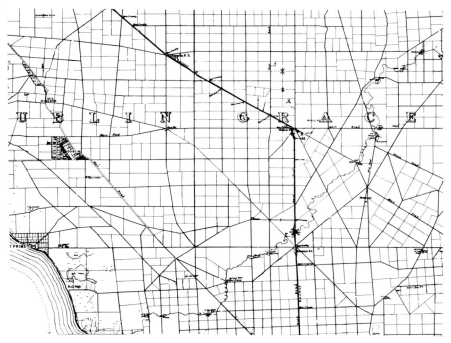

Fig. 33. Typical 160-acre survey patterns in the hundreds of Dublin, Grace, and Port Gawler, County Gawler. The early 80-acre sections in the south had to be enlarged to 160 acres in the more difficult mallee-covered lands to the north and because of a directive not to place roads at intervals of less than one mile apart. Major road junctions and townships are located in what were the open 'plains' in the mallee scrub. The area in the extreme west was not surveyed until it was included in the Dublin Agricultural Area after 1869, hence the larger sections. (S.A. Lands Dept. 1 : 126,720. By courtesy of Director of Lands : S.A.)

The increase in section sizes during these years was rapid and did not go without protest from the smaller landholders. Farmers near Mintaro sent a petition to the Surveyor-General expressing concern that land to the north of the town, for which they had been 'waiting for years to purchase', was to be surveyed 'in blocks of from 300 to 700 acres . . . which would preclude ourselves and others of limited capital from purchasing sections', and therefore requested that it be laid out in 80-acre sections. Similarly, in the hundred of Kondoparinga, near Strathalbyn, small-scale farmers thought it 'a disappointment and disadvantage' that adjoining land was to be surveyed into larger sections as they would not now 'have the chance of adding another section to their property'.[52]

The matter was discussed in the House of Assembly which belatedly reaffirmed that it was 'desirable to dispose of the Waste Lands in 80-acre sections', and the Surveyor-General was requested not to bring forward for sale 'sections containing more than 160 acres, without *previously* making a special report of the reasons which, in his opinion, render a deviation from the rule expedient'.[53] These instructions were amplified a few days later after the Surveyor-General had written to the Commissioner of Crown Lands asking what he should do with an application for large sections in the South-East. The 80-acre system, he was told, was appropriate for land 'adapted to agricultural purposes', but if the land was suitable for grazing only then the requests for large blocks could be considered. If large blocks of up to 640 acres were surveyed they should be laid out in such a way that they could be 'readily sub-divided' if the need arose. The directive to ask for special permission to survey large sections prior to doing the work was modified a few days later; the decision could now be left to an officer of the Survey Department 'on whose judgement a considerable reliance can be placed'.[54]

The ways in which this judgement was exercised in practice can be illustrated by many examples of decisions made during the next few years. Basically, there was a continued pressure to increase the size of sections and the reasons for this were three-fold: first the variable nature of the country, secondly, the requests by pastoralists for surveys and large sections, and thirdly, the need for easy lines of communication.

The Effect of Land Variability.

There was a growing awareness that not all land was of equal value and that South Australia was not 'a terrestrial paradise where there is [*sic*] neither rocks, sandy deserts nor mountains'.[55] Yet, the minimum price of £1 an acre was still in force in the late 1850s, and it implied some common basic level of land quality. Towards the end of the decade, however, soil characteristics became more important determinants of section size, which, said the Surveyor-General, 'averaging 80 acres in the agricultural Districts increases to 640 acres, the maximum size of sections, where the soil is of a poor character'.[56] The need for larger sections was greatest in two classes of country; first, in the areas of broken relief in the eastern portions of the Mount Lofty Ranges, and, secondly, in the sandy, mallee-covered plains. When preparing a plan for the subdivision of the hundred of Alma, Goyder purposely made the sections in the Ranges 'measurably larger than those on the plains, the lands being rough and strong and less accessible', a course of action which he intended to continue in the survey of portions of Clare, Julia Creek, Tungkillo, North and South Rhine, and portions of the South-East, which were to have '80 acres except where the land is of a poor nature where it will be desirable to survey in larger blocks'. Similarly, a request by George Glen to the Department for the survey of 5,000 acres in County Hindmarsh into 'such large blocks as you could possibly allow' because most of the land was 'stringybark and stoney ranges and none of it at all fit for agricultural purposes' was treated sympathetically.[57] All of these examples show up in Fig. 20 as areas of irregular sections of more than 80 acres but less than 160 acres.

In the lighter soils of the plains the same latitude was shown. A request for a block of 500–600 acres at Sandy Creek was granted as the land was 'of a poor and sandy nature', and Goyder recommended to the Commissioner of Crown Lands that mallee land in the hundred of Mudla Wirra be surveyed into large blocks, 'the land is of a very poor character and thickly covered with very dense Mallee-scrub, I do not think that it is the least likely that it would sell in 80 acre blocks'. A similar application about 'scrubby' land of 'inferior quality' near Port Gawler resulted in the survey of gridded 640-acre blocks, but laid out in such a way that the land could be subdivided into smaller sections if necessary[58] (Fig. 33).

The Effect of Requests

A great problem which the surveyors had to contend with was the dishonesty of pastoralists who, in order that large sections could be marked out, either depreciated the quality of the land which they wanted to be surveyed or just asked outright for large sections.[59] Large sections were cheaper to fence, more adaptable to extensive stock-management and harder for the smaller farmer to buy at the auctions.

Although the examination of survey procedure is not the main concern here it is essential to know how requests for survey fitted into the survey system and how the pastoralists holding a commanding position used the system of requests for the purpose of getting larger sections for themselves. Land was surveyed either as part of the Government's programme of expansion from the cores of settlement, or on request from any *bona fide* applicant for a survey of up to 640 acres, whether or not it was in a hundred.[60] If surveyors were in the locality, and it was convenient, the land would be surveyed. As was often the case in land matters in South Australia, there was a discrepancy between the theory and the implementation of governmental directives. While many requests were for blocks of land of less than 640 acres, it seems that in practice the Survey Department was prepared to survey much larger amounts, probably because of the assured revenue which would result. This gave the pastoralists a great advantage over all other buyers. During the ten years between 1857 and 1866, the survey of 294,151 acres was asked for. One example must stand for many. J. Ellis, a pastoralist with interests north of Adelaide asked to purchase 'about 6,000 acres on the Light, if surveyed along the N-South Banks say, upwards from my section No. 637 in the direction of Red Banks. I am also desirous of purchasing about 1,000 acres of the Wood north of the Light if surveyed in the part I may point out.' The tendency was for these requests for the survey of very large areas of land to be accompanied by requests for large sections.[61]

Some pastoralists were downright misleading in the information which they gave the Survey Department about the quality of the land to be surveyed, while at other times they were quite open and blatant in their requests for large sections. As an example of the first, Hawker asked for the survey of 3,000 acres in blocks of 640 acres. When the surveyor examined the country he found that the land was not as stated, 'only adapted for pasture, being rough hilly country and none in the river flat', but, quite to the contrary, 'first-rate land'. It was surveyed into 80-acre sections with an occasional upland area in 350–400-acre section.[62] B. Leake, from near Penola, was more open about what he wanted : 'the squatters of this district are the largest purchasers of land—and I think their applications ought to be attended to, 80-acre sections are of little use—cannot fence them [because of (?)] so many roads'. A little later, when asking for a 13,899-acre survey of his run, Leake said 'I hope you will not [survey (?)] 80-acre sections on my Run at Nalang . . . If you are obliged to measure 80 acres, I wish to limit my application to four square miles . . .'.[63]

There were two courses open to the Government : first, to subdivide any existing large blocks, and secondly to designate stringently the quality of the land, and, as a consequence, survey appropriately sized sections on it. In the South-East, existing square-mile blocks were cut up.[64] Some pastoralists objected; John McIntyre of Mount Schank said :

> 'It will completely upset my arrangements . . . I may remark that most of the land fit for agricultural purposes is already surveyed and sold and it is hardly gain for the Govt. to cut off the few acres of middling land that is on one end of my applica-tion, 3 miles of it is of little use to any one except for grazing.'[65]

Against such people were arrayed the numbers of the 'small capitalists' who wanted the land in the runs to be 'surveyed into 80-acre sections to suit small purchasers and the publick [sic] in general'.[66] The problem of classifying the land as being of either pastoral or agricultural use was subjective and open to a great amount of variation, and, although the Surveyor-General re-issued 'positive instructions' once more to the surveyors that large sections could not be marked out unless 'it is proved that the land is not fit for agriculture'; it was a losing battle.[67]

The Effect of Roads.

The third reason for the general increase in the size of sections during the 1850s was associated with the laying-out of the roads, which were, of course, an integral part of the survey system. The gridded pattern of the 80-acre system gave rise to a network of roads that was often impracticable in hilly country, (Fig. 34), and there were also too many roads, all of which needed double fencing, were costly in their upkeep and wasted land.

FIG. 34. A vertical view of 80-acre section grids west of Birdwood, in the Adelaide Hills. The grid of roads runs around each group of four sections on the flatter land in the east and there has been an attempt to continue the grid across the broken and uneven topography in the west. (By courtesy of Director of Lands : S.A.)

But all too often, the grid of roads around four 80-acre sections was still surveyed irrespective of terrain features thereby giving too many roads; 'a thing uncalled for on such bad land', said one settler near Truro.[68] The stated object of the survey during the 1850s was to provide a network of roads and eventually to close those that were not used as the 'ultimate direction of traffic could only be determined after the complete occupation of the country'; [69] then the surplus roads could be sold. But the population as a whole was well aware of the implications of this policy. The Clerk of the District Council of Gumeracha wrote to the Surveyor-General to say that if roads under survey in the district 'are run out in straight lines as usual, they will be useless to settlers in consequence of their being carried over very steep hills', and complaints of surplus and unsuitable roads became common.[70]

It is clear that by the late 1850s Freeling was aware of the problem; he told surveyors in the Pinkerton Plains area, north-west of Gawler, 'not to mark out parallel lines at lesser distances than one mile apart' unless the topographical features of the country made it necessary to deviate from the rule in order to give access to land already surveyed or to get a 'good natural line of communication'.[71] Although a grid pattern of sections was adhered to in this area, inevitably the sections were much larger and were nearer to 160 acres in size (Fig. 33). But the legacy of unusable roads remained, and contemporary views were summed up in a satirical, mock-biblical piece written by the editor of the *Border Watch* entitled 'A too common chapter in South Australian history', the first paragraph of which is reproduced at the head of this chapter. It continued

'And it came to pass that as they measured the land only in straight lines, turning neither to the right nor to the left, lest their calculations should become disordered and themselves be lost; so did they mark out beautiful roads thirty cubits in width that went nowhere, others ran over perpendicular mountains or through impassable swamps, many went into deep watercourses or hideous caverns, and some did terminate in the depth of the ocean . . . and the people were exceedingly glad, but the working bullocks lifted up their voices and wept.'

'Now these men of learning became after much toil and hard

practice very skilful in the mysteries of land measuring after their fashion—that is to say in straight lines; for to measure a piece of land in any shape, or no shape at all, they held to be a departure from sound judgement and sinful thing to contemplate. And a chronicle of these days hath related that one rash man not having the fear of the theodolite before his eyes did leave the paths of rectitude and right-angle to make a better road across a gully, and was seen no more.'

The article must have struck a chord with many and it led to complaints, which Goyder was not prepared to let pass. A few weeks later he sent a memorandum to all his staff:

'Officers-in-charge of field parties are instructed to exercise the greatest care in laying off the best lines of road. The Surveyor-General wants it to be distinctly understood that he will suspend officers laying out an impracticable road and recommend his immediate dismissal to the Responsible Minister.'[72]

In every way the desire for uniform sections in small sizes was superseded by the desire to achieve the best line for roads and a reduction in their number. The recognition that different types of land demanded different survey arrangements was also important. The efforts of 1857 to stem the tide of section enlargement were of no use, and the gradual disintegration of the '80-acre system' was symbolic of the changes that were occurring through all facets of the economic and social life of the colony as the original, conscious plan of an ordered and controlled settlement and society was being questioned, and being replaced by new goals and plans.

Flexibility, 1860–85

Detailed information about section size decreases after 1860, although the general trends become increasingly clear to follow because there was greater governmental direction, and less was left to the discretion of the surveyors in the field. Sections generally tended to be larger. Table IV (based on Fig. 31) sets out the percentage of sections for various sizes by 5-year intervals.

Table IV

Sizes of Sections Surveyed (by percentages) in Hundreds Declared
for Selected Years, 1860–90

(100 acres = 40·496 ha; 640 acres = 259·0 ha)

Year	Suburban lands (less than 40 acres)	Rural sections (in acres)				
		0–99	100–319	320–639	640–1,279	1,280+
1860	19·1	26·7	38·3	12·2	1·0	2·6
1866	16·7	21·6	51·8	9·5	0·4	—
1870	41·0	5·0	45·4	7·5	0·2	—
1875	24·4	19·5	21·0	33·4	1·1	0·7
1880	2·3	8·2	21·8	66·6	0·5	1·2
1885	19·6	7·5	26·6	45·9	8.3	2·0
1890	50·5	1·5	0·5	3·5	1·5	46·0

Source: S.A. Lands Dept., Diagram Books.

Three aspects of the trend towards larger sections are of significance.

1. There was a progressive decline in the number of small
    sections from over 30 per cent in the early 1860s to well
    below 10 per cent in the 1890s. These figures are a little mis-
    leading, however, as there was an accompanying rise in the
    number of small suburban sections (of 2–40 acres) around
    towns, which parallels the growth in town survey during the
    years from 1870 to 1878 in particular (see pp. 366–375).

2. As the number of 80-acre sections declined so the number of
    sections of 100–319 acres increased, rising to a peak of 51·8
    per cent in 1866; larger sections of from 320–639 acres were
    of overwhelming importance by 1880.

3. The really large sections of 640–1,279 acres were relatively
    insignificant, except in the mid-1880s, as little land was taken
    up at the time when they were in vogue. But the sections of
    1,280 acres (2 square miles) became overwhelming during the
    late 1880s and the 1890s, and outnumbered all other section
    sizes from then on.

While the Government still paid lip-service to the idea of 80-acre sections, its surveyors were measuring out 'in the usual manner' routine sections which varied 'from 80 to 160 acres',[73] and were surveying even larger sections for the pastoralists, whose land purchases reached a peak during the mid-1860s. The trend towards larger section sizes was occurring for all the reasons noted before; but now there was a formal recognition of the need for them which was embodied for the first time in land legislation. The Scrub Lands Act of 1866 was designed to encourage the settlement of the difficult lands of the mallee areas. The idea was Goyder's and it was his original intention to survey sections in the Scrub Areas with sizes tending to be larger but no more than 160 acres. The Commissioner of Crown Lands took a very liberal attitude, however, and asked for land to be offered 'in *larger* blocks, from 300 to 600 acres, while a few may be smaller'.[74] Seeing that there was likely to be a general change of policy in favour of larger sections, the Surveyor-General asked for permission to increase all sections to 350 acres, where appropriate, while still keeping the best lands in sections of 80 to 160 acres, and this the Cabinet later granted in 1867.[75]

This was a major change, but it was not the only one. Events moved even more quickly during the ensuing years as the South Australian wheat growers clamoured for more liberal land laws. The upshot of this pressure was the passing of Strangways' Act in 1869 which allowed, for the first time, the purchase of land on credit in farm blocks of up to 640 acres laid out in sections of no more than 320 acres in size, within specially designated Agricultural Areas.[76]

Some of the remarks made during the lengthy debate on the new legislation throw light on the attitudes to the 80-acre system by 1869. The Chief Secretary opened the debate by saying that 'at the present time an 80-acre section is not large enough a holding for a farmer'. Others thought that 'the time for the 80-acre system had gone by' and that 'it might have done in the early days of the Colony when the farmer had the right of commonage', but when all the land was fenced in it was impossible to farm efficiently. The need was to 'change with the times' by getting rid of 'small petty farms' and substituting large holdings 'so that grazing and farming might be combined and the land be occasionally rested'. The Chief Secretary looked ahead prophetically and said that 'farming in the future in South Australia would not be with 80- or 100-acre sections, but with thousands of acres'.[77]

The old charge that the trend towards large sections kept out the smaller farmer and favoured the pastoralists and land jobbers was raised anew the next year in the House of Assembly but the Commissioner of Crown Lands, Blythe, doubted if there were many people in Parliament with 'an undue admiration for the old 80-acre system'; yet, surprisingly, there was a great deal of support for smaller sections, especially when it was learnt in the course of the debate that the Canowie Station had just been surveyed into sections of between 200 and 600 acres.[78] The next day the Commissioner of Crown Lands wrote to Goyder drawing his attention to the outcome of the debate and told him to survey 'land fit for agriculture in blocks ranging from 80 to 500 acres, having a far larger number of small than of large sections'.[79] Whilst a perusal of Fig. 31 and the evidence of the size of sections gazetted for sale in 1870–72 suggest that the number of smaller sections was maintained and even increased, it is clear that Blythe's policy had opened the door officially for the survey of sections larger than those of 320 acres as provided for in Strangways' Act of 1869; and from 1872 onwards sections in the range 320 to 640 acres became increasingly common. Nevertheless the limit of 500 acres was re-affirmed in the Land Act of 1877.[80]

Yet, within a few years of Blythe's advice to Goyder in 1870, the gulf between official policy and routine action revealed itself once more as sections in excess of 500 acres were surveyed. Sometime before May, 1874 Goyder told his surveyors that the size of sections could be increased from between 400 and 500 acres to between 640 and 700 acres 'if such is thought desirable'; and in March of the same year he sent a circular to officers in charge of field parties 'to survey the sections laid off by them in blocks of from 320 to 640 acres, preference being given, where such is practicable, to the largest area'.[81]

In fact it seemed as though everything was working towards the creation of larger sections. The Survey Department's policy of tracing the pattern of major roads within the boundaries of the hundreds, evolved during the late 1850s and early 1860s, was now in full swing, and the irregular pattern of roads created many awkwardly shaped units that were difficult to divide into smaller sections, especially where inferior and rugged ground was avoided by the roads. Almost any hundred designed and surveyed in the Northern Areas, the west coast of Eyre Peninsula, Yorke Peninsula and the Lower South-East between 1869 and 1885 reveals this. The Department was also keen to survey in larger sections as this was quicker (an important point during the 1870s when the demand for land was probably at its greatest but the survey staff numerically at its weakest, since the 1860s) and it was, above all, cheaper. The cost of survey dropped as the years progressed, and later, Goyder calculated the average cost per acre as being: 1840–1, 1s-6d; 1842–51, 3$\frac{6}{10}$d; 1852–61, 9$\frac{1}{2}$d; 1862–87, 6$\frac{1}{2}$d; and 1887–90, between 2d and 3d. He attributed the drop in costs to 'the greater area of sections, which proportionately reduced the number of miles of lines required to be run in marking the blocks on the ground'.[82]

Finally, the question of section size took on a new significance as it became linked with the idea of the desirable size of holdings, so that as the demand for larger holdings increased so did the demand for larger sections. Often it is difficult to disentangle exactly what happened; the words 'selection', 'section', 'holding' and 'farm' were used interchangeably and one is never sure of the basis of the figures of average size that were bandied about. For example, the average size of selections under the 1869 Act was said to be 355 acres, and under the 1872 Act 414 acres. Elsewhere it is said that the average holding size in 1873 was 276 acres, and in 1875 it was 289 acres.[83] Because of the variations in the basis of these figures the best indication of the increase in the size of holdings is given by Table V which consists of the number of holdings and the extent of land in holdings of various sizes for 1866–7 and 1886.

The significant things in this table, from our point of view, are the absolute decline from 2,214 to 1,448 in the number of holdings in the 51–100 acres group and the rise in the number of holdings in the larger groups, particularly those over 500 acres which rose from 874 to 6,024 between 1866–7 and 1886.[84]

One important reason for the increase in section size with holding size was that the 1869 Act limited section sizes to 320 acres (a size frequently exceeded) and holdings to 640 acres; yet, the farmer who wanted 640 acres often found it hard to find the right combination of section size to make up a square mile. If he found two adjacent sections of 300 and 400 acres respectively he could 'go in for one or the other, but could not have both'.[85] The tendency, therefore, was to enlarge the section so that in most cases it constituted a holding, and frequently its size approached that of the permitted holding, i.e. 640 acres. Certainly by the late 1870s two-thirds of all sections surveyed approached 640 acres in size (Fig. 31 and Table V). The situation was eased somewhat, and greater flexibility achieved, by the Crown Lands Consolidation Act of 1877 which allowed holdings of 1,000 acres and sections of no more than 500 acres.[86] There was an additional reason for surveying sections in sizes which approached the size of the holding, namely that it enabled purchasers to avoid competition for contiguous sections at auction, and to obtain what they wanted by one bid.[87]

New Lands and New Patterns

The size of sections became larger from the mid-1880s onwards in response to new needs associated with the expansion into the new lands of Eyre Peninsula, the Murray Mallee and the Upper South-East. The trend in section sizes is depicted in Fig. 31 and percentages for selected years are given in Table VI. The distribution of the large sections in these new areas of settlement can be gauged from Fig. 20.

As pastoral leases in these dry, sandy and scrub-covered areas expired during the late 1880s the land was squared off into hundreds which by this date were the basic land-planning units. The land in the hundred was divided initially into large sections—called 'blocks'—which were let on lease, often as Grazing and Cultivation Leases. The size of the blocks varied from 2,000 to 20,000 acres depending on the type of country, and they were designed to encourage more intensive grazing and some cultivation. These experiments were not a success, and the more favourable portions of the Leases in Eyre Peninsula and in the Murray Mallee were subdivided into smaller units. The land was leased in perpetuity to agriculturists with a right of purchase at 5 shillings per acre. At last, what farmers had been saying for years was recognized officially : not all land in South Australia

Table V

The Number and Extent of Holdings, 1866/7 and 1886

(50 acres = 20·234 ha)

Size	Number of holdings				Extent of holdings				Average size	
	1866–67		1886		1866–67		1886		1866–67	1886
	No.	%	No.	%	No.	%	No.	%	Acres	Acres
1–5	1,188	10·27	2,278	11·61	3,114	0·07	5,236	0·04	2·62	2·29
6–50	2,256	19·51	2,437	12·42	46,016	1·07	53,828	0·43	20·39	22·08
51–100	2,214	19·15	1,448	7·38	169,110	3·95	113,125	0·92	76·38	78·12
101–500	5,029	43·49	7,421	37·84	1,085,325	25·30	2,133,228	17·36	215·80	287·47
500+	874	7·55	6,024	30·72	2,978,790	69·59	9,979,407	81·23	3,408·20	1,656·60
TOTAL	11,561		19,608		4,282,355		12,284,824			

Sources: SAPP, 10 (1867); 114 (1886).

Table VI

Sizes of Sections Surveyed (by percentages) in Hundreds Declared
for Selected Years, 1890 and 1931

(100 a = 40.496 ha; 640 a = 259 ha)

Year	Suburban lands (less than 40 acres)	Rural sections (in acres)				
		0–99	100–319	320–639	640–1,279	1,280+
1890	50·5	1·5	0·5	3·5	1·5	46·0
1895	12·9	4·6	5·2	6·0	7·9	66·5
1901	15·9	—	7·8	13·7	23·5	39·2
1905	—	—	—	3·7	7·4	88·9
1910	24·9	0·9	4·8	4·8	24·4	40·1
1915	8·0	2·0	5·0	3·0	5·0	77·0
1921	9·4	2·5	10·0	0·8	45·1	33·1
1925	10·7	1·7	5·0	—	17·4	65·3
1931	4·3	—	17·3	8·7	13·0	56·5

Source: S.A. Lands Dept. Diagram Books.

was of equal value or of sufficient value to warrant the paying of a
minimum price of £1 per acre.

Between 1885 and 1900 the Government surveyed 13,543,212
acres of 'ordinary lands' in 16,253 blocks with an average size of
8,332 acres, the largest blocks being surveyed between 1886 and
1888. After 1900, the provision of railways and wells in the interior
areas, and the new confidence engendered by fallowing practices
and superphosphate caused a great surge of settlement, and the
Government began to review, once more, its policy on the size
of blocks. The larger blocks were subdivided into smaller sections,
and many surveyed blocks tended to be between 1,000 and 2,000
acres in size. Where the land was dominated by east–west
trending dunes the subdivision was characterized by a sinuous
pattern of roads which snaked through the gaps in the dunes (see
Fig. 28 and pp. 89–90). This form of survey is present in about
100 hundreds in the southern half of the Murray Mallee, parts of
the Upper South-East, and most of the interior portions of Eyre
Peninsula. Where the landscape was undifferentiated by natural

features, straight lines and right-angles predominated (Fig. 29). These two patterns dominated survey from about 1885 onwards, and in this regard, Fig. 20 should be compared with Figs. 15 and 16.

Increasingly the whole idea of block size was associated not only with holding size but with the concept of a 'reasonable living area'. The official attitude during the early part of this century was that the blocks were generally too large. In 1904 the Surveyor-General, Strawbridge, noted that fifty-one settlers in Mortlock and Cummins hundreds in the southern part of Eyre Peninsula had farms with an average size of 1,566 acres. In his opinion this was excessive as 'large areas generally lead to slovenly farms, while small farms as a rule, tend to a better system being adopted at less expense'.[88] But in saying this he was going against the collective experience of the farmers who tended to think that a size varying between 2,000 and 5,000 acres was more reasonable. There were Commissions of Enquiry into the extension of the railways in Eyre Peninsula and the Murray Mallee in 1904 and 1906 and their reports are full of information on holding size.

From 1931 onwards, only 376 completely new sections were surveyed throughout the whole of South Australia, although, of course, there were many subdivisions of existing ones. The climatic limits of land settlement had been reached, expansion was over, and what occurred from here on was the internal re-organization of sections within known limits. The object was to make the best of what was settled, and the intensification of land use led to the subdivision of large and under-productive estates. Some further subdivision of the massive Mallee Blocks occurred, but more importantly, the settlement of ex-servicemen on repurchased estates after the First World War led to much irrigation settlement along the River Murray and, after the Second World War, to medium-sized holdings in repurchased estates throughout Kangaroo Island, the Upper and Lower South-East and parts of Eyre Peninsula.

But, generally speaking, the main lineaments of the pattern of the landscape over most of South Australia had been set by 1920, and they have proved to be very durable features over time, out-living residences and townships in their permanence.[89] In the short space of about 100 years the framework of the new economy and society had been laid over the land, which was now changed beyond recognition.

3. Notes

1. Calculated from the original field books (Diagram Books) of the surveyors, S.A. Lands Department, Adelaide.
2. With the exception of J. M. Powell, *The public lands of Australia Felix* (1970), 32–55, there has been no geographical inquiry in Australia on the form and effect of survey systems to rival studies such as W. D. Pattinson, 'Beginnings of the American rectangular survey system, 1784–1800', *University of Chicago, Department of Geography, Research Paper, No. 50* (1957), and N. J. Thrower, *Original Survey and land subdivision* (1966), Monograph Series No. 4 Assoc. of Amer. Geogr.
3. W. Oldham, *The land policy of South Australia from 1830 to 1842* (1917). The price of £1 per acre was a compromise between the 12 shillings per acre in the disastrous Swan River settlement and the £2 per acre suggested by Wakefield.
4. S.A.A., R.N., 1324/170.
5. D. N. Jeans, 'Territorial divisions and the location of towns in New South Wales, 1826–1842', *Aust. Geog.*, X (1967), 244.
   In N.S.W., townships of six square miles with square mile blocks were surveyed for a few years, but this rectangular system was discontinued after 1826 and a less regular system of English origin was adopted, with parishes of 25 square miles and sections adapted to local conditions of topography and water supply conditions. This hierarchy with variations was used later in Victoria. For the system in Victoria see J. M. Powell, *The public lands of Australia Felix* (1970), 34–37.
6. *S.A. Govt. Gaz.* (2 August 1842); (18 May 1843).
7. SGO, 222/1855 (out); 216/1856 (in).
8. SGO, 627/1857 (in).
9. S. J. and B. Webb, *English local government* (1906), Vol. 1. 'The parish and the county', 284–5.
   H. M. Cam in her authoritative *The hundred and the hundred rolls* (1930), is not prepared to suggest an origin.
10. W. Oldham, op. cit. 27; *SAPP*, 158 (1860), qus. 6 and app. 2.
    The pastoral runs were occupied by squatters with no legal title until the issue of occupation licences after 1842.
11. *Act* 11/1846. An Act to regulate the occupation of Crown Lands. Later

amendments were contained in *S.A. Govt. Gaz.* (29 June 1846). The leased lands continued on an annual basis, but with six months' notice of resumption.

12. *SAPP*, 158 (1860), qus. 17, 41, 104.
13. SGO, 106/1855 (out).
   For other examples see:
   SGO, 349/1855 (out); 678/1858 (out); 965/1859 (out); 1779/1859 (out).
14. SGO, 92/1860 (in).
15. SGO, 172/1860 (in).
   For examples see:
   SGO, 149/1868 (out); 887/1868 (out); for Yorke Peninsula;
   SAPP, 192 (1877), for Kangaroo Island.
16. E. C. Frome, *Instructions for the interior survey of South Australia* (1840), 5.
17. SGO, 33/1856 (in).
18. For example SGO, 1119/1858 (out), for Yankalilla; SGO, 848/1859 (in), for Talunga; SGO, 1393/1859 (in), for Ulooloo. The quality of the surveyors was obviously not of the best. The trouble at Ulooloo arose from the work of Sapper Fargahar whose work had 'to be laid out for him, the roads, reserves and methods of survey being pointed out to him on the ground as well as sketched on his plan.' A little later Faraghar asked to be discharged, which was granted. SGO, 345/1859 (out).
19. SGO, 579/1855 (in).
20. SGO, 1343/1859 (out). See also for confirmatory evidence SGO, 1986/1859 (out), concerning the planning of lines of roads.
21. SGO, 938/1859 (in);
   SAPP, 158 (1860), qus. 15.
22. *SAPD*, (H.A.) (1860), cols. 815–16.
23. *SAPP*, 158 (1860).
24. SGO, 1530/1860 (out), shows that Freeling thought 'it injurious to the public interest' and that 'the Minister in charge is better able to decide the position than the whole of Parliament'.
25. *SAPP*, 118 (1861); see also *SAPP*, 44 (1861) for the date of proclamation of all hundreds to 1861. For examples of proposed hundreds see *SAPP*, 187 (1861); 189 (1861); 197 (1861).
26. For an early example of this see SGO, 1656/1859 (out), where Freeling suggests to the Commissioner that 'the time has arrived when it may be desirable to declare a new hundred north of Kooringa, in accordance with Surveyor Kingston's outline plan'.
27. *SAPD*, (H.A.) (1869–70), col. 1510.
28. *SAPP*, 23 (1870–1), 8.
29. In declaring only seven hundreds the Government thought that it was being

very moderate. It had already rejected a request for the creation of hundreds around Streaky Bay, a request, moreover, which had had Goyder's support. See *SAPD* (H.A.) (1875), cols. 683–4 and 771; and SGO, 2742/1875 (in); various correspondence and reports from 27 July to 29 November.

30. See *SAPP*, 84 (1875) and 17 (1875 Spec. Sess.) for some of the maps of the areas involved.

31. *SAVP* (H.A.) (18 August 1875) and (19 July 1876); for descriptions of hundreds see, for example, *SAPP*, 102, 203, 209, 218 (1876).

32. D. W. Meinig, *On the margins of the good earth; the South Australian wheat frontier, 1869–1884* (1962), 95–9.

33. *Handbook for government surveyors* (1887), 40–1.

34. A. S. Martin, *Aspects of South Australia Lands*, (1958). This first appeared as an article in *The Valuer*, April (1958), 76–86.

35. SGO, 292/1855 (in); SGO, 462/1855 (out).

36. SGO, 217/1860 (out).

37. SGO, 142/1852 (out), and additional information in SGO, 81/1851 (out), and 193/1851 (out).

38. SGO, 646/1869 (out). Permission was granted.

39. SGO, 2742/1875 (in); various correspondence. The Attorney-General's opinion is in letter dated 29 Nov. At this time, Goyder obviously thought that changes in boundaries could take place without recourse to Parliament, see memo, 2 Oct. For examples of boundary changes see *SAPP*, 30 (1875); 236 (1877); 141 (1879).

40. SGO, 261/1856 (in).

41. *SAPP*, 167 (1860).

42. *SAPD* (H.A.) (1861), col. 71; and (L.C.), cols. 194–5.

43. J. M. Powell, *The public lands of Australia Felix*, (1970), 44–5.

44. A. S. Martin, *Aspects of South Australian Lands* (1958), 1.

45. South Australian Land Company, *A Proposal to His Majesty's government for founding a colony on the southern coast of Australia* (1831), 6; E. G. Wakefield, *Plan of a company to be established for the purpose of founding a colony in South Australia* (1832), 4.

46. For the U.S.A. see W. D. Pattinson, 'Beginnings of the American rectangular survey system, 1784–1800', *University of Chicago, Department of Geography, Research Paper, No. 50* (1957); For Canada see W. A. Mackintosh and W. L. G. Joerg (eds.), *Canadian Frontiers of Settlement*, Vol. 2 (1934); For New South Wales see D. N. Jeans, 'The breakdown of Australia's first rectangular grid survey', *Aust. Geogr. Studies*, IV (1966), 119.

47. *British Parliamentary Paper* (1841). Second report of the Select Committee on South Australia, 10th June, app. 34, p. 340, 'Report on surveying, considered with reference to New Zealand and applicable to other colonies

generally', by Capt. R. K. Dawson. This report contains a map of the Adelaide plains surveyed into square mile blocks.

48. D. B. Grigg, 'Small and large farms in England and Wales', *Geography*, XLVIII (1963), 268–79.

49. *British Parliamentary Paper*. First Annual Report of the Colonization Commissioners for South Australia (1836), app. 4, p. 19.

50. SGO, (out) (1839), p. 97. Instructions to the officers of the survey, and SGO, 71/1839, (in).

E. C. Frome, *Instructions for the survey of the interior of South Australia* (1840), 5–9.

For a useful preliminary study of survey policy see J. I. Poynter, 'The cadastral survey of South Australia'. B. A. Hons, Dept. of Geography, University of Adelaide, (1964).

51. Although these statistics are calculated on a different basis from that used to construct Fig. 31, the general trends are confirmed.

52. SGO, 467/1855 (in); 774/1856 (in). The Surveyor-General's memo in this docket is interesting because it states clearly that the first applicant for land was served first, irrespective of the desirability of maintaining 80-acre section sizes.

53. SGO, 357/1857 (in); and CLO, 190/1857 (out), also printed in *SAPP*, 135 (1858).

54. SGO, 462/1857 (out); 360/1857 (in).

55. W. Mann, *Six years' residence in the Australian provinces* (1839), 248; SGO, 1729/1859 (out).

56. SGO, 2185/1859 (out).

57. SGO, 775/1858 (in); 1528/1859 (in); 1914/1859 (out).

For other examples see SGO, 1056/1857 (in); a request for a 320-acre section in North Rhine; and 869/1857 (out), for large sections in the Ranges north of Clare.

58. SGO, 1579/1860 (out); 1924/1860 (out); 1463/1860 (in).

See also 1075/1860 (in), for a request for large sections to be surveyed in the swampy land of the South-East.

59. Early examples of this were requests for two square mile blocks at Kanmantoo, four sections of 500 acres each at the junction of the Rivers Gilbert and Light, and 2,000 acres in Julia Creek hundred, 'in blocks as near as 640 acres as possible,' SGO, 871/1856 (in); 84/1856 (in); 216/1859 (in) respectively.

60. *Act*, 8/1842–43. An Act to regulate the selling of Waste Lands belonging to the Crown. This arrangement, said the Surveyor-General to the Colonial Secretary 'has in every case been adopted by this office'. SGO, 141/1853 (out).

61. SGO, 674/1856 (in); 634/1856 (in). Between 1857 and 1863 Ellis applied

for the survey of 69,000 acres of which he purchased only 14,047 acres. For examples of other requests see SGO, 357/1857 (in), for 17,000 acres in the South-East; 1528/1859 (in), for 5,000 acres in the hundred of Hindmarsh; 1064/1860 (in), for 3,000 acres north of Clare.

62. SGO, 2004/1860 (out); CLO, 1301/1860 (in). For a similar case near Penola see SGO, 2107/1860 (out); and 2161/1860 (out).

63. CLO, 329/1858 (in); SGO, 508/1869 (in). In fact this survey was not allowed as the land was so good that the Commissioner thought it best if an extended notice be given to allow the intending small-scale purchasers time to come and look at it.

64. SGO, 950/1857 (in); 267/1858 (out), with additional details in 498/1858 (out); 204/1858 (in); 594/1858 (out).

65. SGO, 906/1857 (in).

66. SGO, 1059/1857 (in).

67. SGO, 360/1857 (in).

68. SGO, 41/1858 (in).

69. SGO, 1324/1859 (out). See also previous correspondence on the selling of excess roads in SGO, 1057/1859 (in).

70. SGO, 172/1854 (in). Freeling's reply is in 163/1854 (out), 27 April, but there is no indication that he did anything. Other complaints are found in SGO, 558/1855 (in); 43/1858 (in), for roads in the hundreds of Moorooroo, Belvidere, and North and South Rhine; and in SGO, 3403/79 (in), farmers in the Burdett district had appropriated the excess and useless roads and had been farming them for years.

71. SGO, 723/1858 (out), found in 1088/1859 (in).

72. SGO, 64/1864 (in).

73. SGO, 277/1861 (in), on the occasion of allowing pastoralists the privilege of purchasing 640 acres around their homesteads; and SGO, 973/1866 (out).

74. For further details see pp. 139–42 below, and also SGO, 463/1866 (out). In fact, Goyder initially surveyed 280 sections, ranging in size from 14 to 220 acres. See SGO, 425/1867 (out).

75. SGO, 541/1866 (in), and cover notes; also CLO, 1092/1867 (in).

76. *Act*, 14/1868–9, Waste Lands Amendment Act. The terms of credit were extended slightly by *Act*, 4/1869–70, Waste Lands Amendment Act.

77. *SAPD* (H.A.) (1868–9); cols. 531, 543, 554, 1397–8 and 1013 respectively.

78. *SAPD* (H.A.) (1870–71), cols. 1819–23.

79. SGO, 2548/1870 (in).

80. *Act*, 86/1877, Crown Lands Consolidation Act, Part 2; and *Act*, 420/1887, Crown Lands Amendment Act.

81. CLO, 530/1874 (in).

82. *SAPP*, 60 (1890), p. 22 and app. C. The general point was confirmed in 1870 when Goyder estimated that the survey of 1,000,000 acres of land in square mile blocks would cost about 2d per acre, however 'should they smaller, the cost will be proportionately larger', SGO, 1032/1870 (out).

83. *SAPP*, 122 (1877); and CLO, 393/1875 (in).

84. This group consisted mainly of 80-acre section holdings which declined markedly in the older settled counties, e.g. Adelaide, 902 to 612; Light, 404 to 173; Stanley, 140 to 75; Grey, 186 to 120. For the sake of comparison the further breakdown of holdings over 500 acres in 1886 is not shown in Table V, but it is known that of the 6,024 holdings in this group, 4,292 were between 500 and 1,000 acres, and 1,045 between 1,001 and 2,000 acres in size.

85. *SAPD* (H.A.) (1870–71), col. 1118. For the first test case of this ruling, see the application of J. Walter of Booyoolie, to buy 58 acres of land more than 640 acres. It was not allowed. SGO, 1901/72 (in). This regulation was repealed by *Act*, 123/1878, an Act to amend the Laws relating to the Crown Lands of South Australia.

86. *Act*, 86/1877, Crown Lands Consolidation Act.

87. CLO, 530/1874 (out).

88. *SAPP*, 31A (1909), qu. 489; 30A (1909), qu. 196; and 51 (1911), qu. 1755, respectively. See also SAPP, 20 (1912), for further confirmation.

89. M. Williams, 'Simplicity and stability in rural areas: the example of the Pinnaroo district of South Australia', *Geografiska Annaler*, LIV, Series B (1972), 117–135.

4
Clearing the Woodland

'Will any one who knew the country a dozen years ago say we have nothing to fear if the work of destruction goes on at the same rate for some 20 to 30 years to come?' *Border Watch*, 15 Jan., (1870).

'Smoke! smoke! smoke! anywhere, everywhere, nothing but smoke.' *Yorke Peninsula Advertiser*, 11 March, (1881).

Of the many activities which have gone into the making of the South Australian landscape, the clearing of the woodland must have brought about the most striking and widespread transformation. One has only to realize that most of the open country in the agricultural areas of today was once clothed in a dense stand of timber to appreciate the work that has gone into the using and subduing of the woodland during the last one hundred years. We need to make an effort of the imagination to see the forests as they were once (Fig. 35). Despite the radical visual change which has occurred over large areas, however, woodland clearing has not been the most obvious aspect of landscape change. It has been an individual operation carried on by each farmer as he has prepared his block of land, not a concerted governmental programme that has used public funds, and therefore been subject to public enquiry and documentation, like railway-building, irrigation or drainage. Most clearing has gone on unrecorded and has been regarded as a part of the normal farm operations that all new settlers faced when colonizing the land; it was an integral part of the process of 'progress'.

FIG. 35. All this land just east of the township of Karoonda (top) was covered by mallee scrub about 70 years ago. Now only the sand ridges have a few trees left, and even these are not sufficient to prevent 'blow-outs'.

The Extent of the Woodland

South Australian woodland can be classified into four general types : the eucalyptus forest; the eucalyptus savannah woodland; the mallee scrub or woodland; and the mallee-heath woodland. The first two are timber stands with individual trees, and are found in areas of rainfall of about 20 inches or more per annum. The second two are dense scrub-like covers of smaller trees, and are found in areas of lower rainfall or areas of impoverished soils (see pp. 6–13). Some measure of the extent of the various types of woodland can be gauged from Table VII below, which consists of calculations derived from the coverage of vegetation shown in Fig. 5, and contained within the area of the proclaimed hundreds.

Of course, these percentages are a broad generalization and they obscure an immense amount of variety and local detail. The

Table VII

Area and Percentage of Land within Hundreds originally covered by
Various Dominant Vegetational Types

(1 mile^2 = 259·0 ha, or 2.589 km^2)

Type	Sq. miles	Per cent
Eucalpyt Forest (Stringybark)	3,862	6·43
Eucalypt Savannah Woodland	5,249	8·74
Mallee Scrub	35,237	58·67
Mallee-heath	7,070	11·77
Open grass	1,672	2·78
Other (principally saltbush, grass and some scrub)	6,969	11·60
TOTAL	60,057	99·99

Source: based on Fig. 5.

precise mapping of the pre-European vegetation is always
difficult because it relies upon past verbal accounts and the present
day remnants of the original cover. One is on fairly sure ground,
however, with the detailed reconstruction of the distribution of
the mallee scrub. This 'uninterrupted waving prairie' was distinctive in its form and dense in its growth, and therefore usually
had a well-defined and abrupt boundary. Because of this its
distribution was carefully recorded, section by section, by the
surveyors as they came into contact with it from about 1850
onwards. This material from the surveyors' Diagram Books has
been pieced together in Fig. 36 which is an example of the detail
lost in the generalizations of Fig. 5. The mallee cover was by no
means as complete as is commonly thought. Near the coast the
mallee changed to samphire swamp, and along the river courses
tended to disappear and be replaced by open grassy land with
wider spaced trees—the eucalypt savannah woodland or 'arable'
land as the surveyors labelled it. At the foot of the higher rainfall
areas of the ranges mallee again gave way to savannah woodland.
Of great interest is the evidence of the open, largely treeless
'plains'[1] within the scrub. Only the largest are shown in Fig. 36
but there were many smaller ones. These 'plains' may have been

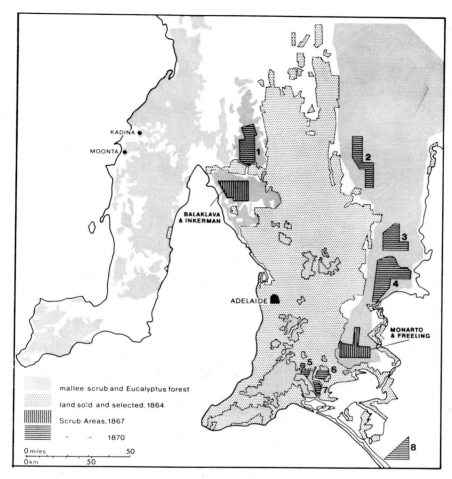

FIG. 36. The original mallee and eucalypt vegetation of the central portion of the settled areas, the location of the Scrub Areas of 1867 and 1870, and the land sold and selected by 1864. Based on S.A. Lands Dept. surveyors' note-books; *SAPP*, 161 (1870–71); and *Act* 25/1870–71. 1. Blythe, Stowe and Hall. 2. Neales and English. 3. Bagot. 4. Finniss and Angas. 5. Kondoparinga. 6. Alexandrina. 7. Bremer. 8. Coolinong.

due to aboriginal clearing by fire[2] but, whatever their origin, they were of great significance for early settlement, being sought out for roadways (particularly road junctions), township sites and initial cultivation.

Whilst bearing in mind the local variations which are concealed in the generalized vegetation map in Fig. 5, and the figures in Table VII which are derived from it, we can gain from both map and table some idea of the magnitude of the task of clearing which confronted the settlers, and so of the scale of change that has been wrought in the landscape.

Clearing in the Areas of Early Settlement

Early descriptions of the Adelaide area all emphasize its attractive qualities for settlers. In 1837, John Morphett described the plain as,

> 'Very picturesque and generally well timbered, but in the disposition of the trees more like an English park than we would have imagined to be the character of untrodden wilds; it is therefore, well suited for depasturing sheep, and in many places, under present circumstances, quite open enough for the plough.'[3]

A more sober, practical and succinct description of the Adelaide plains was given in 1843 by Samuel Davenport, who said that they were 'very beautiful to the eye of an agriculturalist, so much is clear of timber, level for the plough, and a deep soil too'.[4] Thus, agricultural operations could begin without the preliminary expense of 'grubbing' or 'girdling', i.e., ring-barking.

The presence of a few trees on a section was considered desirable as they were regarded as 'an index of good soil and fresh water', and they provided enough timber for 'domestic and ornamental purposes'.[5] But the sufficiency of timber depended very much on whether one's section was near a water course, and some unfortunate settlers did not have 'as much timber as would split into paling for the enclosure of a single allotment'.[6] Consequently, many sawyers' and shingle splitters' camps were established in the eucalypt forests of the Mount Lofty Ranges. The demand for the stringybark wood arose not only from the dearth of timber on the plain but also from the contrast in the quality of the timber that grew in the different areas. The wood of the blue gums was tough, knotted and difficult to work, whereas that of the stringybark split easily and was free from knots and straight in the grain. The supply of stringybark was thought to be limitless;

there was 'plenty of it within seven or eight miles of the town, and if we had 20,000 Emigrants every year, for the next century, there would be enough for them all'.[7]

G. F. Angas, who travelled through the Ranges in 1847 described a sawyers' camp;

'occasionally in some deep glen in the mountain forest there is suddenly revealed a group of busy workmen, with their gypsy-like encampment around them scattered with felled timber and planks on all sides, while the sharp sound of the axe rings echoing through the solitude, proclaiming the dawn of civilization and industry.'[8]

Evidence of their 'free and crusoe [sic] like life' was amply supported by Wilkinson's description in his *Working man's handbook to South Australia*, published in 1849 :

'It is customary with sawyers to ramble about in search of a job, and, carrying their tools with them, to agree with whoever wants their services. They either contract for erecting the building, or charge by the amount sawn, and then, taking provisions and a few cooking implements with them, they make off to the nearest forest to build their hut. This is composed of sheets of bark stripped from the trees, and which will turn the heaviest rain; these make a comfortable little habitation. If it is likely to be a long job, they sink a pit, and choose an eligible place at the side of a bank, to save the trouble of digging. The trees are now felled and dragged by the master's team to the pit, and then they set to work. They are supplied by the master with rations at a fixed rate, which are brought up to them (for sometimes they are six or eight miles from the station) in the owners drays that cart down the sawn stuff. While at work, other settlers will generally agree with them to supply sawn stuff; and in this way they frequently remain in one spot five or six months, and then leave for the town to "have a spree".'[9]

One of the most important uses for the wood was for fencing. In 1839, Stephens made some calculations which suggest that the erection of a substantial fence around one acre of land could cost the astonishing amount of between £35 and £53, which was so expensive that he thought live hedges would be far cheaper. Part of this high cost arose from the need to cart the timber from the Mount Lofty Ranges, which he estimated to be dearer than importing it from Tasmania. But Stephens' calculations were based on insufficient knowledge, and on the undoubtedly high carting costs during the first few years of occupation. Probably Duncan's estimates of 1849 were more typical: he calculated that the cost of establishment of an 80-acre section was £1,024, of which interior and exterior fencing would cost £168, or a little over £2 per acre of land occupied. Even this, however, was double the purchase price of the land. In contrast, Dutton's estimate of 1849, that the 4,500 pieces needed in a 3-rail fence around 80 acres would cost between £60 and £70, was probably more realistic.[10] Whichever estimate one takes, however, two things are clear; the cost of fencing was high but it tended to decrease in time as the supply of wood became more organized.

From the very first years of settlement, timber was cut indiscriminately in the parklands surrounding Adelaide, so that the area between North and South Adelaide, once 'a scene of beauty had become one of ruin and desolation'.[11] The administration tried to devise ways of controlling felling. As the population grew, so the demand for timber increased, and as settlement extended into the Central Hill Country and away from the stringybark forests, greater controls had to be applied to felling. Cutting was restricted to the unsurveyed lands, and £5 licences were issued to sawyers and splitters.[12] But as more and more land was surveyed, so the timber getters had to go further and further afield, and the attraction of the timber on the surveyed but unoccupied land in near localities became great.[13] By 1849, Freeling, the Surveyor-General, wrote to the Governor expressing disquiet at the way in which 'section after section of surveyed land is gradually being denuded of its timber', and therefore of its potential value.[14] The point was simply this: the minimum price of £1 per acre did not help to distinguish land of varying quality but the presence of timber was an obvious sign that one section was of higher value than another. It was not as if the timber-getters grubbed up the trees and left the land in a suitable state for agriculture in the future; they cut them at the most convenient height—about 3 feet from the ground—and these stumps proved to be more difficult to remove than whole trees. (This practice also depreciated the value of the land about to be surveyed.) Accordingly, Freeling wanted licence fees raised to £20 to stop 'fly-by-night' felling, and power to be given to all staff of the Lands Department and of the Colonial Engineer (as well as to the police) to demand the showing of licences from all persons seen cutting timber. He also wanted to give large rewards for information.

Bonney, the Commissioner of Crown Lands, realized that higher licence fees might have the reverse effect and increase illegal cutting because of the unabated demand for timber. Accordingly, he suggested that all land in the densely-settled hundreds of Adelaide, Willunga, Yatala, and Noarlunga, west of Mt Bold, be exempt from the operation of timber licences. This would remove the need to police cutting and the need to prove that the land in question was in fact surveyed, which was a costly business as a surveyor had to be sent to the locality every time there was a charge brought against a cutter. Bonney's suggestion was approved.[15]

The administrative problems of timber-getting were far from resolved, however. In an effort to encourage greater local supervision, the Government handed over power to issue licences to the expanding network of District Councils, or where none existed, as in the South-East and Port Lincoln districts, to the local police and magistrates.[16] But a few years of this new system of administration revealed its impracticability because the District Councils relied upon the Government to police illegal cutting. In any case, they did not restrict cutting within their boundaries as this reduced their revenue; in fact, they may even have encouraged cutting, or, as happened in the District Council of Onkaparinga, issued licences for cutting on land which was surveyed and from which the cutters were clearly excluded.[17]

Eventually, power to issue licences passed back to the Commissioner of Crown Lands who policed the cutting with eight Crown Land Rangers, who, instead of having the 80-square mile territory to supervise, as had been suggested by Bonney in 1849, were responsible for areas between about 4000 and 8000 square miles, in addition to checking for illegal pasturing of cattle in hundreds. Inevitably, with such a large territory to administer, the Ranger could not supervise all areas and much illegal cutting went on. Sometimes, collusion between Ranger and cutters was suspected, as at Mt Torrens where an 'extensive system of illegal timber getting' was known to have been carried out, although nothing was reported. The Surveyor-General said, 'I can hardly believe . . . that the inhabitants of Mt Barker District are a bit more honest than others'. Whatever the truth of this, the local Ranger knew that the trees were 'cut down by night and then cut off in blocks (and removed) for shingles, so I shall lay in wait at night'.[18] The outcome is unknown.

Despite a general tightening of the regulations,[19] illegal felling continued and became well organized. Reports came in of groups of people cutting and splitting at many places throughout the colony.[20] 'It was a common custom of splitters and others holding timber licences to congregate in large numbers in land near which they perceive the Tents of the Surveyors', wrote the Surveyor-General, and when the survey was over, they immediately removed the best timber. Therefore he wanted to preclude all cutting from near newly surveyed land.[21] As noted before, illegal felling reduced the value of sections, and many examples of this occurred. The case of Daniel Parker of Virginia must have been typical of many : he found that 400 acres that he had bought had 'nothing left on the land but a host of stumps, being so completely stripped of timber'. There was not enough wood for him to fence his land.[22]

If individual sections could not satisfy the demand for timber the farmers hoped for a common patch of woodland nearby which would serve their needs, rather like the common timber lots of the medieval and later European experience. Thus 139 persons in Apoinga, Redruth, Waterloo, Kooringa, Stoney Gap, Hamilton and other places, petitioned the Commissioner of Crown Lands not to proclaim as a hundred a piece of ground 4 by $2\frac{1}{2}$ miles to the north of the present Julia Creek hundred as it was the only source of timber 'for fuel, fencing, and mining purposes . . . between Kapunda and Kooringa'. Despite the fact that a large number of woodcutters would be put out of work and £500 per annum lost from their licences, the Surveyor-General was 'disinclined' to accede to the request as the land was suitable for agricultural purposes.[23] Eventually it was surveyed and it was taken up by settlers.

The Crown Lands Department attempted to keep a tight control on timber-getting, and only occasionally allowed concessions to individuals. Such was the request to fell timber for the erection of a Lutheran Church at the Reedy Creek Mine, near Tungkillo, and the unexpected generosity of allowing a special licence to cut wood for fences, free of charge for six months, given to Albert Blandford and his son of Port Lincoln, who could not afford the £5 for a timber licence and who said that they were 'cultivators of a small piece [of] ground, and that about a fortnight ago a Bushfire broke out near our place destroying the greater portion of our crops and the whole of our fence'.[24]

All in all, our knowledge of clearing is slight during these early years for reasons which have already been mentioned, particularly the essentially individual and piecemeal character of the evidence. We do get some indication of the areas of activity from the distribution of licences issued to timber getters in 1861.[25] There were three main areas of concentration; in Fleurieu Peninsula, between Rapid Bay and Encounter Bay, on the eastern sides of the Mount Lofty Ranges in the Echunga-Macclesfield area, and particularly north of Gawler in the foothills between the mallee scrub and the peppermint gum woodland. But this only helps to pinpoint the concentration of the commercial cutters and does little to elaborate the activity of the farmers. One reason why information on woodland clearing remains so tantalizingly slight is that its end result is negative—nothing of it remains. Unlike other landscape changing processes, such as draining, irrigation and survey, there are no enduring monuments of drains and channels, and fences and roads. Only where the woodland vegetation formed a tangible landscape feature that disappeared quickly was the change noticed. Such was the case of the Peachy Belt, a peppermint gum forest which stretched between the Para River and north of Gawler, along the foothills zone. The importance of the Belt, wrote a local correspondent in 1851 'for fencing and firewood, . . . particularly the latter, at no very great distance from Adelaide is almost incalculable. It would seem from its yet dense appearance, to be almost inexhaustible . . .'. But already, commercial wood cutters and agriculturists were making clearings around its edges, and within eight years another correspondent wrote of the cutters and colonists: 'how far they are doing right by waging a war of utter extermination against the timber, I do not pretend to say; but certain it is that unless peace be proclaimed in time, their descendants will look in vain for a tree in that which was once Peachy Belt'.[26] By about 1880 it had all but disappeared. Another example was in the South-East where the timber on the uplands between Mount Gambier and Naracoorte was being cleared 'recklessly' during the early 1860s.[27]

Besides the normal use made of woodland for timber for fencing, housing and domestic fuel, there were two other major demands, first as fuel for smelting copper ore (and firing brick-kilns and lime kilns), and secondly as railway sleepers, about which we know very little.

Copper was discovered at Kapunda in 1843, at Burra in 1844 and Wallaroo/Kadina in 1863. The first two discoveries were at places some distance from the main outport, Port Adelaide, and they were not connected by rail until 1860 and 1870 respectively, although the opening up of Port Wakefield in 1849 and the operation of a fleet of barges halved the distance of hauling by bullock wagon and therefore the cost of transport from Burra to Port Adelaide. Obviously the need was to reduce the bulk of the commodity transported by smelting the ore at the mine sites, as at Kapunda and Apoinga south of Burra, although there was also a smelting works at Yatala, near Port Adelaide. As workable deposits of coal were not present, wood and charcoal were the only fuels available, and in their acquisition much destruction of woodland occurred.[28] Neither the Kapunda nor the Burra Mine was situated in a timber-rich area; Kapunda was in the savannah woodlands of the Central Hill Country where the growth of trees was only sparse and moderate and Burra was on the edge of naturally treeless, grassy plains. Both were a considerable distance from the stringybark forests, although both were within ten miles of the mallee scrub land, a future source of fuel.

The demand for fuel was enormous; it was estimated in 1851 that the three Apoinga smelters consumed 150 tons of wood, and the Kapunda smelters 120 tons daily.[29] This rate of consumption could not continue and it seems that the supply of fuel for smelting reached some sort of crisis in the late 1840s. A plan to form a company to ship the ores to the abundant timber supplies of Tasmania was only one manifestation of this crisis.[30] Others were an invention to improve the efficiency of the smelting process by interbedding layers of ore and wood-chips in the furnace; permission to collect dead wood and fallen timber in the Mt Lofty Ranges for charcoal making, free of licence charge; the employment of aborigines near Blanchetown, and at Wellington to collect scrub;[31] and W. B. Hay's invention to make charcoal in iron retorts at Port Lincoln, where a small plant was established.[32]

However interesting these inventions were they did little for the central problem of fuel supply which had to be solved near to the smelting works (Fig. 11). For example, a contract was entered into in 1849 to cut 1,000 tons of timber in the country around Kapunda although the felling was disallowed on the grounds that it would devalue potential farmland.[33] In 1851 the South Australian Mining Company of Burra asked for permission to have a special licence to cut 70 square miles of peppermint gums and mallee in the Tothill Scrub, a tongue of woodland that extended westwards between Kapunda and Burra, but was refused.[34] One observer in Burra in 1851 described how 'drays loaded with wood were arriving every instant . . . to replenish the forest of cut logs and long wood piled up, circling the whole area of the works and filling every available space'. The average load was 2 tons, but some were up to 5 tons ('and we pity the bullocks', he wrote) and all the wood was coming from the Murray Scrub.[35] As was to be expected, the demand for timber for the pits as well as for the smelting-furnaces gave rise to much illegal cutting—by gangs in private and Crown lands. Eventually the mining company resorted to importing coal from Britain and the Hunter Valley, in New South Wales, and about 6,000 tons were landed at Port Wakefield and back-hauled to Apoinga in the empty drays during the first six months of trading during late 1849.[36] The demand for timber for smelting dropped rapidly, but that for strong timber for underground shoring-up continued unabated, and in the 1870s and 1880s the Wallaroo-Moonta mines got their supplies from the Wirrabara Forest in the southern Flinders Ranges, about 100 miles to the north at a cartage cost of 6 shillings per ton.

The Mallee : Initial Contact

In contrast with the clearing of the savannah woodlands of the plains and foothills around Adelaide and in the South-East, and of the stringybark forest of the central high rainfall portions of the Mount Lofty Ranges, the clearing of the mallee scrub is, perhaps, a more important theme, and is certainly better documented.

Originally the mallee covered more than 58 per cent of the settled portions of South Australia, and when the roughly similar vegetation of the mallee-heath areas is added, it covered more than 70 per cent. In addition to its extent, the density of the timber was so great that any clearing was an impressive sight and radically transformed the landscape. But the importance of the clearing of the mallee was more far-reaching than that. For successful clearing to occur new legislation was needed so that the land could be taken up on easier terms than before to compensate for the expense of clearing it. This legislation, then, was not only the key to the clearing of the mallee but was also of great significance in the development of land legislation generally being the thin edge of the wedge in the Wakefieldian system. Further, the clearing of the mallee on the scale necessary to achieve lasting success depended upon new machinery and new techniques of farming, both invented and first evolved in South Australia, and later to have such a profound effect on scrub clearing in other parts of the Continent.

The earliest appraisals of the mallee lands were not favourable. The scrub lands were described with varying degrees of truthfulness, as 'horrid', 'valueless', 'inferior', 'desert', 'impenetrable', 'waterless', 'barren', 'a barrier to progress', and as 'those lands of the colony which were confessedly the worst—scrubs without water'. In addition, there was something menacing about the mallee scrub; it was thick and impenetrable, devoid of water and landmarks, an easy place in which to get lost and die : it was a place to avoid.

Nevertheless, contact with the mallee scrub had arisen in two ways. Settlement was nibbling away at the edges of the Gawler Scrub, lying to the west and north of Gawler. Clearing and grubbing by hand proceeded slowly and laboriously during spare time and slack seasons,[37] but there was no concerted attempt to penetrate the scrub (Fig. 37). Secondly, the discovery of copper ore at Wallaroo and Moonta in 1862, in the middle of the mallee of the northern part of Yorke Peninsula, forced attention on the scrub in a new way. The need for collecting fuel for the mines has

FIG. 37. Collecting firewood. The need for domestic fuel helped to bite into the woodlands. Walleroo, *c.* 1870.

been mentioned already, and large areas of the surrounding scrub were cut-over, but there was also a need to carve roads through the scrub in order to connect the copper towns with the ports of Clinton and Port Wakefield at the head of St Vincent Gulf, and also with Port Adelaide. Contracts were let regularly for road clearing,[38] and reports were sent to the Surveyor-General by contractors. The costs of clearing varied; half a mile between Kadina and Clinton cost £20, and between 10 and 11 miles between Moonta Mines and Brauns (?) cost £120, which, said the contractor was £3 per mile less than the cost of clearing the track to Auburn 'in consequence of the scrub being lighter in some portions'. Tools were being broken constantly and large stumps left in the ground for want of an efficient grubbing machine. Great difficulty was found in selecting lines for new roads, and the 'plains' were invaluable in this respect. One contractor said of the line between Salt Lakes near Hummocks to the Moonta-Clinton road, 'the country through which the road goes is so thickly covered with scrub that I was obliged to cross it eight times before I could get a satisfactory route'.[39]

But these contacts during the late 1850s and early 1860s were mere pin-pricks in the vast area of scrub lands that covered the State, and they were succeeded by a more general attempt to conquer the mallee after the mid 1860s.

The agitation to open up the scrub lands for settlement arose from the adverse conditions of farming in the 1860s which were years of increasing difficulty. A major problem was that the pastoralists had been so thorough in purchasing land that they blocked northward expansion into the Central Hill Country, so that 'the farming lands of the colony were a kind of oasis, enclosed on one side by the sea, and on the others by the great pastoral desert'. The principle of contiguous survey did not allow settlement to leap-frog over the estates and, in any case, settlers were 'afraid to go beyond this into the open country' for fear of bushfires and the isolated position of their farms.[40] Isolation meant, above all, higher transport charges which decreased the competitive position of South Australia wheat in the world market. To go into the densely timbered, waterless mallee lands was unthinkable while the existing conditions of tenure meant that land cost £1 an acre, before wells were dug or the mallee cleared laboriously by hand.

The first move to open up the scrub lands came from a group of farmers in the Bremer District, east of the Mt Lofty Ranges. For some years, these farmers had been edging eastwards into the margin of the mallee and had proved that the cleared land was productive, but only at considerable cost. Goyder, the Surveyor-General, examined the scrub areas and reported on 24th August, 1866, that the idea of a more liberal tenure was feasible, provided that the experiment was confined to limited areas. It was, he said, a 'scheme that upon the face of it appears simple and one that if carried out will change the face of large areas of the country from hopeless scrub to smiling fertility'.[41]

The Government acted quickly on this report and gathered information on land sold in the northern hundreds, followed by another return on 'unsold and unoccupied land of a scrubby and inferior character,'[42] and then introduced a Bill for the occupation of the scrub lands. The debate which accompanied the Bill went on over weeks and finally, in Committee, the conditions of tenure were fixed; up to 640 acres could be bought at £1 an acre and was to be put up for auction as usual, but if unsold could be occupied on a 21-year lease at a small rental provided that one-twentieth of the land was cleared every year.

The areas to be surveyed under the new regulation were in the Hundreds of Balaklava and Inkerman on the east coast of Gulf St Vincent, and Monarto and Freeling on the Murray Plains to the east of the Mount Lofty Ranges. (See Fig. 36 for their location.) Although the leases were snapped up by the land-hungry farmers there was no guarantee that the settlers could satisfy the regulations which required a minimum amount of land to be cleared and improvements to be made to the property. The real difficulties of the mallee scrub lands soon became evident and of the 132 leases taken out by 1870 only fifty had had any improvements carried out on them, and of those fifty, six were due to be forfeited for insufficient clearing. From sheer necessity settlers expended far more of their initial energy on securing a good water supply by well digging and shelter by building a house during their first year than they did on clearing and cultivating the land.[43] Experience also began to show that not all the land was of even moderate quality; much of it did not repay the cost of clearing, a cost which varied between 10 and 140 shillings per acre according to the nature and density of the scrub. Balaklava, Inkerman and to a lesser extent, Freeling had 'a great amount of inferior sandy land in which the ultimate success of farming operations is very doubtful and in which water is difficult to procure', reported Cooper, the Deputy Surveyor-General in 1868. In addition to these difficulties, a great mistake had been made in Balaklava, Inkerman and Freeling in surveying the new scrub areas between two and three miles away from the existing settlements. The intervening strip of mallee was 'an insurmountable barrier to the occupation of the land already surveyed beyond it',[44] wrote one settler, and it discouraged part-time clearing.

A detailed account of the progress of the experiment in the first four scrub areas is shown in Table VIII. In Freeling, twenty-eight leases were never occupied and improved in any way, and in the remaining six, in which small patches of clearing had been made nearly two years before, the mallee was 'again beginning to

Table VIII

Progress of Survey in First Four Scrub Areas to August, 1870

(100 acres = 40·469 ha)

	Leases taken up	Acres involved	Area which should have been cleared Acres*	Area cleared Acres
Monarto				
Improved	26	5,753	704	842
Never improved	6	1,565	—	—
	32	7,318		
Freeling				
Improved	6	943	92	67
Never improved	28	4,867	—	—
	34	5,810		
Balaklava				
Improved	18	3,926	373	203
Never improved	43	13,439	—	—
	61	17,365		
Inkerman				
Improved	—	—	—	—
Never improved	5	1,592	—	—

*Not necessarily 2/20th of the land as some leases were taken up for less than two years.

Source: SGO 1702/1870 (in) and 1745½/1870 (in).

spring and cover the land'. Forty-three leases in Balaklava were never improved and, in the eighteen that were, only about half of the land that should have been cleared was in fact cleared. Little had been done since the first year of clearing, the greater part of the hundred being too sandy for occupation. 'While so much fair open land can be procured at £1 per acre', wrote Cooper, who inspected the scrub blocks, 'it will not repay a lessee to incur the cost of clearing inferior land; a cost which amounts to about £2 per acre'. The mallee was suckering and growing again on seven of the leases, and their forfeiture was recommended. Inkerman was a complete failure. Only in Monarto was 'fair progress' made, and twenty-six lessees had cleared 842 acres, 138 more than was required, although six leases had to be forfeited.[45] The field maps which accompanied Cooper's reports must be some of the first maps in Australia to record accurately woodland clearance. They are redrawn in Fig. 38.

In review, the early experiment with the Scrub Land Act of 1867 had really done little to promote settlement in the mallee, and also it had done little to prevent the movement of people out of the colony, as was hoped at the time of its passing.[46] Aware of the lure of the newly opened credit purchase lands in the Northern Areas, the Government was not anxious to throw open a great deal more land to the operation of the Scrub Lands Act. Cautiously, ten more areas were declared in the hundreds of Kondoparinga, Bremer and Alexandrina, near the mouth of the Murray; in Neales, English, Bagot, Finniss and Angas, east of the Ranges; in the southern half of Balaklava; and in the hundreds of Blythe, Stowe and Hall during 1871[47] (Fig. 36). As was expected, the public response was poor during the first few months; there was no bid for 17,786 acres offered in Kondoparinga, Bremer and Alexandrina, and of the ninety-four forfeited leases consisting of 24,055 acres in the four original scrub-hundreds of Balaklava, Inkerman, Freeling and Monarto, only ten lots totalling 1,991 acres were sold.[48] All in all, between 1871 and 1877, only 270 leases totalling 112,421 acres were taken up, of which 34,065 acres were subsequently abandoned during the same period (Fig. 39).

Besides the difficulties and costs of scrub clearing, the poor response was also a result of the confusion that had arisen over the lengthy debate accompanying the passing of new land legislation in 1872.[49] So great was this uncertainty that the number of leases issued and acres affected declined steadily after 1872 and none were taken up during 1875, so that the Government had to bring in a new Bill 'to revise' and 'remove doubts' about the Scrub Act.[50] But the removal of doubts about the old legislation was

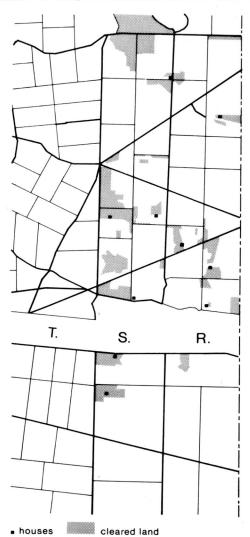

■ houses ▨ cleared land

FIG. 38. Clearing in the Monarto and Freeling scrub areas, 1870. Based on Cooper's sketches, SGO 1702 and 1745½/1870 (in). T.S.R. is a Travelling Stock Route.

not enough to encourage the settlement of the scrub lands; something far more radical was needed before settlers would vie with each other for the 'despised' mallee.

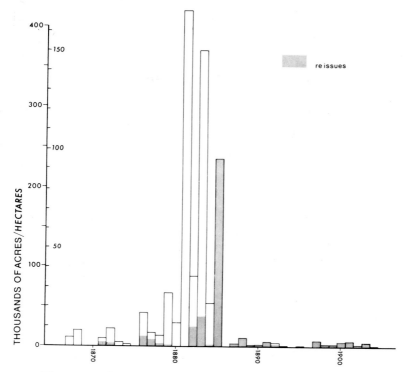

FIG. 39. The area taken up under Scrub Leases, 1867–1904. Based on S.A. Lands Dept. Scrub Lease dockets.

The Mallee : A New Attack

The area of land taken up under scrub lease regulations before 1877 was small compared with the enormous area of over 1·3 million acres that was affected in the new attack afterwards— mainly between 1880 and 1886 (Fig. 39). Not only did the amount of land affected increase, but the locality of the new activity changed—from the mallee fringes of the areas of early settlement to the difficult lands of Yorke Peninsula, with an additional few far-flung outposts in the rest of the colony.

Ostensibly, the new attack in clearing the scrub lands coincided with new legislation of 1877 and 1880 which liberalized the conditions of tenure and extended the area in which new regulations could be applied. The 1877 Act included roughly all the land in the hundreds in which the previous 1867 and 1870 Scrub Areas had been located, together with some new hundreds alongside the Murray and in the Fleurieu Peninsula. The Act allowed the area that could be leased to be enlarged to two square miles, but reduced the amount of land which had to be cleared annually to one-fortieth, and allowed purchase at £1 per acre after ten years. The total amount of land that could be held by one lessee was raised to 3,200 acres.[51] Yet this revision of the Scrub Land Act and the renewed interest in the mallee lands was an outcome of the success of new methods and inventions to facilitate clearing and cultivation which had been pioneered and perfected in the mallee for a decade before, but which were only having an impact in the mid 1870s after being slowly diffused throughout the farming community. Most certainly, the extension of the Scrub Land regulations to thirty additional hundreds in 1880[52] was a direct result of the new techniques. (For the location of these areas see Fig. 40.)

Foremost amongst these new methods to make mallee farming both practical and profitable was the technique known as 'mullenizing', named after Mullens, a farmer from near Wasleys, northwest of Gawler. In 1868 he was cutting mallee for sale to the nearby railway and found that if the trees were cut low enough and burnt off the soil could be opened up by dragging a heavy, V-shaped log, with spikes in it, over the uneven surface of roots and stumps, and sowing seed broadcast. If the underground roots of the mallee suckered, the shoots could be burnt in the stubble after the harvest, and then the mallee roots could be grubbed out later by hand when time permitted. The success of this technique encouraged him to experiment with a cheaper means of clearing, and he discovered that the slender mallee trunks could be knocked down by dragging a heavy roller over the ground, the trash and exposed roots then being burnt and the ground opened up with the spiked log.[53] The same process of burning the stubble after the harvest kept down the suckering roots. How and when the technique of mullenizing was diffused throughout South Australia during the 1870s is not known. In 1879 the editor of the *Yorke Peninsula Advertiser* suggested that the operation of the new Scrub Act would be a failure because of the high cost of clearing and talked as though mullenizing was unknown to him.[54] Yet the

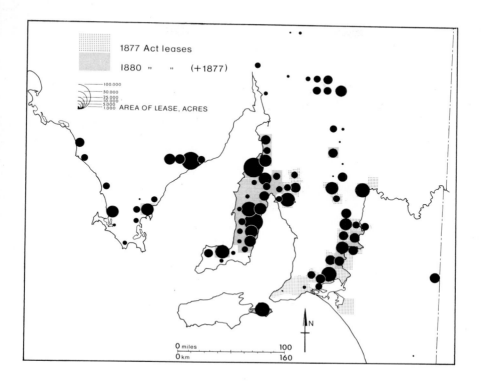

1877 Act leases

1880 „ „ (+1877)

100,000
50,000
25,000
10,000
5,000
1,000 AREA OF LEASE, ACRES

0 miles 100
0 km 160

N

FIG. 40. The areas affected under Scrub Leases, 1867–1904. Based on S.A. Lands Dept. Scrub Lease dockets.

farmers who were already established in the naturally open lands of the Peninsula must have been experimenting with mullenizing for some years, for in 1880 one local correspondent wrote 'I don't think there will be much mallee left standing between this [Dowlingville] and Moonta if the "mullinising" [*sic*] answers as well as it has in the last two years'.[55] Confirmatory evidence of this clearing is given in Fig. 41 which shows the extent of sold and selected land in 1877 in Counties Daly and Fergusson in the Peninsula, and the distribution of mallee vegetation. In most areas, there is a remarkable coincidence between the outer boundary

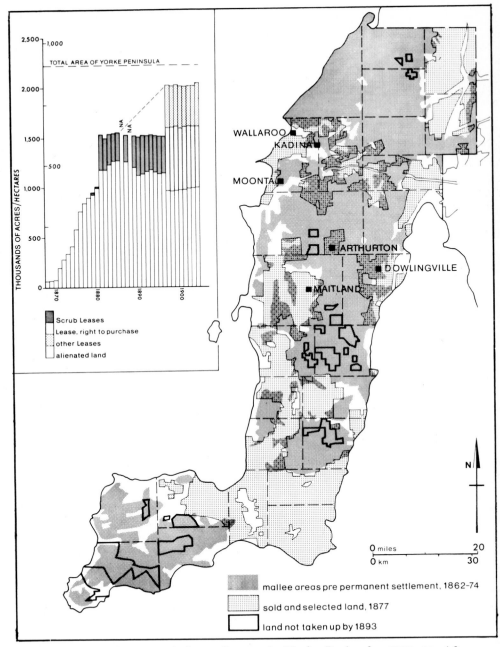

FIG. 41. Settlement and the mallee scrub, Yorke Peninsula, 1877–93. After S.A. Lands Dept. surveyors' note-books, *Atlas of sold and settled lands*, Adelaide (1877); and *SAPP*, 10 (1893).

of land occupied and the edge of the mallee. But around the township of Dowlingville, Arthurton and Maitland, across the centre of the Peninsula, and around the three mining towns and their connecting road to Adelaide, the clearing and the penetration of the scrub were already evident.

In 1880 the Peninsular hundreds came within the terms of the new Scrub Act and this brought increased clearing activity as farmers were said to be preferring the scrub country to the open country. A great change was occurring in the landscape; one person near Ardrossan thought it not unlikely that 'in a few years time scrubby country in the Peninsula will be a thing of the past'. More pungent was the comment of another, 'Smoke! smoke! smoke! anywhere, everywhere, nothing but smoke'.[56]

Initially many farmers on the Peninsula used a small wooden roller for clearing. It was about 9 feet long and 20 inches in diameter with a shaft on one side of the frame. With this 'splendid acquisition' six bullocks could roll down about 5 acres of scrub a day at a cost of between 8 and 12 shillings per acre.[57] However, this roller proved insufficient for the task; it could roll down timber only $2\frac{1}{2}$ inches thick, only half the roller could be used because of the way it was pulled at one side, and the rigid shaft caused the horses and bullocks to be badly knocked about as the roller pitched and swayed over the scrub. Inevitably, larger, heavier and more complex rollers were made which overcame these problems and cleared thicker timber all requiring the power of eight to ten bullocks and calculated to do the work of a dozen scrub-cutters a day[58] (Fig. 42a).

Mullenizing was, as Meinig has pointed out 'an excellent pioneer expedient allowing a crop with a minimum effort and delay',[59] but the problem remained of grubbing out the large stumps which hindered the ploughing of the land. Admittedly, some of the stumps could be left in the hope that with continual cutting and burning, and the assistance of white ants, they would be rendered harmless.[60] Nevertheless, the tradition of clean cultivation and the impossibility of using conventional ploughs over stump-ridden paddocks led to the search for a grubbing machine. Throughout the 1870s the cry was for the invention of equipment that was cheap, efficient and simple to operate, and a number of machines appeared on the market. Stott, an implement

FIG. 42a. Rolling down the mallee scrub with a six-horse team. Pinnaroo, *c.* 1911.

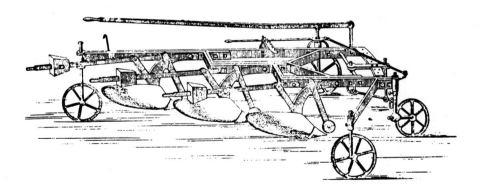

FIG. 42b. The first stump-jump plough—a multi-furrow version made by R. B. Smith of Kalkabury. (Ross, 1881).

manufacturer of Alma Plains, was producing a machine by 1876, as was Spry of Kulpara, who was finding it difficult 'to supply his grubber as fast as they are required', Scobie's grubber appeared in 1878.[61] These were but a few of many invented. Late in 1878, the government offered a reward of £200 for the best grubbing machine adapted to clearing mallee and peppermint gum. A trial was held at Kangaroo Flat near Gawler and fourteen machines of various designs were exhibited and tested; some worked by manual power, and others by horse power. But most of them were slow and expensive to operate and some even broke, and three of the best axemen grubbed 'twice as much in three hours as the best machines did in four hours with the aid of three men and a horse'.[62] Most farmers still looked to the grubber to clear the land with his mattock, an operation which was reasonably economical, even at a cost of between £3 and £4 an acre, when the price of stumps was high enough to stand the cost of freight to Adelaide, or if the land being cleared was within a reasonable distance of a railway, a town or a mining centre, such as Wallaroo, Kadina and Moonta. Despite these potential economies, however, some farmers preferred to leave the grubbed-up roots on the ground to be burnt, as they thought that the manurial value of the ash outweighed the return from firewood sales.[63]

However, another local invention was at hand to overcome the problem of stumps, grubbing and ploughing; it was the stump-jump plough, most probably invented by R. B. Smith of Kalkabury, north of Maitland.[64] The principle of the plough was simple: the mould-boards were mounted on hinged beams which allowed the shares to rise gently out of the ground on meeting an obstruction; by placing weights on the extension of the beams, the share was pressured back into the ground as soon as it passed over the obstacle. This allowed a seed bed to be prepared despite the stumps, and, in time, it destroyed all but the largest roots and stumps (Fig. 42b).

A simple, single-furrow version of the plough was exhibited at the Moonta agricultural show in 1876 and immediately it was seen that it would 'plough over stumps and do away with grubbing'.[65] But initially farmers were unwilling to adopt the plough because it left stumps in the ground and this was thought to be 'slovenly'. A resurgence of interest in the plough occurred in

1880 when land in the Peninsula was opened to settlement by the Scrub Land Regulations. The plough was exhibited at Ardrossan and its performance was such that in the new legislative climate it was forecast that 'some time during the next twelve months all the light scrub in this district will be under cultivation'. Whereas only people capable of investing between £3 and £4 an acre in grubbing could take up scrub land, it would now be brought into cultivation for between 10 and 15 shillings an acre, and a capital outlay of about £21–£23 for a three-furrowed plough. An equally radical change of opinion about the after-growth from the stumps was also evident by this time. Rather than being regarded an annoyance it was thought of as beneficial because after three or four years' harvests, a paddock could be left to regenerate then be cut down and burnt, and the soil 'enriched by the ashes and the action of the fire'. This procedure was followed for many years and was thought to make the scrub farmer 'independent of fallowing and manures'.[66]

The impetus for the widespread adoption of this innovation, however, was a trial of stump-jumpers of various design at Ardrossan in September and at Agery in November, 1880.[67] The demonstration was so convincing that by March of the next year some 70 ploughs were being manufactured in the Dowlingville district alone. The mallee was being cleared, and the roots turned up, and it was thought that the time would soon arrive 'when the sound of the grubbing axe shall be heard no more'. The editor of the *Yorke Peninsula Advertiser* even went so far as to suggest that the farmers of the Peninsula had made 'a great mistake' in holding the stump-jump ploughing match the year before because the obvious efficiency of the plough had 'invited so much competition for the scrub lands that absurd prices have been paid for this class of selection', which worked against the farmer who still had a considerable outlay of money and labour before any 'paying returns' were received from scrub.[68]

When the complementary inventions of the stump-jump scarifier (which scratched open, but did not turn over the soil) for preparing shallow seed beds in the light mallee soils, and the mobile rake for piling up the roots and trash are added to the invention of the plough, it is not surprising that 'a scramble' set in for land. In 1881 alone 430,000 acres were taken up (Fig. 39) and scrub land was 'more sought after than plain land on the Peninsula'. Indeed, previous values were reversed and some said that 'mullenized ground proved the most profitable for the farmer' and a further 457,000 acres were leased during 1882 and 1883.[69] The thrust into the mallee was not confined to Yorke Peninsula; a small nucleus of settlement under scrub leases had been established across Spencer Gulf in the hundreds of Hawker, Mann and Playford, between Arno Bay and Franklin Harbour. The land there was described by one correspondent as 'the most persistently scrubby country I ever saw' so that for the 'old style settlers it is hard country to conquer. But for the stump-jumpers it is a Promised Land'[70] (Fig. 12).

The very sharp drop in the number of acres affected by the scrub leases after 1884 (Fig. 39), was a result of the piecemeal legislative measures brought forward to deal with droughts and depression after 1880. In order to rescue those farmers who had gone too far north during the 1870s the Government passed relief legislation which enabled farmers to repurchase their land at a reduced price, and also allowed any rental paid to the Crown to be credited towards the final purchase money of land. In effect, purchase money could not be repaid in instalments which corresponded with the length of the lease. In addition, lessees had the right to complete the purchase during the last eleven years of the lease.[71]

These concessions, designed as assistance to farmers on ordinary leases, were then extended to the Scrub Leases in 1884, provided the Scrub Lease was surrendered and exchanged for an ordinary one.[72] The Act was passed in November 1884, and during the second quarter of 1885 (the surrender interval stipulated) every outstanding Scrub Lease in South Australia was exchanged for a new lease under the revised conditions (see Fig. 39). The effect of the legislation was different from what had been intended, since, from now on, instead of being a relatively cheap and easy way of developing and clearing the more difficult mallee, the Scrub Lease offered little incentive as a means of subduing the scrub lands: 'We might just as well take away scrub leases altogether and deal with them as with other land', said one member in the House. Increasingly, perpetual leases and leases with right-of-purchase were available for average quality land and were taken up throughout South Australia, and despite concession after concession granted in successive legislation, the Scrub Lease never revived as a means for subduing the scrub. Had the concessions been introduced ten years earlier they would have conferred great benefits : but now they were too late. The reduction in the advantages of the Scrub Leases was so overwhelming that after 1886 only 77 leases affecting 32,510 acres were issued, and all of these being reissues and exchanges of old forfeited leases.

This is not to suggest, however, that the clearing of the scrub lands stopped during this period; only the legislative method of disposing of the scrub lands changed, and clearing went on as before, particularly in the higher rainfall lands of Yorke Peninsula and to a lesser degree in the coastal fringes of Eyre Peninsula, both of which were regarded as agriculturally safe.

A glance at Fig. 41 shows that by the close of 1877, nearly all of the available open land on Yorke Peninsula, with the exception of the less productive coastal fringes, had been taken up, and that farmers were at the very edge of the mallee scrub and in places had already begun to clear it. By 1893, when the next map of land occupation in Yorke Peninsula is available, only small patches were left unalienated and unleased, mainly in the trace-element deficient soils of the 'toe' and the core of difficult scrub lands in the 'calf' of the Peninsula.

The implication is that nearly all the scrub land was subjected to occupation and probably to clearing. In order to give some quantitative expression to the distribution shown in Fig. 41, a graph of the progress of occupation in Counties Daly and Fergusson (the area shown on the map) is also included.[73] It shows that the amount of alienated land rose from 47,084 acres in 1868 (overwhelmingly around the three copper towns in the north of the Peninsula) to 836,161 acres in 1877, the date of the extent of settlement as shown on Fig. 41. After that more land was taken up and a total of nearly one million acres was alienated by 1880 when the Peninsula was placed under the operation of Scrub Leases. From 1880 to 1884 another 639,000 acres were taken up, over half of which was in Scrub Leases, which remained in operation until they were exchanged for right-of-purchase leases in 1897. The great deficiency of this graph is the lack of information about perpetual leases and right-of-purchase leases between their inception in 1886 and when detailed information first becomes available in 1897. The dotted line on the graph suggests the likely effect of their inclusion. Whatever the uncertainties of some of these data, however, one can be sure that, by 1897, 2,085,799 acres of land were accounted for, almost two and a half times the 836,161 acres of twenty years before. Most of these 1,249,638 additional acres must have been mallee land which had to be cleared in order to be occupied.

The Mallee: The Inner Areas

The uncertainty in what we know about scrub clearing during the nineteenth century gives way to accurate statistics from 1906 to 1941, and an abundance of official and newspaper information. During these thirty-four years, 7,134,485 acres of land were cleared of timber, almost as much land as was alienated during the preceding seventy years of the State's history. Clearing went on principally in the two new areas of settlement—Eyre Peninsula and the Murray Mallee—but it also continued in Yorke Peninsula, and, to a lesser extent, in the older settled areas of the Adelaide Hills, particularly in the stringybark forests of Counties Hindmarsh and Sturt. Clearing also went on steadily in the South-East.

The abundant evidence makes possible a minute analysis of the changing activity and its effect on the landscape, hundred by hundred, year by year. Add to these statistical data the evidence available from government reports on agriculture and projected railway routes, parliamentary debates, and at least five local newspapers which flourished and circulated widely in the newly colonized areas of the Murray Mallee and Eyre Peninsula, and the result could be an indigestible morass of local detail. Accordingly it is necessary to change the scale of generalization and take a broader view of clearing, looking first at its fluctuations through time, then its changing location, and finally at the more local details of the methods and techniques of clearing and the resultant change in the landscape.

Fluctuations

The average rate of clearing between 1907 and 1941 was 209, 379 acres per annum, but like all averages, this figure masks great fluctuations (Fig. 43). While the rate of clearing never fell below 100,000 acres, except in 1941, it exceeded 200,000 acres on thirteen occasions with two great bursts of activity between 1909 and 1911, and between 1927 and 1929 well over 1,000,000 acres being cleared during both periods. Nevertheless, whatever the fluctuations in the rate of clearing, the amount of cleared land still increased—it was a cumulative, once-and-for-all process that was going on despite down swings in the graph. The fluctuations are most closely related to the increase and decrease in the wheat acreage, although the peaks of clearing activity anticipate by three to five years, the booms in the wheat acreage, or put another way, the rate of clearing drops while the expansion

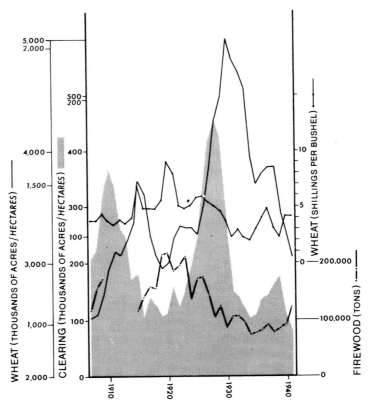

FIG. 43. Clearing, wheat yields, wheat acreage and firewood loading at South Australian railway stations, 1907–41. (*S.A. Stat. Reg.*)

of the wheat acreage continues for several years—something which needs further explanation.

The falling yields and acreages for the decade before 1908 were replaced by eight years of rapid expansion due to the increase in yield that resulted from planting better varieties of wheat, the application of superphosphate, the use of fallowing, general governmental assistance, and the slightly higher than average rainfall, together with the pent-up enthusiasm for land settlement after nearly two decades of stagnation. The rate of clearing began to fall off sharply after 1910, however, the decline probably being brought about by the drought of 1911. Farmers attempted to recoup some of the drought losses by expanding their wheat areas into fallow land rather than expand their acreage into land which had to be prepared for cultivation by the capital-consuming task of clearing.

The decline in wheat acreages during the First World War due to labour shortages and to the problems of exporting wheat overseas, is paralleled by a gradual waning of clearing. Although prices were high between 1914 and 1920 they were not related to domestic conditions but to conditions in the world market to which Australia exported between 60 and 70 per cent of her wheat. However, the high prices were not an incentive to expanding the wheat acreage. This is what Dunsdorfs calls a 'perverse' reaction to prices; farmers tend to expand their acreage during periods of low price in order to recoup losses, (as was done after periods of drought) rather than increase acreage during periods of high price.[74]

After the early 1920s the trough of the period of the First World War was replaced by a general upswing in the amount of land cleared and wheat sown, associated with the effects of increasing mechanization and the encouragement of soldier settlement schemes, particularly along the western railway of Eyre Peninsula and the Pinnaroo line in the Murray Mallee. The high point of clearing activity was reached in 1928, but again it was checked, this time by the droughts between 1928 and 1930, and, from then on, the rate of clearing plunged. Wheat acreages, on the other hand, continued to rise under the stimulus of a guaranteed price. Eventually, clearing was again shelved at the first sign of declining prices and more and more, previously-cleared land now in fallow or lying idle was utilized.

The bubble burst with the Depression, and wheat acreages declined along with clearing activity, but the economic problems of the cleared lands were compounded by a succession of years of low rainfall which particularly affected the newly cleared lands in the more northerly portions of the Murray Mallee and Eyre Peninsula where over-cropping, continual fallowing without a crop cover and the frequent tillage required for moisture conservation had caused a deterioration in the fertility and structure of the soil leading to excessive wind erosion. After the mid-1930s clearing was carried out only in the higher rainfall mallee lands that had previously been untouched.

Locations

Activity was concentrated primarily in the Murray Mallee and in the south-eastern coast of Eyre Peninsula, but there were other areas of significant change on the far west coast of Eyre Peninsula, in Yorke Peninsula and along the line of the Adelaide-Melbourne railway across the Ninety-Mile Desert. In fact, the railways are largely the key to this and to some of the other distributions. The greatest activity before 1914 was in the Pinnaroo lands in the south-eastern Murray Mallee and it occurred immediately after the railway was constructed in 1906.[75] An area of 294,614 acres was cleared in the five eastern-most hundreds in Country Chandos alone, and a further 167,364 acres were cleared in the seven hundreds to the west in County Buccleugh. The further extension of the railway to Paringa in the north-east corner of the Mallee in 1913, and the construction of three branch lines in 1914, one to Peebinga and two towards the Murray with terminals at Waikerie and Loxton respectively, all had their effect in encouraging clearing along their routes in the northern half of the Mallee, (compare Fig. 44 with Fig. 16).

The activity in Yorke Peninsula was the continuation, although less vigorous, of the clearing made twenty years before, which has been examined already. This clearing was not associated with the spread of a railway system but was based on the movement of goods and exports by boat from the many small ports which were strung out along the coast.

Clearing in Eyre Peninsula was similar to that in the Murray Mallee and Yorke Peninsula in that it was based on both railways

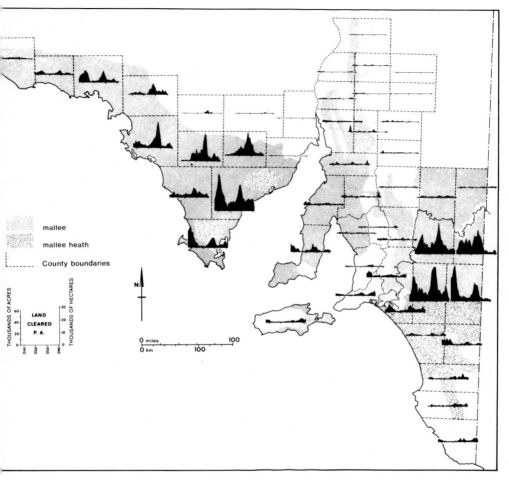

F I G. 44. The progress of clearing, by counties, 1907–41. (*S.A. Stat. Reg.*)

and ports. Along the south-eastern coast in the vicinity of Port Lincoln in County Flinders, and around Arno Bay in County Jervois clearing was proceeding at the rate of about 5,0000 acres per annum by the time the statistics were being collected, but it was the construction of the railway line to Yeelana by 1909 in the eastern portion of the Peninsula and of the line from Cummins to Kimba by 1913 that brought about the real attack on the woodland. The far west coast, however, was very different. Here, in the coastal fringes of Counties Hopetoun, Kintore, Way, Duffrin and Robinson, 235,367 acres were cleared, the whole operation being based on the ports of the area. (See Fig. 16 for the expansion of settlement.)

During the First World War, the rate of clearing dropped to less than one-third of what it had been before, as the colonization of new land declined with the diversion of men and energy elsewhere. The main zones of clearing were now wholly railway orientated; in the north-east portion of Eyre Peninsula, land alongside the railway line to Kimba was an area of moderate clearing, and the clearing along the new railway to Thevenard in the far west, completed in 1915, is just discernible from the slightly higher values along its route. In contrast, there was a decline in clearing in the adjacent coastal regions which were relatively less productive than those newly opened up inland. In the Mallee, settlers alongside the Tailem Bend to Loxton and Peebinga railway lines showed the greatest activity of all in South Australia, with 32 per cent of all clearing between 1915 and 1919 being carried out in these areas.

After the war there was a slight stepping-up of activity between 1920 and 1924 but the location of this was almost the same as in the previous few years, especially in the Murray Mallee, but there was a marked increase of activity alongside the Eyre Peninsula railway lines.

The years between 1925 and 1929 witnessed another enormous burst of clearing activity and a further 1,867,286 acres were stripped of their timber during these five years compared with 2,120,706 acres during the eight years between 1907 and 1914. Although both periods were alike in the massiveness of clearing, the location of activity changed. In Eyre Peninsula there was a marked shift from the coastal hundreds and their ports to the inland hundreds proclaimed along the new railway lines which ran through the relatively better loamy soils of the inner parts of the Peninsula, something which had already been hinted at by the distribution of clearing during earlier years. This shift can be gauged from Table IX.

An equally marked shift from south to north occurred in the Murray Mallee as railway lines allowed penetration further inland from the Pinnaroo line, and again, this can be gauged by

Table IX

Land Cleared in Eyre Peninsula during Two Peak Periods of Clearing

(100,000 acres = 40468·6 ha)

	Coastal		Inland		Total
	Area in acres	%	Area in acres	%	Area in acres
1907—14	697,629	81·1	158,353	18·9	837,982
1925—29	284,497	31·9	607,711	68·1	892,208

Source: S.A. Stat. Reg. (1907–1929).

comparing the number of acres cleared in the southern-most Countries (Buccleugh and Chandos) and the northern-most counties (Albert and Alfred), which together cover the bulk of the Mallee, during the two peak periods (Table X).

Table X

Land Cleared in the Murray Mallee during Two Peak Periods of Clearing

(100,000 acres = 40468·6 ha)

	Southern half		Northern half		Total
	Area in acres	%	Area in acres	%	Area in acres
1907—14	497,978	64·0	280,670	36·0	778,648
1925—29	376,386	46·0	441,474	54·0	817,860

Source: S.A. Stat. Reg. (1907–1929).

The implications of these basically northwards, but more importantly, inland shifts was to bring the scrub farmer into the lower rainfall mallee lands where seasons were more precarious. The result was a retreat from these areas and a decline of new clearing as their marginality became increasingly apparent during the mid-1930s, particularly in the northern and north-eastern

Murray Mallee hundreds and along the western railway line in Eyre Peninsula. There was a corresponding tendency to concentrate clearing in the middle high-rainfall land of the Peninsula.

During the late 1930s these patterns of retreat are even more striking as clearing became more concentrated in the south and the west of the Murray Mallee and the south and central parts of Eyre Peninsula. New areas of clearing became evident in the high-rainfall zones in Kangaroo Island and Fleurieu Peninsula (Counties Carnarvon and Hindmarsh respectively) and along the railway line through the deep sands of the Upper South-East. But this attack on the most difficult of the scrub lands is another story which is intimately bound up with the increase in the knowledge of soil chemistry; it is a story that belongs rightly to man's attempts to change the character of the soil.

Processes

The whole process of clearing during the early years of this century followed a familiar pattern, although a great deal more is known of that pattern than was the case in the Yorke Peninsula settlement during the previous century. The crucial factor in clearing such large areas was the cost, which could amount to a large figure on holdings that usually ranged between 640 and 2,000 acres and frequently were very much larger.

The cost appeared to vary mainly with the size, type and density of the mallee. An average cost often quoted was between 3 and 7 shillings per acre for small mallee which covered the greater part of Eyre Peninsula and the Murray Mallee; but larger mallee, such as that on the east coast of the Peninsula and in a few localities near Pinnaroo, could cost between 12 and 13 shillings per acre to clear. The very large trees on the eastern side of the Ranges, particularly in the vicinity of Robertstown, could not be rolled down and had to be cut at 25 shillings an acre.[76] The cost of purchasing heavy equipment for such a short part of the farming year deterred many farmers from doing their own clearing; many had their land cleared by contractors, others by the commercial firewood gatherers.[77] As a result, scrub cutters were in great demand and were being offered up to 12 shillings for every acre cleared in the Fowler Bay district. Sometimes, however, the better-off farmers had their own equipment and would offer '3 shillings per acre to any good bullocky' who would like the job of rolling down the scrub.[78]

One spectacular, but apparently short-lived, innovation in equipment, was a steam traction-engine for rolling (Fig. 45). One was at work in the Tintinara district in the Ninety-Mile Desert some time before 1908, and attracted so much attention in Pinnaroo and the adjacent Victorian Mallee that a similar model was

FIG. 45. The Pinnaroo 'monster', c. 1910.

eventually purchased by the Victorian Government. It had two massive rollers, weighed 35 tons and ran on its own rails. It cut a swathe 66 feet wide, cleared an average area of 40 acres a day, and had even been known to do 60 acres in one day, at a cost of between 2s.-6d. and 3s. per acre. There was little wonder that it was 'cheaper, quicker and more effective than horse-flesh'. To this cost had to be added another 1s.-6d. per acre for the preparation of the ground for ploughing. The result was spectacular and it was an awesome sight to watch 'this powerful great thing stalking about in the mallee crushing everything before it'. It is known that the machine cleared 16,000 acres during 1910, but little is heard of it afterwards. The 'monster' consumed 3 tons of wood per day (an easy thing to supply in the mallee) but it also used 800 gallons of water, which was much more difficult to supply away from the wells, and in all probability this was the cause of its disappearance. In any case it was too expensive for the average settler.[79]

Conventional rollers continued to be used for a long time in the mallee-lands,[80] but they did not completely prepare the land for cultivation, and essential costs—particularly those of stump-grubbing—were deferred until time and money were available. The stump-jump plough, while allowing cultivation to occur on the partially cleared land, did not, in fact, pull out as many of the roots as was hoped, particularly in the areas of the heavier mallee in Eyre Peninsula and in parts of the Murray Mallee. The wear and tear on machinery was said to be three times greater, it was estimated that it took 20 per cent more time to seed and harvest a crop on ungrubbed land; and crops grew poorly within 1–4 yards radius of large stumps. 'When everything was taken into consideration', wrote one farmer, 'he was quite satisfied that grubbing though more costly at the start was cheaper in the long run.'[81]

The old quest for an efficient grubber began again and many farmers exchanged ideas on various leverage methods that they had employed now aided by steam tractors.[82] Finally in 1918, the most promising methods were put to the test on the Government Experimental Farm at Minnipa on Eyre Peninsula. The results can be summarized as follows:

	Average cost per acre
Brown's Forest Devil (a lever system worked by two men)	£2-1-11
Jelbart Tractor (direct pull)	£2-0- 8
Jelbart Tractor (action on a winch)	£2-0- 4

All of these worked at a rate of about half an acre a day (Figs. 46 and 47).

Thus the true costs of complete clearing were really about £2 an acre more than the commonly quoted figures, and could range between £2-10s and £3-10s an acre.[83] When price changes are taken into account, the improved methods and machinery of grubbing were barely more efficient than those in operation on Yorke Peninsula nearly forty years before (Fig. 48).

Another innovation, more lasting and important than the steam tractor, was the simple procedure of logging the scrub rather than

FIG. 46. Grubbing out stubborn mallee roots with a two-man winch.

FIG. 47. The winch could also be used for pulling over larger trees which could not be 'mullenized' or rolled down.

rolling it. Rolling tended to break off the stem of the trees either at, or slightly above ground level, leaving jagged pieces sticking up, which injured the horses and bullocks, and, of course, left many roots to be grubbed out. Logging, on the other hand, consisted in dragging a heavy log through the scrub. The log rode up the stems of the trees and exerted leverage on the whole tree, thus causing it to topple over and the root to be pulled out of the ground. A further development was the construction of a V-shaped cradle of logs which ran on wheels and which had a high breaking rail, 8 feet from the ground and staggered forward to supply the necessary leverage. Costs of initial clearing by logging were usually less than those of rolling by anything up to 2 shillings per acre because of the reduced need for grubbing as a result of half or more of the roots coming out of the ground. With a strong team of horses or bullocks, 15–20 acres could be cleared in a day, or up to 40 acres in very light scrub. Further to this reduction in costs, the log could be assembled for a couple of pounds, whereas a roller cost £20.[84] Mention is made of logging in 1911 in the hundreds of Verran, Roberts and Kimba on the eastern coastal areas of Eyre Peninsula, which suggests that it might have been invented there. Its localized nature was noted at the time and it did not spread either widely or rapidly throughout the Peninsula. By 1915 references to logging become more numerous, but still in the eastern area, near Kimba.[85] As a technique it came very much into its own in the 1920s with the advent of powerful tractors; and references to rolling decrease. By 1928, costs of logging with a tractor were said to be between 1s.-11d. and 2s.-7d. per acre, but this was for tractor fuel alone and did not take into account machinery and labour costs.[86]

Yet another innovation was referred to in 1911 but was not taken up widely; it was the knocking down of stubble and mallee shoots with a 20-feet anchor chain. It was not as effective as a roller, but it was a quicker method; it being possible to clear 40 acres a day.[87] After 1945, chaining replaced rolling and logging as the most common means of clearing.

But variables other than the type of the mallee and the type of machinery entered into the cost of clearing—such things as the quality of the 'burn', the availability of water and feed for stock, the availability of stock itself, and the ability to sell the timber and roots for firewood, which in turn depended on the proximity of railways and ports with access to the main market, Adelaide.

The quality of the 'burn' was important to the success of clearing. If it was a hot one the subsequent costs were minimal as it cleared the fallen timber on the land and even burnt stumps enough for ploughing to commence. If it was a poor burn due to wet weather or changes of wind then the reburning or removal of trash could add anything from 2 to 5 shillings per acre to the initial cost of clearing. As an example of the task an 'extra-good' burn resulted in only 2 days of 'stick-picking over 100 acres of land. Much of this back-breaking work, which usually employed the whole family, was done away with after the invention by J. C. Campbell of a scrub-rake which gathered and lifted the trash. One person and two horses could clear up to 12 or 14 acres a day, 'thus doing the work of at least a dozen men'.[88]

Because of its direct financial results reckless burning was sometimes resorted to, farmers waiting for fierce northerly winds to fan the fire along so that 'get-a-ways' did great damage to neighbouring property and stock. Thus, it appeared to one correspondent in Shannon Hundred in Eyre Peninsula that it did 'not matter whose you burn, so long as it burns your own well'.[89] When the burning of the stubble after the harvest in order to kill the suckering mallee roots, to 'sweeten' the ground, and to prepare a seed bed for the next harvest was added to the burning of the rolled-down mallee, then the result was to place the countryside under a great pall of smoke : 'How many thousands of acres have been reduced to ashes is hard to calculate', wrote a Pinnaroo resident, 'but according to the amount of smoke and ashes that have been floating around and enveloping the town, it could be easily believed that there was no scrub left in the district.'[90]

Another important factor in the cost of clearing in the inner mallee areas at this time was the availability of working-horses and bullocks and of the feed and water they needed. At present, we take so thoroughly for granted the mechanization of labour that it is sometimes difficult to appreciate the dependence on draught animals in the working economy of a pioneer area. For example, it was calculated that it would cost £737 to establish a 300-acre farm in the fairly thick mallee of the Pinnaroo area in 1912.[91] Of this total, £222 (30·1 per cent) was accounted for by horses and associated items (although bullocks could have been bought for £8–£10 each), and £100 (13·6 per cent) by implements; the remainder for preparing the land for cultivation, fencing it, and building a house. But besides the cost of purchasing the horses there was also the question of the availability of water and food. Often water for stock had to be carted to the farms until such time as the wells were dug, and if it was carted the horses needed feed, and if the mallee was not cleared (by horse) there was no grass for feed. It was estimated that a farmer who lived more than ten miles from the railway needed 10 or 11 mature horses (at anything between £30 and £50 each) for three months of the year in order to cart wheat to the railway during which time no clearing would be done. Ideally, he needed 20 horses, but their feed would have taken up half of the cleared block. The mallee farmer was often caught up in a vicious circle of events and often the only way out was to buy feed, but usually only at a very high cost.[92]

It was not surprising, then, that as a result of this cost factor many farmers skimped their clearing and left many stumps in the ground. They were accused of 'slumming', but in reality they were only deferring their capital expenditure in order to get immediate returns from their land. The stump-jump ploughs removed far fewer stumps than was hoped, and those stumps that remained suckered so that shoot-cutting or 'sucker-bashing', as it was called, at a cost of up to 5 shillings per acre for the next few years was necessary, despite frequent burning of stubble. Grubbing was still the best answer, but still the most expensive.[93]

There was one other way in which the scrub farmer could reduce his costs and that was to sell the firewood rather than burn it on his paddocks, as was the usual practice. 'Enterprising men' realized that their wood was ultimately marketable when they had the time to transport it to the railheads, and therefore they stacked it around their holdings while others used it for burning limestone.[94] Sometimes the jagged mallee roots were stacked to make quite effective fences, some of which still exist today, but more elaborate pioneer structures, such as barns and even the dwellings, the outer walls daubed with mud, have long since disappeared.

The main market for the wood was Adelaide, and the main

form of transport for this bulky low-cost commodity was the railway. The annual amount of wood moved between 1906 and 1914 was between 110,000 and 120,000 tons, and after that time the tonnage rose rapidly to reach an all-time peak of 217,421 tons in 1928 (Fig. 43). Statistics on the loading of firewood at each station and halt in the State have been collected almost without a break since 1881 and it is possible to identify the major zones of supply at any time. Whereas during the 1880s and 1890s (annual) loadings were in the vicinity of 70,000 to 80,000 tons and came from the mallee areas served by the Hamley Bridge–Balaklava–Wallaroo Railway, north-west of Adelaide, and the Eudunda–Morgan line, north-east of Adelaide, with a constant supply coming from the stringybark forests in the Adelaide hills, after 1906 the supplies from the north-west line almost disappeared and loadings on the new Murray Mallee lines rose dramatically (Fig. 49). The Adelaide hills,[95] and the Eudunda–Morgan line (with the new spur to Robertstown constructed by 1914) continued to supply large amounts, the loadings at Morgan being the greatest in South Australia, it served as a railhead for commercial timber gatherers working in a wide area east of the Ranges and beyond into the unsettled country, and also as an off-loading point for steamers coming down the Murray. So important was Morgan that the price at that township was usually taken to be the ruling price in South Australia.

The rate of clearing and the rate of firewood movement do not coincide (Fig. 43), and this is born out by a more detailed analysis of selected hundreds and stations in the Murray Mallee, and in Eyre Peninsula. There was an almost directly inverse relationship between clearing and loading which suggests that the pioneer farmer had little time or inclination to supply wood while he was clearing the land, getting in his first crop, and carting the wheat to the railhead. Once the pressure of establishing himself was relaxed, however, the farmer could afford to attempt to get the extra income, particularly if the sale of roots coincided with a deferred programme of grubbing, as was often the case. Perhaps more important was the fact that in times of drought and low yields the sale of firewood proved to be a source of *essential* income, and loadings increase significantly during such times of stress, sometimes encouraged by governmental action in the

FIG. 48. Rolled, grubbed and ready to burn. Northern Murray Mallee, *c.* 1900.

FIG. 49. The valuable products of the mallee lands—wheat and mallee roots.
Pinnaroo station yard, 1922.

lowering of freight rates as a drought relief measure, e.g., the
rate from Lameroo was lowered by 2s.-5d. per ton in 1912.[96]
Therefore, firewood loadings cannot be used as a detailed indication of clearing, although it would be true to say that, if large-

scale clearing was going on and there was a nearby railway line giving easy access to Adelaide, that area would be a major source of firewood in due course.

The return from selling the wood, at Eudunda for example, varied between 4, and 10 shillings per ton, depending upon the season and the demand. Cartage to the railhead could cost as much as 5s.-6d. per ton. A better break-down of costs is that from Pinnaroo in 1912 where wood delivered to the railway yards gave a return of 6s. to 6s.-8d. per ton, but to that must be added the freight to Adelaide at 8s.-11d. per ton, cartage in Adelaide at 2 shillings which with sundry other charges meant that the wood sold retail at 28 shillings, a fairly constant price for the next couple of decades. The yield from chopped medium-sized mallee derived from cut-over land was said to be 10–12 tons to the acre, but that could rise to 20 tons per acre for 'roots and all'. The whole topic of firewood is a fascinating one that would repay closer analysis.[97]

It would be unprofitable to write again about the processes of clearing during the 1920s and 1930s. Not only would the topic be repetitious because its ·main characteristics have already been described but it was obviously of little interest to the local inhabitants since they recorded so little about it. The novelty had worn off and so had much of the enthusiasm: 'Another year gone by with not much noticeable alteration in McClachan and surrounding hundreds', wrote the Lock correspondent of the *West Coast Recorder*, 'a marriage or two, a birth or two, a death or two, a few more hundred acres cleared, a few more miles of sheep-proof fencing . . . two or three new stone homes built . . . this outlines the main events of the past twelve months.'[98]

Indeed, life and interests, as reflected in the local newspapers, had changed. The 'annals of scrub farming' no longer consisted of 'wheat growing and playing football' as they had before.[99] and one is left with the impression that the main topics of news were the latest model cars, the state of the roads, the latest film show and the advent of radio. The whole content of the newspapers changed. Whereas up to the early 1920s they were intensely parochial, reflecting every facet of local life yet with a remarkably well-informed coverage of world news, they now lost their local interests and much of their overseas news, and became just metropolitan-orientated South Australian papers that happened to be printed locally. Undoubtedly the wider circulation of Adelaide newspapers and the increasing trend for innovation and change to be concentrated in Adelaide had something to do with this, but one also feels that the change in the content and the format of the local newspapers was more fundamental; it reflected a disenchantment with the harsh and often unrewarding realities of pioneering life in the mallee lands which became more and more pronounced with years of economic depression and mounting problems of erosion and soil deterioration.

Two or three themes stand out during these years, however. First the mechanization of farming was beginning and trucks were replacing drays. Advertisements appeared in 1923 for a Chase tractor—'work it by day and night, it never tires, makes full use of every hour'—a point not lost on the farmer who wanted either to catch the rain for seeding or for harvest in a wet spring.[100] By 1925 'the passing of the horse' was a common topic, and references to tractors became more and more frequent, while 'power farming' competitions were held.[101]

It would seem that the initial penetration of machines was mainly on already cleared land and for the purposes of harvesting, and it was not until the advent of crawler tractors, first referred to in 1928, that the mechanization of rolling, logging and stump-pulling came into its own.[102] Even so, bullock-teams and horse-teams were still surprisingly common. Writing in 1939 one farmer in Pinnaroo said that tractors were introduced into the district in 1927 and twenty were in use initially. By 1932, the number had risen to twenty-three, but had then dropped to seventeen because of the problems of bogging-down in the clay in winter and in the drifting sand in summer, and because of the lack of mechanical knowledge on the part of most farmers. The number of horses remained steady at 1,800, and the writer forecast that the number would remain the same 'for many years to come'.[103]

One other reason why information on clearing becomes less is that clearing itself became less important, and the over-riding concern was how to make the already cleared land pay its way during the periods of physical and economic deterioration.

Drought and sand drift in the light soils plagued the mallee farmer, and, until suitable rotations and pasture crops were introduced in order to maintain, and even to restore, soil fertility and correct erosion the mallee farmer battled on as best he knew.[104] Rising costs and falling prices, with the loss of overseas markets, were the basis of much of the distress and poverty of the mallee farms, and until these righted themselves the farmer had little incentive to clear new land, and was more concerned with making his existing holding pay. Economic stress had revealed the marginal character of many of the farms. Articles such as 'Financial results of two years farming on a Murray Mallee farm', and 'Costs of production and land values in the Mallee areas over 20 years' were typical of many in the *South Australian Journal of Agriculture* at this time and were indicative of the mallee-farmer's concern.[105]

Indeed, as with the discussion on the location of clearing after 1941, so the discussion on the process of clearing becomes but a part of the whole change in farming attitudes after the mid-1930s, that arose from an increasing appreciation of soil limitations and possibilities. The need was to call a halt to the 'making' of new land by clearing it of its timber, and to capitalize on what was already cleared by improving the quality of that unseen thing, the soil itself. The need was to reappraise the physical environment and stop expansion, retreat from the edges of cultivation, and re-structure the farms and the economy. If clearing did need to be carried out on the lands deficient in trace-elements, then it was an incidental accompaniment to the rectification of those deficiencies. From now on, the clearing of the woodland was basically the story of 'changing the soil' (see pp. 321–324).

4. Notes

1. Many place-names exist today with the element 'plains' in the name, at places which are not particularly level. Their origin lies in the openness of the locality compared with the surrounding dense scrub. In many ways the usage is analogous to the Anglo-Saxon 'field', meaning a 'clearing in a wood' when the name remained long after the wood disappeared.
   E. Ekwall, *The Oxford dictionary of English place-names* (1935).
2. C. R. Harris, 'Mantung—A study of man's impact on landscape', unpublished B.A. Hons. thesis, University of Adelaide (1968).

3. G. C. Morphett, *The life and letters of Sir John Morphett* (1936). Also quoted in J. Stephens, *The land of promise* (1839), 12.
4. B. S. Baldwin (ed.), 'Letters of Samuel Davenport, chiefly to his father, George Davenport, 1842–1849', *South Australiana*, VI, Part I (1967), 24.
5. H. Duncan, *The Colony of South Australia* (1850), 22.
   For similar comments on vegetation as an indication of soil fertility, see W. S. Chauncey, *A guide to South Australia* (1849), 20 and 26.
6. W. Mann, *Six year's residence in the Australian provinces ending in 1839* (1839), 250.
7. W. Smillie, *The great south land* (1836), 22;
   It is significant that when the Governor of South Australia was asked to send seeds of economically useful plants to the Cape Colony he sent those of the 'Mt. Lofty stringybark and common wattle'. CSO, 2471/1855 (out).
8. G. F. Angas, *Savage life and scenes in Australia and New Zealand* (1847), 44.
9. G. B. Wilkinson, *The working man's handbook to South Australia* (1849), 74–5. By 1846 there were 420 sawyers and splitters in South Australia, which was about 3·2 per cent of the labour force and only slightly less than the number of miners.
10. J. Stephens, *The land of promise* (1839), 22;
    H. Duncan, op. cit. 20.
    F. S. Dutton, *South Australia and its mines* (1849), 203.
11. S.A.A., 1045, p. 112. Reminiscences of Miss C. E. Clark.
    For the destruction of trees see *S.A. Gazette and Colonial Register* (30 June 1838) and *The South Australian* (1 and 15 Sept. 1838).
    For the prohibition on cutting see *S.A. Gazette and Colonial Register* (13 Oct. and 30 Nov. 1838).
12. Not all people approved of the new licence fee. Farmers in the Willunga area protested that it had caused a doubling of timber prices and that as a consequence 'the expense of fencing a section is now more than the upset price of the land . . .'. CSO, 627 and 912/1849 (in).
13. CSO, 718/1843 (in); 884/1843 (out), 27 June, concerning illegal timber getting at Mt Barker.
    See also *S.A. Govt. Gaz.* (26 Jan. 1843).
14. CSO, 2037/1849 (in). See enclosed letter from a Mr H. Burslem of Kooringa which describes 'the immense destruction of timber now being committed on the surveyed lands'.
15. CSO, 2094/1849 (in).
16. CSO, 2169 and 3275/1855 (out).
17. CSO, 3184/1856 (in); 3992/1855 (in).
18. SGO, 136/1858 (in); 410/1858 (in).
19. Amended regulations were printed in 1859 (*SAPP*, 144 (1859)) under which licences remained at £5 if issued annually, or £3 if issued half-

yearly, neither being transferable. Licencees were restricted and were not permitted to cut 'on any waste lands leased for pastoral or any other purpose; nor on any lands surveyed for sale, or public roads or reserves', neither could they camp on waste lands or depasture their draught stock, except where absolutely necessary. In the next year, the licencees were requested to state 'within a reasonably limited area the locality in which they intended to operate', which was specified in their licence. (*SAPP*, 29 (1860), 1). In 1866 cutting was prohibited within 2 miles of a government township. (*SAPP*, 16 (1866–7)). See SGO, 395/1869 (in) for an example of this near Meningie township.

20. For example SGO, 91/1859 (in) referring to Saltaire, near Port Augusta; 1315/1859 (in), referring to Yorke Peninsula; and SGO, (1863) (out), in Mobilong hundred.
21. SGO, 2102/1859 (out).
22. SGO, 1116/1857 (in).
23. SGO, 838/1866 (in). This was probably the remnant of the Tothill Scrub mentioned on p. 135.
24. SGO, 1140/1869 (out); 26/1868 (in).
25. *SAPP*, 190 (1861). There were 112 annual, 168 half-yearly and 211 quarterly licences issued in 1861 compared with only 47 licences in 1857; SGO, 169/1857 (in), List of timber licences, 7 March.
26. *S.A. Register* (3 June 1851); *Adelaide Observer* (30 July 1859).
27. Ibid. (2 Dec. 1865); *Border Watch* (15 Jan. 1870).
28. *The South Australian* (4 August 1848) and (2 Nov. 1848). The Yatala works closed after the Apoinga smelters were established successfully. See D. Pike, *Paradise of dissent* (1957), 338, for the search for coal in South Australia.
29. *S.A. Register* (3 and 8 July 1851).
30. *The South Australian* (29 Sept., 6 and 10 Oct. 1848).
31. CSO, 1338/1849 (in); 1679/1849 (in).
32. CSO, 1648/1851 (in); 2666½/1851 (in); 3624/1851.
33. CSO, 2037/1849 (in); 2049/1849 (in).
34. CSO, 683/1851 (in); 892/1851 (out); 1359/1851 (in); 1156/1851(out).
35. *S.A. Register* (8 July 1851).
36. S.A.A. Legislative Council Papers (1849). Report of the Harbour Commissioners, 'Lipson's Report on Port Lincoln.'
37. *S.A. Register* (3 June 1851); *SAPD*, (H.A.) (1867), Col. 1447.
38. For example, *S.A. Govt. Gaz.* (8 August 1864). SGO, 233a/1863 (in); 72/1864 (in).
39. SGO, 209/1862 (in); 233a/1863 (in); 72/1864 (in).
40. *SAPD*, (L.C.) (1865), cols. 258–64; *SAPP*, 73 (1865), App. See also pp. 32–37 above.

41. SGO, 463/1866 (out).

42. *SAPP*, 49 (1866–7); 155 (1866–7).

43. See *SAPP*, 172 (1868–9); SGO, 1702 and 1745½/1870 (in).

44. SGO, 800/1867 (in).

45. A. Prosser on lease 264, was allowed to give up his lease because he was 'utterly unable for want of means to carry out conditions . . . in clearing'. SGO, 220/1869 (in).

46. *SAPP*, 124 (1867).

47. For detailed plans see *SAPP*, 161 (1870–71); and also *Act*, 25/1870–71 : an Act to extend the provisions of the Scrub Land Act 1866. One obvious place where some success might have been expected was around the Yorke Peninsula mining townships, but the Government would not survey these lands in case they contained minerals, (see SGO, 2511/1872 (in)).

48. SGO, 1190/1871 (in).

49. *Act*, 18/1872, Waste Lands Alienation Act. Part of the confusion arose because, during the passage of the Bill, the Government also tabled another Bill to deal with the scrub lands in which the regulations would have been liberalized to allow up to 3 square miles to be taken up with residence or occupation qualifications. It was never passed. *SAPD*, (H.A.). (1872), col. 734–53.

50. *Act*, 17/1875, an Act to revive certain Enactments relating to scrub lands. The regulations are published in *SAPP*, 39 (1876). In *SAPD*, (L.C.) (1875), col. 1389, the Chief Secretary said that the original Scrub Acts 'had been accidentally repealed'.

51. *Act*, 86/1877, Crown Lands Consolidation Act. A new departure was contained in Clause 57 which allowed any land remaining unsold for 5 years to be offered in blocks of 1,280 acres for 10 years at an annual rent of 6d per acre, with the right of purchase on the expiration of the lease at £1 per acre. Therefore 'difficult' land outside specified Scrub Areas could be taken up on similar terms to the Scrub Lands. For examples in Southern Eyre Peninsula see *SAPP*, 32 (1882).

    For pleas by R. B. Smith (the inventor of the stump-jump plough) that Yorke Peninsula land be included in the Act see *Yorke Peninsula Advertiser* (21 May and 4 June 1881).

52. *Act*, 192/1880, Crown Lands Amendment Act.

53. This sequence is based on E. O. G. Shann, *An economic history of Australia* (1930), 221.

    See also A. R. Callaghan and A. J. Millington, *The wheat industry in Australia* (1956), 319–20, and photographs on, 150–1;

    E. Dunsdorfs, *The Australian wheat-growing industry, 1788–1948* (1956), 155–7.

54. *Yorke Peninsula Advertiser* (2 May 1879).

55. Ibid. (24 Feb. 1880).

56. Ibid. (7 June and 11 March 1881).

57. R. D. Ross, 'Scrubland cultivation in South Australia', *Proc. Roy. Agric. Hort. Soc. S.A.* (1881–2), 33.

58. *Yorke Peninsula Advertiser* (9 Nov. 1880; 28 Oct. and 11 Nov. 1881).

59. D. W. Meinig. *On the margins of the good earth: the South Australian wheat frontier, 1869–1884* (1962), 104.

60. W. Harcus (ed.), *South Australia: Its history, resources and productions* (1876), 130.

In 1890, Goyder reported that the roots needed to be removed 'as upon considerable areas left uncultivated during the last few years, the young mallee is coming up as thickly as ever'. *SAPP*, 60 (1890), 19.

61. *Farmer's Weekly Messenger* (28 August 1874); and *Yorke Peninsula Advertiser* (21 Sept. 1877) and (16 April and 30 August 1878).

For greater detail see R. D. Ross, op. cit., 35–6.

62. *Garden and the Field*, IV (1878–9); *Farmer's Weekly Messenger* (6 Sept. 1878).

63. *Yorke Peninsula Advertiser* (4 July 1879; 9 Jan. 1880).

64. Smith's claim seems quite clear, although many others put forward requests for rewards. See Callaghan and Millington, *op. cit.*, 320–1, and R. D. Ross, *op. cit.*, 31–2, and comments in *Yorke Peninsula Advertiser* (17 June, 1881). The principle of lifting the shares out of the ground on meeting an obstruction by bearing down on the handles of a plough was known from an early date. Designs with back wheels which acted as a fulcrum for the movement were in use in Scotland since the early nineteenth century and were known as 'grubbers', 'scarifiers', 'extirpators' or 'tormentors'. It is possible that Smith knew of these and that they were the inspiration for his invention. See Society for the diffusion of useful knowledge, *British Husbandry* (1837), Vol. I, 29 *et seq.*

65. *Farmer's Weekly Messenger* (17 Nov. 1876).

66. *Yorke Peninsula Advertiser* (4 and 21 May 1880); *Garden and the Field*, XVI (1890–1), 114.

67. *Yorke Peninsula Advertiser* (2 July, 21 Sept., 12 Nov. 1880). Smith's, Whittacker's and Murdoch's ploughs were tested.

68. Ibid. (31 May, 23 Aug. 1881).

69. Ibid. (1 Nov. 1881; 14 Feb. 1882).

70. Ibid. (28 March 1883).

71. K. R. Bowes, *Land Settlement in South Australia, 1857–1890* (1968), 239–243;

Act, 275/1882, Crown Lands Amendment Act.

72. *Act*, 318/1884, Agricultural Crown Lands Amendment Act. Part II relates to Scrub Leases.

73. This graph is compiled from a variety of sources in the *S.A. Statistical Register* (1868–1904).

74. E. Dunsdorfs, op cit., 364–7;
    SAPP, 10 (1923), 44.

75. See *SAPP*, 124 (1901), for the recommendation for the line to Pinnaroo and *SAPP*, 22 (1902), for the Royal Commission on the Pinnaroo Lands.

76. *SAPP*, 51 (1911), qus. 1183 and 1315; 30 (1909), qus. 114 and 197; (1909), qu. 30; 51 (1911), qus. 1319, 1562, 1653 and 1720; and 23 (1911), qus. 10 and 53.

77. *Pinnaroo and Border Times* (9 August 1912), However, logging changed this in later years.

78. *West Coast Recorder* (17 July 1912).

79. *Pinnaroo and Country News* (19 June, 20 Oct., 27 Nov. 1908; 9 April 1909);
    Pinnaroo and Border Times (14 April 1911).

80. *Pinnaroo and Country News* (19 August 1910). References to conventional rollers and rolling techniques abound during these years, for example, *SAJA*, XII (1908–9), 185 and 407. Similar descriptions may be found in Vols. XV (1911–12); XXVI (1922–3); and even as late as XXIX (1925–6), 635.
    C. P. Hodge, 'Hints to settlers starting in Mallee Lands', *SAJA*, XXV (1921–2), 204–11, gives a lengthy description of rolling.

81. *SAJA*, I (1897–8), 957; and VII (1903–4), 299, respectively.

82. For example, *SAJA*, XI (1907–8), 196; XVII (1913–14), 1083.

83. *SAJA*, XXIII (1919–20), 438–43; *West Coast Recorder* (29 Oct. 1919).

84. *SAPP*, 51 (1911), qus. 1269 and 1274–81.

85. *West Coast Recorder* (3 May 1911); *SAPP* 51 (1911) qu. 1498; (24 March 1915; 7 Sept. 1919).

86. *SAJA*, XXXI (1927–8), 864–5; and *Murray Pioneer* (11 Nov. 1927).

87. *SAJA*, XIV (1910–11), 954.

88. *SAPP*, 30 (1911), qu. 2; 51 (1911), qus. 1270 and 1273;
    West Coast Recorder (5 April 1911);
    Pinnaroo and Country News (17 May 1912);
    SAJA, XV (1911–12), 974.

89. *Pinnaroo and Country News* (19 Feb. 1909: Pinnaroo); (26 Feb. 1909: Geranium); and (19 March 1909; east of Lameroo).
    West Coast Recorder (6 March 1912);

90. *Pinnaroo and Country News* (23 Feb. 1912) and for general comments on burning see:
    SAJA, XVI (1912–13), 82;
    C. P. Hodge, 'Hints to settlers starting in Mallee Lands', *SAJA*, XXV (1921–2), 204–11.

91. *Pinnaroo and Border Times* (9 August 1912).
   For similar calculations see *SAJA*, XVI (1912–13), 83;
   Pinnaroo and Country News (10 March 1911).
92. See *SAPP*, 30 (1911), qu. 53 and other comments on commencing
   farming in *SAJA*, XVI (1912–13), 182.
93. *West Coast Recorder* (18 April 1917);
   Murray Pioneer (4 March 1927); and for stubble burning and shoot
   cutting see *West Coast Recorder* (30 August 1911 and 29 May 1918).
94. *Pinnaroo and Country News* (10 July 1908);
   West Coast Recorder (17 July 1912); and SAJA, XVI (1912–13), 80–1.
95. Although 20,000–30,000 tons were being loaded annually in the Hills
   during the 1920s there was virtually no clearing in these areas, which
   suggests that commercial thinning was practised. However, the yield
   from stringybarks was in the vicinity of 30–40 tons an acre so that the
   clearing of relatively small areas would give high tonnages.
96. *Pinnaroo and Country News* (3 May 1912).
   For another example see *Murray Pioneer* (30 August 1929).
97. *Pinnaroo Border Times* (14 June 1912);
   SAPP, 23 (1911), qus. 14, 20, 49–51, 63–6, 74, 117, 124 and 140.
98. *West Coast Recorder* (6 Jan. 1925).
99. Ibid. (27 May 1924).
100. Ibid. (1 Jan. 1923). At a cost of £395 it was the equivalent of a team of
   8 horses. An additional advertising bait was the fact that every horse
   replaced released enough pasture for 10–15 sheep, which could each
   return 9–10 shillings in wool alone.
   SAJA, XXXII (1928–9), 884. A Ford truck cost between £155 and
   £203.
101. For two good examples see *West Coast Recorder* (13 Jan. and 14 April
   1925); for tractors see *West Coast Recorder* (13 Oct. and 23 Nov. 1926).
102. *SAJA*, XXXIII (1929–30), 922–3; XXXIV (1930–1), for accounts of
   trials with crawler tractors for clearing in Koppio and Pygery on Eyre
   Peninsula.
103. *SAJA*, XLII (1938–9), 672.
104. *SAJA*, XLII (1938–9), 670–1;
   R. L. Griffiths, 'Rotation and cropping methods', *SAJA*, XXX (1926–7),
   1122–7.
105. A. J. Perkins, *SAJA*, XXXV (1931–2), 728, 1066, 1168 and 1316;
   T. H. Vowles, *SAJA*, XL (1936–7), 354–6, respectively.
   For other similar articles see A. J. Perkins, *SAJA*, XXXVII (1933–4),
   635, 768 and 928.

5
Draining the Swamps

'It is comparatively easy to say and show what ought to be done, but it is not so easy, looking at the importance and area of the district, to say, with the limited means at command, how best to begin'. *SAPP*, 48 (1864). Report by W. Hanson on works in the South-East.

If an area of Australia has a water problem, more often than not it is a problem of water deficiency rather than one of water excess. Yet, in the South-East of South Australia there is a large area of about 6,500 square miles, or about one-tenth of the total settled area of the state, over much of which the accumulation of surplus water has produced a distinctive landscape characterized by sheets of standing water, swamps and waterlogged ground. The efforts made to convert the swamp to productive paddock through draining are an obvious focus of interest for any study of the settlement and colonization of the region (Figs. 50 and 51).

Draining is one of the major 'resource-converting' techniques or processes whereby man changes the landscape to produce a new visual scene. The object of the change is to raise the production of the land and establish new agricultural and pastoral pursuits, which means new crops and animals, new farms, and new towns and patterns of communication. But the changes are more far-reaching than that, for draining is the conscious alteration and control of the natural hydrographical features of the landscape. Swamps become dry land, water-tables are altered, old drainage channels are regraded and re-orientated, and new ones dug. More basic, but probably less obvious, are the changes in the biotic features of the landscape. One major vegetative cover may be replaced by another, and the soil structure disturbed and eventually

FIG. 50. Flooding. The hundreds of Comaum and Peacock, *c. 1955*.

FIG. 51. The drained landscape. Improved pastures on the flats in the hundred of Symon.

altered, while the elevation of the land surface may be permanently changed with the irreversible shrinkage and wastage of organic soils.

'A Watery Waste'

In order to understand fully the nature of these changes, it is perhaps best to consider first the physical features of the South-East which give rise to the problem of defective drainage. They are three in number : the impeded natural drainage, the presence of excessive ground water, and fairly high rainfall.

The natural drainage is impeded because of the configuration of the principal surface features of the region, which consist of a series of low 'ranges' separating valleys or 'flats', as they are known locally, both running approximately parallel to the coast (Fig. 52). The ranges consist of Tertiary and Quaternary sands and gravels which probably were former coastal dunes now left stranded as the sea has retreated by successive stages to its present position after readjustment to phases of eustatic movement. The loose, unconsolidated sand dunes of the Younghusband Peninsula (which separates the Coorong from the sea) and the coastal dunes further to the south, mark the latest stage in the process, while those inland are older and the sand has become lithified into dune-limestone. The ranges are up to 100 feet above the surrounding flats. The flats consist of a great variety of soils ranging from black spongy peats to grey-black clays overlying limestone (rendzinas), to sandy soils overlying clay (meadow podsols), all characterized by poor drainage.[1]

Each flat is at a progressively higher level than the adjoining one to the west, the most easterly flat at Penola being about 200 feet above sea level, the most westerly being drowned and forming a series of lakes along the coast. Not only does each flat decrease in elevation from east to west but it is also slightly tilted, about 2 feet per mile, from the south-east to the north-west. The natural drainage of the flats is towards the west until one of the low ranges is encountered, when the water is deflected towards the north-west along the eastern side of the range. A sluggish and ill-defined water course is formed which either gravitates slowly towards a natural outfall at Salt Creek on the Coorong or stagnates

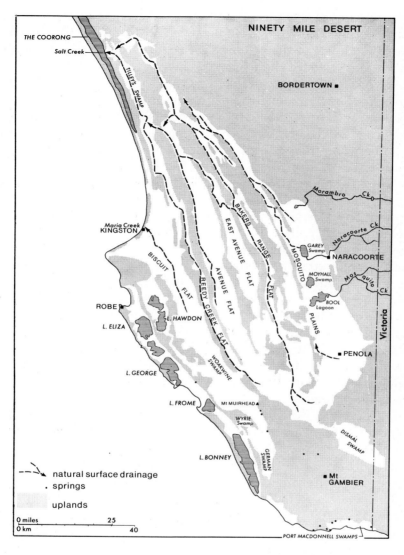

FIG. 52. The natural drainage of the South-East.

and evaporates in one of the great swamps on the edge of the Ninety-Mile Desert. Prolific vegetative growth in all water courses reduces their effectiveness in evacuating water.

In contrast to these ill-defined natural water courses which attempt to evacuate the surface water, there are the well-defined courses of the Morambro, Naracoorte and Mosquito Creeks which contribute much of the water to the region, and discharge it in the easternmost flats of the Mosquito and Naracoorte Plains.

Although the surface drainage of the South-East is so imperfect, there is an underground drainage system which is continuous and efficient. A large amount of water sinks into the porous rocks which underlie much of the region and adjacent parts of Victoria and the water moves slowly towards the coast and the Upper South-East. It lies at about 5–6 feet below the surface of the flats in the summer months but with greater rainfall during the winter, it rises and reaches the surface at or about a peak in September and causes widespread flooding. In places the underground water comes to the surface in the form of strongly flowing and continuous springs. Most occur along the Tartwaup fault, a major structural break in the country, which has disrupted the lines of the underground drainage and caused the water to reach the surface. The most important springs are the Snuggery and Racecourse Springs, east of Millicent and Tantanoola and south of Mount Muirhead at the base of the Reedy Creek Range while other springs are situated at Ewen's Ponds on the edge of the Port MacDonnell swamps. Needless to say, the continuous flow of water from these springs into the flats greatly increases the flood problem.[2]

Thirdly, the rainfall of the South-East is fairly high, though not excessive. The annual rainfall decreases from 32 inches at Kalangadoo in the south to about 22 inches at Naracoorte, 42 miles to the north (Fig. 3). About two-thirds of the rain falls during the winter months from May to September.

The combined effect of the impeded drainage and the slight fall of the land, the presence of ground water and, of course, the rainfall has been to create many large permanent swamps and to cause most of the remaining area of the flats to be inundated for long periods, water sometimes being known to bank up to 12 feet deep on the western side of a flat throughout the winter months. Until the present there has barely been a year when water has not lain many feet deep over the surface of the land or at least the flats have been so waterlogged as to be unusable for depasturing stock, let alone for cultivation. The area shaded in Fig. 52 shows the extent of land which is free from flooding. The remainder is ground which has a drainage problem, varying in degree from seasonal waterlogging and flooding to permanent swamp. An early estimate of the extent of standing water is given by Goyder's valuations of runs in 1864.[3] The amount of land under water in the western portion of the central flats—Biscuit and Avenue Flats —rarely fell below half of the area of the run, and the cover was as much as two-thirds in Avenue Flat and up to three-quarters in the northern or Blackford end of the flat (Fig. 53). The absence of leases in the East Avenue and Baker's Range Flats was a measure of the permanence of the water cover in these two areas. Further east the Mosquito Plains were drier, being between one-third and one-half only covered by water. Dismal Swamp, on the border with Victoria, stood out as another area of extensive flooding. Only the coastal strip of lands, the Bordertown District (the Tatiara), and the eastern and southern uplands were reasonably dry, but still having, up to one-third of the land under water in some localities. In these circumstances it is not hard to believe the tale that bets were offered for the first person who could navigate a punt from the Dismal Swamp on the Victoria border, to Goolwa and the Murray Mouth.[4]

The first move to drain a portion of the South-East occurred in 1863 and it arose solely from a desire to improve communications with Adelaide after the threatened secession of the District from the rest of the Colony on the grounds of its neglect. The inhabitants of the District had many grievances. Foremost they felt isolated and neglected by the Government in Adelaide, a centre which was separated from them by a four and a half days' hard coach journey over the swamps of the Lower South-East and the forbidding Ninety-Mile Desert of the Upper South-East. On the other hand, Melbourne, which was similarly 300 miles from Mount Gambier, took only two and a half days to reach by coach, mainly because of better roads.[5] It was also alleged that money received from local land-sales was not being spent by the Government in the South-East.[6] Generally speaking, at this time agricultural settlement had not extended far enough for settlers to be forced into contact with the swamps and to feel the need to drain them so that deficient draining was not yet a cause of complaint. The issue of separation from South Australia had been raised in 1861

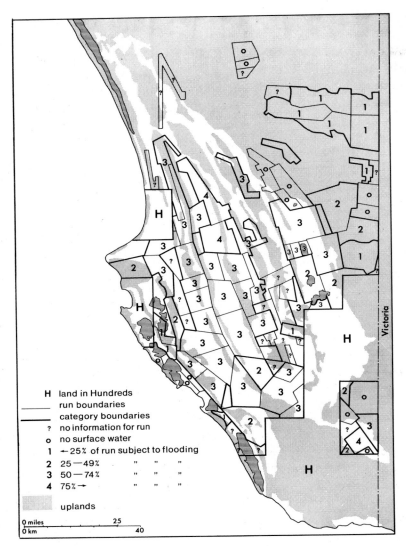

Fɪɢ. 53. Flooding in the South-East, 1864. Based on *SAPP*, 86 and 126 (1865–66).

at a time when discontent at the neglect by Melbourne of the Western District of Victoria was causing similar agitation across the border. These moves culminated in the proposal that the two Districts should secede and form a new state called Princeland.[7]

The South Australian Government was apprehensive of losing this distant but valuable portion of the Colony, and hastily agreed to investigate some of the complaints. A team of government officials, headed by Hanson, was sent to the District in April, 1863 to report on the condition of public buildings and roads and to suggest what ought to be done to improve them. Among many proposals, they recommended the enlargement of the natural outfalls of Maria and Salt Creeks, by which means it was hoped that the accumulation of water on the flats would be lessened, and communications westwards from the wool-producing districts to the coastal outports would be made easier.[8]

These limited objectives were soon replaced by the wide ranging aims and remarkably clear analysis of Goyder, the Surveyor-General. He saw draining not only as a means of aiding general traffic and road building in the District, but also a means of creating new agricultural land and doubling the area available to the stock holder.[9] He quickly and accurately assessed the true causes of flooding and the direction of the movement of water in the different parts of the District; the experience he had gained in assessing the runs some years before being most valuable,[10] In addition to the enlargement of the natural outfalls at Maria and Salt Creeks, he suggested that two new cuttings be made through the narrow coastal ranges that separated the German Swamp and Mount Muirhead Flat from Lakes Bonney and Frome (Fig. 52). These two cuts would, in Goyder's view, achieve startling results in the drainage of the coastal swamps at a 'moderate expense'. They were to be regarded as experimental forerunners of a more complex and comprehensive scheme of drainage to be implemented once a careful survey of the levels of the flats had been undertaken and 'the result placed beyond mere speculation'. If the cuts were successful, then they would demonstrate the practicability of forming straight drainage channels, cut at right angles to the direction of the flats to the sea. With what was to be characteristic acumen and foresight Goyder had perceived immediately the most effective way of draining the South-East swamps. It was unfortunate that these proposals for a wider scheme were to lie dormant and basically untried for the next fifty years. Whatever the future was to hold, however, there was a growing realization among the local inhabitants and the

Government alike that the draining of the swamps was both possible and desirable.

The implications of these limited experiments had not been lost on the inhabitants of the South-East. But the failure of the Assembly to provide money for draining revived the old grievances of neglect and financial meanness. The editor of the *Border Watch* was shrill with indignation; 'Something should immediately be done', he wrote, 'a few thousand pounds judiciously laid out in drainage works would nearly double its [the District's] resources'. Those who were well acquainted with the District knew that:

> 'many of the runs were not able to carry one-half the stock they would carry were there any means of draining off the surplus water. They know that the immense flats, which are at present under water four or five months of the year and are consequently nearly useless, would if drained carry immense herds. They have seen how in a few dry seasons the grass increases—how ten blades would spring up where only one grew before. And they have seen it all disappear again after a wet season or two and sour vegetation spring up instead.'[11]

The example of the Maria Creek cutting, 'though confessedly small and inadequate for the body of the water', was plain for all to see, and as the Creek had been 'running all the year' it needed only to be enlarged and carried farther back into the swamp to drain a larger extent of the country. With no prospect of a start to draining, separation from the Colony was urged before all the land was sold, unless the 'little Rundle Street politicians' turned their attention 'to draining this district of something besides its money'.[12]

Yet another Government inspection of the South-East was carried out, but it seemed that Goyder's vision had been replaced by the original and more limited objective of improving roads and maintaining the telegraph line with Adelaide; proposals to enlarge the natural outlet from Tilley's Swamp to Salt Creek, to cut two channels through the coastal ranges near Narrow Neck, one near Lake Hawdon, and another in the swamps behind Port MacDonnell were all to be undertaken 'as a cheap means of saving expense on roads, many of which would be without further outlay for a considerable time'.[13]

The local editor looked at the coming season with gloom:

'With the setting in of another winter, and the apparent probability that we shall soon have before our eyes the picturesque but not very pleasant prospect of a vast district extending from Lacapede Bay to Port MacDonnell and nearly as large as Denmark, converted into a great Lake, with only Mount Gambier and the minor ridges looking up as oases amid the watery waste, the minds of settlers are set a-speculating as to whether or not the South-Eastern District could be drained.'[14]

The Coastal Cuts

The pessimism of the inhabitants of the South-East lifted with the cutting of the Narrow Neck outfall in 1864 (Fig. 54). This cut was one of those suggested by Goyder and was so called because a narrow strip of coastal dune bayed back the water of the Cootel Swamp, which lay behind as deep as ten feet during the winter months. When the cut was completed the pent-up water 'roared and leaped through it like a mountain torrent' into Lake Frome. The resident engineer was jubilant, 'I am glad to say' he reported, 'this bids fair to be a great success, *in fact it is*'. The level of the water in the swamp dropped by over two feet by mid-December, and he looked forward to seeing 50,000 acres of 'as fine agricultural land as any in the Colony' becoming available almost immediately. The further widening and deepening of the cut and the excavation of a short drain into the swamp behind were necessary before all the water was removed, and by the end of the year only 'a few inches' remained. The editor of the *Border Watch* considered the results satisfactory and mused on the thought that the lower end of the swamp, which had 'never been trodden dry shod by man, can be walked over as freely as any of the stubble fields of Mount Gambier'. The Salt Creek cut was also completed and water was flowing strongly out of Tilley's Swamp.[15]

The actual benefit of dry land, and the potential benefit of the elimination of coast disease because of the cuts through the coastal ranges and the improvement of the natural outfalls were

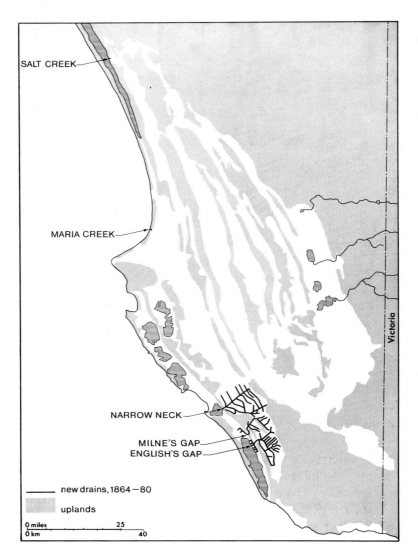

F IG. 54. Drains, 1864–80.

so great that surveys were put in hand immediately in order to locate other likely places for new cuts. Land was withheld from sale in anticipation of the higher price it would fetch when it was drained completely.[16] But despite the preliminary activity nothing was done because the Government became concerned with the plight of the pastoralists in the northern part of the Colony, who were suffering from the severe drought of 1864–65. Cries of neglect were heard again, and the dormant image of Princeland resurrected. A Select Committee was convened quickly to inquire into aspects of the communications, draining and settlement of the South-East; but it was a holding operation; no recommendations were made, and it issued a flabby report that left all the decisions to the Government.[17] However, the Government had not been entirely idle. A week before the Committee's report was made public it transferred the administration and development of the drainage to the Surveyor-General's office. Goyder now had unhampered control over a project about which he was personally interested and enthusiastic. The emphasis in draining changed from the piece-meal improvement of communications to a more comprehensive policy of land settlement over a large region.

Goyder decided to concentrate activity in the Mount Muirhead Flat because of its favourable combination of factors that would foster the success of his plans. The soil of the Flat was of 'superior quality', a large area was capable of being reclaimed at a comparatively small outlay, and the Flat was near to existing areas of settlement, particularly to the port of Grey Town on Rivoli Bay. In addition, the Narrow Neck cutting was an example which could be followed and was a starting point from which new drainage works could be extended. Approximately 600 square miles of the coastal swamps were surveyed and their levels, and soil and vegetational characteristics recorded. Two new outfalls were cut through the ranges at Milne's Gap and English's Gap by the end of 1867, and 23 miles of new drains were excavated back through the Wyrie and Pompoon Swamps (Fig. 54). As a result of these works the level of the water in the swamps fell dramatically, but the land was still boggy and 'horses and cattle could hardly venture on the deep spongy soil'. A much more intensive network of local drainage channels was required, and the seepage of water from the higher flats to the east needed to be diverted before cultivation could start.[18]

Goyder had already thought of this, and he had planned for the short drains to be the precursors of a more ambitious scheme to reclaim over 800 square miles of the flats to the east, in the southern ends of the Avenue and Baker's Range Flats, the Mosquito Plains and the Dismal Swamp, all of which he thought to be of 'sufficient richness for the purpose of agriculture'[19] (Fig. 55). Unfortunately, the drains were never completed because of their cost and because of the doubts that were expressed by 'the sceptics, cavillers, and croakers' over the feasibility of the scheme. Moreover, Goyder was transferred to organize the survey of the Northern Territory. The *South Australian Register*, thought it 'monstrously unbusinesslike to relinquish the undertaking in its present condition' and a waste of the money spent so far. 'In the meantime', commented the *Border Watch*, 'land sale after land sale takes place by which almost another hundred thousand is shovelled into the Adelaide Treasury . . . Ministers doubtless chuckle at the success of their little game in the provinces'.[20]

When it seemed as though the draining would languish once more, the coastal swamps were declared an Agricultural Area under the Waste Lands Amendment Act (Strangways' Act) of 1869 mainly as a move to placate the South-East residents who saw all the Agricultural Areas being created in the North (see Fig. 55 for their location). This legislation allowed land to be bought on credit, which, in theory at least, would result in competition for the land from the farmers. Nevertheless, one of the regulations for the sale of land in the Agricultural Areas was that the price of unsold land was to be lowered after successive land sales. For example, in the Mount Muirhead Area the price was fixed at £6 an acre on 2 July, 1871 and was lowered progressively at each land sale until it reached a minimum of £1 per acre by 25 August, 1872. An almost identical arrangement held true for the Mayurra Agricultural Area.[21] However well these regulations worked in stimulating competition for land in the other Agricultural Areas they were singularly inappropriate to the swamp land of the South-East. Settlers would not take up flooded or waterlogged land at high prices but were content to delay buying until the price of land fell. Yet, as the Government was committed legally to sell the land for agricultural purposes it needed to be drained at a cost which varied between 16s.-0d. and £2-0s.-0d. per acre. Therefore the land had to be sold during the first few months of offering in order to recoup the costs of drainage, which were estimated to be about £15,000. Even if the land was sold

at its lowest price in an undrained state, it was realized that this
was only postponing the potential trouble as the credit selector
would probably expect in time that the Government would construct the drains to his holding through intervening unsold land.[22]

The Government had unwittingly committed itself to extensive
and immediate draining activity, and, realizing that the sooner
something was done the easier and cheaper it would be, it withheld from sale and drained the land in the Mount Muirhead and
Mayurra Agricultural Areas. Goyder's larger scheme for draining
the whole of the southern portion of the South-East was abandoned
in favour of a more limited objective of making dry the coastal
flats. In all, about 178 square miles of land were dealt with. The
land was opened for credit selection in August 1872, and the
price was to be no less than £2-10s. per acre so that the cost of
draining could be recovered.[23]

A new landscape was created in the swamps when the new
network of 67 miles of drains was completed and functioning. The
network was extended bit by bit throughout the next decade to
give the pattern shown in Fig. 54. Roads were made on the earth
thrown up from the drains and they crossed the swamps like
causeways. Goyder envisaged 'steam cars' using them like
railways on embankments, particularly between Rivoli Bay and
the inland portions of the swamps near Penola. Once the the land
was selected, new farms were built and sited carefully on slight
rises to be out of the reach of possible flood waters, and the
sections arranged so that some would be on dry land.[24] The new
towns of Millicent, Rendlesham and Hatherleigh were established,
symbols of the progress and wisdom of draining the swamps.[25]

Despite the fact that some of the land was still not drained
properly (which was going to cause trouble during the ensuing
years) enthusiasm at the transformation of the swamps ran high.
With the expectation that the drainage system would be extended
northwards, the hundreds of Rivoli Bay and Lake George were
proclaimed along the coast in 1871 and the land surveyed, subdivided and opened for sale. The surveyors then shifted their
activities to areas farther north, and marked off the hundreds of
Mount Benson, Bowaka, and Murrimbina in the badly flooded
lands around the port of Kingston, a policy which some people
thought 'very suicidal'.[26]

While settlement with draining was going on in the coastal swamps near Millicent, settlement without draining was going on in the swampy lands in the new Agricultural Areas of Naracoorte, Binnum, Glen Roy and Jessie in the eastern borders of the South-East (Fig. 55). Here nearly half a million acres of land were laid out by the surveyors, who were hard pressed to keep ahead of the demands. The capabilities of these Agricultural Areas had been boosted notoriously during late 1869, and many farmers on the eastern side of the Mount Lofty Ranges, on the edge of the impenetrable mallee, had seen them as the solution to their problems of insufficient land for the creation of larger farm holdings. But they found that most of the best land in the Agricultural Areas has been 'dummied' flagrantly by local pastoralists,[27] and that there was little good land left unless they were 'mad enough to take land in the flats, which, in ordinary winters are covered from six inches deep in water'. Many of the settlers just kept on moving and went to Victoria, where land had long been open to credit purchasing; the stream of wagons and drays at Naracoorte being reminiscent of 'the old times when the people were all going to the diggins'. Some 200 families were counted going over the border in the space of a month.[28]

Many did stay to try their luck on the flats, and while some were successful many had disastrous results. A section by section return of crops planted and land ploughed, with an account of the state of their drainage, showed that large areas were under deep water and much of the rest of the planted crops were either damaged in some way by moisture, or the land was so wet that it was not occupied at all. Such descriptions as 'in a perfect state of slush', 'saturated with water', and 'this section nearly all under water', were common.[29] By 1872 the Naracoorte Farmers' Club petitioned the Government for relief, saying that the district was in a 'deplorable state' and needed thorough draining. As far as this part of the South-East was concerned, the working of Strangways' Act had been 'a complete failure'.[30]

After 1872 there was much speculation about what to do next in draining the swamps, but very little was done, because of the expense entailed in draining, with its need for careful prior survey, costing and planning, and because of the relative ease and success of settlement in the Northern Areas. As a consequence, it was recommended that no further extension of drainage work be allowed until the Millicent drainage system was perfected and the results placed beyond doubt and the land of the existing settlers drained adequately. In addition, there was the problem of the subsidence of the organic soil because of wastage and shrinkage with draining. The surface of the Wyrie swamp sank by 18 inches and many of the drains lost their fall, and this necessitated re-grading and deepening throughout the whole drainage system. The delicate decision of whether or not to lower the outfalls was postponed because it was thought that such action might lead to an increase in the velocity of the flow of the water and con-sequently to an increase in the scouring of the peat.[31]

All these practical problems gave rise to the more general question of the maintenance and after-care of the existing drainage system. Generally speaking, the maintenance of the minor drains was the responsibility of the person through whose land they passed, but this system was haphazard at best. In 1875 the South-East Drainage Act provided for the appointment of Boards to supervise the care, control and management of the local drainage systems. These Boards had the power to levy and collect rates to pay for maintenance, which caused no controversy in the coastal swamps as it was obvious to all settlers that their very existence on their farms depended upon the removal of water. It was realized, however, that if the area to be drained was extended to other flats, then the drains of the existing coastal systems might be used as the major outlets for new systems further inland. Therefore, in 1877 the control and maintenance of the 'Main Drains' was taken from the local Boards and placed under the supervision of the Commissioner of Crown Lands, and the minor drains were administered by a new authority, the District Councils, with special drainage duties.[32]

From time to time during the years of the 1870s suggestions were made about extending the drainage system, which, while they came to nothing, are of interest because they help us to understand the contemporary view of the problems of draining, and the solu-tions that were feasible within the resources and organization of the time. These suggestions are also of significance because they mark a progression of ideas and events that culminated in a change in the locale and scale of draining after 1880.

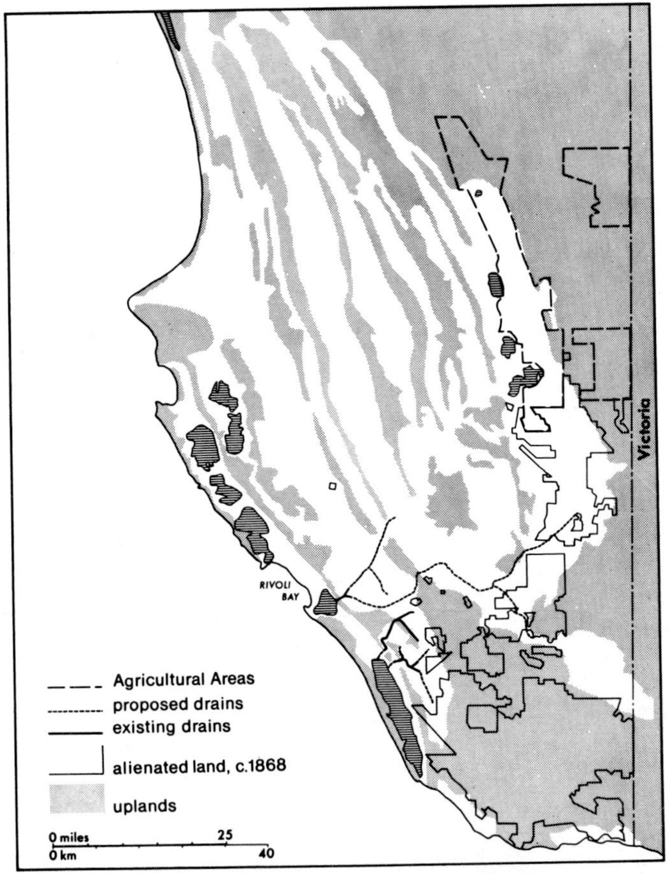

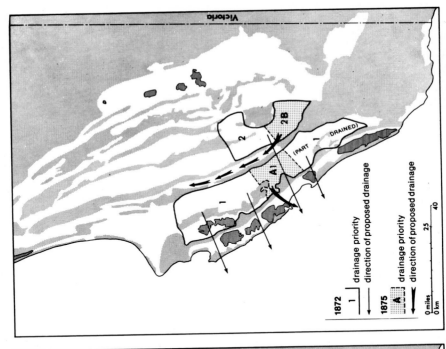

FIG. 55. Alienated land, 1868; Agricultural Areas, 1869; and Goyder's drainage scheme, 1869. Based on *SAPP*, 88 (1869–70).

FIG. 56. Draining priorities, 1872 and 1875.

In 1872, it was suggested that the Millicent system should be extended northwards into the 170 square miles of the physically similar Woakwine Swamp and its continuation into Biscuit Flat (Area 1 in Fig. 56) and also extended eastwards into about 140 square miles of swampland in the southern end of Avenue Flat (Area 2 in Fig. 56). In both areas the water was to be evacuated by a system of transverse east-west drains. But nothing was done, as it was generally agreed that first the Mount Muirhead-Millicent system had to be completed before any extension was carried out.

By 1875, after three more years of experience in operating the Millicent system, and in view of the ever-increasing cost of draining, new, modified, and pared-down proposals for extension were put forward. The object of these proposals was to concentrate on those parts of the country which were not already sold and which were 'immediately remunerative'; and to avoid becoming involved in the indiscriminate draining of large areas as in the past. Moreover, it was realized that economies in draining could be achieved by concentrating activity near existing nodes of settlement and communication networks. The nearest outfall and the shortest length of drain were the desired objects, hence, the southern end of the Woakwine Swamp could be drained by transverse drains, but the area immediately east of the Mount Muirhead Flat, so it was thought, could be relieved of its surface water most easily and cheaply by opening up the sluggish natural water course of Reedy Creek which gravitated northwards (Areas A1 and 2B in Fig. 56). This was the first time that the expedient of opening up these inland water courses had been suggested.

But a new factor was entering into the question of draining that was to alter the whole focus of interest. The farming population questioned more and more the Government's assessment of land quality and its control of settlement expansion and the clamour for land in the inland swampy areas was growing greater with the increased liberalization of the land laws.[33] The question came up frequently in the House, and the Chief Secretary, Blythe, replied:

'this matter had been referred to the Surveyor-General over and over again, various Commissioners of Crown Lands had visited the land and made recommendations, the matter had been considered by the Cabinets, and it had been thought advisable to hold the lands over until a system of drainage had been decided upon.'[34]

Goyder foresaw that there were two possible consequences of opening up these inland areas before draining took place : either the land would fall into the hands of the pastoralists rather than the agriculturist small holders, or, if the latter did buy it they would clamour for necessary drainage works.[35] But the pressure on the Government was relentless, particularly after the announcement that a railway line was to be constructed from Naracoorte across the inland swamps to the coast at Kingston. The settlers 'memorialized and importuned the government' to offer the land 'until further refusal became impolitic'.

The Government, which has so carefully controlled all settlement in the swamps now seemed to abandon all pretence of restriction and in 1876 opened up 744 square miles of land in a block of six new hundreds (Minecrow, Townsend, Joyce, Ross, Bray and Conmurra) in the north central portion of the region, in what was some of the worst flooded land of the whole of the South-East (Figs. 57 and 14). 'Of all the country I have seen, that is the worst', wrote the editor of the *Border Watch*, 'nothing but sand, scrub, and wet flats all the way.'[36]

By 1878, little of the land in these hundreds had been taken up, and that which had been alienated had been dummied badly by the pastoralists. The inevitable, so it seemed, now happened. Those settlers that had established themselves found the land too wet for use and petitioned the Government for drainage. The Government saw the folly of its liberal policy, and immediately withheld all land from sale in the South-East. The Resident-Engineer, Rogers, was asked to provide a plan for the draining of the flats.[37] Rogers' report embraced the whole of the flats and he suggested a scheme of priorities in areas for drainage which would be either partial or complete, depending upon the agricultural potential of the land.

His suggestions are summarized in Table XI and Fig. 58. The scheme envisaged some drains emptying into the sea, and other drains emptying into Reedy Creek which was to act like a great sewer, taking the water northward to Salt Creek.

Table XI

A Scheme for Draining, 1878

(10,000 acres = 4046·86 ha)

No. and priority	Region	Acres.	Complete or partial drainage	Cost per acre £ s. d.
1	Mount Muirhead Flat, South	39,500	C (finished)	2– 1–0
2	Mount Muirhead Flat, Narrow Neck	52,000	C (in progress)	2–8
3	Mount Muirhead Flat, German Flat	6,000	C	15–0
4	Biscuit Flat, Woakwine	60,000	C	1– 5–0
5	W. Avenue Flat, Mt McIntyre	{ 46,000	C	1– 0–0
		16,000	P	5–0
6	W. Avenue Flat, Mt Benson	60,000	C	1– 5–0
7	W. Avenue Flat, Mt Scott	35,000	P	5–0
8	W. Avenue Flat, Avenue Range	58,000	P	5–0
9	E. Avenue Flat, Baker's Range	61,000	P	5–0
10	Biscuit Flat, Konetta	64,000	P	5–0
11	Biscuit Flat, Kingston	155,000	C	2– 0–0
		652,500		
	Port MacDonnell (not in scheme)	4,570	P	1– 0–0
		657,070		

Source: SAPP, 112 (1878); 203 (1878).

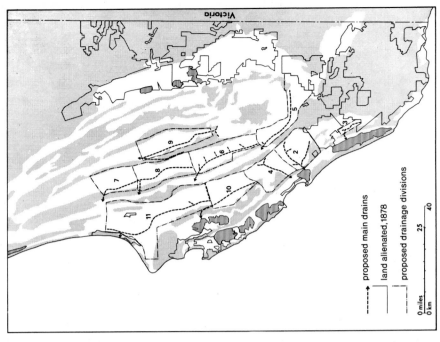

FIG. 58. Roger's scheme for draining, 1878. Based on *SAPP*, 203 (1878).

proposed main drains

land alienated, 1878

proposed drainage divisions

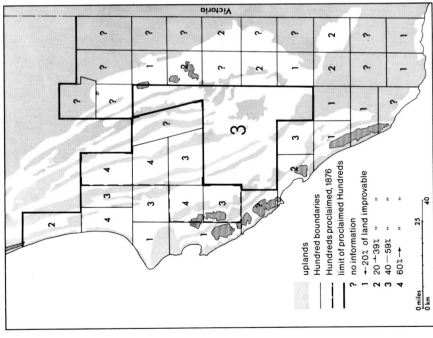

FIG. 57. Flooding in the South-East, 1876.

uplands

Hundred boundaries

Hundreds proclaimed, 1876

limit of proclaimed Hundreds

? no information

1 —20% of land improvable

2 20 —39% „

3 40 — 59% „

4 60% → „

Playford, the Commissioner of Crown Lands, wanted to push ahead with all of Rogers' plan because in his opinion it was

'not good policy to sell the only dry spots in the District, selling perhaps at the same time some of the land through which the drains will have to be taken therby [*sic*] having to repurchase at High Prices.'

A total of £81,000 was set aside for the draining of areas 3 and 4,[38] but before anything could be done heavy rains throughout 1879 and 1880 set the flats awash, and the situation of the settlers deteriorated further, particularly that of the people in the inland northern swamps; it was one long tale of melancholy and failure. While the Crown was sympathetic to the plight of the farmers in the 'drained' area around the Millicent swamps[39] and promised the long awaited deepening of the main outfalls, it had little consideration for the settlers further north. The Commissioner of Crown Lands said that he

'did not hold himself responsible for the results complained of, as the lands had only been offered after repeated memorials from the residents and contrary to the convictions of the department; the people, therefore, had only themselves to blame'.[40]

The situation in the flooded swamps was directly analogous to that at the same time in the drought-stricken North where the Commissioner similarly put the blame squarely on the selectors in almost identical words:

'This northern country was urgently asked for on the rep-representation of practical men, who ought to know what amount of rainfall were [*sic*] necessary for the successful cultivation of wheat. After considerable pressure this land was resumed from the squatter, and placed on the markets for selection. It was not fair then to charge the Government for mistakes the men had made themselves with their eyes wide open'.[41]

Who was to blame; the Government which had traditionally guided settlement and set itself up as an arbiter of land quality through its whole system of survey and allocation of land for selection, or the selectors who had either been deluded by the appearance of the swamps during the summer months, or even encouraged to select by the many plans and half promises of action which they implied? It was a difficult question that was not to be solved easily. The Government, after all, was elected and had resisted the pressure to open up the land until, in its own words, further resistance became 'impolitic'. More important than the apportionment of blame was the decision of what was to be done. Once more, all land was closed for sale pending another investigation of what to do, and, in the meantime, some settlers were allowed to re-select in the drier southern portions of the region, and others had their lease rentals revised.[42]

The Inland Answer

By 1881, the enthusiasm for draining had evaporated just as surely as did the water from many of the swamps during the summer months. It seemed as though action was paralysed by the realization that all the South-East needed draining now, because of the way in which settlement had spread so widely throughout the swamps. To be sure, the droughts from 1881 to 1883, which checked the boom of settlement in the frontier of the Northern Areas caused much depression, both in morale and in economic activity, but one might reasonably expect that this devastating experience of water deficiency would have led to an accelerated effort to aid settlement in the humid environment of the South-East. But it was not to be. Wheat was not grown easily in the South-East, and wheat had become both the symbol and the reality of prosperity and settlement expansion; the South-East remained the Cinderella region of South Australia.

In retrospect, one can fairly say that one phase in the draining of the South-East was ending and that another was beginning. Two of the most obvious signs of this second phase were the changes in the locale and direction of the drainage system (Fig. 59). Prior to 1881, the location of the drainage works, and of most plans for extension, was coastal. This resulted in the improvement of natural outfalls and the cutting of new outfalls throughout the coastal ranges, together with the creation of an experimental drainage system in the swamps nearest to the coast. After 1881,

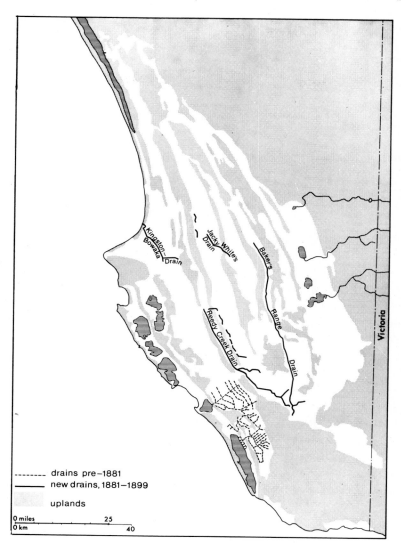

FIG. 59. Drains, 1881–99.

on the other hand, attention shifted to the draining of the inland flats by improving the flow of water along natural water courses. The direction of the drainage system changed too. The draining of the coastal swamps had resulted in the cutting of channels at right angles to the ranges in a south-westerly to north-easterly direction, but now the draining of the inland swamps by the improvement of the natural channels in the flats resulted in the emergence of a north-west to south-east trending drainage pattern. This emphasis upon the inland answer to problems of draining was the mark of these two decades.

The changing locale and direction of draining were also influenced by contemporary beliefs about the agricultural value of land in the South-East. It was known that rainfall decreased northwards, with an adverse effect on farming, but this knowledge was supplemented by the widespread belief that the soils of the flats to the north of a line from about Beachport to Penola (with the exception of the drier eastern border uplands) were of such indifferent quality that they were of use for nothing except grazing, and poor grazing at that. Therefore, it was felt that the northern inland flats, because of their low agricultural potential, needed only a partial and inexpensive drainage system, in contrast to the thorough and expensive drainage system of the coastal swamps. Cheapness of draining could be achieved, so it was thought, by opening up the natural water courses along the flats, and by improving the northerly flow of the water towards the Maria and Salt Creek outfalls. If these outlets were unable to cope with the flood waters it did not matter greatly, since, the accumulated water would soon soak away and evaporate in the useless flats on the northern edge of the region, bordering the Ninety-Mile Desert. As a consequence, straight, direct cuts across the ranges to achieve maximum fall and the rapid evacuation of the flood waters gave way to long winding channels with little fall; and the idea of 'soak away' drainage or evaporation drainage which merely exploited the natural system grew in popularity. The shifted emphasis in draining was underlined by the abandonment of the long-awaited reclamation of the coastal Woakwine swamp (for which £81,000 had been voted by Parliament late in 1878) in favour of work on the inland swamps.[43]

The first work on these inland 'National' drains, as they were called, was the excavation of Jacky White's drain to relieve the flats in the vicinity of Lucindale, which had been the scene of the worst flooding throughout the late part of the 1870s (Fig. 59). It was followed by the regrading and enlargement of 47 miles of the southern half of Reedy Creek, a natural inland channel, together with the removal of obstacles in the remaining 50 miles of the channel to Salt Creek. The outcome of these works was unexpected, although not entirely unpredictable, namely to increase the amount of flood water in the already badly inundated flats around Kingston.[44] One selector said:

'Now we are actually worse than ever I have seen it. It means utter ruin to many and as there is no outlet for our surplus water its utterly futile for us poor selectors to attempt in any way to improve our position without the Crown cuts a drain up through our District'. [sic][45]

Eventually, the Kingston-Bowaka drain was dug to relieve Biscuit Flat of the increased flood water originating from inland, which was carried to a new and improved outfall at Maria Creek.

Once more the framework of rural settlement ran ahead of the draining system, but at least this time with some semblance of a plan. The Government attempted to relate land settlement to draining by proclaiming new hundreds only when drainage works were under way within their confines. In this way the progressive proclamation of hundreds occurred from south to north in the area of the inland flats as the natural drainage channels were improved. Kennion, Short and Riddoch were proclaimed in 1883 in the south, followed by Symon, Smith, Fox and Coles in 1885, Spence in 1886, and then Landseer, Peacock, Woolumbool, Marcollet and Parsons in the north in 1888. In all, over 1,400 square miles were opened up in the space of four years and there was now nowhere settlement could expand except in the northern low-rainfall fringe to the District (Figs. 15 and 57).

This rash of survey seemed reckless in the face of what had happened in the South-East during earlier years, for, although the proclamation of the hundreds ensured the sequence of settlement, it did not necessarily promote the occupation of the land. The Government, however, was well aware of the dangers inherent in proclaiming hundreds and was concerned lest the land should fall into the hands of the pastoralist and 'help to swell the large estates' of which there were in this District, by 1880, fourteen over 5,000 acres, eight over 10,000 acres, seventeen over 20,000 acres, two over 40,000 acres, and one over 80,000 acres. This was not an unwarranted concern for many of the credit lands in the past had been sold to the pastoralists because the selectors 'had found that the seasons had been against them, the land was not thoroughly drained and the result had been failure'.[46]

Therefore, after 1884, it was decided that no swamp land could be alienated permanently but was to be sold at auction for a limited period of fourteen years at a rental which included the value of the land and the improvements made upon it, which could include draining.[47] The lease system gave the Government some control over the progress of settlement, and of course, enabled it to recoup the costs of present as well as any future draining works. But generally speaking the move did not encourage much settlement.

Towards the end of the century it was evident that all was not well with the inland drainage system, and the negligible benefits which the drains conferred prompted much thought, debate and investigation from 1889 to 1899. Once more, Goyder quickly summed up the position by pointing out that the inland works were all but useless because their outfalls were far away; consequently the fall of the drains was too gradual to produce a moderate flow, let alone the rapid evacuation of the flood water from the high rainfall areas of the south. Not only were the existing works inefficient but there had actually been a deterioration in the drainage condition in some parts of the region as the flow of water from the higher flats in the south and east was now definitely destined to find its way north and west by the new channels on the lower flats. It was likely that this dangerous situation would be made worse in the future by proposals of the Penola District Council (with the aid of a government subsidy to Councils for draining) to reclaim land by excavating drains which would lead towards the west and let surplus water spill on to the lower flats. If the experiment was successful (and later petitions and complaints proved that it was)[48] then other authorities and individuals in the 750 square miles of the flats between Naracoorte and the Dismal Swamp might try to do the same.

By 1890, Goyder produced a new, grand plan for the draining of the South-East. Surprisingly, it did not incorporate all his previous proposals, and it was an uneasy compromise between opening-up the north-flowing natural water courses and cross-cutting the ranges (see Fig. 60). The scheme would have entailed the reconstruction or excavation of more than 330 miles of major drains, and would have affected about 3,500 square miles, at an estimated cost of over £970,000.[49] But the plan satisfied no one. The cost of 'such an elaborate drainage system' was out of the question during these depression years and was rejected immediately; it was clear that the Government was looking for a cheap method of draining and had wanted merely to 'open the mouth and gaps of natural water courses'.

A Commission was appointed. It issued a 170,000-word report which after considering in detail what had happened prior to 1892, and outlining the contemporary state of the flooding, added very little that was new. It was a disappointing result; the recommendations were minor and local, and consisted of the expenditure of a mere £26,000 on the Mount Hope-Furner drain and cutting, on a cutting from the Avenue Flat to Reedy Creek in the vicinity of the Wilmot Swamp, and on an embankment near the Kingston-Robe road to hold back the flood waters.[50] But these were mere palliatives, and none of the proposals, except that for the Mount Hope-Furner drain (which was not excavated) would have helped the flood situation. Indeed, they may well have aggravated it since the cutting at the Wilmot Swamp would probably have swelled the water in Reedy Creek, which would then have had to find its way to the sea as best it could, probably via the Kingston–Bowaka area, and so worsened conditions there.

Goyder retired in 1894 and the responsibility for the drainage passed from the Survey Department to the Department of Public Works under Moncrieff. He made his general convictions clear by advocating that a general scheme of drainage should be decided upon before any further works were undertaken as, in the last resort, the successful draining of every area was dependent directly upon the successful draining of some other area. 'At present', he said, 'there is a want of a system and the main effort of occupiers on the higher levels is to get rid of the water regardless of the direction which it may take, or the damage it may do at lower levels. This should be stopped'. In his opinion the need was for long, straight, east-west trending drains.

By 1895 Moncrieff's report on the drainage was complete; he wanted to open up and improve the north-south trending natural water courses. Central to his scheme was the 'hitherto unrecognized

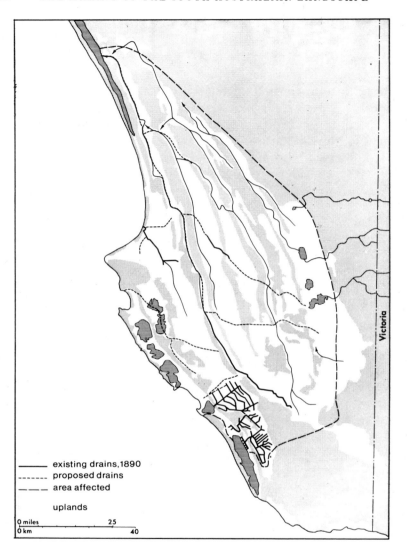

existing drains,1890
proposed drains
area affected

uplands

0 miles   25
0 km   40

FIG. 60. Goyder's scheme for draining, 1890. Based on *SAPP*, 64 (1890).

outlet' of the Baker's Range Drain revealed by his new and thorough survey. Moncrieff wanted to spend £200,000 on this and other drains (Fig. 61) but the Government eagerly sanctioned the partial improvement of the Baker's Range drain only, at a cost of £50,000, as a fortuitous answer to the prospect of expen-

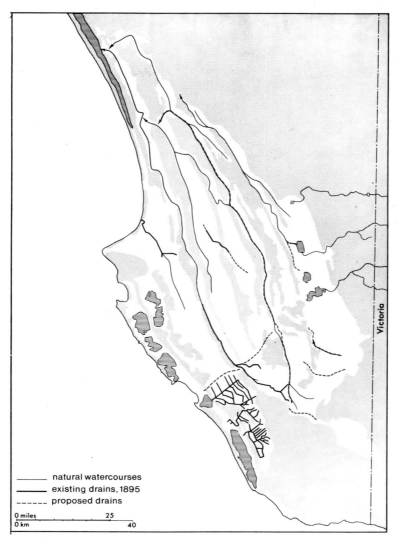

natural watercourses
existing drains, 1895
proposed drains

0 miles   25
0 km   40

FIG. 61. Moncrieff's scheme for draining, 1895. Based on *SAPP*, 104 (1895)

sive cuts through the ranges in a westerly direction.[51] This natural, but ill-formed water course was regraded and enlarged to take away water from the higher eastern flats. The effect was generally favourable but it fell short of the dramatic improvement in the flood situation that was hoped for. The major significance of the drain was perhaps not appreciated fully at the time; it acted as a diversion for water flowing from the east to the west, and with the stop banks constructed later in the gaps in Baker's Range, the drain prevented flooding in the country to the west.

The century ended with one more attempt to find a solution to the problem of draining. In 1889, Moncrieff suggested a list of works that ought to be done throughout the flats, but, despite the promise of improvement that the implementation of even a part of the plan would have given, it became one more scheme to criticize and reject. Clearly something was very wrong.

The physical and technical problems of draining in such a large area were real enough and should not be underestimated, but the administrative and financial problems were proving to be almost as difficult to overcome. These problems loomed larger during the last decade of the nineteenth century because the drainage network had been expanded and the need for co-operative work and for maintenance became more pressing. The core of the problem lay in the Government's attempt to achieve two conflicting aims. On the one hand, it wanted to plan and work towards a comprehensive and regional drainage scheme (with associated maintenance) with its own departments providing the guidance and solutions. On the other hand, it was not prepared to finance these schemes wholly out of public funds, and wished to inspire enough local interest for the works to be financed by locally raised revenue. Many members of the House 'did not agree with the expenditure of public money to enhance the value of private properties'.[52]

Since 1876, the administration of the compact coastal swamp areas had been vested in the three Drainage Boards of Mayurra, Mount Muirhead and Tantanoola, which received some government grants, but could and did levy drainage rates. In 1885, the Districts were given 13,550, 8,250, and 6,000 acres of common land respectively, the proceeds from the letting of which were to be used for the upkeep of the drains in each district. As new areas of drained land came into being away from the coastal swamps, some form of maintenance had to be provided, and in 1887 powers of drainage supervision were given to Local District Councils, which could also apply to the Government for a subsidy for public works, which included draining.[53]

None of the new Councils was prepared to proceed with new

drainage works, however, and they scarcely kept up with essential maintenance, so that it is not surprising that both the Royal Commission of 1892 and Moncrieff's report of 1893 recommended new legislation to give the Government the authority to construct new drains and to raise the finance locally. A new Bill was introduced into Parliament enabling the Government to raise an assessment on the increase in the value of the land through draining. The 'betterment' or 'benefit' principle was hard to administer fairly and it was disliked intensely by landowners in the South-East, so the Bill did not get past its second reading.[54]

A new bill was introduced in 1895 which allowed the Commissioner of Crown Lands to make whatever drains he thought necessary out of government money, all plans to be laid before Parliament first and to be approved by the House.[55] The maintenance of both minor and 'main' drains, even the power to construct new drains, was taken away from the Drainage Districts and given to District Councils. But not one Council asked for an advance from the Government for the construction of works, being unwilling to incur a liability that would benefit a few ratepayers only, and also being unwilling to consider schemes that were not confined wholly to their own administrative area, an almost impossible proviso in land drainage. Therefore, without the co-operation of neighbouring District Councils, desirable drainage works could not be undertaken successfully on a local basis. Drainage administration, maintenance and finance were labouring under a tangle of inept laws and inadequate finance.

During the closing years of the century debate raged in both Parliament and the Press on what to do next in the draining, the relative merits of the Butcher's Gap opening near Kingston and the Mount Hope-Furner drain being bandied about in the hope that at least one would be started, completed and 'form part of a great and harmonious whole'. The question was reconsidered by yet another Royal Commission which sat during 1899.[56] It seemed as though the amount of work done was in an inverse ratio to the number of words spoken and written.

By the end of the century the state of the drainage in the South-East, with the exception of the coastal swamps, was little better than it had been nearly forty years before when draining started. True, the land near the new drains was better, but between and away from them conditions had not really changed. The flats still flooded regularly every year, and even pastoral activity was severely limited. A member of the parliamentary party that inspected the District in 1900 said that 'for two days they were travelling through water all the time', and he marvelled 'how the sheep and lambs . . . could live in the flooded country'.[57] The sheets of water, stretching further than one could see, were a monument to the inactivity of nearly twenty years and a standing reproach to the Government.

State Involvement

A third stage in the development of the pattern of drainage in the South-East opened with the passing of the South-East Drainage Act of 1900.[58] This Act embodied the recommendations of the Royal Commission of the previous year, and it enabled a significant advance to be made in the draining of the region. But there was more to the change in the pace of activity than administrative re-organization and improvement. There was, generally, a resurgence of interest in land development after the hiatus of nearly twenty years. It coincided with the emergence of the country from economic depression, the stimulus of Federation and the realization on the part of the State Government that it had to take the lead in fostering rural settlement by providing essential developmental services prior to, rather than in the wake of, settlement. Such State involvement was halting and reluctant at first, but gathered strength over the years.

In addition, some people were obsessed with the notion of the neglect of the South-East, and, with vestiges of the old colonial mentality, they feared the diversion of all the District's produce to Victoria now that tariff barriers were down. D. J. Gordon's *Shall we hold the South East?* published in 1902, and A. J. Perkin's *An enquiry into South Eastern conditions*, (1904), were indicative of these attitudes; but whatever else they achieved these publications did stimulate interest in the region. Moreover, the desirability of focussing on the merits of the South-East at a time when attention was being diverted to the mallee lands seemed only sensible to those whose memories went back to the 1880s :

'Better by far increase the occupation of the waste land in known country with assured rainfall by opening better railway facilities and by carrying out drainage works than in running the risk of creating another "drought-stricken" district by going to Pinnaroo.'[59]

By the Drainage Act of 1900, the Government partially solved its problem of local initiative, and was able to construct drains on receipt of a petition from a majority of landholders representing three-quarters of the value of the land likely to benefit from draining, on condition that the landowners would agree to repay the cost of the drains, with interest, over a period of forty-two years. This took the onus of responsibility away from the Government and passed it on to the landowners, a thing which the Government was glad to do owing to the administrative and financial tangles of the previous twenty years which had hindered the expansion of the artificial drainage system.

The requests by landowners for Petition Drains, as they became known, were not as quick as one might have expected, largely because there existed few main drains and outfalls into which the Petition Drains could be led. The local landowners were neither able nor prepared to construct the major cross country drains needed to take the water from the local drainage projects to the sea. The first and most important of the Petition Drains was the long advocated Mount Hope Drain, constructed in 1905 (Fig. 62). It skirted the edge of the Woakwine Swamp, but its effect was limited for it should have been cut through the Reedy Creek Range to tap the accumulated waters in the fertile areas of Reedy Creek and south Avenue Flats. Three other minor Petition Drains followed in the next few years.

But the Petition Drains were only of minor help in solving the problem of flooding, a problem which was aggravated by a succession of extremely wet seasons between 1906 and 1910. The floods goaded the local proprietors into action and they formed the South-East Drainage League in order to present their case for draining to the Government. Finally, a scheme of drainage was prepared by Moncrieff, which was accepted by a two-thirds majority of the land holders affected, and, after much amendment, it was put into operation in 1911. Under this scheme the

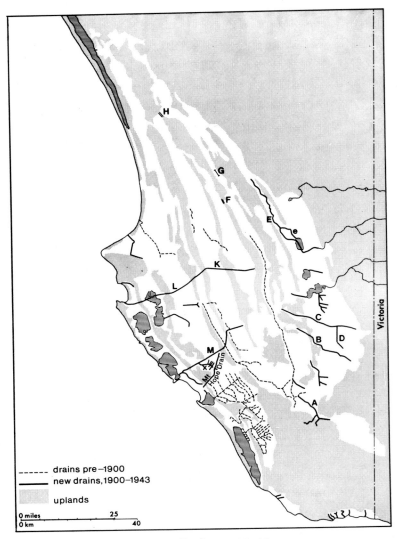

FIG. 62. Drains, 1900–43.

Government and the landholders each paid one half of the cost of the works, which eventually reached the staggering amount of £450,000. The landholders contributed their share from a rate based on the benefit due to drainage, administered by a new Drainage Assessment Board made up of government officials and elected representatives of the landholders. In addition, the administrative problem was simplified when the drainage powers of the Local District Councils were transferred to a Drainage Management Board.

The Scheme Drains, as these new drains became known, were designed to set the main lines of the drainage, and individual proprietors could later construct subsidiary local drains to them. The pattern of new drains is depicted in Fig. 62. Drains B, C and D helped to relieve the higher eastern flats by conveying water towards and into the Baker's Range drain. Petition Drains which now became a feasible proposition, like the Bool Lagoon outlet (1909), Robertson's and Seymour's drains (1910), and the Grey-Monbulla drain (1911) did the same. The water of Naracoorte Creek which emptied into Garey's Swamp was taken northwards by Scheme Drains E and e, in a similar fashion to Baker's Range drain. The effectiveness of the Baker's Range drain in evacuating water northwards was aided by G Cutting, and the overflow of that water into the western, lower flats was prevented by embankments F and H. The head of the Baker's Range drain was extended by the construction of Drain A to tap the Dismal Swamp, and the Glencoe Petition drains (branching to the south) were added later (1916).

The most spectacular and significant achievement of the Scheme Drainage was the excavation of the combined K-L Drain for forty-two miles across the ranges and flats, and the parallel Drain M for about thirty miles (Fig. 63). These two drains fulfilled the hopes of settlers in the Reedy Creek, Avenue Flat and other flooded areas nearer the coast by providing direct outlets to the sea. Immediately, other drains were constructed : the Bray drain, relieving upper Biscuit Flat and leading into Lake Drain L, via Lake Hawdon; and similarly Sutherland's Drain leading into Drain M. In addition to these works, the Lake outfalls were improved, the Lake George outlet in 1914, the Lake Frome, and the Lake Bonney outlets in 1915.

Figure 62 shows that the Scheme Drains had radically changed the established pattern of drainage. The whole District was now divided into two basic drainage areas on either side of Baker's Range. To the east, the drainage of the upper eastern flats and freshwater channels was caught in the Baker's Range drain and

F I G. 63. Drain L cutting, where the drain cuts through the Woakwine Range, about five miles east of Robe. The cutting is about 120 feet deep, but has been widened considerably since this photograph was taken.

carried north-eastwards. To the west, the long-advocated system of a number of independent outfalls with generally east-west trending drains cutting back inland through the ranges was now established with Drains M and K-L as the main arteries. The north-south drainage of the western flats (e.g. by the Reedy Creek and Avenue Flat channels) was broken by these new drains and reoriented towards the west. With perhaps the exception of the Mount Hope drain, the Petition Drains were of local importance only and had merely filled in some of the gaps in the new pattern. The direction and method of the draining of one area only was still in doubt, and that was the Kingston-Lucindale country. Originally a Scheme Drain, Drain J, was planned to link Jacky White's drain to the coast, but its excavation had been abandoned owing to the high cost of the Scheme Drains generally. It remained to be seen whether future work would lead the flood waters of this area either to the coast or north into the wastelands.

Despite the expenditure of nearly £1,000,000 on the drainage of the South-East from 1900 to 1920, the situation had not improved as much as was hoped. The new drains allowed an extension of the pasture grazing season in some localities, but they had been ineffective in fostering permanent pastoral activities and agriculture. An intricate system of minor drains between the major drains was needed for this. Undoubtedly the burden of maintenance and repayment for the Petition Drains and Scheme Drains hung heavily on the landowners, so that they had little opportunity or incentive to construct the subsidiary side drains. It is possible, also, that many landowners were dilatory in making improvements because they foresaw that substantially better drainage and land improvement might lead to the repurchase and subdivision of their estates; this had already happened from 1904 onwards in the eastern upland portion of the South-East, and it was being keenly discussed and advocated during the 1920s for the western and central areas.[60]

The Depression and then World War II put an end to all idea of further work, as is shown by the fact that only 64 miles of new drains were completed between 1920 and 1945, compared with 175 miles during the preceding eight years.

The pause was probably justified and necessary, however, for although some major works had been implemented, a basically piecemeal approach still prevailed. There were now four sets of drains, those in the coastal swamps near Millicent, and those excavated as National, Petition, and Scheme Drains. Each type of drain was financed in a different way, and the administration of the drainage was still divided amongst various authorities. There was still no permanent body to plan for the future and to co-ordinate individual schemes. Above all, the potential of the swamps had never been accurately and scientifically assessed so that even if the land was drained of water in the future there was no guarantee that it was worth the outlay of money and effort. This was a question that had constantly nagged the Government in the past, and explains, partially, its insistence upon local initiative in draining based on the local knowledge and assessment of the land. Thus, for the next two decades, discussion and inquiry ranged over the whole field of administration, finance, the classification of the land, and the delimitation of aims. Five major reports were issued, probably amounting in total to over 1,250,000 words and it is these verbal forests that must be cleared in order that we may see some of the timber.

The impetus for reassessment and investigation came with yet another Royal Commission in 1923, which considered past measures and future possibilities. It recommended that a thorough survey of administration, engineering, contouring, land values and land quality be undertaken for 'securing a reliable basis for a comprehensive policy of drainage and land settlement in the South-East'.[61] Administratively, the Commission wanted to see one body having control over all the South-East. This aim was partially achieved in 1926 when the Irrigation and Drainage Commission was given control of the drainage, but the Millicent and Tantanoola Districts decided to remain apart, and their drainage was administered by their District Councils. By 1931, the administration of the South-East drainage passed to newly constituted, semi-independent Drainage Board which had control of all areas (except Millicent and Tantanoola once again, an exception that has lasted until the present). The Board instituted a common system of rating throughout the region based on an 'assessment of the increase in the fee simple value which had occurred to all land . . . from draining and draining works', which, although reviewed and appealed against many times, still stands.

From the point of view of drainage improvement, the 1923 Commission concluded that the Scheme Drains had not conferred the degree of benefit that had been expected. The Commission, therefore, came around to the view expressed by both Goyder and Rogers nearly half a century before, that the land capable of improvement, or more correctly worth the cost of improvement, was limited, and that activity should be restricted accordingly to the most rewarding areas, that is to say, to the southern ends of the western most flats between Kingston and Millicent, the activity edging northwards, step by step, as each portion of the drainage scheme was completed and proved successful. The land classification surveys, carried out both immediately before and during the years that the Commission sat, confirmed that the potentially most rewarding areas were in the south-west. The relative amounts and proportions of the five categories of land in each area are shown in Table XII.

Armed with this information, the subsequent Closer Settlement inquiries in the South-East concluded that a maximum of 1,290 more farmers could be accommodated, 290 by draining, but 1,000 without draining.

But nothing happened; the time was not propitious for intensi-·fying rural settlement and yet another Committee produced a report in 1936 on the general development of the South-East. It concluded that as the number of holdings that could be created without draining was about four times as great as the number with draining, 'no further public expenditure on drainage would be justified', particularly until the Government either owned or had an option over the land in the areas concerned.[62] The repurchase of the land became a *sine qua non* of all future schemes. Despite the fact that the years from 1920 to 1945 had done nothing to alter the pattern of draining and improve conditions in the flats, the years had led to the amassing of an enormous amount of information, so that greater things could be accomplished later.

A Comprehensive System

In 1944, the inactivity of the inter-war period ended as significant advances were planned for the draining and settlement of the South-East. The reason for this change was the desire to settle ex-servicemen on the land after the war. The detailed investigations of previous years into the possibility of draining and settling the flats made the South-East an obvious place for undertaking such a project, especially when the advances in pasture improvement and the rectification of trace-element deficiencies were taken into account. A further extensive inquiry from 1944 to 1948 resulted in the strong recommendation that a comprehensive and efficient system of drainage for the South-East was 'not only practicable but desirable'.[63] As if to underline the desirability of drainage, severe flooding affected the flats in 1946 and 1947.

Before the construction of new drains was begun some important innovations in the administrative, financial and land settlement

Table XII

Classification of Land in the South East Flats, 1925

(To Nearest 1,000 acres)

(1,000 = 404·68 ha)

Type of Agric. land	Area 1 Blackford Flat	Area 2 Kingston-Beachport	Area 3 Lakes Area	Area 4	Area 5 Minecrow Flat	Area 6 Avenue Flat	Area 7 Reedy Creek	Area 8 Drain M to Dismal	Total	% of all land classified
Good	8	12	5	4	3	7	7	23	69	9·5
Very fair	19	89	5	5	31	13	9	96	267	36·9
Fair	8	39	4	2	17	37	16	43	166	22·9
Fairly poor	—	28	5	1	6	27	4	12	83	11·5
Poor	4	39	3	1	4	16	3	29	99	13·7
Undifferentiated	40	—	—	—	—	—	—	—	40	5·5
TOTAL LAND	79	207	22	13	61	100	39	203	724	100·0

Source: SAPP, 64 (1925).

aspects of draining were made. Draining was to be a purely governmental undertaking, so avoiding the disputes between landowner and Government which had paralysed activity at times in the past; and the Government was to be able to acquire compulsorily any land it needed for the implementation of the scheme. The project for draining was submitted to the Commonwealth Government for inclusion within the scope of the War Service Land Settlement Act, and so national funds were made available for draining. In this way, the State Government had complete control over all aspects of the draining and settlement of the South-East. This was the only way in which a successful, comprehensive drainage scheme could be effected. The local, piecemeal attitude disappeared as draining became a truly State affair with Federal financial backing.

It was decided to concentrate activity in the 400,000 acres of land liable to inundation in the Western Division, which consisted of the flats west of Baker's Range, and in 1948 drainage work began.[64] It would be tedious to describe in detail the drains, banks, and sluices that have been constructed in the last twelve years. Figure 64 tells the story better than words can. Nevertheless, it can be seen that the flats south of Drain K-L, i.e. Reedy Creek Flat, Avenue Flat, and Biscuit Flat, have all been provided with an intricate network of new drains, totalling about 316 miles in length, which produce a density of drainage channels approaching that of the Millicent-Tantanoola area, and give thorough drainage. This work is now complete. To the north of Drain K-L, work has been completed recently on the draining of the Kingston-Bowaka flats and the northern end of Avenue Flat in the hundreds of Minecrow and Townsend. The long-awaited connection between Jacky White's drain and Maria Creek is complete with the construction of the Blackford drain, which is also being extended through Avenue Flat. This drain will bring much needed relief to the area. The network of subsidiary drainage channels north of Drains K-L is not as dense as in areas to the south because the rainfall, and consequently the volume of flood water, is less. Besides the new drains excavated since 1944, nearly all old drains have been regraded, widened and generally improved (Fig. 65).

In 1960, work started on the draining of the 730,000 acres of floodable land in the Eastern Division of the South-East, that is

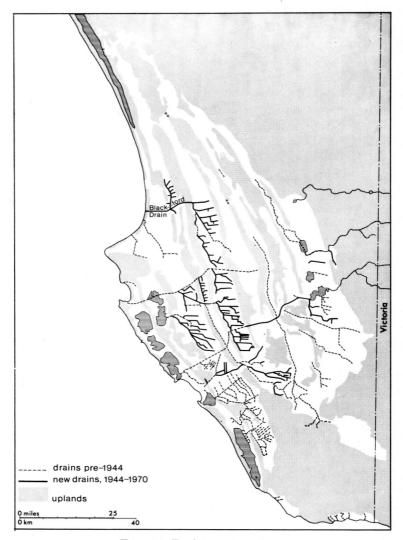

drains pre–1944

new drains, 1944–1970

uplands

0 miles _____ 25

0 km _____ 40

FIG. 64. Drains, 1944–1970.

to say, east of Baker's Range. The first stage of the project consists of the construction of a drain from Mosquito Creek at Struan, via Bool Lagoon into an enlarged Drain M to the sea at Beachport. Thus Drain M now carries water coming from Victoria for about fifty-five miles across the ranges and flats of the

FIG. 65. A typical drain in the flats, wide and shallow so as not to lower the water table too much.

South-East. With the completion of this work artificial drains have completely re-orientated the natural north-west and south-east trending drainage system towards the west, except for the northern portion of the Eastern Division, which still drains on the 'soak away' and evaporation principle.

As a result of these new drains, the north flowing water of the Western Division has been intercepted at several points, and diverted to the sea by the shortest course possible. This has brought into existence a series of artificially created drainage basins, each with its own outfall and almost dendritic pattern of drains. There are seven main drainage systems in the Western Division now, besides several smaller ones.

The 'watery waste' of just over one hundred years ago has disappeared with the completion of the artificial drainage system. It is hard to find much standing water on the flats these days, except for that in individual swamps, too unproductive and too small to be worth the expense of draining. Indicative of the change that has come over the District is the concern of naturalists to preserve Bool Lagoon from the effects of Drain M, for this unique aquatic environment is in danger of disappearing or at least being drastically affected, and with it will disappear the flocks of long legged swamp birds that nest and mate in this almost inaccessible and distant spot of the South-East.

Elsewhere, the wide shallow drains have led away most of the surface water, and water-tables have dropped significantly. Most drains are dammed by timber baulks during the summer in order to preserve some of the valuable drinking water from flowing to waste in the sea. Further north, in the vicinity of Naracoorte and Padthaway, good quality stock water can be obtained at shallow depths by the aid of windmills, but lately it has been realized that the underground water is available in quantities that are sufficient for irrigation. In the late 1950s large diameter bores were drilled and yielded flows of up to 200,000 gallons per hour. Initially this water was used for the uncontrolled flooding of existing annual pastures and lucerne paddocks, but now it is led into graded bays bounded by check banks and is also used for supplementing water supplies to the very large acreages of vineyards that have recently been planted in the vicinity. All this is not without its effect upon the water resources of the region. Underground water supplies are being depleted and they are not being replenished rapidly, because so much of the water that formerly flowed northwards in the flats is now diverted westwards out to sea.

Indeed, everything points to the fact that the draining of the South-East has gone about as far as it can or should, and that this epoch in the making of a significantly large and distinctive portion of South Australian landscape has all but drawn to an end.

5. Notes

1. The best and most accessible accounts of the physiography, hydrology and soils of the Lower South-East are in L. K. Ward, 'The underground water of the south-eastern portions of South Australia', *South Australian Department of Mines, Bulletin*, 19 (1941);

R. Sprigg, 'The geology of the South-East Province, South Australia, with special reference to Quaternary coastline migrations and modern beach developments', *Geological Survey of South Australia, Bulletin*, 29 (1952);

E. P. D. O'Driscoll, 'The Hydrology of the Murray Basin Province in South Australia', *Geological Survey of South Australia, Bulletin*, 35 (1960);

G. Blackburn, 'Soils of County Grey, South Australia', and 'Soils of Counties Macdonnell and Robe, South Australia', Publications Nos. 33 (1959), and 45 (1964) respectively of *C.S.I.R.O., Soils Division, Soils and Land Use Series.*

2. In addition to the underground water near the surface there is deeper artesian water flowing through deep beds of sands laid down between impervious clays. This water is tapped for domestic and stock purposes.

3. *SAPP*, 86 and 126 (1865–66).

4. E. Ward, *The South-Eastern District* (1869), 46.

5. *Border Watch* (17 June 1864).

6. *SAPP*, 118 (1860); *Border Watch* (3 May 1861).

7. *Border Watch* (16 Oct., 17 May, 2 August, 9 Sept. 1861); and (21 March, 18 April 1862).
   Anon., *Residents of the South East* (1861), (pamphlet);
   A map of the proposed new state in the Mitchell Library, N.S.W., Map No. M2/806/fax/1862.

8. *SAPP*, 41 (1863). Already (13 August 1862), W. R. Coulthard, the Assistant Engineer and Architect, has prepared a plan for the deviation of the Maria Creek, and for a cutting from the head of the Creek into the swamp behind. By this means he hoped that a large tract of the land in the neighbourhood would be drained and that a sufficient fall of water would be achieved to keep the mouth of the Maria Creek free of sand and sea-weed. This is perhaps the first clearly documented proposal to excavate a drain in the South-East, although it is known that Seymour, a pastoralist, had cut through the rise on the margin of the Bool Lagoon to allow water from the Mosquito Creek to enter it, and that a minor cut had been made through the coastal belt at Port MacDonnell in order to drain the swamp that lay behind. See, EAO, 32/1862 and 84/1862 (out).

9. SGO, 23/1863 (in).

10. Milne, the Commissioner of Crown Lands, wrote of Goyder as follows; 'the great amount of consideration which that gentleman has given to the subject, joined to his intimate knowledge of the country, the situation and extent of the lagoons and the direction in which the surplus water flows, must render his opinion as to the feasibility of draining a large portion of the district of great value', *SAPP*, 41 (1863).

11. *Border Watch* (4 March 1864).

12. Ibid. (3 June and 22 July 1864);

13. *SAPP*, 48 (1864).

14. *Border Watch* (3 June 1864).

15. Ibid. (29 April; 28 Jan. 1865);
    SAPP, 181 (1864).

16. EAO, 346/1864 (out).

17. *SAPP*, 65 (1866–67).

18. *SAPP*, 30 (1867); 142 (1867);
    Border Watch (30 Nov. 1867).

19. *SAPP*, 88 (1869–70), appendix; SGO, 133/1868 (in).

20. *S.A. Reg.* (17 July 1869);
    Border Watch (15 Aug. 1868).

21. *SAPP*, 31 and 32 (1871).

22. *SAPP*, 88A, (1869–70); SAPD, (H.A.) (1869–70), col. 217, and (H.A.) (1871), col. 745.

23. SGO 1891 and 1389/1870 (out); SGO, 520/1869 (out);
    SAPP, 107 (1871);
    Border Watch (8 April 1871).

24. At this time, unless the sections were adjoining a selection could not take up two sections, which caused much hardship in the swamp—see SGO, 2770/1872 (in).

25. For details of the changes see *SAPP*, 107 (1870–71); 107 (1871), and various reports in *Border Watch*, e.g. (8 Jan. 1870), (14 Sept., 16 Oct., 4 Dec. 1872), and (1 and 7 March 1873).

26. *SAPP*, 61 (1870–71). This was part of a much larger scheme of hundred survey throughout the whole of the west central part of the flats, but which was eventually disallowed. See *SAPP*, 51 (1870) for details.

27. *SAPP*, 124 (1876); 41 (1877).
    See also G. L. Buxton, *South Australian Land Acts, 1869–1885* (1906), 45–49.

28. *Border Watch* (12 Feb. and 6 April 1870);
    SAPD, (H.A.) (1870), col. 1480;
    See J. M. Powell, *The Public Lands of Australia Felix* (1970), 244–46 for their subsequent settlement in Victoria.

29. *SAPP*, 200 (1870–71); 172 (1872).

30. *SAPD*, (L.C.) (1872), col. 2057 and (H.A.) (1876), col. 1531, respectively.

31. *SAPP*, 38 and 68 (1875). For further complaints of damage due to subsidence, see 163 (1877), and for lack of maintenance of the drains, see 131 (1876).

32. *Act*, 21/1875, and 85/1877. The Mount Muirhead Drainage Board was established in 1876, and the Tantanoola and Mayurra Boards six years later.

33. The Waste Lands Amendment Act of 1872 (*Act*, 18/1872) opened all land south of Goyder's Line to credit purchase at 10% deposit and repayment within 6 years. *Act*, 22/1874 made all land in South Australia available for credit purchase.

34. *SAPD* (H.A.) (1874), col. 1025.

35. *SAPP*, 168 (1874).

36. See *SAPP*, 53 (1876); 218 (1876); 237 (1877);
Border Watch (12 Feb. 1870).

37. SGO, 501/1878 (in).

38. SGO, 501/1878 (in).

39. *SAPD* (H.A.) (1880), col. 1998.

40. *SAPP*, 196 (1880).

41. *Port Augusta Dispatch* (30 Dec. 1881), quoted in D. W. Meinig, *On the margins of the good earth: the South Australian wheat frontier, 1869–1884* (1962), 85.

42. Already under *Acts* 275/1882, 318/1884 and 444/1888, the Crown had to give relief in the form of the revision of payment to occupiers of badly flooded lands.

43. Anon., *The South Eastern District of South Australia in 1880* (1881), 25. A collection of articles written originally for the *S.A. Register*.

44. *SAPP*, 129 (1884); 96 (1886).
For a general description of the flooded areas of the South-East at this time see *S. A. Observer* (10, 17 and 24 Feb. 1883).

45. SGO, 155/1885 (in).

46. Anon. *The South Eastern District of South Australia in 1880* (1881), 51–55; *SAPD* (H.A.) (1883), col. 305.

47. *SAPD* (H.A.) (1883), cols. 303–306; 459–462; 615–622; *SAPP*, 45 (1884).

48. *SAPP*, 149(1893) and 32 (1894), petitions from Lucindale and Kingston respectively.
See also *SAPD* (H.A.) (1894), col. 773.

49. *SAPP*, 64 (1890).

50. *SAPP*, 35 (1892).

51. *SAPP*, 104 (1895). A preliminary report is in *SAPP*, 136 (1893).

52. *SAPD* (H.A.) (1890), col. 1595.

53. *Acts* 340/1885, and 469/1887.

54. *SAPD* (H.A.) (1894), col. 772, et seq.

55. *Act*, 629/1895.

56. *SAPP*, 19 (1899).

57. *SAPD* (H.A.) (1900), col. 604.

58. *Act*, 737/1900

59. D. J. Gordon, *Shall we hold the South East?* (1902), 21.

60. See *SAPP*, 10 of the years from 1904 to 1920, (the Surveyor-General's Annual Report) for the early repurchases, and *SAPP*, 36 (1915), 71 (1925), 55 (1926) for schemes for the western and central flats. See also *SAPP*, 37 (1920), 'A report by the Engineer-in-Chief on present conditions'.
61. *SAPP*, 55 (1923).
62. *SAPP*, 32 (1936).
63. *SAPP*, 17 (1948).
64. This section is based on the Annual Reports of the South Eastern Drainage Board, usually *SAPP*, 6, in every year.

6
Irrigating the Desert

'The banks of the Murray are not dead but asleep—it wants but the enterprise of man to awaken them to exuberant life'. S. Australian Director of Agriculture, *SAPP*, 10 (1903–4).

The impact of irrigation on the landscape of South Australia was late in its occurrence and limited in its extent. Putting aside the many passing references to the desirability of irrigation that occurred from time to time during the early years of settlement, no serious moves were made to apply supplementary water to the land until the early 1880s, and even then little was done until after 1900. Figure 66a shows that the total amount of land affected by 1910 was only about 3,000 acres, which rose to about 50,000 acres by 1950, and to 168,000 acres by 1966—a total which despite its recent rapid increase is not expected to rise much more because of the limitation of water resources.

Compared with the other activities of man in changing the landscape, such as scrub clearing, survey and swamp draining, which have affected either all or large parts of the land surface of the State, irrigation has affected only about 0·31 per cent of the land within the hundreds. Not only is the amount of land affected small, but the impact on the landscape is even more limited than at first appears. Most of the land irrigated away from the River Murray consists of individual paddocks of pasture crops scattered throughout the State (Fig. 66b), but concentrated mainly in the Adelaide Hills, the Central Hill Country and the Upper and Lower South-East. Even within these areas the paddocks are rarely found in contiguous blocks but are scattered almost randomly within individual holdings, their main function being to extend the stock carrying capacity of the properties by supplying extra feed

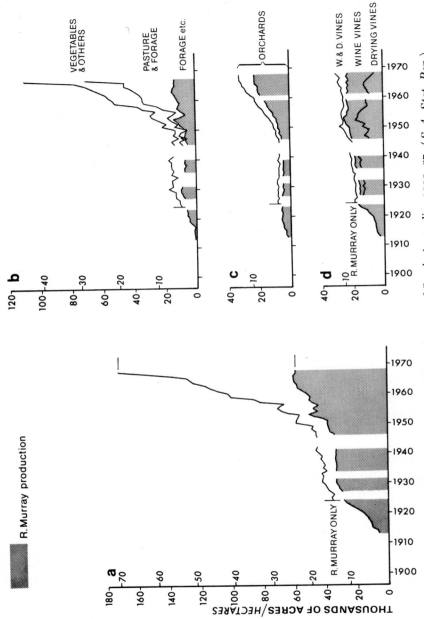

FIG. 66. Crop production in the irrigated areas of South Australia, 1900–67. (*S.A. Stat. Reg.*)

throughout the dry months of the year. As a result, they are rarely seen and barely appreciated. The two exceptions to this scatter of individually irrigated blocks, are the concentration of vegetable growing near Virginia, on the Gawler Plains north of Adelaide, and the irrigated pastures, and more recently vineyards, around Padthaway in the Upper South-East both areas being dependent upon underground water supplies.

But it is along the River Murray, where irrigation is concentrated in specific localities, that the visual contrasts between irrigated and non-irrigated land are stark and significant (Fig. 67). These contrasts occur in land use, intensity of cultivation, density of rural population, and the prosperity of the urban centres which these areas support. When one is approaching an irrigation area through the mallee lands, greens replace browns as the predominant colours; trees and shrubs of the orchards and vineyards replace wheat and sheep (Fig. 66c and d); the townships are more prosperous, and the ubiquitous pipes, sprays, and irrigation and drainage channels remind one constantly of the reasons for these changes. Although the area affected is small it is the intensity of change which merits attention, a change only equalled perhaps by that of urban creation. It is these irrigated lands and the process of their creation that are the subject of this chapter.

Like the draining of the swamp lands in the South-East the irrigation of land alongside the Murray has been achieved by the conscious alteration of the hydrological features of the landscape. The level of the river water has been altered by pumping, the flow of the water has been redistributed by a network of artificial channels, and the water table has been changed where the ground has become saturated. Sometimes the changes are unintentional, for example modifications of the soil structure by rising salt in over-irrigated areas. Of all the rural landscapes made by man, in a sense, it is the most artificial and the one most likely to revert to its natural state if the irrigation works are not regularly maintained to continue this transformation. The magnitude and potential impermanence of these modifications has meant that co-operative action has long been recognized as an essential prerequisite for irrigation settlement. In this the irrigation farmer alongside the Murray has much in common with other

FIG. 67. The Waikerie irrigation area. Waikerie township and the River Murray are in the top left-hand corner. The bushy trees on the left are mainly oranges, but the planting of wine grapes (on the right) has been undertaken more recently. Open irrigation channels run alongside the roads, and drainage water is passed through bore holes in the cavernous limestone which underlies most of the area.

'hydraulic' societies, whether it be with the rice farmer in South-East Asia or the polder farmer in Holland or the Fens.[1]

The need for co-operative action in planning and maintenance probably goes some way to explain the lateness of large-scale irrigation in South Australia, an environment otherwise potentially suitable for irrigation. Individual action in the settlement process had long been the norm and was bound up with ideas of the inherent value of the independent yeoman agriculturist and when large scale irrigation was first proposed during the 1880s, the Government was willing to encourage private ventures but not to become involved itself. But the very nature of large-scale irrigation necessitated overall control of the maintenance of works and the rational regulation of water, together with substantial financial backing, all of which only the Government was capable of providing. Until the Government was ready to commit itself under changed circumstances after 1900, irrigation could not proceed on any large scale. The need for co-operative action and overall control had one further effect. Unlike the individual, piecemeal affair of woodland clearing, for example, which escaped public attention, irrigation schemes became the subject of engineering reports, feasibility studies and similar inquiries. This contemporary official comment helps considerably in understanding the impact and extent of irrigation on the landscape.

Beginnings : 1880–1905

Causes of Interest

The early 1880s were a period of agricultural depression in South Australia arising from three consecutive years of drought and of progressively declining yields caused by continuous cropping in phosphate-deficient soils, and falling wheat prices aggravated the effects of the depression. The result was unemployment, not only amongst farmers but also amongst city-based workers dependent upon the prosperity of the rural areas. There events stimulated an interest in irrigation. Water supply was uppermost in people's minds, and it was not surprising, therefore, that attention turned first to the high-rainfall areas of the Adelaide hills and the South-East,[2] and then to the River Murray. The Murray was the Colony's largest supply of water, and until this time it had been viewed solely as a means of navigation and trade into the adjacent colonies, remaining untapped for the supply of domestic and irrigation water.

Depression had one other effect. The continual decline in land sales caused the Government's finances to dwindle and it was unable to promote works to alleviate the extensive unemployment.

In 1884 the Government sought to minimize distress by levying a tax on real and personal property in order to raise funds.[3] At the same time there was a popular move towards land nationalization which led to the formation of the *Land Nationalisation Society*, in 1884. Those concerned wanted to copy the ideas of A. R. Wallace and Henry George on the public ownership of the land and the buying-out of private owners.[4] Some of the initial supporters of land reform found these policies too extreme and, in 1884, G. W. Cotton, a member of the House of Assembly and a socialist reformer, became involved with the Homestead League and was the originator of the idea of Workingmen's Blocks. The Blocks of twenty acres or less were thought of as a solution to the problems of poor wages and irregular employment, and as a means of combating what Cotton saw as a coming working–class revolution.[5] But the realities of the South Australian climate made intense cultivation in small blocks difficult without supplementary water supplies, and many of the blocks taken up were a complete failure. Only those in the Adelaide Hills, centred around the newly created township of Mylor were successful. Increasingly, the idea of small holdings became linked with that of irrigation.

The move for agricultural reform and experiment in South Australia was aided by the development of irrigation in other parts of the world, particularly in the U.S.A. and in the neighbouring colony of Victoria. For example, the Reverend M. Wood Green, a member of the Homestead League's executive, visited the U.S.A. and subsequently wrote a number of articles on what he saw, entitled 'Irrigation—the hope of Australia'.[6] In Victoria events were already moving quickly; the first organized water schemes were begun at Echuca and in Warenga Shire in 1882, and by 1886 an Irrigation Act was passed in Victoria which led to the creation of ninety Water Trusts by 1900, including some twenty-one irrigation trusts and many private schemes, the most famous of which was the First Mildura Trust, founded by the Chaffey Brothers from California.[7] In addition to these practical examples of irrigation elsewhere in the world, there was also the South Australian Government's participation in the draining of the South-East Swamps, which the supporters of irrigation could point to as an example of the use of public funds for the preparation of land for settlement.

Despite these precedents, however, the Government was not prepared to get involved in the financing or administration of irrigation works during a difficult economic period; its solution to the problem was to encourage and facilitate private ventures. But there was another side to the problem. The Government saw the Murray primarily as a means of navigation to the other colonies and therefore as a source of trade and revenue; irrigation was undoubtedly considered as a secondary use of the river (Fig. 17). In fact, railway construction to the river by the other colonies was causing a diversion of trade away from South Australia, so that from the mid 1880s onwards navigation declined and was by no means as important as was supposed. This fact took a long time to be appreciated and both private and governmental attitudes to the form of interest and involvement in the River Murray continued in the old way. Given this situation, it was not surprising that irrigation was not considered seriously, especially as it might interfere with navigation.

Plans and Projects

The first scheme for irrigation was in 1884, when a Mr Bevilaqua wanted to irrigate 25,000 acres of land in the Hundred of Stuart, north of Morgan (Fig. 68). The Government was sympathetic to his request, but offered only a fifty-year instead of a ninety-nine-year lease, at 1s.-0d. per acre which was double the rent requested. This deterred Bevilaqua from further action,[8] nevertheless, the Conservator of Water was asked to make a rapid survey of the area to be irrigated and he reported favourably upon the scheme, but a more careful survey six months later convinced him that the soil was not suitable for irrigation and that parts of the Hundred of Eba would be better.[9]

A debate in Parliament showed that although a majority of members seemed in favour of legislation to promote irrigation there was no unanimity on the question of governmental versus private enterprise as the agency of change. Agreement was reached, however, that, provided the Conservator of Water was in favour of the idea, 'steps should be taken at some point in the River Murray to raise and distribute by drains or otherwise, sufficient water to irrigate not less than 1,000 acres of land', to be let out to agriculturists and small-scale graziers.[10] Supplementary reports

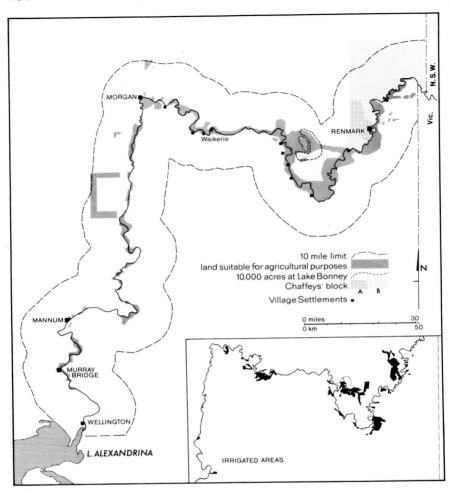

FIG. 68. Irrigation alongside the River Murray during the 1890s. Based on *SAPP*, 86 (1892); 135 (1893); 73 (1894). The inset map shows the extent of irrigated land at present.

were called for on soils and engineering problems and these were generally favourable concerning the possibility of starting irrigation, either in the river flats north of Murray Bridge near Mannum or on the upland ground near Morgan. The unknown and unresolved issue was the working cost of such a scheme, particularly that of pumping, and much detailed study was given to the possibility of utilizing the motive power of the flow of the river to raise the water. The aim was for the Government to 'make a fair start' so that private enterprise would see the possibility of success and then relieve the Government of further anxiety.[11]

Renmark

The Government's anxiety about making even a token gesture towards promoting irrigation was assuaged by the appearance of the Chaffey Brothers who had practical experience of irrigation in California. They had been invited to Victoria by Alfred Deakin in 1886 and had attempted to establish Mildura, but because of difficulties did not proceed further. They were then asked to come to South Australia to start a settlement at Renmark. Generally speaking, both people and Parliament were delighted that practical farmers with a knowledge of irrigation had been invited to the Colony. In the agreement of July 1887, the Chaffey Brothers were given a licence to lease 30,000 acres (Block A) with the possibility of a further 220,000 acres (Block B), and the right to draw off two feet of water for every acre irrigated (Fig. 68). In return they were to establish a technical institute of agriculture, a school and experimental farms.[12]

The town of Renmark was laid out on the usual uncompromising grid pattern, and it and the pumping station were located beside the river. The irrigation channels and roads extended northwards into the mallee in a roughly fan-shape. The number of acres irrigated was 2,700 in 1896, which rose to 3,200 in 1900, 3,700 in 1905, and 4,993 in 1910, altogether a much more modest increase than had been expected. The main emphasis was on growing fruit for canning and drying with the aim of reducing South Australia's imports of these products and, hopefully, of exporting them in time. The main crops were apricots, currants, sultanas and lemons.

The contrast between the irrigated and non-irrigated land was considerable. One writer pointed out that people were prepared to pay £11 per annum rental for vineyards, but 'over the fence where the country is in its natural state, the passer-by would label it "desert" and would not pay a rent of 11d per square mile'. It was a 'conquest' and a 'contrast', in the eyes of most, and undoubtedly a success. With such results, public enthusiasm ran high. The

Adelaide newspapers, the *Observer* and the *Register*, between 1888 and 1890 were full of articles, commentaries and correspondence on the virtues or defects of irrigation, and its connection with unemployment, small blocks and other land settlement schemes. One might say that people had 'water on the brain'. It was estimated that 2,000,000 acres would be available for irrigation alongside the Murray which awaited only 'the enterprise of the capitalist, the agriculturalist and the horticulturalist'.[13]

Lake Bonney Scheme

Encouraged by the success of attracting the Chaffey Brothers, and conscious of the popular demand to promote settlement in small holdings as a means of relieving distress, the Government at last toyed with the idea of establishing its own irrigation schemes. In 1889, the irrigation of 12,000 acres near Smithfield, north of Adelaide, supplied by the South Para River, was proposed. The scheme was rejected, mainly because it was thought that there were many areas in the high-rainfall Ranges that could be taken up and developed at lower cost without governmental financial commitment.[14] Meanwhile, attention had shifted again to the Murray, and, during the same year, two reports were published on the possibility of spending £30,000 on developing 600 ten-acre blocks to the west of Lake Bonney. This particular area was chosen because of the storage potential of the Lake and also because it had been the location of an investigation and proposed settlement by the Melbourne-based 'Lake Bonney Irrigation Company'. The company had requested governmental permission to go ahead and had had its proposal and the site inspected by a Parliamentary committee, which was impressed enough with its potential to ban the company and reserve the land for a Government sponsored irrigation scheme. Once again, the Government was being led by private initiative.[15]

Interest and controversy in irrigation mounted throughout 1890 and 1891, and became so great that eventually the Government had a fairly detailed survey made of all land suitable and available for irrigation within ten miles of the River Murray (Fig. 68). The survey was disappointing to the optimists who had dreamed of an irrigation empire in the Murray valley; the chimera of 2,000,000 acres of irrigated land was dispelled. Of the 1,763,000 acres of land within the twenty-mile strip, 1,397,500 acres were considered of use for extensive grazing only, 154,000 acres were useful for both grazing and cultivation and 103,000 acres were of use for cultivation only, with a further 108,000 acres suitable for cultivation but subject to periodic flooding. However, although the area of potentially irrigable land was far more limited than was once thought, at least the location of the most suitable areas had been identified. They were concentrated in the great Pyap loop of the Murray. This practical confirmation of the suitability of the Lake Bonney scheme prompted the Government to enlarge to 10,000 acres its original proposal for settlement there by the irrigation of the higher ground to the south and east of the Lake (Fig. 68). As cautious as ever, the Government obtained further reports from the Engineer-in-Chief and the Conservator of Water, both of whom supported the feasibility of the scheme; legislation was passed to enable the Government to make the necessary works and lease the land, the whole scheme to be both a practical example and an encouragement to private ventures.[16]

Co-operative Settlements

But the Government was too slow off the mark, and as the prolonged planning phases dragged on, private initiative intervened once more. As the number of urban unemployed continued at a high level, a group of them made a request to establish a communistic settlement to accommodate 250,000 people within ten years at the now much publicized Lake Bonney site. This was an alternative to emigrating to Paraguay and attempting to build an ideal society in which land and labour were shared. Like so many irrigation schemes before it, the proposals of the 'New Australians' came to nothing, and two months later, on Christmas day, 1893, they set sail from Port Adelaide to Paraguay. No sooner had this attempt languished than another group of unemployed asked for 20,000 acres of land at Lake Bonney, a request which was taken more seriously by the Government than that of the 'New Australians', but which, eventually, was equally ineffective in producing any lasting results.[17]

The attempts of the unemployed to relieve their distress by co-operative action were not without results, however, for the Government saw in their suggestions a means of bringing 'idle hands and idle lands together'. With almost indecent haste legislation was put through Parliament to facilitate the establishment of a modified form of co-operative settlements called the 'Village Settlements'. These could be formed by an association of twenty or more people of a minimum age of 18 years who conformed to certain rules. They were granted land on perpetual lease and the Government gave up to £50 to each of the villagers so that they could establish themselves. In all, thirteen Village Settlements were created, eleven of them along the Upper Murray and based on irrigation—Murtho, Lyrup, Pyap, New Residence, Moorook, Kingston, Holder, Waikerie, Ramco, Gillen and New Era (Fig. 68). Because of the character of these settlements, the early emphasis was upon self-sufficiency; land in the surrounding mallee areas was cleared and the greater part of it given over to cereal cultivation (i.e. 2,379 out of 3,215 acres cultivated in all settlements) with relatively small amounts of irrigated fruit crops (Table XIII).

The Government had believed the Lake Bonney Scheme to be economically sound, but nothing had materialized; on the other hand, it had seen the Village Settlements merely as a means of meeting 'a pressing exigency' and as being of temporary significance. But during the closing years of the nineteenth century the Village Settlements were in fact the more important of the two projects.

Government Involvement

By a complex process of trial and error over a period of ten years from 1885 to 1895, a number of irrigation nuclei had been established along the Murray which were to remain the cores of future developments. But the contribution to irrigation of these settlements was not merely locational. Although Renmark and the Village Settlements had started out as predominantly private ventures, slowly the Government became more and more involved in them, despite its resolve to stay aloof. In the case of Renmark, the control and administration of the water became too important to be left to a private company and it seemed necessary

Table XIII

The Village Settlements, 1895 and 1900

(100 acres = 40·469 ha)

	Land held (acres) 1895	Cereals (acres)		Irrigated and other crops (acres)		Population		Subsequent history
		1895	1900	1895	1900	1895	1900	
Murtho	2,000	140	91	91		53	Disbanded 1899–1900	
Lyrup	14,000	300	418	267	200	346	110	
Pyap	10,485	268	744	85	47	274	83	1905, reverted to private ownership
New Residence	4,000	70		25		92	Disbanded 1896–97	
Moorook	3,200	140	380	43	67	109	20	1905, reverted to private ownership
Kingston	4,800	205	400	65	33	145	71	1911, reverted to Government
Holder	7,540	500	1,500	88	48	227	102	1903, reverted to private ownership
Waikerie	3,340	300	1,000	27	43	117	78	1910, reverted to Government
Ramco	3,685	64	500	11	53	36	49	1910, reverted to Government
Gillen	10,000	200		12		134	Disbanded 1895–96	
New Era	2,095	160		29		103	Disbanded 1895–96	
Nangkita	1,894	15		20		26	Disbanded 1895–96	
Mt Remarkable	932	77		73		93	Disbanded 1895–96	
TOTAL	67,971	2,379	3,033	836	491	1,755		

Sources: SAPP, 113 (1895); *SAPP*, 37 (1900).

to place this under the control of a Trust, established by Parliamentary Act. This move was supported by the majority of the landholders.[18] Undoubtedly, in becoming involved with the administration of the water at Renmark, the Government was influenced by its need to balance the conflicting uses of the Murray, lest irrigation should ultimately reduce navigability.

In addition to aiding in these administrative problems, the Government became committed financially. The Chaffeys became bankrupt in 1892, and some of the original irrigation culverts and channels were constructed faultily. Because the Government had become concerned in the administrative aspects of the settlement and had shown initial support for the scheme it was then partially (although unfairly) blamed for the financial problems that beset Renmark. In consequence, the Government initiated a lengthy inquiry in order to clear itself of responsibility and to investigate the financial matters. The outcome was that grants of £3,000 and £16,000 were made in 1897 and 1899 respectively in order to put the scheme on a sound footing[19] (Fig. 69).

In a similar way the Government became deeply involved in the Village Settlements through the guarantee of a grant of £50 to each settler once he was established. Yet the schemes were not as successful as was hoped because many of the villagers had no agricultural experience, only 81 out of 544 having any agricultural background, and these included gardeners, station-hands, dairymen and bushmen, as well as farmers and farm-labourers. All villagers found difficulty in co-operating successfully, and many left the Settlements.

In time the financial difficulties became acute and the cost of supplying water to the remaining villagers increased. A Parliamentary inquiry in 1895 into the working of the Settlements resulted in the reduction of rents and the establishment of a more efficient administrative system with a director of irrigation to give technical advice.[20] But even this did not help, and, whereas Murtho, Lyrup, Pyap, New Residence, Moorook, Kingston, Waikerie, Ramco, Gillen and New Era (together with Mt Remarkable and Nangkita which were located elsewhere in South Australia) had 598 villagers in 1893, the number dropped to 440 in 1895, and by 1900 New Era, Mt Remarkable, Nangkita, Gillen, New Residence and Murtho had been dissolved. Undoubtedly, human nature was the main element to be reckoned with and was of no less importance 'than quality of soil, suitable climate and available water supply'. Eventually the land of the Village Settlements was re-allocated to individual leaseholders, and then the settlements began to improve.[21] Figure 73a depicts the layout of one of these Village Settlements at Waikerie, and Fig. 70 the pumping station.

The century ended with one more attempt to extend the irrigated area, this time not in the Murray Valley but on 45,000 acres in the Gawler Plains, the scene of a previous proposal in 1889. The Government was once more understandably reluctant to become involved but did guarantee to provide 2 per cent of the capital per annum, with a right of purchase after seven years and an Act was passed to set up the scheme. It was a now familiar story of limited support of a private enterprise to carry out a public work. The overseas capital that was needed to make the scheme operational was not forthcoming. The Government took no further risk and the scheme flopped.[22]

In fairness it should be recognized that the Government was lukewarm towards irrigation not only because it wished to avoid financial and administrative entanglements during a difficult economic period, and its blindness to the economic realities of the decline of the use of the river for navigation, but also because it became aware increasingly that South Australia was but one of the three users of the River Murray, and that before irrigation could proceed successfully agreement had to be achieved over the apportionment of this common resource. Efforts to achieve co-operation between the colonies over the use and regulation of the River during the nineteenth century had revolved around the clearing of obstacles in the channels and the easing of tariffs which restricted trade. By the 1890s, however, a new element entered into these deliberations, that of irrigation in the up-stream colonies, which South Australia feared because it might lower the level of the Murray and prevent navigation. This concern also entered into the calculations over the feasibility of irrigation within South Australia. For example, Jones, the Conservator of Water, had cautioned in 1894 that before money was spent on the Lake Bonney scheme a firm understanding on the allotment of water to South Australia should be reached first. Not until the Murray Waters Agreement of 1914 was the Government sure of

FIG. 69. Lining irrigation channels with concrete, Renmark, 1889.

FIG. 70. The pumping station at the Waikerie Village Settlement, for lifting water up the side of the cliff, *c*. 1890.

its supply of water for irrigation, and therefore willing to commit itself whole-heartedly to new schemes.

Government Activity

The second phase in the development of irrigation occurred after 1905 and was characterized by direct government involvement. Whereas previously the Government attempted to provide the legislative framework within which private development could operate, it now became an active agent of change. This policy was part of a general drive to participate directly in agricultural expansion in order to stimulate the economy after the depression of the 1890s and the drought of 1902.

From 1885 onwards, the development of Workingmen's Blocks and then Homestead Blocks became an accepted part of land settlement and became linked with the development of irrigation. These ideas were further extended in the Closer Settlement Legislation of 1897 and 1902,[23] which provided for the re-purchase of large freehold estates in the high-rainfall areas and their subdivision into medium-sized holdings. This legislation was then applied to a few large estates alongside the River Murray that contained areas of swamp land. The swamps were reclaimed and then used as irrigated land.

The Swamps

The technical problems and costs of pumping water into the completely dry areas alongside the Upper Murray were good reasons for the reluctance of the Government to participate in irrigation schemes. In the swamps alongside the Lower Murray, however, the problems were fewer, although they were under-estimated initially. Nearly all the swamps were arcuate in shape and lay on the inner sides of the large swinging meanders that characterize the broadening flood plain of the Murray below Mannum. Each swamp area was strictly limited in its extent by the river on one side and the abrupt break of slope to the upland on the other side. It was a relatively simple matter to build an embankment from one end of the high ground to the other and thereby exclude the flood water. Irrigation water could then be supplied cheaply and easily to the reclaimed swamps by syphoning it over the embankment or letting it through sluices in the embankment, the natural slope of the swamp away from the river then ensuring the gravitational spread of the water.[24]

Already, by 1881, private reclamation of swamps had begun, acting as a spur to government action.[25] This was on the Wellington estate of the then Governor, Sir W. F. D. Jervois, who drained 3,320 acres for grazing (Fig. 71). To what extent the water was completely excluded is difficult to say, for without pumping there must have been inundation during the winter months. In all probability the embankment merely excluded the

FIG. 71. The Jervois Swamps beside the River Murray, looking south towards Tailem Bend. On the opposite bank lies an area of partially reclaimed swamp and some unreclaimed swamp. The characteristic linear arrangement of the farmsteads on the sloping land of the old river bank shows up clearly, each farm consisting of a narrow strip of reclaimed land in front, and upland behind. Irrigation water is let through the river side embankment to irrigate the pastures strips or 'bays' as they are known.

minor surges of the river and helped to extend the grazing season. Other schemes followed. For example, in 1884, G. W. Schultze of Mannum wanted permission to embank the swamp on the opposite side of the river to the town.[26] In 1889, the Morphett Brothers reclaimed 650 acres at Woods Point, to which was added another 350 acres by 1902. Other schemes completed at an early date were those of Macfarlane at Wellington (700 acres) and Cowan at Glen Lossie near Murray Bridge (800 acres).[27]

These schemes served as practical examples of what could be done with thorough draining. When the water was excluded the 'entangled jungle of rushes, reeds and other water-loving plants' died and was replaced by a coarse herbage. This was eaten down by sheep, which were light enough not to sink into the mud and which also helped to consolidate the ground. By the next season, when the ground was drier, it was ploughed and then allowed to dry further before the planting of any crops. Morphett's experiments showed that the ground was too wet for growing wheat for human consumption, although the crop could be grown and supplied green to the stock. Better still was the growing of onions, barley and lucerne, while potatoes, mangolds, pumpkins, maize and sorghum had all been cultivated successfully. Eventually, however, the swamps were given over to pig-rearing and dairy cattle, as grass was the best crop to withstand either accidental flooding, prolonged wetness due to seepage, or incorrect irrigation practices. The form of land use has not changed to the present.

The obvious success of these schemes prompted the Surveyor-General to suggest in 1904 that the 'important departure' into swamp draining should be undertaken by the Government now within the new framework of the Closer Settlement Legislation, an action he had advocated as far back as 1887.[28] The first areas taken up for reclamation were the Burdett and Mobilong Flats which were embanked and drained by 1906, and some land was leased during the following year. In 1905, work started on the Monteith and Long Flat areas and reclamation was completed by about 1908. Mypolonga Flats were next. Government activity had expanded sufficiently by 1910 for control to be passed from the Surveyor-General's department to a newly created Irrigation Department, under the direction of McIntosh, who had been the irrigation expert assigned to the Village Settlements.

The initial response to the reclamation of the swamps was enthusiastic, 'What was formerly a deep swamp or lagoon of little value but for a few head of stock during the summer', wrote the Surveyor-General of Monteith Flat, 'is now a deep black soil flat of over 1,000 acres capable of intense culture.' He calculated that there were 170,000 acres of similar land alongside the Murray, which, at 10 acres for every family of four, were capable of supporting a population of 68,000.[29] Others, like Gordon, the River Murray publicist, went further, and suggested that Lake Albert could be reclaimed and that 40,000 acres could be made available for irrigated settlement. The 100,000 acres of Lake Alexandrina were discussed, and the analogy of the Zuider Zee project, then being planned and widely spoken about, was not lost on the Murray boosters.[30] But these were just dreams; the soil of the lake floors was poor and would not have repaid draining, and, in any case, there were the problems of embanking the Murray and keeping the salt water from seeping into the lakes during periods of low river flow.

Work on the swamps proceeded slowly after the early years of the century and there was no new reclamation between 1910 and 1917. Further swamp reclamation was limited to either side of the core area around Murray Bridge where the river levels were known; and the extensive swamps further upstream could not be reclaimed with any assurance of success. The Barrages near the sea to maintain the lake levels and exclude the sea water were not completed until 1940 and the locks to regulate the levels above Mannum were not completed until well after 1920.

Unfortunately, despite the early and successful examples of private reclamation alongside the Murray, some important lessons were overlooked initially. In the first place, the embankments of the first government schemes were constructed entirely from swamp soil, which was so peaty in places that on drying, it shrank, cracked, and let water in. The centres of the first embankments had to be excavated and a core of sand and clay from the upland placed inside, and later embankments were made entirely from these materials. The original costs of between £650 and £1,020 per half mile of wall were now increased by anything up to 50 per cent.[31] More serious was the fact that no provision was made for the drainage and removal of the surplus water that accumulated in the swamps through rainfall, seepage and particularly through excessive irrigation. New drainage channels had to be excavated and pumps installed in every swamp. Another deficiency was the failure to purchase adjoining high ground in some of the reclamation areas so that there was a lack of suitable dry sites for houses and farm buildings, and for the stock when waterlogging became too great. Finally, there was the problem of the settlers themselves and their over-zealous application of water to the swamps. Flood irrigation was a reasonable method 'in sandy soil areas like parts of Renmark, Waikerie and the high lands on the river', but led to the ruin of clay and organic soils. People had been told for so long that water was the only ingredient missing from South Australian agriculture that they virtually drowned the crops and increased the salt in the soil. Sluices were opened for hours on end and the water lay on the already waterlogged bays and took days to pump out.[32] This is a problem that is not completely solved even at the present time.

Most of the early problems were eventually overcome with money, time and experience, and settlement progressed fairly satisfactorily. The Government assisted in the clearing, grading and fencing of the land, as well as with the construction of drainage and irrigation channels, and tanks. By the very nature of their origin each swamp was physically distinct from the next, and therefore each was administered by a separate irrigation trust, which was composed of representatives from the Government and the settlers. The swamps surveyed and reclaimed after 1917 came under the Soldier settlement legislation.

Landscape

The similarity of the physique and of the utilization of the swamps has had an effect in producing distinctive landscapes of minute subdivisions which recur, in one form or another, along the Murray below Mannum. The stages and processes by which these landscapes came into being can be seen in the examples of the Mobilong Swamp near Murray Bridge, an early, small-scale reclamation under the Returned Soldiers settlement schemes, and the more complex Jervois Swamp further downstream.

In 1886, the Mobilong Swamp (Fig. 72a) was reclaimed by the

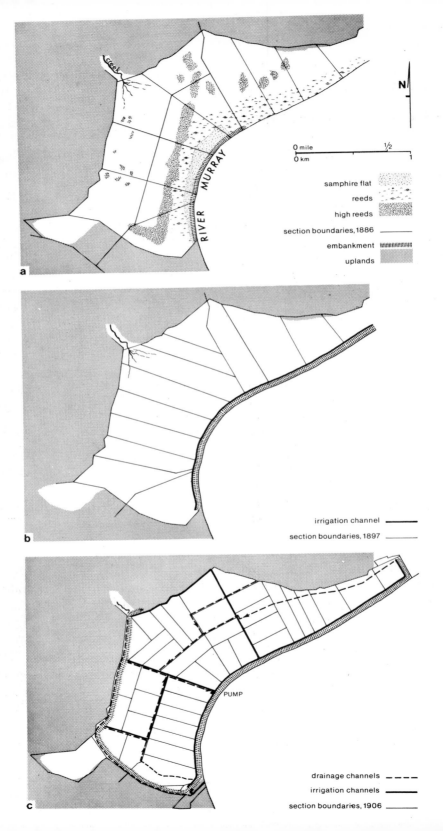

a

samphire flat
reeds
high reeds
section boundaries, 1886
embankment
uplands

b

irrigation channel
section boundaries, 1897

c

PUMP

drainage channels
irrigation channels
section boundaries, 1906

building of a low embankment which made it 'dry at ordinary low river'. Three new access roads were constructed into the swamp and the land was divided into 14 rectangular paddocks of between 32 and 56 acres in size. In 1897 the embankment was raised and strengthened and the swamp reclaimed sufficiently for irrigation. The sections were re-surveyed so that 11 of the 13 new blocks had a river frontage to allow the ingress of water (Fig. 72b). By 1906 the swamp was taken over by the Government for Closer Settlement. The embankment was extended around the southern and western sides of the swamp to preclude flooding from incoming streams, new irrigation channels and roads were constructed, and a pumping station installed to get rid of excess irrigation water. The swamp was surveyed for the third time, and the result was 28 sections ranging in size from 10 to 13 acres (Fig. 72c).

Figure 71 is an aerial view of Jervois Swamp and portions of the Wellington Swamp to the south, and the Wood's Point Swamp to the north. The swamp was unusual in its extensive area and in its early survey in 1841, with further subdivision in 1868. At this time the land was probably being used for summer grazing only. As the Jervois swamps are said to have been reclaimed in 1881 one must surmise that a low embankment was constructed alongside the river edge in order to exclude the water at flood time. In 1923, the area was purchased and subdivided for ex-servicemen, and, so that the largest number of farms possible could be accommodated in the space available, the sections were surveyed into strips (or 'bays') of three sizes: 3–4 acres, 8–10 and about 25 acres. The strips led from the river edge and back into the upland, where houses, barns, dairies and yards were situated. The result was, and is, a minute subdivision of the landscape and a distinctive settlement morphology. A linear pattern of houses stretches out along the junction of the high and the low ground to give a polder-like landscape. The impression is enhanced by the level, green swamp bays with their herds of black-and-white Friesian cattle. Numerous sluices in the embankment let the water into the swamp from where it drains gravitationally towards the Centre Drain which runs through the middle of the swamp and

---

FIG. 72. The transformation of the Mobilong Swamp, just north of Murray Bridge, a: 1886, b: 1897 and c: 1906. Based on records in the S.A. Lands Dept.

collects the surplus water which is pumped out of the swamp further downstream.

Upstream Irrigation

The Government's interest now began to move from the swamps upstream to the run-down Village Settlements. By 1905 only Lyrup, Kingston, Waikerie and Ramco remained of the original eleven Murray Village Settlements, with a total of 73 lessees and a population of little over 300. Even these settlements were having difficulties, and in 1908 the residents of Waikerie and Ramco requested the Government to assist in replacing the worn-out and obsolete pumping equipment. The Government was willing to grant the request provided more acres were planted with citrus orchards and drying vines in order that the fullest use would be made of the new pumping equipment. Ramco was joined to Waikerie and the total area of the combined settlements increased to 2,900 acres.[33] The immediate results were encouraging, and, as in the case of the swamp areas downstream, enthusiasm ran high. 'Water is the golden key that unlocked the lands of Western America' wrote Gordon in 1908, 'There is no reason why history should not be repeated in South Australia.'[34] Less flamboyant than Gordon's words, but a practical example of confidence, was the acquisition of 200 acres at Berri in 1909 for the establishment of a completely new irrigation scheme. In the succeeding years the Government took over and renovated the abandoned and run-down Village Settlements of Moorook, Kingston, Holder and New Era. The Cobdogla Irrigation Area was surveyed in 1912 and finally offered for lease in 1918. These government-initiated schemes were paralleled by many private developments, such as the irrigation of nearly 1,000 acres at Pyap and more than 2,000 acres in a large number of smaller ventures along the river. The concentration of activity around the great loop of the river was so marked that the Director of Irrigation commented in 1912 :

'We may look forward at no great distant date to see one continuous irrigation district from Overland Corner to beyond Renmark, with the back lands above the irrigation contours and within reasonable distance of the frontage for dry farming purposes.'[35]

The expansion of irrigation was facilitated by the Government in two ways. Legislation was passed which allowed the reservation of land alongside the river for irrigation and the expenditure of money on permanent improvement works. The Government was prepared to administer the schemes until development reached a stage where an Area Board with Local District Council powers could take over.[36] Secondly, and of importance not only to the upstream irrigation areas but also to the downstream swamps, there were moves to settle the interstate question of riparian rights, culminating in the River Murray Waters Agreement of 1914. This was necessary because of the irrigation already carried out and because of the prospect of new schemes. South Australia had to divest itself of the notion that navigation was a more important use of the River than irrigation. At the 1902 interstate conference on the use of the Murray water the South Australian delegate had all but excluded irrigation from his consideration. This emphasis on navigation can be partly explained by the fact that navigation was the one South Australian right to the river which was acknowledged by the other States. Moreover, the Federal constitution guaranteed the right to unfettered interstate trade. These were two legal aspects of the situation that were played to the full by South Australia and they explain the interest in navigation long after the river trade had dwindled to insignificant proportions. But the success of the swampland irrigation and the widespread irrigation activity in Victoria prompted a reappraisal of water resources. The Government pressed for the locking of the Murray not purely for navigational purposes now, but for the planning of irrigation schemes because locking helped to store water and to regulate river levels, an essential consideration in the embanking of swamps.[37] It also advocated the building of barrages across Lakes Alexandrina and Albert to stop the inflow of salt water up the river. From 1903 to 1910 negotiations with the other two States achieved very little,[38] but by 1911 agreement was reached on the development of the Lake Victoria storage which would supply South Australia during times of drought. Further meetings and further development of schemes followed,[39] and the interstate conference of 1914 finally culminated in the Murray Valley Waters Agreement of 1914 between the three States and the Commonwealth, which led to the creation of the Murray Valley Commission, defined storage and control projects, apportioned costs and distributed water withdrawals. From 1915 onwards, one can say that for the first time South Australia was confident of a minimum supply of water, and this assurance was a great impetus to the further expansion of irrigation after the First World War.

Landscape

The landscape created by the new irrigation areas in the Upper Murray was a very marked contrast to that which existed before. Figure 73 depicts the area of the Waikerie irrigation settlement. In 1893 the original Blocks, 7, 8, 9, of 3,683, 3,340 and 13,507 acres respectively, were surveyed across the undulating mallee-covered sand dunes. In 1895, portion of Block 8, between the floodable Hart's Lagoon and the cliff edge, and described as being of 'red sandy soil on clay', was cut up into twenty 10-acre sections for the new co-operative Village Settlement of Waikerie (Fig. 73a). Section 1, slightly larger than the rest, contained the residence of the Irrigation Commissioner and became the nucleus of the township. But the new sections were too small and by 1908 were enlarged by the annexation of the former common lands nearer to the river.[40]

By 1910 the Government took over the settlement and the adjoining Ramco settlements. Expansion was to the south in the sand dune area and the new irrigation channels snaked around the dunes (Fig. 73b). This resulted in an irregular and distinctive landscape pattern. As a result, certain areas could be irrigated but some proved too high, and, in fact, the full benefit of the channels was not achieved. By 1918, new channels were constructed in these non-irrigated areas and new subdivisions were made. The final map (Fig. 73c) shows the present position.

Soldier Settlement and Expansion

A new phase of government involvement leading to a great increase in the irrigated area arose out of the events of the First World War. Just as defence and recruitment were considered a national responsibility so was the re-establishment of the returned servicemen—particularly their resettlement on the land. The

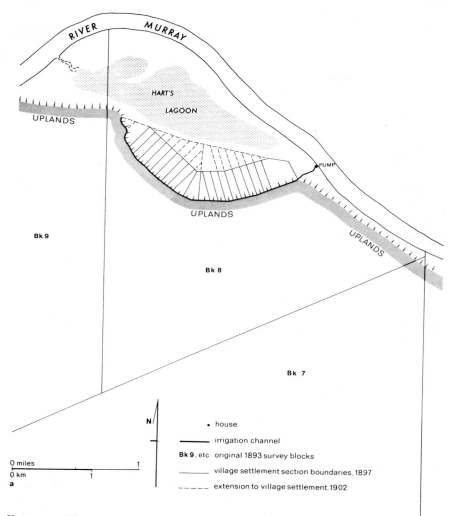

FIG. 73a. The transformation of the Waikerie irrigation area, 1890. Based on records in the S.A. Lands Dept.

states organized the settlement and the Commonwealth provided the funds. The Soldier Settlement legislation was an adaptation of the existing Closer Settlement legislation which had been so successful in the swamp reclamation schemes. After 1910 the Government had acquired powers for the compulsory purchase of large estates and the subsequent subdivision of the land into small

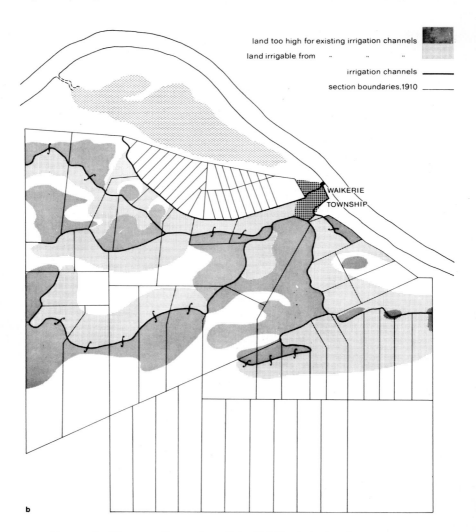

land too high for existing irrigation channels

land irrigable from   "   "   "

irrigation channels

section boundaries,1910

WAIKERIE
TOWNSHIP

b

FIG. 73b. The transformation of the Waikerie irrigation area, 1910.

blocks let on perpetual lease, and, after 1915, these powers were reserved exclusively for the purchase of land for the ex-service-men.[41]

New irrigation schemes were developed at Cobdogla (Loveday and Nookamka Divisions) Cadell and Chaffey (Ral Ral Division) and Waikerie after 1918, in addition to many smaller projects in the Upper Murray area such as the extension of Berri and

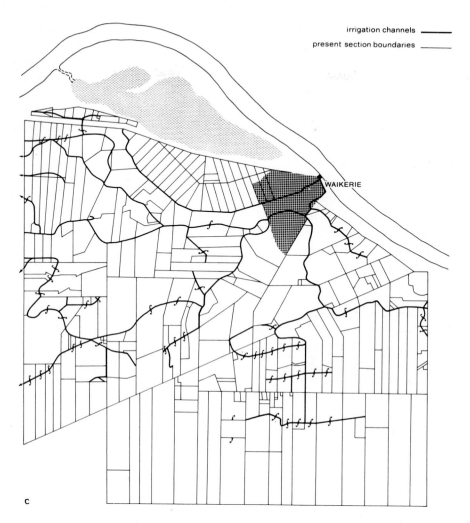

irrigation channels _____

present section boundaries _____

WAIKERIE

c

FIG. 73c. The transformation of the Waikerie irrigation area, 1965.

Moorook. Continued reclamation in the swamps also occurred at
Pompoota, Neeta, Wall, and Cowirra, all near Mannum, and
after 1924 at Baseby Flat, while the partially reclaimed swamps
nearest Lake Alexandrina at Wellington, Jervois and Woods
Point were re-subdivided and drained. In all cases the Government
paid for the major works, planted two-thirds of the ground (in the
upstream settlements), provided houses and made cash advances.

Soldier Settlement reached its peak of activity in 1923 and then slowed down as the number of ex-servicemen dwindled and the costs involved far exceeded the original estimates. After 1924 (when 1,068 settlers, including 587 returned soldiers, had been placed in the Upper Murray, and 241, including 56 returned soldiers, in the Lower Murray swamps), the Government decided to curtail expansion and to develop further areas only in special circumstances. By 1925, the losses on the schemes were estimated to exceed £3,000,000.[42]

The losses were the result of the over-expansion and optimism during a phase of high prices and ready markets during and immediately after the war, and the consequent failure to assess the practical economics of irrigation schemes. Optimism had been boundless once again; the Director of Irrigation calculated that between 110,000 and 160,000 acres of land were available for irrigation and that 'in the not too distant future the Murray Valley will carry a population equal to the present State population [560,925 in 1926] and yield an agricultural revenue equal to the present State revenue'.[43] Official government handbooks issued in 1926 still told of the opportunities offered by the river valley for 'thousands of additional settlers to make themselves at home'.[44] But in reality, by 1925, when the majority of the orchards and vineyards were coming into production, the local markets for dried fruit were saturated and overseas prices for most primary produce had fallen badly with a particularly severe effect on the River Murray irrigation settlements. The effects of these changes can be seen also in Fig. 66 which shows how the acreage of irrigation crops barely rose from 1925 to 1946.

It is not proposed to consider the intricacies of the Government's enormous involvement in Soldier Settlement Schemes once more after the Second World War as they are largely repetitious. However, a few points are of importance in this expansion. In the first place, South Australia felt that its quota of water, now assured since the building of the Hume Dam in the headwaters of the Murray, and other storages, allowed a greater expansion of irrigation than hitherto. A Committee appointed to consider the development of irrigation reported in 1941 that only about 25 per cent of the potential was being fulfilled. Secondly, a more satisfactory agreement was concluded with the Commonwealth

Government over the financing of the Soldier Settlement schemes compared with the almost haphazard arrangements which existed after the First World War.

Renewed government confidence led to a great increase in the acreage irrigated, which was concentrated around the great loop of the Murray at Loxton, Loveday and Cooltong. Over 8,000 acres were developed for irrigation, and consisting mainly of orchards but also of vineyards, with an increasing emphasis on wine grapes rather than drying grapes (Fig. 66). About 334 new holdings were created by 1955. The new settlement schemes were more successful than their predecessors because a sounder technical knowledge existed than ever before. Settlers were selected more carefully, market prospects for crops were investigated and surveys of blocks and plantings were carried out on a micro-scale so that every variation of soil and slope was taken into account to facilitate water or frost drainage.

While this expansion of government-sponsored irrigation along the Upper Murray was proceeding between 1945 and 1955 there was a parallel expansion of privately sponsored irrigation. The completion of the Barrages in 1940 and the conversion of Lakes Alexandrina and Albert to moderately fresh water allowed the enlargement of the irrigated pastures around the Lakes. The amount of land affected was not fully known until recent detailed returns were compiled showing that there were 3,477 acres in 1970. There has also been an enormous increase in private irrigation along the Upper Murray, particularly immediately west of Waikerie, much of it resulting from the acquisition of large estates by wineries which were pushed out of the vineyards in the vales south of Adelaide by the metropolitan sprawl.

The expansion of metropolitan Adelaide has also been responsible for the expansion of another irrigation area, this time away from the River Murray, in the Gawler Plains north of Adelaide. Here vegetable growers, displaced from the old market gardens of Lockleys, Campbelltown and Marion in the Adelaide Plains have established over 11,000 acres, dependent on sprinklers and pumped ground water.[45] Interestingly enough, this vegetable growing region covers roughly the same area as the 1896 proposals for an irrigation colony.

The Future of Irrigation

It seems unlikely that the areas of concentrated irrigation in the Gawler Plains and along the River Murray will get much larger in the future. In the Gawler Plains over-extraction of the ground water has led to an increase in salinity and a lowering of the sub-surface water levels with a consequent threat of invasion of the storage beds by sea water. Unless treated water from the metropolitan sewage works at Bolivar can either be pumped down into the ground or used for spray irrigation, it is difficult to see how the acreage can be maintained, let alone expanded.[46]

In the Murray Valley the future of irrigation seems equally as limited since total water extraction from the river is now at a critical level. The building of barrages and the consequent reduction of the salt content of the lower reaches of the river allowed the construction of pipelines to deliver domestic, stock and industrial supplies to many towns and rural areas. The first pipeline was from Morgan to Whyalla and Port Pirie. It was completed in 1944 and has recently been duplicated. A second was from Mannum to Adelaide, completed in 1961 and it is currently being supplemented by another pipeline from Murray Bridge. Two other pipelines have been completed recently running from Tailem Bend to Keith, in the Upper South-East, and from Swan Reach to the Barossa Valley. The demand which these pipelines serve is mainly domestic and industrial, and will rise with an expanding urban population, which in the Adelaide metropolitan area is expected to increase by 650,000 between 1970 and 1991, to reach a total of 1,814,000.[47]

In order to understand this critical balance between use and supply it is best to look first at the amount of water available. Under the Murray Valley Waters Agreement South Australia is entitled to an annual flow of 1,254,000 acre-feet. In most years the flow of the Murray exceeds this, but in some years it is dangerously close to it, and the 1,254,000 acre-feet must therefore be regarded as the practical planning and accounting limit. Out of the normal entitlement, a monthly total of 47,000 acre-feet (or 564,000 acre-feet per annum) must be allowed down the river to maintain flow, to prevent stagnation and saline blockages and as to compensate for evaporation losses.

From the remaining 690,000 acre-feet, approximately 350,000 acre-feet are already used for irrigation and it is thought that current plantings and a better system of licensing with metered withdrawals rather than the estimated withdrawals as at present will reveal a higher actual consumption nearer to 450,000 acre-feet, above which it must not rise. The limitation becomes more evident when one realizes that this leaves a margin of only 240,000 acre-feet available during a critical year. Already domestic, stock and industrial uses fluctuate between 30 and 100,000 acre-feet (the amount depending upon the rainfall in the Adelaide Hills catchments) and they are calculated to rise to 325,000 acre-feet by 1991.

No new licences to irrigate have been issued since 1968 and it is difficult to see any opportunity for increasing irrigation in the future, even when the South Australian entitlement is raised to 1,500,000 acre-feet with the building of the Dartmouth Dam storage on the headwaters of one of the Murray tributaries in Victoria. From the point of view of this study this limitation means that the rural irrigated area will not increase in size to become any more important than it is now.

The critical nature of the water supply problem is increased when the evaporation losses from Lakes Alexandrina and Albert (which are specifically excluded from the Murray Waters Agreement) are taken into account. Their total loss is between 500,000 and 700,000 acre-feet per annum. Increasingly, official thinking is that this loss of water is too great to be tolerated and that in future a new barrage should be built across the Murray at Wellington and the lakes allowed to become salt. What would happen to the irrigation areas around the lakes if such a course of action were taken, is not easy to see. It might be too costly to irrigate them by a reticulated water system and the irrigation landscape might be reduced in size as these areas were phased-out of intensive production.

In contrast to this stagnation and ever potential decline in the size of the irrigated areas, that other, and most artificial landscape of man's creation, the metropolitan area of Adelaide, will increase in size and importance. With its well-watered parks and domestic gardens, maintained in a luxuriant and lush growth throughout the four or five dry summer months by water pumped from the

River Murray, Adelaide will become the largest irrigation area in South Australia. The domestic landscape preferences of a people derived predominantly from the well-watered margins of North Western Europe are being reproduced in a semi-arid environment, one of the closest geographical analogies to which is Algeria on the edge of the Sahara Desert.

6. Notes

1. K. A. Wittfogel, 'The hydraulic Civilizations', in *Man's role in changing the face of the earth* (1956), ed. W. L. Thomas, Jr. 152–164.
2. Anon., *Our inheritance in the Hills* (1889);
   Anon., *The South-Eastern District of South Australia in 1880* (1881).
3. *The Adelaide Observer* (25 August 1883).
4. A. R. Wallace, *Land nationalisation, its necessity and its aims* (1882);
   H. George, *Progress and poverty* (1883).
5. J. B. Hirst, 'G. W. Cotton and the Workingmen's Blocks', unpublished B.A. Hons. thesis, University of Adelaide (1963);
   the blocks were created under *Act*, 363/1885, Crown Lands Amendment Act.
6. *The Adelaide Observer* (19 May and 4 August 1888).
7. See J. Rutherford, 'Interplay of American and Australian ideas for the development of water projects in Northern Victoria', *Ann. Ass. Amer. Geog.*, LIV (1964), 88.
8. SGO, 5970/1884 (in); and 7044/1884 (in).
9. *SAPP*, 158 (1884); and 73 (1885).
10. *SAPD* (L.C.) (1884), cols. 1300 and 1690.
11. *SAPP*, 73A (1885).
12. *SAPD* (H.A.) (1887), cols. 251–63 and 299–314.
13. D. J. Gordon, *Handbook of South Australia: progress and resources* (1908), 220;
    H. J. Scott, *South Australia in 1887–8; a handbook for the Centennial International Exhibition, Melbourne, 1888* (1888), 73.
14. *SAPP*, 25 (1889).
15. *SAPD* (H.A.) (1888), cols. 1267 and 1496; (1889), col. 246.
16. *Act*, 599/1894, Lake Bonney Settlement Act.
    See also *SAPP*, 86 (1892); 135 (1893); and 73 (1894) for details.
17. *SAPD* (L.C.) (1894), col. 2535;
    Act, 584/1893, Crown Lands Amendment Act.

18. *SAPP*, 156 and 157 (1893);
    Act, 578/1893, Renmark Irrigation Trust Act.
19. *SAPP*, 110 (1892); 37 (1899).
20. *SAPP*, 113 (1895);
    Act, 627/1895, Village Settlements and Reduction of Rents Act.
21. *SAPP*, 37 (1900);
    The Report of the Interstate Waters Conference (1902), 24.
    See also H. J. Finnis, 'Village Settlements on the River Murray', *Proc. Roy. Geog. Soc. S.A.*, LX (1959), 87.
22. *SAPP*, 111 (1896);
    Act, 668/1896, Gawler Plains Irrigation Act;
    SAPD (H.A.) (1896), 932–3 and 939.
23. *Act*, 688/1897, Closer Settlement Act;
    Act, 802/1902, Crown Lands Amendment Act.
24. A. J. Perkins, 'Irrigation on the Murray: utilisation of the swamp lands', *SAJA*, VI (1902–3), 492.
25. For these experiments and other earlier ones in 1851 near Wellington see *SAPP*, 90 (1860), qus. 331, 346, 510 and 511. The reclamation of the swamps was first thought of for producing fruit and dairy items for the river steamers.
26. SGO, 7608/1884 (in).
27. S. McIntosh, 'Irrigation and reclamation', *SAJA*, XV (1911–12), 812.
28. *SAPP*, 10 (1905), 15.
29. *SAPP*, 10 (1909), 17.
30. D. J. Gordon *The 'Nile' of Australia, nature's gateway to the Interior* (1908), 50–1.
31. *SAPP*, 86 (1913).
32. *SAPP*, 10 (1909), 17; 10 (1910), 18.
33. *SAPP*, 10 (1909), 18; 10 (1910), 19.
34. D. J. Gordon, *Handbook of South Australia: progress and resources* (1908), 218.
35. S. McIntosh, 'Irrigation and reclamation', *SAJA*, XV (1911–12), 809.
    See also D. J. Gordon and J. V. H. Ryan (eds.), *Handbook of South Australia* (1914), 158 for similar comments.
36. *Act*, 953/1908, Irrigation and Reclaimed Lands Act.
37. *SAPP*, 10 (1906), 15. The Surveyor-General in his report said, 'Until the question of locking the river has been definitely settled and the position and heights of the various locks decided, it would not be advisable to attempt any reclamation works above Mannum, and in fixing the height of the locks, the question of water levels ought to be very carefully considered as by high locks enormous areas of our swamp lands could be inundated and rendered useless'.

38. *SAPP*, 55 (1903); 59 (1905); 79 (1905); 25 (1906); 29 (1910).

39. *SAPP*, 37 (1911); 16 (1912); 60 (1913); 65 (1913).

40. SGO, 283/1902 (in).

41. H. Lelacheur, 'War Service Land Settlement in South Australia', un-published M.A. thesis, University of Adelaide (1968), particularly Ch. 1.

42. Aust New Zea. Ass. Adv. Sci., *Handbook of South Australia* (1924), 54; *SAPP*, 10 (1925), 5; and 69 (1925).

43. A. J. Perkins, 'The rise and progress of the South Australian fruit growing areas on the River Murray', *SAJA*, XXV (1925–26), 496.

44. Anon., *South Australian handbook of information for settlers, tourists and others*, 5th edition (1926), 87.

45. D. L. Smith, 'Market Gardening at Adelaide's Urban Fringe', *Econ. Geog.*, XLII (1966), 19.

46. *North Adelaide Plains: progress information on the ground-water situation, Jan. 1969*, Department of Mines, Adelaide, (1969);
    R. G. Shepard, 'The hydrology of the North Adelaide Plains Basin', *Mining Review*, Dept. of Mines, No. 125 (Dec. 1966).

47. This section on the future of irrigation is based on:
    (a) *Annual Reports of the Engineering and Water Supply Department, S.A.* (1962–69) and the *River Murray Commission Reports* (1918–69);
    (b) H. L. Beaney, 'Water for South Australia', *S.A. Education Gazette* (1 Oct. 1970), 3–12, from which the projection of future demand has been obtained;
    (c) personal communication with officers of the Engineering and Water Supply Department, Adelaide.

7
Changing the Soil

Soils are not always to be correctly judged from appearance, even by the most experienced eye'. *SAPP*, 20 (1868–69), app. VIII.

'The farmer, to successfully co-operate with an environment which is not always smiling must be resourceful and provident, and have initiative, keenness of perception and personal experience, or the ability to apply the experience of others.' R. W. Peacock, in *Report of the First Interstate Dry Farming Conference*, Adelaide (1911), 90.

The previous chapters on surveying, clearing, draining and irrigating all dealt with obvious, visible and tangible facets of man's making of the landscape, and thereby of the creation of new geographical arrangements. All of these activities have taken place as an outcome of rural settlement and colonization, in order to grow crops and graze animals. Throughout the preceding discussion, however, one important change in the landscape has been either subsumed or ignored—that is, the resultant change in the character of the soil. Admittedly the fact that the soil could be modified, almost as an accidental side-effect of human action and 'interference', has been recognized in the discussion on exhaustion and over-cropping, clearing and erosion, draining and shrinkage, and irrigation and rising salt. But the purposive changes in the soil environment through fertilizing, fallowing, the rectification of trace-element deficiencies, and the introduction of leguminous plants to restore and raise fertility, all of which have been instrumental in altering the landscape to a greater or lesser degree, have not been explored. The simple fact is that Australian soils are poor and infertile (none more so than South Australia) and there is a widespread distribution of podzolized, laterized and solonized soils, usually deficient in phosphorus, in nitrogen and often in other minor but essential elements and nutrients. In the rectification of these deficiencies lies the clue to much of what we see around us.

Clearly, an investigation into changing the soil takes one into the sphere of resource appraisal as well as of resource use. What did officials and farmers think of the environment of South Australia; what was 'actual' and what was perceived; what were the farmers' attitudes to the soil and how did these affect it; what mode of farming did they adopt, and what did they learn about the environment that in turn affected their mode of farming? The ideas contained in such questions are not new; they have been implicit in what has been written already but in this discussion on soils they have an undeniably important role in the explanation of landscape changes. Such a treatment involves the history of agriculture and ecological change brought about by technological innovation, adaptation and introduction, but the object in view is to select those aspects of history and ecology which will highlight man's role in learning about and changing the soil, and which, in turn, played a part in the evolution of the South Australian landscape through the extension and intensification of the landscape.

Six main phases and associated themes stand out for consideration and form a ready framework for understanding how the character of the soil was understood and how the soil was changed. These six phases straddle, and yet, in a sense, unite a number of themes more fully developed by others : for example, Callaghan's and Millington's schema for delineating the metamorphosis of farm land in Australia, Donald's periods of adaptive and purposive change to the environment, and Dunsdorfs' themes of the development of wheat growing. A finer division has been used here than by any of the other authors, but the common ground and coincidence of dates of significant change can be seen from Table XIV.

First, there was a period of initial assessment of the environment which began in 1836 with first settlement and lasted until about 1850. During these years, ideas were formed about the soils and climate, and there was a gradual recognition of differences of

Table XIV

Themes of Agricultural Change

Year	Williams	Callaghan and Millington	Donald	Dunsdorfs
1970				
1960	'A valuable weed'	Permanent system (Pasture phase)	Favourable change	International domination and Governmental intervention
1950				
1940	Exploitation to conservation			
1930	'When our soils have gone we too must go'		Maladaptation to the environment	Rapid expansion
1920		Temporary system (Wheat phase)		
1910				
1900	Phosphates fallows and parasites			
1890			Mainly disadvantageous change	Declining yield
1880		Pioneering phase (Sheep pasture)		
1870	Falling yields and dying stock			Insufficient expansion
1860				
1850				
1840	Initial assessment			
1830				
	Changing the soil	Metamorphosis of farm land	Attempted adaptation and purposive change of environment	Australian wheat-growing

Source: Based on Callaghan and Millington (1956); Donald (1965); Dunsdorfs (1956).

soil type and fertility, which led to the selection of the more favourable areas for agriculture. Undoubtedly, however, it was the climate which most impressed the pioneers and suggested limitations to agriculture, and the significance of the soil was underestimated and not understood. During this initial appraisal an exploitive system of wheat farming had evolved in South Australia, and, as settlement expanded northwards between about 1855 and the droughts of 1881 the theme of exploitation became more marked. Acreage increased enormously but yields declined (Fig. 74). A parallel theme during the early part of this phase was the recognition of coast disease in stock. This problem while not solved at this time did lead to a closer look at the quality of the soil and its cause was later identified as a deficiency in soil micronutrients. From about 1880 to 1900, there followed a period of reassessment during which soil deficiencies, particularly of phosphorus, were recognized and rectified, but the true cause of coast disease still eluded the scientists. The practice of fallowing for nitrogen release and moisture conservation also became firmly established during these years.

The pattern of thrust, pause and reassessment was repeated during the next half century when superphosphates and fallowing created a new confidence that the character of the soil was understood and that climatic limitations were less important than previously assumed. But drought and economic adversity coincided with a widespread deterioration of the environment through soil exhaustion and erosion, a result of the rapid breakdown of soil organic matter and soil structure after frequent fallowing. From the mid-1930s until after the Second World War there was a significant change of attitude as conservation and regional concentration replaced exploitation and expansionism, and the need to make the best of the soils within the known climatic limits was recognized. Finally, since 1945, the widespread introduction of pasture crops has stabilized the soil, renewed and boosted its fertility by increasing its nitrogen content and has caused a radical change in the mode of farming. Closely associated with this change has been the opening-up with the recognition of widespread deficiencies in trace-elements, of the last areas of unsettled and 'difficult' land in the high-rainfall parts of South Australia—in Kangaroo Island, the Upper South-East, the ranges in the Lower South-East and the tips of Eyre, Yorke and Flerieu Peninsulas.

That all these innovations and discoveries relating to the soil had their beginnings and were first elaborated in Australia—in the State of South Australia—heightens their significance for this study of man's fashioning of the landscape.

Initial Assessment

Sir John Morphett's recollection, on arriving with a party of immigrants at Port Adelaide in 1836, of 'the disconcerted and dismal look with which most of the first party regarded, from the deck of the ship, the dried and scorched appearance of the plains, which to their English ideas, betokened little short of barrenness' contained all the ingredients of the pioneers' appraisal of the environment during the opening years of settlement.[1] Although a Mediterranean type of climate had been inferred for this part of southern Australia from the observations of the earliest explorers, the summer season still came as a shock to the English mind, and it took many years of experiment by the cultivators to fit their traditional agricultural practices into the new regime of seasons. The process of acquiring local knowledge still continued into 1840 and the facts of climate were dominant in this learning process.[2] This was not surprising, for, as Karen Moon points out in her review of early perception and appraisal of the South Australian landscape, climatic matters were readily experienced and easily observed and therefore written about copiously. From 1840 onwards, the detail and the description of the climatic characteristics had been amassed sufficiently, so that, after 1845, explanations of changing weather patterns were advanced in terms of latitude, elevation, aspect, nearness to the sea and the interior.[3]

Soils, on the other hand, received much less attention than did the climate which impinged so markedly upon the English mind. Nearly every early report was enthusiastic about the soils on the east side of Gulf St Vincent, but consistently submerged soil evaluation in a description of the vegetation and a discussion of the aesthetics of the scenery. Knowledge of the soils advanced slowly, therefore, and it was not until 1846 that the initial impression of the sameness of the soil in all areas was dispelled and Dutton could say that the soil 'varies, as it does all over the world'. Most writers agreed that the Adelaide Plains consisted of 'rich', 'reddish' soils underlain by limestone, with black organic alluvium in the valleys and near to the creeks. The soil was:

> 'Not to be surpassed by any in the world; a plough may in places be driven through it for miles without the slightest obstruction; not even a pebble being met with'.[4]

The coast was 'sandy', and 'brown' and 'stoney' soils were said to cover the Mount Lofty Ranges.

In the absence of any accurate soil analysis, fertility was often described in terms of the vegetation; for example, Morphett said that blue gums were 'a sign of good land', a point reiterated by Chauncey in 1849 when he said that 'the character of the soil may be judged by the trees found growing on it'. Such reasoning goes a long way to explain the comments of the reporter of the *South Australian Register* who witnessed a ploughing match on open ground near Salisbury in 1851 where 'the fine, rich mellow soil was revealed for the first time'. He could only wonder why 'the greatest part of these plains had been passed over by settlers choosing land'.[5] But climate was still an important element in the explanation of any observed soil characteristic. Advice to maintain and increase yields by manuring was met by a stubborn prejudice as 'no one dared to manure land, as the hot winds would be sure to blight the grain just as it was ripening', and when new land was broken up in the Willunga, Para and Gawler districts and produced good crops averaging 22–25 bushels per acre during the first year, the change was attributed to the reduced incidence of hot summers and of the 'sirocco blight', not to the nitrogen released from the virgin soil.[6]

Falling Yields and Dying Stock

Expansion and Exploitation

The first thoughts about the soil, other than those about its colour, texture and vegetation cover were prompted by the concern that the high yields attained during the early years of farming would decline with exploitive farming. In 1846, Dutton attacked the poor agricultural practices then evident, and thought that it was 'high time that the farmers . . . should bestir themselves' to use artificial manure and to stop burning straw, and apply it to the land instead, in order 'to call forth the full energies of those mineral manures contained in the soil'. The lack of manuring was consistently attributed to the scarcity of manure; because it was not necessary to house stock during the mild winters their droppings were not easily collected. In any case, there was so much natural pasture available that there was no need to cultivate root-crops or English grasses and cart them back to the stock-yard and stall, another fact which worked against the collection of manure. Some farmers did adopt a form of fallowing by grazing horses and cattle on the 'self sown stuff' that grew after the harvest in January, and then they ploughed it in during the succeeding winter so that the ground was ready for the next crop. Others practised a more complex fallow and rotational system of intermixed fallow, cropping and grazing, but the system involved a great deal of labour and tillage. Such rotations were not common, and, as early as 1851, Lancelott could say that 'most Australian farmers pursue the unsure system of growing nothing but wheat year after year until the soil is "run out".' Inevitably, the 'overwrought land' required protracted fallowing and manurial dressings sooner or later, and yields declined so badly on the Adelaide Plains that trench ploughing to 'turn up some virgin soil' was being resorted to.[1]

Obviously, the early 1850s were the beginning of what Meinig has called 'a new kind of farming' in which the ideal of a self-supporting peasantry, carefully maintaining soil fertility and keeping stock, was replaced by a commercial view of farming for the production of one commodity for profit—a change which reached its apogee after 1869 when the credit selection system allowed easy expansion and sundered any emotional ties to the land that might possibly have existed. The transition between the two ideas of farming was not sudden, and it is doubtful to what extent the theoretical ideals of labour-intensive smallholdings ever existed. In 1862, Sinnett still talked of 'peasant proprietors', but noted that many were utilizing their spare time and their drays for carting wood, stores, and ores between the mines, the ports and Adelaide in order to earn money for essential commodities, often food, which they did not produce on their own farms.[8]

What happened about farming practices and attitudes during the 1850s and 1860s is not known exactly, but the high average yields of the early years dropped slowly with the movement of farmers into the Central Hill Country and areas of less reliable rainfall and inherently less fertile soils. Indicative of this decline in yield was the move, throughout the early 1850s, to import guano found on Flinders Island in Bass Strait.[9] But little was done, and the fertility of large areas was depleted 'for the lack of timely attention to the warnings of science'. Many people offered advice, particularly the local 'experts' who were influenced by the European experience of the well-tilled small farm. As early as 1862, Andrews, the editor of *The Farm and the Garden* despaired of the farmers' resistance to advice, and it was a theme which was to be repeated throughout the rest of the century and still rings true today :

'. . . farmers are communicative enough in ordinary conversation, though they exert themselves so little in diffusing information either at club meetings or through the medium of published letters. We have seldom talked to an intelligent cultivator of the soil without learning something from him; and we are convinced that the habit of diffusing information through more extended channels is only wanting to effect its very general circulation.'[10]

He was right, they did have something to say, but they usually said it to each other. Farming was a practical art which tended to be learnt through trial and error and conversation with neighbours, and, at this stage, it could not be learnt from books and newspapers and by taking the advice of 'outsiders' and 'experts'.

The mean yields of wheat (indicated by the quin-quennial values in Fig. 74) continued to fall. They were affected particularly by the drought of 1865–66 when the yield dropped to 8·74 bushels per acre, but more so by the incidence of rust in wheat in 1867–68 when the yield dropped to 4·69 bushels per acre. The Royal Commission appointed to inquire into diseases in cereals attempted to evaluate the relative importance of farming practice, disease, climate and soil in the incidence of rust, and concluded that it was a fungoid disease little affected by any of the other factors.

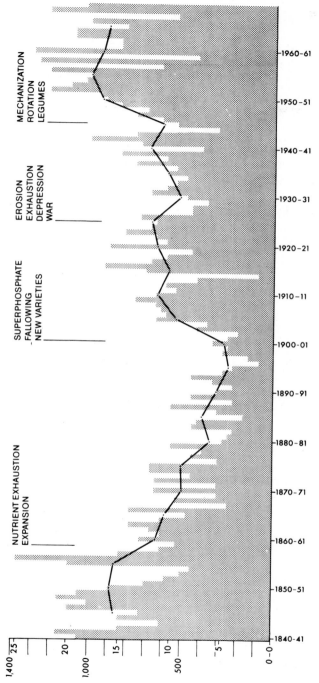

FIG. 74. Annual wheat yields and quinquennial running mean, 1839/40–1966/67. (*S.A. Stat. Reg.*)

Nevertheless, the answers to questionnaires sent out to 638 farmers showed that of the 978 paddocks enumerated, 652 were cropped without interruption, 50 per cent for at least three years without rest, 25 per cent for between four and six years and 25 per cent for longer periods, the longest being twenty-six years at Mount Barker.[11] Fallowing was known but not widely used; there were 153,727 acres of fallow to 801,571 acres of cropland at this time, a ratio of about 1 : 6.

The Commission commented, however, on the lack of knowledge about the soil and on the fact that only about half a dozen analyses had been made, 'so that science, so far, [had] lent practically no aid at all in instructing South Australian farmers as to the adaptation of their lands to the growth of particular crops'. Yet, the Commissioners were convinced that a vast tract of wheat country was gradually being robbed of its 'phosphorus and other constituents' which were essential to healthy growth, and that there was scarcely anything in the form of manure being returned to the soil, 'leading to a sure diminuation of average yield'.[12] But so long as the decline in yield could be offset by increasing the acreage of the farm, and the labour costs reduced by increased use of machines, the adverse effects of the farming system were ignored. The stripper, invented in South Australia in 1846, was used widely, and by 1867–68, 89 per cent of the wheat crop was harvested by machinery which had its effect on yields. The Government Statistician said a few years before:

'. . . the main cause of the low average . . . yield is that much land is sown with wheat which is not of the description best adopted for the successful cultivation in ordinary seasons of that cereal—a state of things doubtlessly owing to the numerous small freeholders and tenant farmers being compelled, whatever the situation or the nature of the soil, to cultivate the crop raised with the least labour, and capable of being gathered by machine.'[13]

Nothing changed, however, and the level of the yields throughout the 1870s was barely maintained because of the rapid expansion of the area under crop, from 556,687 acres in 1869–70 to 1,750,971 acres in 1880–81. When Anthony Trollope passed through the northern wheat areas during the autumn of 1873 he said :

'The ordinary cockatoo [small-farmer] knows nothing of the word fallow and attempts to produce nothing but wheat. Year after year he puts in his seed upon the same acreage and year after year he takes off his crop . . . He does his work without any attempt to collect manure or to give back to the land anything in return for what he takes from it. He even burns the stubble from his fields finding it to be easier to do so than to collect it that it may rot and then be ploughed in . . . He ploughs and reaps and sells; and ploughs and reaps and sells again. He employs his energies in the one occupation with no diversification of interest.'14

Trollope was reasonably accurate in his description, although his use of, and emphasis upon, words like 'fallow', 'manure' and 'diversification' was clearly influenced by his knowledge of English agricultural practices and by the advice that the local experts were ladelling out at the time.

The need to isolate and investigate the problems, both real and imagined, which were besetting agriculture, and to disseminate knowledge was taken up in 1874 when Sir Henry Ayers suggested the establishment of a Department of Agriculture, as Victoria had just done, and New South Wales was contemplating doing.15 But the ensuing debate in the House revealed the deep cleavage of views between those who felt that science had a contribution to make and those who believed nothing could surpass 'practical experience'. Nevertheless, a Commission was appointed to examine the best means of providing agricultural and technical education, and it recommended the establishment of a Department of Agriculture, a number of experimental farms in new areas of settlement, and a model farm, all under the supervision of a Professor of Agriculture, who would have sufficient staff and facilities for the collection and distribution of information, and for research and education in agricultural matters.16 In that very year *The Garden and the Field*, under the energetic editorship of Molineux, began publication in an attempt to circulate information among people interested in agriculture, but even its editorial comment at this time was very disparaging of the Commission's Report; 'We do not suppose anything will come of the matter . . . the idea suggested in one's mind by the term professor is a large salary, a lot of red tape and an easy chair'.[17]

The lack of enthusiasm for scientific knowledge and the means for its dissemination is not difficult to understand when the success of the rapid expansion in the Northern Areas, based on folk experimentation, is remembered. By trial and error the farmers had settled the region despite all the forecasts of the experts. Even more than before, the farmer regarded himself as a 'self-made man', and his land as a business investment which had been acquired for relatively little outlay and which was being made to yield a profit. Locally invented machinery, shallow and minimal seed-bed preparation, and the provision by the Government of railways and jetties, all kept down costs by minimizing labour requirements. Abundant virgin land at £1 per acre on credit helped to maintain yields by enabling a constant increase in farm size. Goyder had warned of this dangerous trend towards a kind of 'shifting cultivation' after seeing what had happened in Victoria :

'it may be a question how far much of the legislation in land almost offers a premium to the exhaustion of the soil by giving new or virgin soil in exchange for worked-out land. It is not difficult to suppose that too liberal land regulations may not so much induce fresh immigration as a shifting population from a locality partially exhausted to another with a similar soil in a state of nature, for it cannot be denied that under a system of liberal credit, with small cash payments, opportunity is given to the selector to abandon his holding when it is cropped out, not only without loss, but as a matter of fact, with great profit to himself.[18]

In every way the advice of the self-styled experts was rejected. Diversification distracted attention from wheat which was profitable to grow and simple to cultivate. Rotations did the same thing as they implied stock rearing, and manuring on the scale needed to have any effect was impossible without large flocks and herds. Thorough tillage was also less economic than 'scratchings'. Agricultural experts and of agricultural information were neglected with an indifference and disdain that was as 'reprehensible as it was unaccountable'.[19] So long as deficient yields could be made up by expanding into new areas the farmers stubbornly refused to indulge in the theoretical improvements, particularly as they could point already to a remarkable record of change and experiment in the form of adaptation to new seasonal regimes, new tillage techniques, new implements and the whole array of settlement facilities throughout the Northern Areas, all of which the pundits had declared impossible.

However, the drought of 1880–84 brought the unlimited expansion to an abrupt and harsh end, and the low yields of the 1870s were now depressed still further to 4·96, 4·57 and 4·21 bushels per acre in 1880–81, 1881–82, and 1882–83 respectively (Fig. 74). It was slowly dawning on the minds of the more thoughtful that folk experimentation had gone about as far as it could, and that the limits of settlement had been learnt. Now the need was to assess carefully the capability of the land within the known limits of rainfall and this meant learning about the soil. A scientific basis for farming was necessary, but how to break down the attitudes of over forty years' exploitation and expansion, how to awaken the farmers from 'the stagnation under which they now labour—no meetings for the discussion of farming topics, no lectures, no clubs or anything else'[20]—these were the problems that troubled the minds of thoughtful men.

Coast Disease

The copper–cobalt deficiency in the soil in some of the areas of early pastoral settlement in the high-rainfall areas of Eyre and Yorke Peninsulas and parts of the South-East produced severe losses of stock. Because of the location of the affected areas, and because of the way this deficiency showed in the stock the affliction became known as 'Coast disease'. This was an unfortunate name which for a long time misled investigations into its cause, and delayed the acquisition of knowledge about the soil.

In 1861 the Government Inspector of Runs, described the disease as follows :

'On the coastline from about ten to fifteen miles back the stock on many of the runs are subject to what is there termed the coast disease, generally attributed to a poisonous herb, but I believe it has never been determined what it is. Sheep sometimes die very suddenly, and in great numbers, at other times they linger long previous to death. Cattle are affected but not to the same extent, though at times there has been great mortality among them. Strange to say, horses do not appear to die from it, but get a disease of the legs which brings off the whole hair.'[21]

The Inspector of Runs had been outlining conditions in the South-East where the disease was more serious and more widespread than elsewhere. Here the pastoral stations were situated on the trace-element deficient calcareous sands of the 'ranges' which stood above the surrounding flooded flats, and therefore stock were restricted to the poor pastures of the worst affected areas (Fig. 75a). Sir Samuel Davenport and George Glen, who held the Mayurra Run situated on the narrow ridge between the Wyrie Swamp and the flats at the north end of Lake Bonney, suffered badly from the loss of stock. In the latter part of 1848 they asked Ferdinand von Mueller, a chemist who had recently arrived in Adelaide, to collect and identify plant specimens, in the hope that he might find the cause of the disease. He found nothing noxious but made the astute suggestion that the grass was deficient in nutrients and recommended the removal of stock from 'infected' to 'unaffected' pastures; this proved beneficial if done frequently enough (Fig. 75b).[22]

It is not surprising that the one obviously unusual aspect of the South-East—the flooded flats stretching away for miles on end—came to be regarded as the cause of the disease, which was likened to malaria. After surveying and assessing for rating purposes all the runs in South Australia, and noting the incidence of the disease and foot rot[23] Goyder reported that the disease was unknown near parts of the coast 'where there are well defined water courses or natural outlets to drain the country'. But the disease was present invariably where there were

'no defined water courses to drain the adjacent country and where the water is deposited in large swamps or basins having no regular outlet and where vegetable decomposition takes place and miasmata so rapidly generated in a climate such as ours . . . It is only necessary to experience the effusion arising from the disturbed surface at the edge of the swamp to readily

FIG. 75a. Coast disease. The effect on animals.

FIG. 75b. The effect of adding trace-elements to pastures, South-East of South Australia. The natural pasture is on the left and plots with trace-elements of copper added, are on the right; that on the extreme right is growing a clover crop.

comprehend how injurious such exhalations must necessarily be to animal life.[24]

This was a widely held view and 'coastiness' and 'rot' were attributed to the 'vegetable putridity of the surface of the soil'.[25]

The outcome was that Goyder recommended the establishment of a comprehensive system of drainage in the South-East and during the next five years draining was begun (see pp. 187–191) It had little effect on 'coastiness', and when the *Select Committee on Drainage Works* met in 1872 a typical question to a witness, and his answer were: 'Do you think, Mr Johnson, that there has been any diminution in the coast disease since the country has been drained?—I tell you the coast disease is as bad as ever and I am a great sufferer by it . . . but what is the cause of it I do not know.'[26]

Mr Johnson's perplexity was well founded; the swamp explanation was obviously not valid. The editor of the *Border Watch*, a shrill critic of the Government, had never believed completely in this explanation, although he had used it as an additional weapon to induce the government to spend money on draining. But he could think of nothing 'more telling against our progress in agricultural knowledge than the existence in our midst of coast disease for the last 20 years without ever a serious attempt having been made to find out what it was or provide a remedy'. Probably as a result of this outburst Dr Muecke of Tanunda was persuaded to do field work in the South-East, and, after discarding quickly the noxious-plant theory, discovered that there was an over-abundance of salt and iodine in the soil of the affected herbage. He suggested, therefore, that the remedy lay in improving the soil itself, by manuring or by ploughing which would 'drive away the coast disease'. In addition he thought that 'hospital paddocks' sown to lucerne or wild oats, and trough water in which was dissolved sulphate of iron and a little citric acid with 'a few bitter herbs such as juniper berries and then coal dust' would be beneficial.[27]

Although the correct diagnosis and cure were far away, further careful observation helped to elucidate some of the characteristics of the disease. Ward noted that similar effects on stock were reported from the Western District of Victoria and even beyond

Melbourne, but in all places the disease seemed to assume its severest form on the dry lands from August to November, or in the spring season, when the feed grew quickly after the rains, especially on the light warm sandy soils. This, Ward thought, favoured the theory that the origin of the disease lay in the poverty of the feed at certain times and on particular soils; but, at any rate, he felt that :

> 'Something ought to be done to prove the bane, in order that the antidote may be supplied. The disease renders a large tract of country comparatively valueless for grazing purposes, and the cost of detecting its origin—and surely that is not impossible—would be money well expended in the interests of the community generally.'[28]

But there was no concerted effort to combat stock deaths and deterioration during the 1870s and 1880s when South Australian attention was focused firmly on the drive to the Northern Areas, on the fortunes of wheat growing, and, later, on the devastating effects of the droughts. Farmers merely learnt to prevent excessive deterioration in stock by the constant movement of sheep from 'infected' to 'hospital' paddocks within the framework of enlarged holdings.[29]

Coast disease was another limitation of the environment that had been learnt about but was far from being completely understood. Unlike the problem of declining yields its solution lay a long way off, for the character of the soil still had to be identified as the causal factor.

Phosphates, Fallows and Parasites

Writing in 1904, A. J. Perkins looked back over the progress of agriculture during the previous twenty-five years. He said that it was

> '. . . now a matter of history that with us agriculture in the past tended much, to our cost, to overstep the northerly boundaries fixed by Nature . . . In particular of our now historic error it may well be said that it is only recent times that have clearly defined to us the limitations of our climatic

conditions . . . and while there is no earthly influence that can apparently modify local climate, the farmer who can handle his own soil with judgement has the making of it in his own hands.'[30]

Undoubtedly the years between 1880 and 1905 were a period of reassessment and research. The 'historic error' and the recognition of climatic limitations, combined with the ever declining yield, eventually caused a marked change in the emphasis of farming from expansion to the 'handling' of the soil. Already the scepticism of the editor of *The Garden and the Field* about professors and colleges had changed to active enthusiasm,[31] and the new College and experimental farm were approved by the Government, and land acquired at Roseworthy in 1879. By the time the droughts of the 1880s were under way, J. D. Custance had been appointed the first Principal.

Superphosphate

It is clear that Custance's initial task was to prove the value of Roseworthy and this he attempted to do by conducting a series of experiments which showed the beneficial effects of fertilizers on wheat yields. That such experiments were necessary was surprising, since Laws and Gilbert at Rothamstead had proved the value of superphosphate as far back as 1857.[32] But the South Australian farmer had evolved a different sort of agriculture based on expansionism; Roseworthy and Rothamstead were of no interest and were equally distant from his mind as each other. In order to make an impact on the farming community, Custance first had to dispel many prejudices about fertilizer and a deep-seated hostility to 'advice'. It was not as though artificial fertilizers were unknown. Superphosphate of lime was available in small quantities, but was a manure the nature of which 'not one in a hundred perhaps of our farmers know anything about'. Nitrate of soda, bone dust and particularly guano, which was mined in small quantities in South Australia,[33] were perhaps better known but little used as they were 'dear, scarce and in a degree uncertain in their action'.[34] Basically, there was deep distrust of artificial fertilizers.

As could have been foreseen, the experiments at Roseworthy,

which began in 1882, confirmed the value of bone dust and guano. Yields of 26 bushels per acre (compared with a State average of only 4·21 bushels) underlined the need for phosphorus and nitrogen to increase yield. Custance was at pains to break down the widely-held theory that the fertilizers were ineffective because of the lack of humidity. The season of 1882–83 was very dry and the experiments proved 'if any proof be required, that it is not *altogether* the season that is the cause of bad crops'. His experiments had one other result which was to be significant later on as he demonstrated that yields rose and that harvesting was easier if the seed was drilled rather than sown broadcast. The problem was to find suitable implements to do this; no local implement-manufacturer yet produced a drill because the farmers were not convinced of the value of the experiment.[35]

Custance had no way of disseminating the results of his experiments through the farming community other than by personal visits to farmer groups. The Government lent little support; he was the sole appointee. The opening of Roseworthy was indicative of attitudes; 'We have seen a Government mud-barge launched with more ceremony' wrote the editor of *The Garden and the Field* with disgust. The farming community was either indifferent or hostile to new ideas and for the next few years Custance 'suffered patiently insult, abuse, misrepresentation—gross misrepresentation—without a word'.[36] He was driven to a more and more extreme position by the attitudes of his opponents and in his last years before resigning in 1887 he dropped his cautious, politic tone and loaded all his experience in a broadside attack on their stubborn prejudices. But the mass of innovations which he suggested was too great and the early and valid experiments were now forgotten as Custance sounded more and more like the 'experts' of the 1860s and 1870s, recommending alien forms of farm management applicable to countries on the other side of the world, but not to South Australia.[37]

Really Custance had run ahead of contemporary opinion which still held that the success of a crop depended entirely on the climate, not on the unseen, impalable ingredients of the soil.[38] As late as 1889 an authoritative account of 'The Position of Agriculture' in South Australia contained the following statement, full as it was of self-deception and comforting thoughts.

'In South Australia we have not a forcing climate and owing to the lack of moisture the crops are able only to take up a very small portion of the elements of the fertility of the soil in any one year and a balance therefore remains over for the next crop. In England and New Zealand and other places where they have a plentiful supply of moisture the soil is forced to make greater efforts and the crops are much heavier than in this colony and after such efforts there is a corresponding demand from the soil for change and rest . . . We can never expect to get high averages but it is not the fault of the land, it is the lack of moisture. I am certain had we the rainfall we could produce as good an average as any one of the other colonies. In moist climates land sooner becomes exhausted, so what we lose in the average we gain in the continued fertility of the soil.'[39]

But in all fairness to the farmers, while Custance was able to demonstrate the success of fertilizer within the confines of the trial plots at Roseworthy, he had not been able to demonstrate that the practice was economic for the selector on his block, many miles away from a railway or port. The manufacturing cost, the transport cost, the quality, and the method of applying the superphosphate to the paddocks were all unsolved problems. Lowrie, successor to Custance at Roseworthy, while noting that superphosphate on hay had 'paid well', and confident that the manuring of crops would ultimately prove to be profitable, had to admit that 'so far, as general practice, we have not demonstrated it to be so'. As late as the 1894–5 season, the Minister of Agriculture was doubtful about the worth of phosphates and expressed the old prejudice about the weather:

'In districts where only wheat is grown we will say, as we have said before, that it is doubtful whether the extensive use of artificial manures would be profitable practice and that in districts handicapped by a small rainfall we are assured that it would not be profitable.'[40]

He was right: although superphosphate had been manufactured in South Australia since 1883, a low demand and insufficient raw material hindered production on a scale capable of lowering costs, and imported fertilizers were at 'excessive' prices which precluded large-scale adoption.[41] In the now traditional way the advisers told the farmers how to manufacture their artificial manure on their own farms but this ran counter to the whole ethos of the kind of agriculture that had grown up in South Australia. The farmers were sceptical and had every reason to resist the innovation because the recommended level of application put it out of their reach. Custance had recommended $1\frac{1}{2}$ cwt of nitrate of soda and 5 cwt of mineral phosphate per acre, which, at a price approaching 6 shillings per cwt, meant a cost of nearly 40 shillings per acre over wheat farms ranging between 300 and 600 acres in size.[42] The farmers could not stand that outlay in the competitive world wheat market. It was a confirmation to some of the meddlesome folly of the experts.

Adoption was not speeded even by the founding of the Bureau of Agriculture in April, 1888, and the establishment of many branches which provided the farmers with the opportunity of discussing and giving reports on agricultural matters, including fertilizers. A lengthy parliamentary discussion on the quality of fertilizer, and subsequent legislation to regulate sales and content were of little avail. Paradoxically, the means of changing the soil once more lay with the wheat farmers themselves, who, when faced with new problems, experimented, adapted and developed a new facet to the farming system that met the peculiarities of the South Australian environment.

Declining yields in the Northern Areas and the delimitation of settlement throughout the 1880s had, to a certain extent, been compensated for by the rapid settlement of the high-rainfall lands of Yorke Peninsula, which had been largely bypassed in that great northward thrust. On the Peninsula, mullenizing and the stump-jump plough had led to the occupation of 639,000 acres in Counties Daly and Fergusson between 1880 and 1884 and of about another 1·2 million acres by 1894. In a sense, the need for fertilizer had been postponed because of the availability of new virgin land, which might partly explain the refusal of the farming community to heed Custance, despite generally falling yields. But by the mid 1890s, dwindling yields plagued the Peninsula farmer too. In the heat of pioneering, the Correll Brothers of Minlaton had experimented with drilling wheat in order to increase their yield, and then hit upon the simple idea of mixing small quantities of superphosphate with the seed (Fig. 76). The old Swedish drill they had been using was inadequate, and, because of the lack of a suitable local implement, they imported from the United States the 'Farmer's Favourite Drill', which cost £35 in South Australia. Their next harvest yielded 22 bushels per acre, and once more, local experiment had proved superior to advice.

FIG. 76. A modern version of the Corrells' simple system of mixing super-phosphate with seed.

The impact of this pioneer expedient, comparable in its simplicity and effectiveness with the scrub-roller and the stump-jump plough, was immediate and widespread. Only one year after the Minister of Agriculture had reported that he doubted if fertilizing could ever be profitable, he noted that there had lately been 'a very observable trend among farmers towards the use of manures', which he ascribed to the propaganda emanating from Roseworthy. But fertilizer had been adopted because of example and not because of words, and the 'splendid results' of the Correll Brothers induced about one hundred neighbours to buy drills and fertilize 30,000 acres during the next year. The Minister later had to admit that it was not until 'a few farmers took the matter up and proved it paid individuals as well as Professor Lowrie backed up by public funds [that] it made any headway'.[43] In May 1897, Lowrie travelled extensively throughout the agricultural areas and found that 'farmers were everywhere considering the subject', when only a short time before they had 'ridiculed the topic'. Now the Agricultural Bureaux proved their value as points for the dissemination of information, and by 1898–99 the innovation had spread to Balaklava, Bute, Gawler, Gladstone, Jamestown and the South-East.[44]

With practical experience came greater knowledge, and it was proved that the quantity of fertilizer needed per acre was 'ridiculously small', i.e. between 70 and 90 lb per acre (Fig. 77a) which immediately put the new system within the reach of most farmers, at an average cost of about 5 shillings per acre, plus labour and machinery costs. It was also proved conclusively that the mixing of the fertilizer with the seed did not produce 'rust' in the resultant crop during moist seasons, nor 'blight' during dry seasons. Old prejudices were laid aside as folk experimentation was triumphant again. It was with pride that the Minister could now say :

> 'We believe we are correct in claiming for South Australia the credit of inaugurating what is practically a new system of manuring.'[45]

The rapidity of the diffusion was remarkable. By the time the House was discussing measures early in 1898 to appoint an Inspector of fertilizers to control the manufacture and quality of superphosphate, 50,000 acres of wheat and fertilizer had been sown by seed drill and 'this year it was expected 200,000 acres would be sown by that means'.[46] This estimate was not far off the mark, and official statistics after 1900 show the constant rise in the acreage fertilized, a rise which averaged 157,000 acres per annum for the fifteen years up to 1915. The use of fertilizer fell slightly during the First World War, and then rose steeply to a peak of 4·9 million acres in 1930 (Fig. 77c). An even more convincing picture of the adoption of fertilizer is given in Fig. 77b which shows that by 1910, 80 per cent of the cropland was fertilized

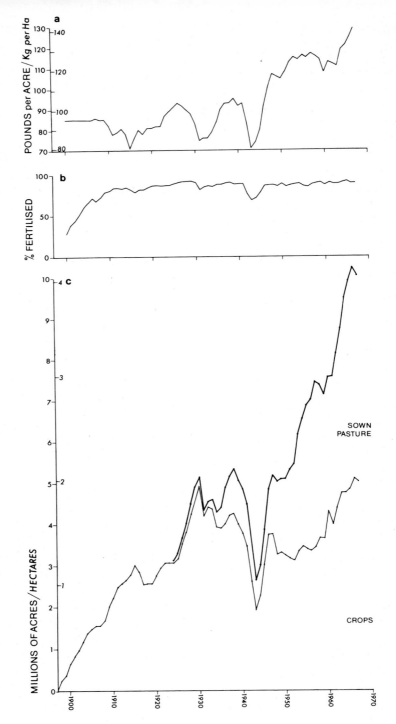

FIG. 77. (a) The rate of application of superphosphate per acre, (b) the percentage of cropland affected, and (c) the number of acres of cropland and pasture treated annually, 1898–1968. (*S.A. Stat. Reg.*)

and that a saturation point of between 85 and 90 per cent was reached after 1920, a level below which it did not fall except during the years of retrenchment and scarcity during the Depression and the Second World War.

But the immediate result was that wheat yields rose[47] (Fig. 74), the old agricultural areas were redeemed, and the way seemed open for the colonization of the low fertility soils of the Murray Mallee and Eyre Peninsula. 'Man and Superphosphate have truly converted the wilderness into smiles' wrote a correspondent of the *West Coast Recorder* in 1911,[48] and it seemed that at last the farmer knew how to 'handle' his soils and transform the landscape.

Fallow

Throughout the period of the great debate on fertilizer there was a parallel debate on the role of fallowing in raising crop yields. The purpose and value of fallowing were imperfectly understood by the South Australian farmer and expert alike. It was done for a number of reasons : to give the land a 'rest' or a 'spell', to turn the weeds down and control them, and to turn the 'goodness up'. Similarly, the evidence is that there were many types of fallow : 'maiden' fallows, which were newly cleared land, fallows which were often burnt stubble, bare fallows, which were cultivation fallows, and sometimes there were even pasture fallows. In 1890, Lowrie suggested that 'rest' and weed control were the main reasons for the fallows which had evolved over the previous few decades as a result of

'wheat after wheat, until the growth of weeds and exhaustion of the virgin wealth of our soils brought about the necessity of an alternation of wheat and bare fallow, which in turn, as soils became less and less responsive, was succeeded by our present practice of wheat, rest and bare fallow—one crop in three years.'[49]

However, Table XV seems to suggest that Lowrie's estimate of about one-third crop to two-thirds fallow was not true of any part of the colony in 1890; and that fallow fluctuated around 20–30 per cent of the cropland. The situation he described was not reached until 1906, and then for very different reasons.

Contemporary comment on fallowing was as confused as it was

copious. While it emphasized the importance of rest and the control of weeds it is also obvious that farmers had been, and were, experimenting with aspects of moisture retention.[50] On the whole, the farmers showed an ignorance of soil physics, but their observations, which were now recorded through the activities of the Agricultural Bureaux and published in *The Garden and the Field*, showed an awareness that there was some relationship and interaction between the climate and the soil, and that the success of cultivation was not a function of rainfall alone. An early and unusually perceptive comment came from a Mr Goode of the Alma district who suggested that 'dirty' (weed infested) land should be either scarified at least twice or the weeds kept down by sheep because the weeds caused moisture loss. Early breaking-up also facilitated the storage of winter rain; 'spring or summer fallow seldom yields like winter fallow'. One anonymous contributor to the column 'Grains of Advice' said that he had noticed that a loose broken surface was much cooler than a solid caked one when the sun was shining on it; therefore, the lesson seemed simple—'if the surface is kept constantly loose the soil will be cool and the hot moist air will deposit moisture because the soil is cooler and because the air can come in contact with it'. Another went so far as to suggest that an opened soil only dried out if it was too wet, for the air kept the soil 'in an equilibrium between wet and dry'.[51] Indeed, for some the atmosphere was 'a vast treasure house of wealth to plant life' and the soil under fallow 'had a surfeit of atmospheric gases which renewed its vitality'.[52] Nevertheless, soil chemistry was still subordinate to climatic factors.

By 1891, a Mr Barker of the Port Broughton district suggested that cultivation fallows 'stored up moisture and conserved it for future crops'; and the *Farm Calendar* that year advised that the subsoil be broken up and 'left still below' to allow deep root penetration for water; while the loose surface was supposed to absorb water from the air at night, provided that the subsoil was not 'full of hard clods which will keep the ground so open that all the moisture will evaporate through the interstices'. From these comments one can see that the old exhortation to plough deeply to aerate the soil and turn up the 'goodness' that had drained down to lower levels was being given a new significance. If the land was ploughed '8 to 9 inches deep instead of scratched we should hear less of drought' said a Mr Grasby of the Woodside branch of the Agricultural Bureau.[53]

By 1892, Lowrie was convinced that fallowing was the answer to declining yields; a winter ploughing and two or three spring and summer scarifyings were insufficient because 'bare fallow is really the working and knocking about of the soil not directly for the sake of providing a tilth for a seed bed but specially to increase the weathering action of the atmosphere . . . [and to keep] the surface open and so retain moisture'.[54] It seemed as though the farmers of the early 1890s were looking at the time-honoured practice of fallowing as the only way in which to increase yields in the absence of fertilizers, which had yet to be proved a practical proposition. They felt that existing fallow practices could be improved, and during these years of experiment, observation and recording they groped towards the idea of moisture conservation, for the rain was a physical phenomenon which they appreciated all too well. But at this point the Correll Brothers proved the value and ease of applying artificial fertilizers, and the interest in fallows was diverted from moisture conservation back to the preparation of the seed-bed. The Corrells emphasized the need to smother the weeds, for if one was going to the expense and effort of buying a drill and fertilizer then the preparation of a good seed-bed seemed worth while :

'First we fallow and keep the weeds in check with the aid of sheep. When the first rains fall the following winter scarify, or plough and if cloddy, roll. About May, if the seeds of weeds have germinated the land should be ploughed as lightly as possible, turning the rubbish under and following with the drill.'[55]

It is significant that the Corrells also realized that fallowing released accumulated chemicals, although the land had to be fallowed 'for many years continuously to free as much phosphoric acid as is contained in one cwt of good superphosphate'. They also recognized the value of sheep, and although there were many who still viewed sheep on the wheat farm with horror, there was an increasing appreciation of the advantages of flocks :

'A flock of sheep will clear as much fallow in one day as a man, a team of horses, and a scarifyer would do in a week, and do the work better because they will pick up all the weeds along side the fences and in the corners that would go to seed otherwise, and blow over the paddock ready to grow up with the wheat.'[56]

Thus, the Corrells' new 'system' of fertilizing, keeping sheep and early fallowing soon became a 'necessary sequence' that hardened into a formal agricultural practice by about 1900.[57] Instinctively, so it seemed, the farmers had once again hit upon an innovation that was to prove effective. By the beginning of the century new patterns of agriculture were emerging with a three-year rotation of wheat, self-sown grasses and adventitious herbage, and fallow. This was modified in the moister areas to include forage crops, and so farms in these areas could support a larger flock of sheep. In the drier areas a five-year rotation was often followed : wheat, wheat or oats, stubble and self-sown grasses, grass and herbage and fallow.[58] Fallow played an important part in all of these rotations in its various functions as a method of weed-clearing, nitrogen release, rest and rejuvenation, and conservation of moisture in the soil and as a means of making the best and most even use of labour and animal power by preparing seed-beds before the crucial, short, hectic seeding period. These systems were the forerunners of the practices of rotation used in the land use zone that we call the wheat-sheep belt today.[59]

Something of the immediate impact of the Corrells' new system can be gauged from Table XV in which the amount of land in fallow is expressed as a percentage of all cereal crops by regions. Fallow increased by nearly 50 per cent between 1896 and 1900 in the Central and Lower North which were the main wheat-growing districts, and by 1904 had nearly done the same in the Upper North. By 1901, the Minister of Agriculture thought that fallowing was no longer a matter of debate as it had been some years before, and that, wherever possible, farmers should fallow land in preference to leaving it in stubble. The only point on which there was room for debate was the best depth at which to plough.[60]

The excitement over fertilizers and the rise of rotations with stock had not entirely quelled the interest in fallows for moisture conservation, particularly amongst those farmers on the outer

Table XV

Percentage of Fallow to Area of Cereal Crop

	Districts				
	Central	Lower North	Upper North	South-East	Western
1890	24·4	26·8	29·6	7·0	17·0
1896	23·5	29·2	26·7	4·8	4·9
1898	31·6	40·8	40·4	2·2	9·9
1900	37·7	47·3	41·5	3·3	10·1
1902	43·5	54·1	36·8	4·3	15·1
1904	48·9	56·2	51·9	6·3	13·6
1906	53·9	66·7	60·3	7·4	12·4
1908	50·2	61·6	57·4	6·6	17·8
1909	53·3	69·7	63·4	5·3	18·5

Sources: 'Fallowing in South Australia' and 'Fallowing' by W. L. Summers, *SAJA*, VIII (1904–5), 141; and XI (1907–8), 56 respectively; *SAPP*, 43 (1910); W. L. Summers, *Notes on Agriculture in South Australia*, (1908).

edges of the wheat belt where the rainfall was low and variable. Instead of worrying whether their yield was going to be 10 or 20 bushels to the acre, these farmers were grappling with the problem of whether the yield would be 5 or 10 bushels per acre, or, as so often happened during a bad year, with the problem of a yield so low that it did not even pay to harvest the crop. To these farmers the idea of moisture conservation held an attraction that probably far outweighed that of fertilizers for they could see the next paddock further out, and the next and the next, and it was hard to accept that they were not wheat-growing lands. When Lowrie said that 'thorough fallowing is . . . a means of conserving moisture sufficient to equal an increase from 2 to 3 inches of rain in the succeeding season' it struck at their hearts as well as at their pockets.[61]

Lowrie was only putting into words something that had been felt to be true by the farmers for many years, and which had been the original impetus to experimentation in fallowing before superphosphate and seed-bed preparation diverted attention. A significant advance in the idea came in 1898 when the dust-mulch was explained by a Mr Torril who said that fallow land should be kept as open as possible during the winter to 'drink in the rain' and store it for the future crop, and that the ground should be brought to 'a fine tilth during the summer and the top kept loose so that evaporation may be retarded as much as possible'. The whole question of moisture conservation was given an added urgency with the drought of 1901 which told with widespread and devastating effect. Typical of the reaction to it was the opinion of one farmer from Robertstown, just east of the Ranges who said:

> 'Many farmers after twenty years residence in this district are no better off now than they were when they settled here first; and it is possible that another twenty years more will not improve their position unless they change the method of working their farms.'[62]

Therefore, when the American technique of 'dry farming' first began to be mentioned in Australia in 1906, the idea initially aroused considerable interest. It was not a new technique in South Australia for there had already been two or three decades of experiment and practice along these lines. In 1914 Lowrie could look back on it and say that farmers had been 'actively practising the operation long years before "dry farming" ... was ever suggested'.[63] But the significance of dry farming lay in the fact that the early practice of fallowing for moisture conservation was given an air of scientific respectability and, more important, the stamp of official approval which led to the encouragement and extension of existing fallowing practices.

The principal exponent of dry farming was H. W. Campbell who first experimented with the technique in North Dakota and then at Cheyenne Wells, Colorado, in 1894, drawing his ideas from F. H. King, Professor of Agricultural Physics at the University of Wisconsin, who put forward the idea that the soil particles formed a mass of capillary tubes. These tubes lifted the moisture in the soil until it reached the surface where it was lost by evaporation. Laboratory experiments suggested that this conception of soil physics was true and that the lifting of the water could be stopped and the loss halved either by breaking the tubes or by pulverizing the subsoil, and covering the soil with a dust-mulch.[64] The first Australian contact with Campbell was undoubtedly through McColl of Victoria in 1906, and these ideas were expounded at length in South Australia in the same year by Mr T Pearce, the Minister of Agriculture, in a talk to the farmers of Whyte-Yarcowie. The method of keeping the subsoil firm and the surface fine was to work over the land with a double disc harrow after rain when the soil was neither too wet nor too dry. The land was ploughed so that the fine soil on the top was turned down to form the seed-bed. The plough was followed by Campbell's 'sub-packer', an implement with wedge-shaped wheels which firmed and pulverized the soil and left the surface loose (Fig. 78). The surface was then harrowed.[65] 'Who can under-estimate what it will mean to South Australia and the great area it will add to that portion that can be successfully occupied for agriculture?' asked Pearce in a burst of rhetoric :

'In our present system so much depends upon whether the amount of rain falls at the proper time, and every year the anxious times come in the shape of dry spells when the plants stop growing and very often go back . . . Now . . . if instead of this experience every year we know that when we put in the crop, even with a light rainfall, it will continue to grow and come to maturity, how much better will be the lot of the outside farmer?'

It was exhilarating stuff, but what effect it had upon the farmers who had been experimenting along these lines for decades is hard to say. Certainly, after 1912, the topic of dry farming *per se* was barely discussed by the Agricultural Bureaux, while fallowing for moisture conservation was. It seems that it was the administrators and the officials who were caught up in the dream of unlimited conservation of rainfall, never realizing that Campbell's experiments were all in areas of rainfall in excess of 12 inches per annum, while they were mainly talking about areas in South Australia with well below that amount. An immediate mark of government interest was the establishment of an experimental farm of 4000 acres at Hammond, at about the point where the frontier had retreated after the drought of 1880; and the Department of Agriculture bought a sub-packer. Deeper cultivation was urged

FIG. 78. Rolling and compressing a harrowed field to conserve moisture. The plains north of Adelaide where the town of Elizabeth now stands (see Fig. 113).

for a new reason; every inch meant another 200 tons of soil particles per acre at the disposal of the crop.[66] The Surveyor General was sent to the United States to get further details of dry farming and came back 'perfectly satisfied of the practicability of conserving moisture by tillage' so that part of the previous year's rainfall could be utilized for crop growing. In his view dry farming meant the possible extension of cultivation into between 3 and 4 million acres of new land with a rainfall between 10 and 15 inches, 'entirely outside the limits of reliable rainfall where wheat is now successfully grown'. The Assistant Director of Agriculture added his authority to the topic and said that he thought that 'the evil effects of drought' could be countered by 'the good effect of dry farming'.[67]

Undoubtedly, the temporary cult of dry farming together with the lasting practice of fallowing was a factor in the official encouragement of settlement in the dry interior areas of the Murray Mallee and Eyre Peninsula where 1·6 million acres of land were cleared between 1906 and 1918. However, as the frontier of cultivation pushed northwards the coincidence of slightly above average rainfall gave results which were wrongly ascribed to moisture conservation. Around Loxton, for example, the loose friable soils were said to be 'unusually retentive of moisture', and although 'dry spells' were to be expected frequently, the advice given was that 'the farmer on the River who fallows wisely and well may expect to come through them without serious loss'.[68] These were just the areas of the worst drift erosion in later years. Nevertheless, the fad of dry farming had led to a greater acceptance of the importance of moisture conservation in the farm operation.

Parasites

The success of superphosphate in combating phosphorus deficiencies in the soil and in raising yields was not lost on those concerned with coast disease. One member of the House expressed the wish that 'some agricultural chemist would tell them what chemicals were lacking in the vast areas of at present useless land in the South and the South-East'.[69] He said this because there were hints from farmers that the different quality of the feed was related in some way to certain types of country. For example, a Mr Slattery of Eyre Peninsula believed that the disease was nothing more than anaemia caused by an insufficient amount of iron in the soil, so 'consequently that mineral cannot exist in the plants growing thereon'. He had good results from dressing the affected pastures with sulphate of iron and sowing them to white clover which 'took it up'. The next year, a Mr Brown of Port Lincoln added support to this hypothesis saying that there was no doubt in his mind that the disease was caused chiefly through the 'want of iron in the soil, as is proved by feed growing on iron-stone country being the only cure for it'. But after putting iron sulphate in water tanks he found no improvement in his stock, 'which goes to show that there is something besides iron required'.[70]

It looked as though the investigation of the disease was going forward along the right lines and that the botanical and miasmatic explanations were being abandoned with the development of soil chemistry. But just at that point, the development of veterinary science and the discovery of microscopic worms in sheep diverted attention towards a parasitic explanation of the disease.

Since the mid 1870s liver fluke had been recognized as a debilitating disease in sheep, particularly in those in the South-East, and large flocks were destroyed to prevent the spread of the infestation. A direct causal connection between fluke and coast disease was never voiced; nevertheless, the swampy environmental conditions were suspected as the cause of both. The discovery of worms in sheeps' stomachs in 1899 by the Stock Inspector, T. H. Williams, was thought to account for 'one of the so called forms of coast disease [and] was mainly caused by bad water'.[71] The supposed correlation between worms and coastiness became stronger throughout the succeeding years, as is shown by article after article in the *Journal of Agriculture*. The veterinary officers of the Department of Agriculture constantly underlined the connection and expressed alarm at the prospect of the spread of the disease from purely stock-rearing areas to cereal-growing areas with the development of mixed farming.[72] Salt, slated lime, sulphate baths and drenches of copper sulphate were prescribed increasingly, but, while helping to get rid of intestinal worms, they did not reduce coastiness. Practical farmers remained sceptical. In an article entitled 'Coast disease as the stock-owner sees it', one Eyre Peninsula farmer recounted :

'I tried the blue-stone remedy for sheep the past summer but it proved a decided failure. It is a well established fact that removal to the iron stone country is a sure cure for coastiness, but no-one knows why. It is beyond the power of the ordinary stock-owner to find it, yet there must be a reason and we are of the opinion that our agricultural stock officers should concentrate their efforts on this problem [the effect of the iron stone country] so that a remedy, applicable to the coasty lands might be discovered.'

Once more the official reply was 'worms'.[73]

For a while great hopes were pinned on the improvement of pastures with the application of superphosphate, but this too proved an ineffective antidote to the strange and crippling disease.[74]

'When our Soils Have Gone, We too Must Go'

After 1906, the twin themes of fallowing and fertilizer came together and there was a new confidence that the soils of the State were understood and mastered at last so that they would yield their greatest harvest, especially with the new wheat varieties bred by Farrer. It seemed as though a new partnership between farmer and scientist was being formed. 'With the use of phosphates and other manures and a scientific system of farming', said the Surveyor-General, Strawbridge, 'hardly any class of land can be said to be valueless for agricultural purposes', and the train loads of fertilizer trundling into the Pinnaroo district seemed to confirm this.[75] After the doleful warnings of Goyder to the settlers moving north in 1876, Strawbridge's enthusiasm in 1910 over the settlers in the Murray Mallee and Eyre Peninsula seemed to mark a new official attitude and an encouragement to expansion. To him, and to many like him in positions of authority, the expansion of the agricultural frontier seemed 'inevitable' as science aided by technology unlocked the lands in a new way. But the expansion was also 'essential'; South Australia still had a rural-based economy, and as the Director of Agriculture realized 'increased wealth we must have, and if we cannot get it from the soil where can it possibly come?'[76] (Fig. 79).

'Rural territorial expansion' was still an unquestioned aim in the mid 1920s despite the droughts of 1914 and 1918. The farmers were not only exhorted to apply more fertilizer, select better strains of wheat, and heed all advice, but also to indulge in 'effective and honest tillage'.[77] The Government outdid itself in surveying and offering land, building railways and sinking wells to encourage the settlers forward. Seasons of above-average rainfall and a high demand and price for wheat all compounded the optimism of the northward-bound settlers and of the government officials alike.

But the frenzy of activity was creating problems—problems not new in kind but certainly in degree. These problems were all to do basically with the soil itself; with the deterioration of soil, its structure and fertility, and the creation of large areas of drift and gullying. They arose through frequent cultivation in response to fallowing and the rising demand and high prices of the boom from 1906 to 1926. In every way, the official policy up to the mid 1920s was leading to a drastic deterioration of the physical environment through erosion.

In retrospect Campbell's theory of dry farming and the practice of fallowing to conserve moisture were both unsound. Any

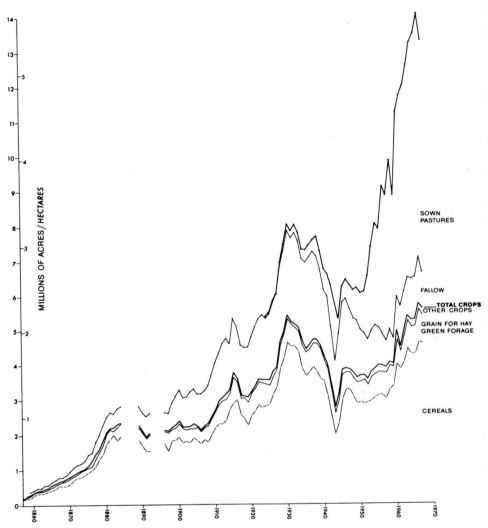

FIG. 79. Area under crops in South Australia, 1855–1968. (*S.A. Stat. Reg.*)

moisture saved by frequent cultivation was due to the increase of
organic matter at the soil surface and particularly to weed control,
not to the mulch cover on the soil. The evidence is that in most of
the soils of the south eastern portion of Australia the surface will
be depleted of moisture during the summer season whatever is
done.[78] Deep ploughing and frequent cultivation (up to twelve

times a year) coupled with long fallows caused the destruction of the soil structure and depletion of fertility through the ultimate loss of nitrogen. The loss in South Australia under average climatic and soil conditions was about one ton of organic matter per acre per fallowing, and it was this organic matter, of course, which absorbed any moisture and resisted the beating action of the rain. But excessive fallowing had one other effect: if the fallow was left uncultivated the soil surface became hard and impenetrable, and this led to a decrease in the amount of water absorbed, to an increase in run-off, and consequently to sheet erosion and gullying. If cultivated, the soil became powdery and was subject to drift.[79]

In addition to these general and basic misconceptions about the soils and the economic incentive to crop as much as possible there was the problem of the farmers themselves in what was, for many of them, a new, untried environment in the inner areas of the Murray Mallee and Eyre Peninsula. While some farmers came from areas in which similar conditions prevailed, such as Yorke Peninsula and the plains on the east coasts of the Gulfs, there were many who migrated into the Murray Mallee from the Adelaide hills, the Barossa Valley and the Central Hill Country and brought with them cultivation methods well adapted to the high-rainfall areas, but disastrous in the sand hills and low rainfall of the mallee lands. As late as 1932, the Agricultural Instructor in the Murray Mallee could still say that 'much still remains to be learnt concerning the correct handling of mallee soils'. The severity of drift in the region was described at an inquiry in 1938, as being 'a measure of mismanagement in the past as much as of natural liability'.[80]

Not once did official opinion suggest either that optimism, expansion and exploitation were to be questioned or that frequent fallowing and tillage were detrimental. Even as the prolonged droughts between 1928 and 1930 got under way, the Director of Agriculture thought that the wheat acreage would be further increased from 2·7 to 3·9 million acres and the average yield raised so that at no time had 'the prospects ahead of wheat growing appeared brighter in this state'.[81]

The disastrous economic conditions and distress which prostrated the rural community after the slump of 1930–31 were countered by now familiar arguments—high costs could best be offset by expansion with more fallowing to aid nitrification and conserve moisture, and with the application of more super-phosphate, the latter being the very thing that the farmer could not afford to do after drought and years of low returns (Figs. 77a and c). Such was the prevailing state of the official mind that 'progress' was gauged solely by 'new areas won to cultivation or placed under crop'. To admit anything else was 'retrogression' and South Australia would 'lose ground and standing', although it was never specified where and with whom.[82]

It was only with the steady downward trend in the area of land under crop by nearly 1,000,000 acres between 1930 and 1935, preceded by five years of declining yields (Figs. 79 and 74 respectively), that the idea slowly penetrated the official mind that there was an economic problem which was as much of a bar to expansion as was drought. The uncomfortable thought struck the Minister of Agriculture that, possibly, by encouraging the settler to attempt 'to farm land that is only fit for grazing purposes' at a time of extreme economic and environmental stress, the Govern-ment might be causing the permanent deterioration of the environment. He had to admit grudgingly that 'if such be the case it may ultimately be said that some good did come of the economic depression of the early thirties'.[83]

The last loud cry of the boosters was heard early in 1935 when Perkins gave what was probably to be his last pronouncement before retiring as Director of Agriculture. His stand was un-equivocal; he could not subscribe to the idea that farmers could 'afford to slide out of wheat growing or even to curtail the area sown to any appreciable degree'. He was now in possession of detailed statistics of wheat production, yield, costs and returns for each farm. The gross return per acre for the seasons 1930–34 was only £1-3s.-1d. which could not possibly balance operating costs which rarely fell below £2-0s.-0d. per acre. He calculated that 11,135, or 82·78 per cent of the wheat farms were run at a loss with an average return of £1-8s.-4d., and only 2,316 were run at a profit (Table XVI). The explanation seemed clear; there was nothing wrong with the land, it was 'the natural consequences of faulty and slovenly farming practices', namely, too little fallowing :

Table XVI

Analysis of Holdings growing Wheat in South Australia, 1925/26–1932/33 (1927/28 excluded)

Yield per acre	No. of holdings	% of all holdings	% of area in holdings	% of production	Average yield bushels	Average return per acre
Non-paying farms						
> 6 bushels	3,647					
6–11 bushels	4,267	82·8	87·3	71·1	7·93	£1 8 4
12–17 bushels	3,221					
TOTAL	11,135					
Paying farms						
18–26 bushels	2,011					
27–32 bushels	248	7·2	12·7	28·9	22·03	£2 11 0
32+ bushels	57					
TOTAL	2,316					

Source: A. J. Perkins, *SAJA*, XXXVIII (1934–35), 716.

'There is no other practice that has had a greater influence for good on our mean yields per acre; fertilizers, quality and quantity of seed, time of sowing, treatment against disease, etc., count for little or nothing unless the land has been adequately fallowed in the preceding season.'

The 'chief sinners' were in the Murray Mallee and Eyre Peninsula where the fallow was only 32 and 58 per cent respectively of the wheat crop in 1932/33 compared with 82 per cent in the Central district and 84 per cent in the Lower North (Table XVII).[84]

Table XVII

Percentage of the Wheat Crop grown on Fallow
1924/5–1940/1

	Central	L.North	U.North	S.E.	Western	M. Mallee	State
1924/25	81·5	87·2	90·4	63·6	35·2	40·6	66·8
1926/27	82·0	87·2	84·5	59·8	29·6	43·3	64·0
1928/29	82·9	88·4	76·4	55·8	28·9	40·4	58·4
1930/31	79·5	84·9	64·0	46·6	27·0	34·6	51·4
1932/33	81·8	84·1	55·3	60·3	31·9	57·7	59·5
1934/35	86·8	90·9	69·8	71·3	42·9	72·0	70·0
1936/37	86·4	89·9	65·0	60·5	47·5	74·5	71·7
1938/39	88·2	90·8	80·0	56·6	55·8	75·4	76·1
1940/41	89·1	93·7	81·8	46·4	57·5	80·8	79·2

Source: S.A. Stat. Reg.

Fallowing was something which the farmers could understand and cope with—it needed no more capital, only more labour—and in their battered state they were ready to listen to any easily applied advice that would help to salve their wounds, especially when it came as the swan-song of a person widely respected by the farming community. Up went the fallow to an all-time high in both of the offending regions: down went the fertility and the stability of the soil. Perkins's figures were only too right in the terrible story that they told, but his analysis of causes was wrong. He had looked at the farm statistics in aggregate without looking at their spatial implications.

The emphasis on fallowing to counteract deficient and variable rainfall, and on frequent fallowing to raise yields in the absence of cheap nitrogenous fertilizers led to a serious problem of erosion. Erosion was of two kinds, the drift in the sandy mallee soils of the new areas of colonization in the Murray Mallee and Eyre Peninsula, and severe gullying and sheet-wash erosion in the red-brown earths of the old established Northern Areas. There was also a serious erosion problem in the pastoral areas, associated with overstocking and with the depredations of rabbits.[85]

The problem of drift had long been known, and seemed to be regarded as an almost necessary evil of farming the light soils, thereby receiving surprisingly little comment. Goyder had recognized the danger of clearing the sand ridges in the Balaklava-Inkerman area as early as 1867, and later, fallowing became the cause of the same problem. In 1898, farmers near Port Germein complained of drift arising from the working of light soils to a 'very fine tilth', and others in the same district noted that land had been denuded of 10 inches of top soil and that drift had covered a 4 foot fence.[86] But this was nothing compared to later experiences in the Mallee. By 1899, the Minister of Agriculture was advocating tree-planting as a means of soil control and even contemplated legislation to penalize owners of drifting land. The problem was compounded by those people who deliberately encouraged drift, like those in the Balaklava area who contended that 'it made the adjoining lands produce better crops'.[87] Traffic obstruction became a serious problem in some areas and the suggestion was made that fallows should not be allowed within three chains of a road.[88] Any windy weather caused a problem, and as one correspondent at Pinnaroo, a not particularly badly affected area, put it; 'crops anywhere within coo-ee of a sand ridge are being inundated with drift sand'.[89] It was a common and widespread complaint for which there was abundant evidence in later years (Figs. 80 and 81).

The incidence, and the consequences for drifting sand and even the remedies for it were recognized by the Department of Agriculture, but no one seemed to perceive that constant fallowing was the basic problem, and, even if they did, they were not game to voice their disapproval of an almost hallowed tradition which for many seemed the only way of increasing yields. Only a few people

FIG. 80. A dust storm over the Murray Mallee.

FIG. 81. The effects of wind erosion. This mallee stump stands about 6 feet above the level of the ground, supported by the roots. The sandy soil around it has blown away.

queried events, W. J. Spafford advocated sowing lucerne, sub-
clover and rye to stabilize light soils, and planting fast-growing
native trees to arrest blow-outs. With regularity, R. L. Griffiths,
the Agricultural Instructor in the Murray Mallee, wrote articles
on this particularly badly affected region, and while emphasizing
the need to cultivate light soils only occasionally, not to burn
stubble, and to sow oats to be grazed and then ploughed in before
fallowing, concluded that 'only a modification of cultivation
methods that reduces the drift menace is worth adopting', without
ever going so far as to condemn fallowing.[90] But by 1936 the last
desperate activities of the 'soil-stirrers' in the Mallee, as they
hoped for something to turn up, reached such proportions that
many were forced to walk off their farms and it seemed as though
the wholesale abandonment of the area around Loxton was
imminent. As Griffiths said succinctly, 'when our soils have gone,
we too must go'.[91]

It seems as though the problem of drift erosion was treated
very much as a local one relating to the Mallee only, although
there were reports of drift elsewhere in Yorke and Eyre Peninsulas.
It tended to be ignored because the Mallee was an area of low
productivity and no one expected anything but drift in the sand-
dune country. In any case, the average person considered soil drift
more as a problem of blocked roads and railways, rather than
fundamentally as a problem of worn-out and mismanaged farms.

But a new element entered into the situation. The Arthurton
Branch of the Bureau had noted that 'some of our heavier soils, in
fact some of our best land, is showing signs of drift', and further
north, in the red-brown earths of the Northern Areas, sheet
erosion and gullying were becoming increasingly common. Prolonged and continuous fallowing and cultivation struck all soils
alike in time. Surprisingly, however, even with the new aid of
radio broadcasting after 1937, an extended technical service and a
re-vamped and more attractive *Agricultural Journal*, it took a long
time for farmers and public alike to appreciate that the very
bastion of safe wheat growing was threatened from within. Even
the Report of a Soil Conservation Committee which had been
formed in 1937 to investigate all types of erosion, and which
prepared maps that are an invaluable record of soil deterioration
(Fig. 82), seemed to have little impact. As late as 1941, the

Conservator of Soils said that the problem in the Northern Areas was 'only just being recognized'.[92]

Exploitation to Conservation

It was to his credit that at the eleventh hour A. J. Perkins changed his views, and with as much zest as he had proclaimed the expansionist, exploitative philosophy, he now sponsored the cause of retreat and conservation. The first stage in this significant change of view came on July 3rd, 1935, when he was asked by a Ceduna farmer to explain the significance of Goyder's Line of rainfall. After summarizing the history of the Line, he said to his local audience:

'I know the Line is not absolutely perfect and that when we have been blessed by a succession of favourable seasons there has been a tendency to overlook it, if not to criticize it unduly. It is true too, that we have not hesitated, when the mood was on us, to go outside the Line, and attempt to farm out of bounds and sometimes successfully . . . I am further of the opinion that much of this country must revert to sheep and cattle.'

He analysed the production of counties outside the Line between 1906 and 1933 and concluded that 'at no conceivable price for wheat could such yields [less than 5 bushels per acre] be looked upon as profit earning to the farmer or of particular value to the community'. The excursions beyond the safety of Goyder's Line had led to the discovery of the utmost margins of cultivation. The trouble was, however, that having discovered the 'limitations of this territory we are still exceedingly loath to recognize . . . [them] in a practical manner'.[93]

Before May of the next year, Perkins had analysed the yields for each hundred from 1914–15 to 1934–35 and plotted them on a map together with Goyder's Line and the mean April–November isohyets (Fig. 83). Every hundred beyond the Line had a yield below 12 bushels per acre, as had not a few within it. These were the very areas in which reports of erosion and declining yields had reached alarming proportions. With a remarkable change of heart Perkins thought that the wheat farmer was not to blame for the situation, and no one knew better than the Director of Agriculture how the farmer had been encouraged to take-up these areas. Drought assistance was 'in reality . . . no assistance at all' and the need was to help the occupants of unprofitable wheat farms to convert their holdings to livestock enterprises upon which wheat would occupy only a very secondary and occasional position.

'I have not in view so many miniature station properties which could not possibly succeed, but farms upon which sheep husbandry would be practised on relatively small areas . . . Crops would still have to be raised but not for sale, but for consumption by livestock. I have suggested a flock of 600 ewes, and I realize that some of the properties in question were not sufficiently large for the purpose. This would simply mean the necessity of merging two or more farms into one, and the transference of some families to other districts'.[94]

Here was the dawning recognition of the limit of available land and a definition of the difficult marginal lands in which erosion, declining yields and low returns had to be rectified by new means of farm enlargement and raising stock on rotations. It was essentially a climatic argument that still took little notice of the soil, but its true significance lay in the fact that it questioned past assumptions on farming and on the environment, and opened up the way for the expression of new attitudes and the experimentation with new solutions to ever mounting problems.

In the next year, A. R. Callaghan, Principal of Roseworthy College, was encouraged to say:

'The land itself may be the temporary property of the individual but it represents the heritage and wealth of the State, and accordingly should be maintained in a progressive state of production and not be allowed to deteriorate through misguided systems of agriculture'.[95]

This attitude that the soil was a national asset held in trust for future generations was revolutionary, and was, perhaps, the beginning of conservation in South Australia. But at this point in time, the implications were more limited, but nevertheless clear: it was the responsibility of the community at large to put the farmer into a state of security so that he no longer needed to exploit his farm and ruin it, as he had before 1936.

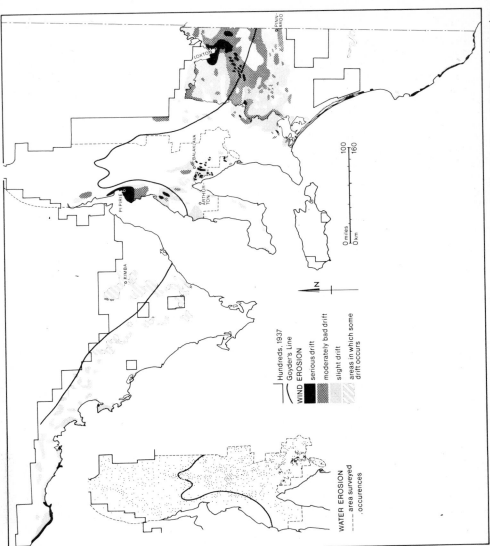

FIG. 82. Erosion in the settled areas of South Australia, *c.* 1937. Based on *SAPP*, 40 (1938).

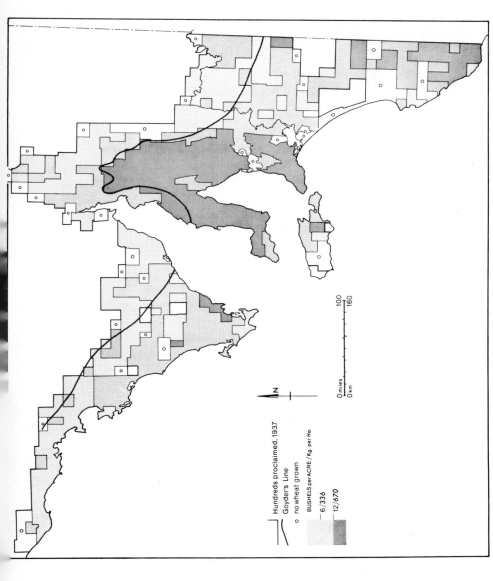

Although official attitudes about the soil changed, it was to take a long time before popular attitudes followed suit. The poor response to measures for the control of erosion baffled some :

'We are at present spending colossal sums of money to prevent this country from falling into alien hands but at the same time allowing this other enemy, just as dangerous, to apply a "scorched earth" policy which if unchecked will ultimately render it almost unusable to anyone.'[96]

The slow acceptance by the farmers of the facts of erosion and of the remedies for it was, perhaps, not too difficult to understand, for such an acceptance needed two confessions : that a problem existed, and that it existed because of exploitive mismanagement of the soil in the past. In the high rainfall areas the process of erosion was slow and crept up on the wheat grower. The gradual depletion of soil fertility, the loss of the soil and the siltation of the creeks were insidious. As one farmer explained :

'These factors will go on and cause no misgivings to any one but economists and conscientious agricultural advisers, but when the farmer is unable to cross the gullies [with his farm machinery] then and then only will he begin to worry.'[97]

Detailed surveys of some of the wheat areas carried out later on showed just how bad soil erosion was. In the hundred of Belalie, in the Upper North, 76 per cent of the arable land had lost more than one quarter of its surface soil, and gullying was severe.[98] The fatalism of the acceptance of erosion by many farmers was as good an indication as any of their basic lack of knowledge of the soil. The need was to stimulate their 'soil consciousness' and attitude of responsibility. The consequences of the bare fallows of the previous fifty years were slowly reaching a climax ; as one observer put it figuratively, 'The Prince Charming disguised as the wheat crop has been dancing with Cinderella, the soil; but each dance brings the clock nearer to midnight'.[99] The problem was brought home, both metaphorically and literally, to the majority of the people in the State by a series of frequent and spectacular dust-storms over Adelaide during the summer of 1944. Immediately soil erosion was 'elevated to first class news status', and the battle of dissemination had been won.[100]

But when the farmer did see that a problem existed and began to worry about it, what was he to do? The advice given by the Conservation Committee of 1937 had been almost irrelevant; its advice had been to stop clearing, to sow down hill-sides to grass, re-afforest upland areas and to contour bank the fields, but it had said nothing about discontinuing the ruinous and exploitative practice of bare fallows and wheat, and replacing it with a rotation based on leguminous pastures with associated livestock and cultivation. In any case, as one observer said, there was still a very deeply rooted 'grain-complex' in the farming community, and the farmer was reluctant to break away from a system in which he was thoroughly trained and to undertake alternatives of which he had only an elementary knowledge. What was needed was a revolution in farm management, which was a far more important and fundamental innovation than any either contemplated or taken up before. Diversification meant new watering places, fencing, buildings, stock, and fodder reserves, all of which meant capital. The problem was how to get the farmer to accept these changes when his capital was gone, and his debts enormous, and his initiative blunted by the bludgeoning effects of drought and poverty, and hindered in some cases by a section of the farming population who still rejected the evidence against long term monoculture and fallowing.[101]

It was natural, therefore, that the first measures taken to combat erosion were those of contour-ploughing and banking which could be accommodated within the existing systems of farm management. Yet the measures were obviously ineffective against drift in the lighter soils, and even in the Northern Areas, where eventually about 250,000 acres were contour banked, such engineering devices to handle surplus water were treating the symptoms and not the causes of erosion, and were useless unless accompanied by 'sound soil husbandry'.

There were two possible solutions. By 1944, Chepil, in Canada, had proved the value as a means of countering wind-erosion, of leaving the 'trash' on the surface after fallowing. This practice needed a drastic re-orientation of the values of the South Australian farmer who had been exhorted for decades to indulge in 'clean' and 'honest' tillage, and burn his stubble; but by the early 1950s the innovation was well accepted because of its obvious benefits.

The other solution was more basic, and it was one which required a complete revolution in agricultural methods. In order to re-habilitate the fertility of the soil as well as to stabilize it the need was to 'find a means of re-establishing the original plant cover and . . . [to] . . . find fresh pasture species suited to the locality and learn how to treat them properly'. Until such species could be found, and rotations accepted so that more and better pastures were associated with wheat growing it was felt that there was 'no hope for our soils'.[102] The progress in adopting pastures was "depressingly slow"[103] and it was not until the mid 1950s that the "take off" occurred.

'A Valuable Weed'

The deterioration in the quality of the environment of the soil and in the state of agriculture generally during the 1930s seemed all too real to farmers and experts alike. Yet, discoveries and innovations had been, and were being, made which when combined were going to dispel the gloom. These discoveries centred around the development of leguminous pastures, which have helped to restore the fertility of the worn out and eroded soils of the wheat growing areas (Fig. 74), have replaced native pastures, and in association with the other important discovery of micro-nutrient or trace-element deficiencies in so many of South Australia's soils, have led to the 'opening-up' of the last difficult areas of the State. With these changes the age old dichotomy in Australian agrarian affairs between livestock and cultivation, usually symbolized by the terms 'pastoral' and 'agricultural', has disappeared and been replaced by more diverse and intensified agricultural practices which make a more productive and efficient use of the land than ever before.

Pastures: Origins

The origins of the changes go back a long way and are associated with the previous themes of coast disease, fertilizers, fallows and erosion. As early as 1898, William Farrer, the wheat-breeder, was convinced that the South Australian 'system' of wheat and fallow had led to 'the impoverished condition of the once famous wheat lands'. In his view the deterioration of the soil and the reduction in wheat yields could be arrested only by a more rational system of soil management based on experiments in cultivation methods, better yielding wheat breeds, a better understanding of fertilizers and 'trials of leguminous plants for green manuring' with which he had been experimenting in a 'small and desultory way'.[104] Unfortunately, Farrar's early leads were not followed up, neither was the early success of applying superphosphate to natural grasses, probably because the farmers were mesmerized by the prospects of increased wheat yields with superphosphate. Even when stock prices were described as 'tip-top' during the early years of the century, and the advice given was to grow grasses and fodder crops and double stock numbers, the farmers could not be weaned away from wheat. In any case superphosphate had undermined any trend towards diversification and soil rehabilitation by pastures, for the common view was that stock were only worth keeping on cereal farms for manurial purposes to improve wheat yields, an improvement now being achieved by superphosphate.

Besides the inveterate prejudice of farmers against stock rearing there was a basic problem in the lack of a suitable fodder crop. Generally speaking, the native Australian perennial grasses were not well adapted to grazing and trampling by sheep and cattle. They were erect and brittle, and suffered damage from defoliation. The taller species of *Themeda* (Kangaroo grasses), *Panicum* and *Stipa* were almost eliminated from an early date. The shorter species of *Danthonia* (Wallaby grasses) and *Stipa*, although moderately nutritious, formed an incomplete and sparse cover which was incapable of providing enough feed, and which disappeared if the soil fertility levels were raised and faster growing grasses and taller species competed for light and water. Imported sown grasses from Britain, such as *Lolium perenne* L (Perennial rye grass), *Dactylis glomerata* L (cocksfoot), *Trifolium repens* L (White clover), and *Trifolium pratense* L (red clover) were adapted only to favourable high-rainfall areas located in the Adelaide Hills and the Lower South-East. The real need was for a sown pasture that was suitable for the long dry summer and wet winter growing season of the settled parts of South Australia.[105]

A now almost familiar story of individual experimentation occurred. As far back as 1889, Amos Howard, a nurseryman and farmer, recognized the potential value of a Mediterranean annual legume, subterranean clover (*Trifolium subterranum L*), which had been introduced by chance in the hill pastures around Mount Barker in about 1880. Howard managed to harvest the seed, which was a difficult technical problem as it is either buried or lies on the surface of the soil, and he vigorously advocated its use as a fodder crop. His increasing confidence in its grazing potential is reflected in the titles of his letters to the *South Australian Advertiser*; the first was 'A valuable weed', the second 'A new fodder crop'.[106] Between about 1906 and 1912 Howard was very active in publicizing the virtues of his discovery, but his propaganda went unheeded for nearly a quarter of a century as the community was not ready to adopt the innovation.[107] During this time the whole of the research effort of the Department of Agriculture into the problems of agriculture went into wheat and grains, with only a minor interest in veterinary science after 1900.[108] Pastures were neglected completely since all interest was focused on the northward thrust into the Murray Mallee and Eyre Peninsula where clearing, burning, fertilizing and fallowing all commanded more attention.

But there was one large area of the state in which grain was of declining importance and pastures and stock were clearly a more efficient way of utilizing the land—that was in the high rainfall lands of the Lower South-East. Here, the emphasis on farming was slowly narrowing down to the one major issue of pasture improvement, both on the 'ranges' or uplands, and on the wet and seasonally inundated 'flats'. The indifferent success of the drainage schemes up to 1920 and the desire to establish ex-servicemen on small holdings carved out of the old large re-purchased freehold estates had made farmers and officials alike take a close look at the farming practices of the region. Inquiry after inquiry came around to the same inescapable conclusion that settlement density could be increased only if adequate land classification and soil surveys were undertaken, and pastures, herds and flocks upgraded. The emphasis on stock also made the solution to the problem of coast disease of outstanding importance. Indicative of these changed attitudes was the decision to convert the Kybybolite Experimental Farm[109] to a pastoral and mixed farming concern in 1919, after fourteen years of indifferent success as a cereal farm and orchard. Experiments were begun immediately, under the direction of L. J. Cook, with rotations, the top-dressing of pastures and the cultivation of forage crops. By the 1921–22 season, the beneficial results were apparent. The application of 1 ton of lime and an annual dressing of 1 cwt of superphosphate per acre was found to double the stock carrying capacity of the pastures at the farm. The weeds and the poorer grass species were replaced by more nutritious plants, particularly clovers, and the stock matured earlier, were better developed and produced better quality wool. Trials with the new annual legume, subterranean clover, showed that it was well adapted to the poor acidic soils of the region and was able to raise the fertility by fixing large amounts of nitrogen in the soil, thereby making way for the high fertility grasses such as the Mediterranean annual *Lolium rigidum* (Wimmera rye grass) and the perennials *Phalaris tuberosa* and *Ehrharta calycina*. Cook's work was important in extending the commercial uses of the pasture legumes throughout Australia and in pioneering the 'sub and super' form of farming[110] (Fig. 6).

From about 1923 onwards the frequency with which the subjects of fodder and grasses appear in the *Journal of Agriculturel* is indicative of their rising importance, and statistics on sown pastures began to be collected from 1924 onwards. At last there was the beginning of the recognition, however slight that grassland needed to be seen in the same light as cropland. Nevertheless, most developments of 'sub and super' during the pre-war years were still in the high rainfall podzolized soils of the South-East and the Adelaide Hills and not in the wheat lands where the need for them was possibly the greatest. Despite the constant exhortation and definite statements that 'the nodules of leguminous plants contain nitrogen-fixing bacteria' clovers as an answer to the loss of nitrogen through fallowing and the incipient erosion were not widely recognized.[111] The number of acres of sown pasture rose steadily from 64,212 in 1924/25 to a pre-war peak of 362,816, fifteen years later, but most of this acreage was in the Adelaide hills, and the total was insignificant when compared with the total area in crops throughout South Australia. The planting of clover obviously had little effect on the ruinous fallows which rose from 1,787,521 acres to 2,429,161 acres during the same period.

But it is in the years since 1945 that the great revolution has come about. Sown pastures have risen from 390,297 acres to 6,713,167 acres in 1967/68, and have outstripped all other forms of cropping (Fig. 79). The effect of this deliberate change cannot be measured in area alone, as the main significance of this widespread adoption of leguminous crops has been the doubling, even trebling, of the stock carrying capacity of the land and the rehabilitation and increased fertility of the soil for crops—in short, a radical transformation of the landscape in the old established agricultural areas. But the effect of the leguminous pastures has been greater still, for they have been an essential ingredient in the reclamation and settlement of completely new areas.

There are probably two main reasons for this spectacular increase in the area of sown pastures: the widening array of leguminous crops for all types of soil and climate, and the understanding, at last, of the soil deficiencies which produced coast disease in the Lower South-East in particular, and the stunted mallee-heath vegetation of the high-rainfall lands of Kangaroo Island, the Upper South-East, and the tips of Fleurieu, Yorke and Eyre Peninsulas.

Pastures: Varieties

The Mount Barker subterranean clover was restricted to the long growing season in the Adelaide hills, but the beneficial effects of legumes have been extended with new varieties, discovered and introduced since 1930, which are adopted to a shorter growing season. For example there is Dwalganup and Geraldton clover from Western Australia, and Bacchus Marsh, Yarloop and Clare clover, and, since 1945, Palestine Strawberry clover for the poorly drained high-rainfall areas in the Lower South-East—the reliability of the early spring rainfall being the main key to the type chosen. All these varieties are suited to the hard red-brown earth soils with a slightly acid to very acid reaction, situated in the 16- to 22-inch rainfall areas of the Central Hill Country, the Lower North and the Mount Lofty Ranges, and to other acidic soils in the Lower South-East. These clovers correct soil structure and counteract low fertility. They are difficult to establish initially, and need to be re-sown after each cropping phase.

On the loamy mallee soils with a loose friable structure, which extend throughout the 12- to 20-inch rainfall areas of Eyre

Peninsula, the Murray Mallee, Yorke Peninsula and the coastal plains, annual medics such as Barrel Medic (*Medicago tribuloides*), Harbinger Medic, Commercial Barrel Medic, and yet newer varieties such as Hannaford Barrel, Jemalong and Paragosa, are better adapted, being able to thrive in the alkaline, lime rich soils. They volunteer profusely, even after a few crops, because they produce a very hard seed that withstands the summer drought.

In both types of soils the trend is now to achieve 'balanced pastures' by mixing the legumes with perennial grasses, first to stop clover induced infertility and 'phalaris staggers' in sheep, diseases which occur with the predominance of one of these grasses in the sward. In addition, balanced pastures are more nutritive and botanically stable, and help to stop weed growth. Furthermore they help to overcome the problem of over-fertility in the soil through excessive accumulation of nitrogen.

Similarly, in both types of soils, adequate applications of superphosphate are essential for the establishment and growth of the pastures, but the application of fertilizer per acre varies according to the type of crop and the character of the soil. In the sandy mallee soils, 1–2 cwt of superphosphate are applied per acre for both crop and pasture; on the heavier red-brown earths, $\frac{3}{4}$ cwt is needed for crops and $1–1\frac{1}{2}$ cwt for pastures.[112] Whatever the type of soil, however, the application of fertilizer has risen markedly from a pre-war peak of 95 lb per acre fertilized in 1939, to 130 lb per acre in 1967, the increase being mainly attributable to the top-dressing of pastures (Fig. 77c). This is borne out by looking at the distribution in Fig. 84 of superphosphate applied per 1000 acres of cropland in a sample year, 1960. While heavy applications of between 200 and 400 lb per 1000 acres have been made to the wheat lands in Eyre Peninsula, the North and the Pinnaroo District, even greater amounts than 400 lb per acre are found in the predominantly pastoral areas of the Adelaide Hills and the South-East, and parts of Yorke Peninsula with very intensive rotations of barley and barrel medics. The South-East has many hundreds where the application exceeds 600 lb per 1000 acres, and two with over 700 lb per 1000 acres.

The natural build-up of nitrogen is evident in all types, but it is greater in the alkaline 'medic' soils than in the acid non-medic or 'sub-clover' soils. It is ironical that excessive fertility is now a

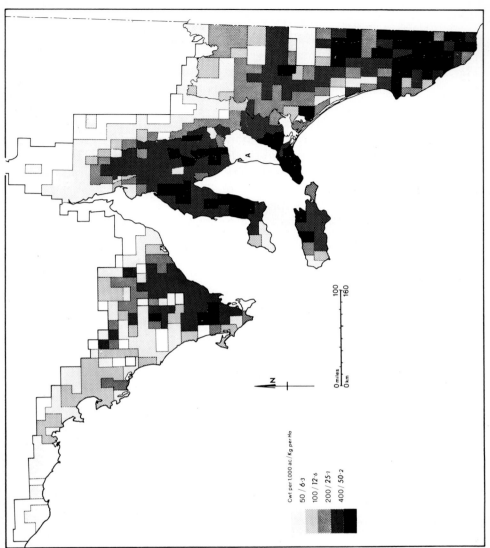

Cwt per 1,000 ac / Kg per Ha

50 / 6·3
100 / 12·6
200 / 25·1
400 / 50·2

F IG. 84. The application of superphosphate by hundreds, 1960.

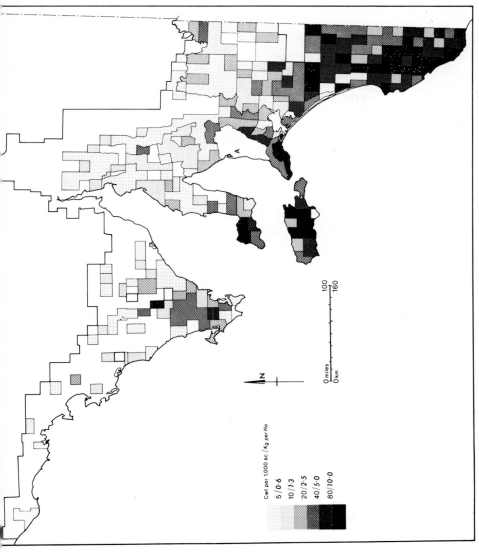

Fig. 85. The application of superphosphate with trace-elements added, by hundreds, 1960. (County Adelaide excluded)

problem that has to be counteracted by more cropping. As Donald points out, the number of crops that can, and has to, be taken in any period has become greater than the 50 per cent of the fallow-wheat-rotation, or the 33 per cent of the fallow-wheat-oats or fallow-wheat-rest rotation practised before. In the case of Yorke Peninsula,

'a two year rotation of barley and leguminous pastures (*Medicago tribuloides*) has given such a continuing increase in fertility that it is being replaced on many properties by a pasture-wheat-barley rotation with two crops in three years.'[113]

Detailed examples abound of the increase in rural production which has arisen from this higher fertility,[114] and one only must stand for many. French has analysed increases in the barley and wheat yields, and the number of sheep and yield of wool for an area of about 12,000 square miles covering Yorke Peninsula and the settled areas north of Adelaide, for three 10-year periods, 1931–40, 1941–50, and 1951–60.[115] In Table XVIII, the changes by 1951–60, expressed as a percentage of the figures for the decade 1931–40, are outlined for two typical Counties, Daly in the northern half of Yorke Peninsula (a medic area), and Light in the Central Hill Country (a sub-clover area). There has been a more than two-fold increase in production in nearly every case. The

Table XVIII

Production in Two Counties for the 1951–60 Period, expressed as Percentages of 1931–40 Values

	County Daly—Medic area		County Light—Sub-clover area	
	Wheat	Barley	Wheat	Barley
Acreage	60	212	43	230
Production	102	384	49	277
Bus./ac.	171	181	114	121
Sheep numbers	200		190	
Wool production	273		247	

Source: French (1968).

visual results have been striking; there are more stock, the amount of fallow has decreased to 1,062,880 acres by 1967–68, and there are more crops.

Trace Elements

The recognition that many of the soils of South Australia lack minute quantities of essential mineral elements such as copper, zinc, cobalt and molybdenum, has been another major factor in the recent reappraisal and changing of the soil. This discovery takes us full circle, for it was coast disease, the physical sign in stock of trace element deficiencies, which aroused curiosity in the soil over 100 years ago and stimulated serious interest in soil characteristics. That it took so long to elucidate the secret of these soils is not difficult to understand; whereas fallowing, fertilizing, dry farming, the cultivation of leguminous pastures and even soil erosion control were all measures of achieving change which were largely the result of practical experiment, aided at times by scientific knowledge, coast disease was beyond the scope and understanding of the farmer. Many of the previous measures of purposeful change had arisen out of the routine operations of the farmers, which had always included some experiment, some innovation, and some refinement of practice through trial and error. It must be admitted that the relationship between iron-stone country and freedom from the disease was an empirical observation of great significance. But it was neglected, and the antidote to coast disease lay solely in the laboratory; its discovery was a triumph for the agricultural scientist.

The idea that coast disease was of a parasitic origin persisted into the late 1920s. The creation of the Council for Scientific and Industrial Research in 1926 led to a new attack on the problem. C.S.I.R., in conjunction with the Waite Agricultural Research Institute of the University of Adelaide, began work on problems of animal nutrition and animal disease, and this research programme included the study of mineral deficiencies in pasture. Some of the earliest tasks were to investigate the composition of pastures in terms of their protein, mineral and vitamin content; the regeneration of natural pastures; and the relationship between the growth of stock, the nature of pastures and the geological characteristics of the countryside.[116]

An important discovery was made by R. G. Thomas who surveyed the distribution of coast disease on Kangaroo Island in 1929 and found a close correlation between its occurrence and the highly calcareous deposits along the coast. This discovery aroused the interests of those working on animal nutrition who were concerned particularly with calcium and phosphorus deficiencies, for at this stage, coast disease was thought to be related to these deficiencies. A survey of the South Australian mainland completed during 1933, further emphasised the correlation between the occurrence of coast disease and geology which had been discovered earlier on Kangaroo Island. Attention was thus focused on the relationship between the herbage, potential nutrient deficiency and coast disease.

During 1932–33 the C.S.I.R. was also working on the incidence of steely wool (*Enzootic Ataxia*) in lambs in Western Australia, and it was soon appreciated that this problem was closely related to coast disease. Experiments with trace elements were carried out in 1934 which established that coast disease resulted from nutrient deficiencies, and by 1935 cobalt was recognized as being an important trace element absent from the diet of 'coasty' sheep.[117]

A second line of attack on the problem came in 1938 from research in pasture development and improvement. The study of pasture defects was considered essential because Australia could not 'afford to neglect to explore the possibilities of territory with an assured rainfall of upwards of 20 in'.[118] Experimental work on pasture deficiencies was carried out in the field at Robe in the Lower South-East, and in the laboratory at the Waite Institute. 'Coasty' pastures at Robe were shown by Riceman and Donald to respond favourably to copper applications. The failure of cereals in the same area was shown to be similar to 'reclamation disease', known on the sandy reclaimed soils of Europe, and was attributed to copper deficiency by Piper.[119] (Fig. 75b).

Through work on the twin problems of animal nutrition and pasture development came the solution to the elusive problem of coast disease, which by 1938 was recognized as the symptom of trace element deficiency, particularly deficiency of cobalt and copper. From these initial discoveries came a more comprehensive appreciation of the characteristics of the last of the unfavourable lands of South Australia in the South-East, Kangaroo Island and the tips of Eyre, Yorke and Fleurieu Peninsulas. For example, Riceman's discovery in 1945 that oats grown on the Laffer sand responded to applications of zinc was the key to the understanding of the problems of the sparse and stunted vegetation of the Ninety-Mile Desert in the Upper South-East.[120]

The distribution of all known deficiencies and affected areas has been studied in a variety of publications[121] but Fig. 85 which shows the application of superphosphates with trace elements added per 1000 acres of cropland and pastures in 1960, helps to give a summary view of the distribution and intensity of the deficiencies of all types for South Australia. Outstanding areas are Kangaroo Island, the whole of the South-East and the southern extremities of the three peninsulas.[122]

Despite the discovery of the key to unlock these 'difficult' high-rainfall lands, none of them would have been reclaimed without the evolution of new agricultural techniques, governmental financial assistance for land development for ex-servicemen, the use of heavy caterpillar tractors for dragging chains and logs to clear the scrub covered land, the application of large amounts of superphosphate and the sowing of legumes with deep rooting qualities and nitrogen fixing properties, well adapted to the colonization of the loose sandy soils. To all these factors must be added the impact of increased demand for wool from 1952 to 1960, accompanied by high prices[123] which made agricultural development profitable. Hence, the post-war period has been a time of change and radical transformation of the landscape as the character of the soil has been understood better.

In the Upper South-East, the Government leased approximately 300,000 acres to the A.M.P. Insurance Society for clearing, improvement and sale as farms,[124] while the Government itself handled 670,000 acres and created approximately 700 new holdings in other parts of the State by 1962.[125] Of these, 177 are in Kangaroo Island, which must stand as a compact example for the changes in all other areas.[126] Figure 86 shows the area of scrub land cleared by 1958. In a sense, this cleared land serves as a summary statement of all the environmental and landscape changes on the Island, for these are the areas which have had their original vegetation removed and replaced by crops and pasture, and which have had their soils radically altered.

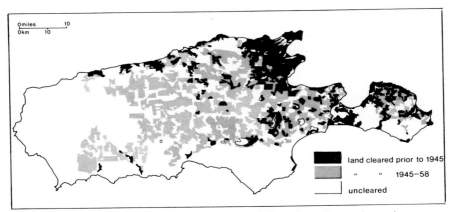

F I G. 86. Clearing in Kangaroo Island. Based on Bauer (1959).

Looking back over the efforts of 130 years to change the rural landscape it seems evident that the process of changing the character of the soil was more widespread than any other, except possibly for survey, ultimately more striking in the visual changes it wrought, except possibly for woodland clearing, and certainly more significant economically than all other activities put together. The story of the changing of the soil straddles and unites all other processes of change, for changing the soil and what it could grow and support was the ultimate aim of the colonizers in their efforts to make the landscape.

7. Notes

1. G. C. Morphett, *The life and letters of Sir John Morphett* (1936), 66.
2. G. Stevenson, 'Three letters on agriculture and gardening in South Australia', delivered to the Adelaide Mechanics Institute, during late 1839, *South Australian Magazine* (1840), 21–56.
   For an analysis of cropping practices and problems at this time see: M. Williams, 'Two studies in the historical geography of South Australia', in *Studies in Australian Geography*, ed. G. H. Drury and M. I. Logan (1968), 71.
3. K. Moon, 'Perception and appraisal of the South Australian landscape, 1836–1850', *Proc. Roy. Geog. Soc., S.A.*, LXX (1969), 41–64.

4. F. S. Dutton, *South Australia and its mines* (1846), 199;
   W. S. Chauncey, *A guide to South Australia* (1849), 24.
5. G. C. Morphett, op. cit., 17;
   W. S. Chauncey, op. cit., 26;
   S.A. Register (13 Sept. 1851).
6. F. Lancelott, *Australia as it is; its settlement, farming and goldfields* (1851),
   Vol. I, 109 and 111–12.
7. F. S. Dutton, op. cit., 219 and 237;
   F. Lancelott, op. cit., 110–13.
8. F. Sinnett, *An account of the colony of South Australia* (1862), 46.
9. CSO, 2354/1855 (in).
   For earlier moves see *SAPP*, 64 (1853).
10. *The Farm and the Garden*, I (1858), 40; V (1862), 56.
11. *SAPP*, 20 (1868–69), app. xxxvi–lxiii;
    E. Dunsdorfs, *The Australian wheat-growing industry, 1788–1948* (1956),
    138–9.
12. *SAPP*, 20 (1868–69), app. viii.
13. *SAPP*, 4* (1862), 5.
14. P. D. Edwards and R. B. Joyce (eds), *Australia by Anthony Trollope* (1965),
    651–2.
15. *SAPD* (L.C.) (1874), col. 599.
16. *SAPP*, 77 (1875).
17. *Garden and Field*, I (1875–76), 120.
18. *SAPP*, 23 (1870–71), 8, quoted in D. W. Meinig, *On the margins of the
    good earth: the South Australian wheat frontier, 1869–1884* (1962), 118.
19. *SAPP*, 20 (1868–69), viii.
20. *Garden and Field* (1877–78), 125.
21. *SAPP*, 101 (1861), 4.
22. The basis of this account is sketchy and is taken from R. Cockburn,
    Pastoral pioneers of South Australia (1927), Vol. II, 76–77. The only other
    information available is that von Mueller arrived in Adelaide in December
    1847 and took a job as a chemist. His first botanical work was a paper to
    the Linnaean Society of London on the flora of South Australia, in 1852.
    He was appointed botanist to the Government of Victoria in 1853.
23. Based on detailed valuations in SAPP, 102–106 (1864); 30 and 30A
    (1865); and 31, 77, 86, 87, 110 and 126 (1865–66).
24. *SAPP*, 137 (1865–66), 1.
25. *Border Watch* (24 March and 3 Nov. 1866).
26. *SAPP*, 34 (1872), qu. 660, et seq.
27. *Border Watch*, (16 June and 18 July 1869).
28. E. Ward, *The South-Eastern district of South Australia* (1869), 19.
29. Anon., *The South-Eastern district of South Australia in 1880* (1881), 61.

30. A. J. Perkins, *An enquiry into South-East conditions* (1904), 28.

31. *Garden and Field*, IV (1878–79), 4–5.

32. J. A. Scott Watson, *The history of the Royal Agricultural Society of England, 1839–1939* (1939).

33. Throughout 1880–82, there was a great deal of interest in guano deposits on the islands off the coast of Eyre Peninsula, such as those near Coffins Bay, the Nyuts Archipelago off Smoky Bay, the Sir Joseph Banks Group off Port Lincoln, and Neptune Island almost midway in the ocean between Port Lincoln and Kangaroo Island. Some nitrates were also found in caves at Mount Muirhead in the South-East. In all cases the deposits were small and expensive to market. *Inter alia* SGO, 54/1880 (in); 3829/1880 (in); 1702/1881 (in); 2508/1881 (in).

34. *Garden and Field*, V (1879–80).

35. *SAPP*, 33 (1883–84);
   Garden and Field, IX (1883–84), 36.

36. *Garden and Field*, X (1884–85), 154; IX, (1883–84), 166;

37. Ibid. XI (1885–86), 95, 102 and 142;
   SAPP, 41 (1887), 24.

38. *Garden and Field*, XI (1885–86), 102.

39. N. T. Grierson, 'The position of agriculture', *Garden and Field*, XIV (1888–89), 128.

40. *SAPP*, 181 (1891), 9; 80 (1895), 13.

41. *Garden and Field*, IX (1883–84), 175;
   SAPP, 127 (1893).

42. *Garden and Field*, XI (1885–86), 142. Custance realized that this was excessive and later reduced it to 3 cwt per acre.

43. *SAPP*, 129 (1896), 19; 115 (1897), 7.

44. *Garden and Field*, XXII (1896–97), 289;
   SAPD (H.A.) (1898–99), 299.

45. *SAPP*, 122 (1898–99).

46. *SAPD* (L.C.) (1898–99), p. 164. With this increased use local production was boosted and imports rose, e.g.,

Date	Local Prod.	Imports	Total
1899	4,000 tons	12,500 tons	16,500 tons
1900	3,400 tons	21,200 tons	24,000 tons
1901	5,000 tons	26,400 tons	31,400 tons
1902	10,500 tons	27,000 tons	37,500 tons

The decline in local production at the turn of the century resulted from the working-out of the high-grade guano deposits. In 1899 the Adelaide Chemical Works began production at Thebarton and Port Adelaide and

the marked rise in production in 1902 was because of the establishment of the Wallaroo Phosphate Company (later amalgamated with Mount Lyell Copper of Tasmania to become Cresco) in the heart of the wheat lands. Production was sustained from then on by imports of phosphate from Christmas Island and Nauru. For the early history of the industry see the Inspector of Fertilizers' Reports, *SAJA*, II (1898–99), 918–19; III (1899–1900), 985–7; IV (1900–1), 969–71; V (1901–2), 922–3;
for the subsequent history see A. R. Callaghan and A. J. Millington, *The wheat industry in Australia* (1956), 91–93; and 143–55;
C. M. Donald, 'Phosphates in Australian agriculture', *Journ. Aust. Inst. Agric. Sci.*, XXX (1964), 75.

47. For a detailed study of wheat fields see E. A. Cornish, 'Yield trend in the wheat belt of South Australia during 1896–1941', *Aust. Journ. Sci. Res., Ser. B*, 'Biological Science', II (1949), 83–136.

48. *West Coast Recorder* (16 August 1911).

49. W. Lowrie, 'South Australian Farming', Paper given, *Agricultural Bureau of S.A., Second Congress* (1890), 8.

50. Anon., *The Australian farmer: a practical handbook for the farm and station* (1885), 26, suggested that rolling helped to press the loose soil together which 'enabled it to more effectively retain moisture, a point of great importance in nearly all parts of Australia'.

51. *Garden and Field*, XIV (1888–89), 11; XV (1889–90), 67; XIV (1888–89), 144.

52. Ibid. XIX (1893–94), 4; XVIII (1892–93), 132.

53. Ibid. XVI (1890–91), 114; XVII (1891–92), 133.

54. *SAPP*, 24 (1893), app. 16.

55. J. Correll, 'Drilling grain crops with fertilizers'. Paper given, *Agricultural Bureau of S.A., Eighth Congress* (1896), 7.

56. *SAJA*, V (1901–2), 991; II (1898–99), 929; and other comments in VIII (1904–5), 706.

57. *SAPP*, 43 (1901), 6.

58. W. Lowrie, 'The farm', *SAJA*, I (1897–98), 137–140;
Idem, 'The position of agricultural practice in the State', in *Handbook of South Australia*, eds D. J. Gordon and J. V. H. Ryan (1914), 115.

59. W. L. Summers, *Notes on Agriculture in South Australia* (1908), pamphlet.

60. *SAPP*, 43 (1901), 6;
SAJA, VI (1902–3), 568.

61. *SAJA*, I (1897–98), 17.

62. Ibid. II (1898–99), 87; V (1901–2), 62–3.

63. W. Lowrie, 'The position of agricultural practice in South Australia' in *Handbook of South Australia*, eds D. J. Gordon and J. V. H. Ryan (1914), 115.

64. It is probable that some form of dry farming was practised in California since the early 1850s, but it was the drought of the late 1880s in the newly settled Great Plains that first led to the adoption of the practice on a large scale. See W. D. Rasmussen (ed.), *Readings in the history of American agriculture* (1960), 34.

65. T. Pascoe, 'Dry farming : Professor Campbell's system of soil culture', *SAJA*, IX (1905–6), 769–71.

66. *SAJA*, XIII (1909–10), 1078.

67. *SAJA*, XI (1907–8), 714, 813 and 913;
Report of the First Interstate Dry Farming Conference, Adelaide, 1911, March 6–8th (1911), quoted at length in A. R. Callaghan and A. J. Millington, op. cit., 114–20.

68. *Pinnaroo and Country News* (19 Nov. 1909).

69. *SAPD* (H.A.) (1898–99), p. 316.

70. *Garden and Field*, XX (1894–95), 288;
SAJA, I (1897–98), 310–12.

71. *SAPD* (L.C.) (1874), col. 1011;
SAJA, III (1899–1900), 981; IX (1905–6), 111.

72. For example *SAJA*, XXX (1926–27), 738 and 860;
A. H. Robinson, 'Stomach worms in sheep', *SAJA*, XXIX (1925–26), 640.

73. *SAJA*, XXX (1926–27), 397 and 860.

74. *First Annual Report, C.S.I.R.* (1926–27);
SAPP, 71 (1925); 55 (1926).

75. *SAPP*, 10 (1910), 12.
See also A. E. Richardson in *Report of the First Interstate Dry Farming Conference, Adelaide, 1911, March 6–8th* (1911), 8, 'the truth has slowly dawned upon the cultivator that his measure of success in the dry seasons is largely determined by the efficiency with which he cultivates the soil'.

76. A. J. Perkins, 'Possibilities of increased production in our rural industries', *SAJA*, XXIII (1919–20), 400.
See also W. J. Spafford 'South Australian agriculture and its requirements from science', in *SAJA*, XXVI (1922–23), 17. Spafford writes : 'The prosperity of South Australia is almost wholly dependent on its agriculture'

77. A. J. Perkins, 'Is rural production on the decline in South Australia and if so what are the factors contributing thereto ?', *SAJA*, XXIX (1925–26), 143.

78. R. J. French, 'New facts about fallowing', *SAJA*, LXVII (1963–64), 42 and 76.

79. For a good survey of erosion problems see R. I. Herriot, 'Making best use of limited rainfall', *SAJA*, XLVII (1943–44), 528–32;
Idem., 'Organic matter in relation to agriculture', *SAJA*, XXXIX (1935–36), 1392.

80. R. L. Griffiths, 'Efficient wheat growing methods', *SAJA*, XXXV (1931–32), 1086;
   SAPP, 40 (1938), 16.
81. A. J. Perkins 'Ten years progress in wheat growing', *SAJA*, XXXI (1927–28), 240.
82. *SAPP*, 43 (1932), 9; *SAPP*, 43 (1933), 6.
83. *SAPP*, 43 (1934), 8.
84. A. J. Perkins, 'Some parting reflexions on wheat growing in South Australia', *SAJA*, XXXVIII (1934–35), 696.
   In the same issue a lengthy technical article by A. E. V. Richardson and H. C. Gurney, 'Nitrogen in relation to cereal culture', p. 954, showed why fallowing was so successful in raising wheat yield but made no mention of the adverse effects of continuous nitrogen loss.
85. F. N. Ratcliffe, 'Soil drift in the arid pastoral areas of South Australia', *C.S.I.R.O.*, Pamphlet No. 64 (1936).
86. *SAJA*, III (1899–1900), 200; II (1898–99), 48.
87. *SAPP*, 79 (1899), 8; *SAJA*, V (1901–2), 723.
88. *SAJA*, VI (1902–3), 321;
   Act, 1598/1923. Sand Drift Act, gave District Councils power to make landowners prevent drift which was dangerous to public roads—now becoming a major problem with the rise of fast traffic on rural roads.
89. *Pinnaroo and Country News* (20 Sept. 1912).
90. W. J. Spafford, 'The control of drifting sand', *SAJA*, XXXII (1928–29), 700;
   R. L. Griffiths, 'Fallowing and cultivation methods for sandy soils', *SAJA*, XXXIII (1929–30), 513;
   Idem., 'Efficient wheat growing methods', XXXV (1931–32), 1086.
91. *Idem.*, 'Wind erosion of soils in the agricultural areas', *SAJA*, XL (1936–37), 25.
92. R. I. Herriot, 'Soil conservation', *SAJA*, XLIV (1940–41), 687–88.
93. A. J. Perkins 'Goyder's line of rainfall', *SAJA*, XXXIX (1935–36), 78.
94. *Idem.*, 'Our wheat growing areas profitable and unprofitable', *SAJA*, XXXIX (1935–36), 1211.
95. A. R. Callaghan, 'The recovery of wheat prices and some agricultural reflections thereon', *SAJA*, XL (1936–37), 923.
96. W. V. Roediger, 'Erosion of farmlands—cause and control', *SAJA*, XLVI (1942–43), 102;
   see also R. I. Herriot, 'Soil conservation : A community problem', *SAJA*, XLVI (1942–43), 376.
97. C. R. Kelly, 'Water erosion', *SAJA*, XLIII (1939–40), 452.
98. C. G. Stephens, *et al.*, 'A soil, land use and erosion survey of part of County Victoria, South Australia', *C.S.I.R.*, *Australia, Bulletin No. 188* (1945).

A still later survey showing equally devastating results was that of G. Blackburn and R. M. Baker, 'Survey of Soils, land use and erosion in the northern marginal lands, South Australia', *C.S.I.R.O., Australia, Division of Soils, Soils and Land Use Series No. 6* (1952).

99. R. I. Herriot, 'The Cinderella of agriculture', *SAJA*, XLVII (1943–44), 57.

100. R. I. Herriot, 'Soil erosion: the present position and what it means', *SAJA*, XLVIII (1944–45), 331.
It is difficult to assess whether or not these dust storms were any more frequent or intensive than previous ones. There are no quantitative data available at the Bureau of Meteorology on solid matter in the air. Nevertheless there is a general agreement by people that the early- to mid-forties were particularly bad, and it is significant that Lowe's report on dust storms deals with the period 1938–42. He considered that the storms were caused by soil particles originating in the cultivation fringes and the dry interior, which were stirred up by turbulence ahead of cold fronts moving across the south-eastern corner of Australia: F. Lowe, 'Dust storms of Australia', *Comm. of Aust. Bureau of Meteorology, Bulletin No. 28* (1943).

101. A good summary article on the financial problems of the farmer at this time is given in O. Bowden, 'Our agriculture at a cross road', *SAJA*, XLVI (1942–43), 351.

102. R. I. Herriot, 'Soil erosion: the present position and what it means', *SAJA*, XLVIII (1944–45), 332;
Idem., 'Soil conservation in relation to methods of production', *SAJA* op. cit., 350.

103. C. M. Donald, 'Innovation in Australian agriculture', in *Agriculture in the Australian economy*, ed. D. B. Williams (1968), 73.

104. From Farrer's letter accepting appointment as wheat experimentalist in the N.S.W. Department of Agriculture (30 August 1898), quoted in, A. Russell, *William James Farrer* (1949), 108–110.

105. See C. M. Donald, 'Pastures', in *Introducing South Australia*, ed. R. J. Best (1958), 149–155;
C. D. Blake (ed.) Fundamentals of modern agriculture (1967), see Ch. 9. 'Pasture production and utilization'.

106. *S.A. Advertiser* (3 Feb. and 2 March 1906).

107. The best summary of Howard's attempts is in D. E. Symon, *A bibliography of subterranean clover together with a descriptive introduction*, Mimeographed Publication No. 1 (1961), Commonwealth Bureau of Pastures and Field Crops.

108. *SAJA*, XXI (1917–18), 931.

109. For its early history see *S.A. Register* (20, 22, 25 and 27 July 1905).

These articles were later reprinted as *Kybyolite Experimental Farm; an agricultural awakening*, Adelaide (1907).

Two local farmers from Naracoorte, S. S. Shepherd and E. C. Schinkel, had already established subterranean clover pastures, and by 1918 A. J. Perkins was advocating dressings of lime and phosphate on these pastures in order to improve their growth. *SAJA*, XXII (1918–19), 641.

110. See in particular, L. J. Cook, 'The improvement of pastures', *SAJA*, XXVI (1922–23), 1042;

Idem., 'Resumé of 12 years' pasture experimental work at Kybybolite', XXXVII (1933–34), 248;

Idem., *An agricultural history of Kybybolite*, (probably *c.* 1957), mimeographed.

D. E. Symon lists another 32 additional articles by Cook on subterranean clover and its effects.

111. See *SAJA*, XXVIII (1924–25), 778; XXVII (1923–24), 380;

W. J. Spafford, 'Some necessary improvements in our farming practice', *SAJA*, XXIV (1920–21), 815.

112. R. J. French and C. L. Rudd, 'Yield increases with superphosphate', *SAJA*, LXX (1966–67), 336.

For an excellent summary see C. M. Donald, 'Phosphates in Australian agriculture', *Journ. Aust. Inst. Agric. Sci.*, XXX (1964), 75.

113. *Idem.*, 'The progress of Australian agriculture and the role of pastures in environmental change', *Aust. Journ. Sci.*, XXVII (1965), 192.

114. See G. D. Weber, 'Clovers will lift soil fertility and production', *SAJA*, LXVII (1963–64), 354;

J. R. Goode, 'Clover leys lift wheat and wool output', *SAJA*, LXVI (1962–63) 358;

C. M. Donald 'The progress of Australian agriculture' (1965) for a review of the literature throughout Australia. Donald would ascribe 48 per cent of the increase in total stock numbers in the period 1947–63 to pasture improvement, the remainder to other factors such as myomatosis, disease control, fodder conservation, fencing, watering, irrigation, improved transport etc.

115. R. J. French, *Soils and agriculture of the Northern and Yorke Peninsula regions of South Australia* (1968). Particularly Table IV, and Figs. 9, 11, 13 of the distribution of increases by hundreds.

116. *C.S.I.R. First Annual Report* (1926–27), 34.

117. H. R. Marston, *et al.*, 'Studies on coast disease in sheep in South Australia', *C.S.I.R. Bulletin No. 113* (1938).

118. *C.S.I.R., 7th Annual Report* (1932–33), 38.

119. D. S. Riceman, C. M. Donald, C. S. Piper, 'A copper deficiency in plants at Robe, South Australia', *C.S.I.R. Pamphlet 78* (1938);

D. S. Riceman and S. M. Donald, 'Copper response on "coasty" calcareous soils in South Australia', *SAJA*, XLII (1938–39), 959.

120. D. S. Riceman, 'Mineral deficiency in plants in the soils of the Ninety-Mile Desert in South Australia', Part 1, *C.S.I.R. Journ.*, *XVIII* (1945), 336;

Part 2, *C.S.I.R. Bulletin No. 234* (1948);

Part 3, *C.S.I.R. Journ.* XXI (1948) 229;

Part 4, *C.S.I.R. Bulletin, No. 249* (1949);

Idem., 'Mineral deficiency and pasture establishment in the Coonalpyn Downs, South Australia', *SAJA*, LIV (1950–51), 132.

121. For example see N. S. Tiver 'Deficiencies in South Australian soils', *SAJA*, LIX (1955–56), 100;

A. Marshall, 'Desert becomes Downs', *Aust. Geog.*, XII (1972), 23.

122. Trace elements do not require reapplication for several years so it may be that the proportion of land treated is undervalued for 1960 but is likely that the location and relative amounts, one area with another, are correct.

123. The *Quarterly Review of Agricultural Economics* gives the following :

1945–46 to 1949–50 average price of greasy wool 38s.-2d. per lb.

1950–51 to 1954–55 average price of greasy wool 90s.-2d. per lb.

1955–56 to 1959–60 average price of greasy wool 61s.-4d. per lb.

124. See M. C. Butterfield, *The A.M.P. Land development scheme*, Australian Mutual Provident Society (1958);

SAPP, 71 (1949).

125. See S. *Australian Government, Land Development Executive, Department of Lands Progress in Land Development* (*non-irrigation*), annual reports 1946 to 1962;

N. S. Tiver, 'Scrub to pasture in the South-East', *SAJA*, LXII (1958–59), 117.

126. For a detailed study of Kangaroo Island see F. H. Bauer, 'The regional geography of Kangaroo Island', unpublished Ph.D. thesis, Australian National University, (1959).

8
Building the Townships

'Alas for poor Hanson! the wheat stacks have vanished,
On the platform is left but a few straggling loads;
The buyers themselves will shortly be banished,
Then Hanson may sigh, for no good luck it bodes.
The streets are all bare, the "pub" is deserted,
The glorious old engines now rust in the bar;
O! ye fates! why was not this sorrow averted?
Sure our town's in the power of some evil star!'

'Hansonia's Lament', by D.D., on the rise of Port Pirie. *Northern Argus* (27 Feb. 1874).

In making the South Australian landscape man has not only cleared the vegetation, changed soils and altered hydrological and drainage features, but he has also built himself a place in which to live. His habitation has either been an individual homestead on the farm, or has been clustered with others in small towns, which impress the traveller to this part of Australia by their appearance and their frequency.

Putting aside the suburban creations around Adelaide and the larger townships, there are about 510 settlements in South Australia that have some pretence of being independent urban entities. This is an average of about one township to every 118 square miles of land within the hundreds. Of course, this mean figure overlooks many local variations and the fact that some of the townships were mere 'paper-towns', some a pattern of pegs in the ground, some surveyed but never offered for sale, and some offered but not bought and subsequently cancelled. Nevertheless, all these townships have been included in the maps and tables as their creation and their plans are indicative of contemporary ideas of town siting and design.

The large number of townships should be no surprise when one remembers the South Australian tradition of planning in survey and settlement matters and of guiding and controlling expansion both spatially and temporally. The township was an integral and logical part of that settlement process, and, of the 510 townships, 370 or 72·5 per cent, were created by the Government in conjunction with rural surveys. Moreover, from the beginning, the emphasis had been to establish a stationary agricultural population on farms of small to medium size and the density of population that accompanied this settlement (given the restricted personal mobility of the nineteenth century) of necessity required a fairly uniform scatter of market centres in order to provide social and retail functions. As Meinig has said, because of our concern for rural matters there has been a tendency for the country township to be 'the forgotten feature of frontier', but, after all, the tradesman was no less a pioneer than the farmer.[1] This tendency to ignore urban matters has run through most Australian regional studies, which have dealt with towns sporadically and set them apart from the main body of work, while the authors have 'written up the highlights of individual towns without worrying about wider significance or inner coherence'.[2]

Yet, towns were not just after-thoughts in land settlement, even from the time of Macquarie in New South Wales.[3] They were the focal points of economic exploitation and the spearheads of colonization; they had inter-relationships one with another through competition, and they had internal patterns which differed. Because towns were such an indigenous part of the settlement process they are included with hundreds and railways as one of the criteria for the geographical over-view of settlement expansion in Chapter 2. True, a few were created before hundreds were proclaimed, but the overwhelming majority (over four-fifths) were created immediately after or within four years of their respective hundreds.[4] But generally speaking, the township is a good indicator of the expansion of settlement.

Creating and Locating Townships

There is an important distinction to be made about townships in South Australia, as indeed there is about towns throughout the whole of the continent, and that is whether or not they are private or government townships. By this is meant whether they were townships created and surveyed as speculative entities, by private individuals or whether they were townships created and surveyed by the colonial Government as part of the total system of either leasing or surveying and disposing of Crown Land (Fig. 87).

The role of the Government in creating and planning townships in South Australia was remarkably comprehensive and it distinguished this nineteenth-century colonization from the speculative turmoil that accompanied urban development in newly settled areas elsewhere—in the United States and Canada for example.[5] Figure 87 shows the location of all private and government townships, the private townships in the immediate vicinity of Adelaide being omitted. As early private township development was speculative and, to a certain extent haphazard, probably more township sites were surveyed than we know of today. It was not so with government townships, each of which was carefully surveyed and recorded on the cadastral plans of the State.

There were 370 government townships and 140 private townships. In the Mount Lofty Ranges and the Central Hill Country which were settled mainly before 1865 (Fig. 10), private townships outnumbered government townships by three to one, and similarly, in a small portion of the Lower South-East there was a roughly one to one distribution of private and government townships. Elsewhere, government townships dominated the urban scene. Their density was so great and their supremacy so well ensured by being the first townships created in the newly colonized areas, that there was little room for the survey of private townships, and, even if these were surveyed, there was little chance of their succeeding as viable economic units with so many near competitors.

Yet, government interest in township creation had not always been so all-pervading. During the thirty years after the establishment of Adelaide the Government took relatively little interest in township creation consciously hoping that private township

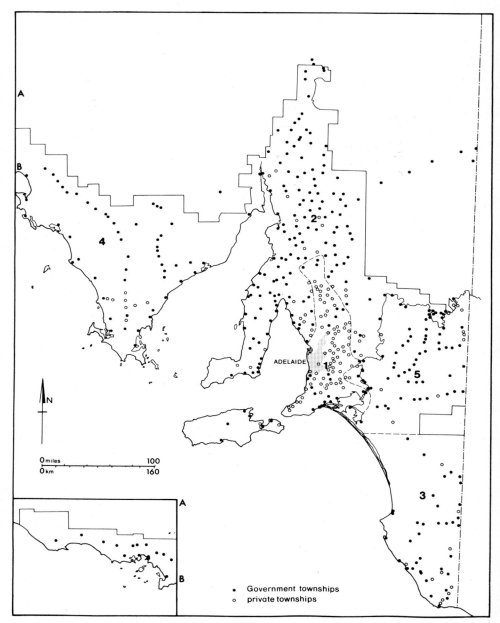

FIG. 87. Private and government townships.

creation would inject much needed capital into the infant settle-ment.[6] At this stage government township creation was sporadic, and, when implemented, was directed at providing a framework of essential ports, service centres and staging posts at widely scattered points, largely in order to serve the expanding pastoral industry. In all, 44 towns were created, including Port Lincoln, Bordertown, Port Augusta, and Robe, which, with others, were later to have great regional importance. Generally speaking, however, up to the mid-1860s, township creation was a secondary consideration, and once the land had been surveyed and sold, official interest in it vanished. This gave the private speculator the opportunity to concentrate his activity in the areas of agricultural settlement where there was about one family to every 80 acres, and, therefore, a need for community facilities. In a few cases where the Government located a township badly the opportunity arose of subdividing the adjacent site. Rarely, however, was there the opportunity of capitalizing on a government township by subdividing adjacent paddocks as suburbs,[7] for the Government surveyed a superfluity of lots in the suburban lands of its own creations, many of which remained unsold for many years.

The Private Townships

Speculative subdivision was rife from the very beginning in the settlement of South Australia and was to be seen first in the swapping of the blocks in Adelaide for enormously inflated prices, and then in the subdivision of the 80-acre sections beyond the encircling belt of parklands where villages 'sprung up like mushrooms'; and it was not long before country sections well away from Adelaide were being subdivided.

The opportunity for speculative promotion of townships seemed so favourable and the profits so obvious that in 1838 the Secondary Towns Association was formed by capitalists in Britain who employed an agent in South Australia to select two Special Surveys in which secondary towns could be laid out, one near the coast and one inland. The instructions of the Association's Board were copious and impossible to fulfil; consequently, the agent spent so much time in trying to find the ideal situations that he missed some potentially good sites which were snapped up by others. He explained: 'There are too many devoted to that object already. The formation of Towns and Villages has become a favourite scheme of the speculative for some time past; although many of them will never have an existence except in name.' Along the banks of the River Murray and on the shores of Lake Alexandrina, six townships were planned 'of which I am doubtful if more than two will ever rise to importance'. With such a large area in which to choose sites and with so many people already attempting to create townships it was little wonder that the agent wrote, 'I am quite at a loss to know where to direct my steps in search of a promising locality'. Eventually, he did decide upon Victoria, near Kapunda, and Wellington on the west bank of the Murray.[8]

It is possible to trace the origins of many of the private townships from collections of subdivisional plans, information in the Lands Titles Office after 1857, and numerous local histories.[9] Each township creation was a story of local initiative and economic opportunism, but their mortality rate was high, and of all those that were born it is probable that as many died as survived their infant years. It is inevitable, therefore, that one concentrates upon the successes which, because of building activity, remained as tangible features in the landscape. The attitude to township creation and to the multiplicity of subdivisions was ascribed by one astute observer to the fact that :

'Young men of spirit were not satisfied to retire into the bush and look after a flock of silly sheep when it was possible to buy a section of land at £1 an acre, give it a fine name as a village, sell the same thing at £10 an acre, for a bill the bank would discount, and live in style at the Southern Cross Hotel.'[10]

Most of the new subdivisions were in the Mount Lofty Ranges (97 out of 140) and within this general location, many were established near the Special Surveys, in the plains immediately north and south of Adelaide, and in the area of German settlement in the Barossa Valley. The origin, growth and subsequent development of many of these early private townships have been described elsewhere,[11] but suffice it to say that by 1840, Noarlunga, Willunga, Strathalbyn, Mount Barker, Nairne, Hahndorf, Balhannah and Gawler ('a very good inn, one public house, police barracks, two smiths' shops, six dwelling houses and thirty-four inhabitants') had been established, and by 1855, other major towns such as Gumeracha, Salisbury, Lyndoch, Tanunda, Angaston, Kapunda and Burra, for example, had been in existence for at least a decade.

The Government Townships

The uncertainty which characterizes some of our knowledge about private townships is dispelled when we come to consider the government townships for which there is ample evidence, giving the date of their creation, their size and the decisions taken in their location, siting and layout. Initially the Government was unsure of its precise role in township creation which was felt to be the responsibility of the speculative developer. But the slowness and hesitancy in involving itself in the process disappeared towards the end of the 1850s when specific needs demanded action.

Of the 44 townships surveyed before 1865 (Adelaide excepted), few were created to serve the agriculturally based population, except, perhaps, the very earliest townships associated with the Special Surveys, such as Wellington East (1841), and Macclesfield (1840). Naracoorte (1859) and Gambier Town (1861) were government suburbs grafted on to the private creations of Kincraig and Mount Gambier, towns where population growth and the prospect of abundant and rising revenue seemed to justify the laying out of government monies and government townships.[12] But, generally speaking, at this time township creation in the agricultural portions of the colony was the preserve of the private person and company and as such was well, even excessively, catered for. Even as late as 1860 the Government was wary of creating townships near those 'already laid out'.[13] The Government was more concerned at this stage with providing towns for two other economic activities that might not attract the private speculator because of their location either in inhospitable regions or at great distances from established centres of population, that is to say, for mining and for the pastoral industry.

In the case of mining towns, Burra was grafted on to the private creations of Redruth and Kooringa in 1857 (Fig. 88). With the discovery of copper in the northern parts of Yorke Peninsula in 1861, Moonta, Wallaroo, Kadina and the associated ports of Clinton and Port Hughes, were laid out.[14] Blinman, another copper town was created in 1864.

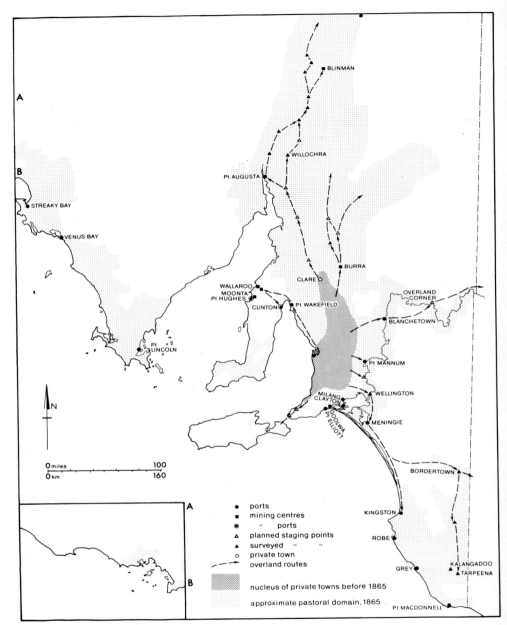

FIG. 88. The strategy of government township creation, c. 1865.

In the pastoral areas the aim was to provide a structure of ports and inland service and staging centres on major inter- and intra-colonial route-ways. Like many of the seemingly ordered land policies of the South Australian Government, that of providing urban centres for the pastoralist and traveller evolved almost haphazardly to begin with, lagging in its response to needs; but by 1859, the policy was formalized and the general strategy implemented.

The first halting moves in this plan were the creation of the ports of Grey (1846) and Robe (1846) as outlets for the rapidly expanding pastoral areas in the South-East. To the north of Adelaide, Port Wakefield was laid out in 1850, and after pastoral settlement had penetrated further north again, Port Augusta was surveyed in 1855. More ports were established in the South-East, at Port MacDonnell (1860) and Kingston (1861). In Eyre Peninsula, Port Lincoln (1840) was the first outlet for the pastoralists, and, as settlement moved along the west coast it was supplemented by Venus Bay (1864) and Streaky Bay (1865).

The promise held forth by the River Murray, during the 1850s, as the supply route and the outlet for the river-fronted runs in South Australia, Victoria and New South Wales was the reason for the creation of another set of ports catering for river navigation. Goolwa (1853) was at the terminus of the river traffic, but, as easy access could not be gained through the sand bars at the mouth of the Murray it was joined by a tramway to Port Elliot (1864), further west along the coast. In 1858 Milang and Clayton were surveyed on the shores of Lake Alexandrina. But the river trade was not the only cause for township creation along the Murray. The lure of Victorian gold temporarily diverted South Australian attention away from the North towards the east, and this meant crossing the physical obstacle of the River Murray. Four major roads led eastwards from Adelaide and townships were located at the termini of three of them—at Wellington (1840), Port Mannum (1864) and Blanchetown (1855)—the fourth township was planned in 1854 but not built.[15] Port Mannum and Blanchetown served as ports for the movement of wheat grown in the eastern Mount Lofty Ranges and then shipped upstream. Wellington functioned as a major river crossing and its importance was enhanced by the creation of Meningie (1866) on the overland route across the Ninety-Mile Desert and the swamps of the Lower South-East.

But after 1858, the piece-meal provision of towns and ports gave way to a new strategy for circulation within the Colony, when the Government wanted to select the sites for at least nineteen townships 'of moderate size on the principal lines of communication throughout the pastoral districts'. The townships were to be spaced at intervals of 20 to 25 miles, about the limit of a comfortable day's haulage, in order 'to facilitate the traffic of the interior and cartage connected with stations, and to accommodate the travelling public by the erection of inns, and other buildings for artisans.'[16] Eventually, Goyder and other surveyors selected seventeen potential sites of about 40 acres in size, twelve in the North following the roads from Clare and Burra which penetrated the pastoral districts, two in the South-East, two in Fleurieu Peninsula and one along the upper course of the River Murray, near the big loop, at Overland Corner. Mainly because of water supply considerations the sites selected finally for the northern towns were at intervals varying between 12 and 52 miles. On the whole, Goyder did not like the idea of creating these townships in the pastoral districts and questioned the wisdom of establishing them because :

> 'The first erection would undoubtedly be an inn which would be the resort of the shepherds and stockmen within reach and whose wages would go in the purchase of ardent spirits, rum and beer, demoralization would ensue and the interests of the squatter seriously affected.'

Inevitably, it seemed to him, these towns would be the 'ruin of the runs' and give reasonable cause for complaint from the pastoral lessees. More practically and certainly, Goyder feared that the return from the sales of the allotments 'would but poorly pay the Govt. the expense they will have incurred in making the surveys'.[17] But neither possible objections nor the likelihood of poor financial returns deterred the Government from deciding to go ahead with the establishment of townships, and Kalangadoo (1859) and then Tarpeena (1860) in the Lower South-East were the first to be established.[18]

The story of the first of the northern group of planned townships,

Willochra, was told fully about two months later. Goyder, then the Deputy Surveyor-General, and his survey party had finished their northern reconnaissance and were returning to Port Augusta in late December during a dust storm caused by a strong northerly wind. They stopped to get water at Ragless' station which was near to one of the sites selected :

'I had pumped up sufficient from the well near the Reserve [related Goyder to Freeling] when the Dust happened to clear away for a few moments and the party were seen from the house and a person sent down to prevent the water being used on the plea that they had a good many sheep to water . . . had the land not been private property I should have taken the water despite his objections . . . We had to give one of the horses all the water in the canteens for the use of the men and shortly after leaving there it fell down from exhaustion. It would be impossible to convey to you an idea of the day and I bitterly felt the want of some accommodation for the poor brutes, and really must respectfully urge upon you the propriety of surveying allotments at this inhospitable abode with the least possible delay.'

Within days, the Commissioner of Crown Lands, Milne, had sent Sapper Elder to the station with instructions to survey a water reserve and eight square miles of the run into a township with surrounding rural sections. The alacrity and severity of the reaction, while showing the very real need that existed for watering places for the public and for stock in the pastoral areas, suggests that the incident had particularly stung Goyder by its injustice and by its lack of comradeship in adversity. It is one of the few insights we get into Goyder's personal feelings.[19]

Of the 1,826 acres of small sections and of the 88-acre township which were eventually surveyed at Willochra, the Surveyor-General later had to report that 'there have been sold 8 half-acre Town allotments and 624 acres (in one section)'. He had to admit the ridiculousness of the situation and said :

'I am not favourable to the declaration of a Hundred in this locality; the country is not agricultural and therefore I conceive that declaring the same into a Hundred will not advance the sale of land there.'[20]

This over-provision of surveyed land in the pastoral townships and the expense incurred for so little return may have been the reason why only one month later the next Commissioner of Crown Lands, J. J. Bagot, forbade further township survey without his approval, and, while there were many suggestions for new townships in the North during the next few years, it was not until late 1862 and early 1863 that the nine townships of Mernmerna, Edeowie, Parachilna, Yarrah, Kanyaka, Hookina, Mount Eyre, Oratunga and Nuccaleena were laid out.[21]

After 1864, a radical change occurred in the policy concerning township creation. The government now branched out in its activity, surveying townships in areas considered suitable for agricultural settlement, the object being to survey at least one township to every hundred. This had momentous geographical implications in both the distribution and density of urban centres. The reasons for the new policy had their beginnings in the late 1850s and were, in many ways, the outcome of the experiment in the 'pastoral townships', which had sold badly and had not returned the cost of survey. The lesson seemed clear : townships should be surveyed where people could, and would be willing to buy them. But there was a complication in this simple logic that the Government did not appreciate. By the mid-1860s, much of the land available for sale in the high-rainfall areas was either near to or on the previously leased runs of pastoralists who were fighting to maintain their position on their territory by large-scale purchasing of rural sections. Therefore, when townships were surveyed the pastoralists bought up the town allotments and eliminated the disruptive elements of the pub, and particularly of the small-scale farmer and the shopkeeper.

For example, when it was suggested in 1860 that Tarpeena be surveyed in the South-East, the local surveyor pointed out that the proposed township would do 'no injury' to the existing and neighbouring township of Kalangadoo (1859) as;

> 'Mr. K. Leake has bought nearly the whole of that township so that it should not interfere with his run, there is not a single house erected there or likely to be.'[22]

Tarpeena was surveyed the next month, but many of its allotments were bought by surrounding pastoralists. The general situation in such rich areas as the Lower South-East was elaborated in another case during the same year. The survey of land between Mount Gambier and Port MacDonnell was being planned. The local surveyor wrote to the Surveyor-General that he had heard it rumoured that it was

'The intention of Mr. Neil Black to buy the whole of the sections, in which case a large proportion of good country suitable for agricultural purposes will be used as a cattle run. Persons of limited means will be unable to bid against so large a capitalist who would go to any amount rather than small farmers should occupy a portion of the land. A deadly feud has existed lately between the holders of runs and small settlers . . .'[23]

Accordingly, in an attempt to ensure the purchase of land by the small holders the Surveyor-General thought it best to survey small sections and reserve land for a township. But it was no use; the small sections were purchased by Black and the township was never surveyed; three months later, after the pastoralists had made a grand sweep of the land auction, the only land left available for a township was on the steep slopes of the volcanic cone of Mount Schank.

A little further to the east, Caveton was surveyed in 1866, but it too was strangled at birth by the pastoralists. Nevertheless, a few smallholders had managed to get individual sections and one settler, William Saunders, wrote to the Surveyor-General requesting that a completely new township be surveyed;

'There is now 12 famlys set down on Sections to reside here all within 3 mils of the 112 section and they all agree that it the most convenient and most likely's spot fore a township in the neighbourhood . . . already there is 28 pounds collected towards Building a school'. [sic]

A few months later Saunders wrote again, but the Government could do nothing; all the land had gone.[24] In the Lower North, Euromina was surveyed in the hundred of Andrews, and similarly it was eliminated.

The blatant purchasing of the townships by the pastoralists caused much resentment. They could not be prosecuted or restrained as there was nothing illegal in their actions, so it was thought best to survey the township in advance of the rural sections with the object of allowing the small man to establish himself before the alienation of the surrounding land took place, and, presumably, to act as a deterrent to pastoralists' purchases. No one really dreamt that the pastoralists would be prepared to buy land at between £5 and £10 per half-acre over town lands that ranged between 70 and 200 acres in size. Thus, in 1865, the Commissioner of Crown Lands wrote to the Cabinet asking for authority 'to lay out in each hundred at least one Government township of say 100 acres with parklands surrounding of say one third of a mile in depth'. Cabinet approval was given, and instructions were sent to the Surveyor-General to lay out towns 'where such has not already been done, and especially where the Surveys and sales are now proceeding'. Goyder thought that the proposed system was 'calculated to do a great deal towards aiding agricultural settlement' and he re-affirmed the need to let township sales precede rural sales since otherwise the object sought 'will be frustrated as in the case of a township laid out on the East Shore of Lake Alexandrina—The whole of which was purchased by the lessees'.[25]

Between July and September, Canowie, Hansborough, Anama, Hilltown,[26] and Davies (now Hanson) were laid out in the hundreds of Anne, Julia Creek, Hart, Milne, and Hanson respectively, but not one of them became a reality (for locations see Fig. 13). In Hansborough, F. H. Dutton bought 77 half-acre lots for £497-15s. within a few weeks, in addition to many thousands of acres of land in the surrounding rural areas. In the other townships there was some purchasing by city folk and smallholders, but the grasp of the pastoralists on the surrounding country damned the townships to extinction. Three years later in Parliament, Mr. Hay said :

'Any Honourable member acquainted with South Australia would know that there were government townships—such as Davies in the Hundred of Hanson, and Anama in the Hundred of Hart—which he would defy anyone, as he travelled through them, to know to be townships. They were townships on the map but not so far as settlement was concerned.'[27]

In the South-East there was an almost similar situation and the editor of the Mount Gambier newspaper, the *Border Watch*, considered that most of the land was in the hands of 'a privileged few' and that 'the rest of the population is shut up in stunted townships unable to produce any of the necessities of life'.[28]

The first experiment of the Government, then, in establishing a township in every hundred that might be agriculturally productive was a failure. That it was so, was not really surprising. While the survey was restricted to selected areas, while sales were still held only in Adelaide and while the land system still called for cash down at auctions, the large-scale pastoralists had the organization, time, and financial backing necessary to buy extensively and expensively in the auction room. It was not until the beginning of credit purchasing in 1869 and the survey of the land outside the high-rainfall pastoral zones of the Lower South-East and the Central Hill Country that the policy of a township to every hundred began to be fulfilled.

Undoubtedly, the action of the pastoralists was the prime cause of the new policy on townships, but since 1859 Goyder had been attempting to achieve greater efficiency and accuracy in the rural surveys by using the hundred as the planning unit for survey and settlement. In the light of these moves it was little wonder that the township was becoming increasingly an integral part of the survey procedure. Moreover, Goyder's concern for the social, educational and religious well-being of the settlers on the frontier was changed to a conviction after visiting Victoria in 1869 to inspect the working of its Land Acts. Urban centres and their associated facilities were, to his mind, a necessary and civilizing part of frontier life, and not a belated afterthought.

Thus the scene was set for the implementation of a programme of surveying one town to each hundred, which really got under way with the massive boom of settlement in the Northern Areas of the Colony, and to a lesser extent in the Lower South-East, between 1869 and 1880. After the beginning of this expansion, not more than a score of private townships were created and the government township represented the bulk of urban development from here on. Nearly every township created was modelled on the predetermined design of the Adelaide town plan, with its central core of townlands, and surrounding parklands and suburban lands. Between 1870 and 1879, 101 townships were created, more than in any other decade before or since, and another 60 were surveyed in the ten years up to 1889, two-thirds of these creations occurring during the first few years up to 1883, before drought finally checked the expansion of settlement.

In fact, of the 196 hundreds proclaimed between 1865 and 1890, 75 had one township, and 26 had more than one township, particularly where there was a port and an inland township, as at Edithburgh and Honiton in the hundred of Melville, Forns and Port Gibbon in the hundred of Hawker in Eyre Peninsula, and Hatherleigh and Beachport in the hundred of Rivoli Bay in the Lower South-East; or where the hundred was unusually large, as was Tatiara with the townships of Bordertown, Wolseley and Custon. Of the 95 hundreds without a township, it is possible that about a dozen of these were served by multiple-township hundreds and by private towns while 9 hundreds had a township before the date of their proclamation. This leaves about 70 hundreds without townships; usually the land in these was not capable of sustaining dense agricultural settlement, for example, the central swamps of the Lower South-East, the southern portion of the Flinders Ranges, and particularly the outer fringes of settlement in the North, where more hundreds were proclaimed without towns after 1878 than with towns.

Therefore, the programme of one town to each hundred was effective in slightly less than two-thirds of those hundreds created between 1865 and 1890, but the comprehensiveness of the policy becomes greater when it is realized that it was applied retrospectively in 46 hundreds which were created before the Cabinet decision and which possessed no town. Certainly the practice became common enough for a typical township design to be included in the diagrams of the ideal hundred design that appeared in the *Handbook for Government Surveyors* (see pp. 85–86).

As Meinig has pointed out, such an arrangement of a township to nearly every hundred has important geographical implications because, as the hundreds were roughly one hundred square miles in size, this meant a fairly uniform distribution of townships at approximately ten-mile intervals, the general result of which would be to place most of the land within a five-mile radius of a town, 'Whether such was a conscious objective of the Government's programme is not clear, but the actual result was not far short of the general schematic pattern.'[29] In addition to Goyder's concern to provide township sites for the well-being of the settlers, there is also some evidence to suggest that the settlers themselves thought that foot or horse travel that exceeded seven miles to a town was too great, as in the case of the hundred of Palmer where the pioneers were 'at last to have the boon of a township in their midst' and no longer have to travel the eight or nine miles to Willochra.[30] Other settlers petitioned for a township to be established on the southern edge of Hynam in the South-East, as it was impossible to send their children to school seven miles away, either to Glen Roy or to Naracoorte. While the Commissioner of Crown Lands thought that it was 'vital to assure the best facilities for the settlers', a better case would have to be made out than this for a new township.[31]

After the droughts of the early 1880s and the economic depression of the 1890s, few townships were created in South Australia. Between 1890 and 1899 there were only thirteen new townships, most of them being surveyed in 1891, in the area out of hundreds along the new railway to Alice Springs (Lindhurst, Copley, Algebuckina, Innaminka) and the railway to Broken Hill (Fig. 15). But between 1900 and 1929 there was another burst of activity in surveying townships, activity when another 119 towns were laid out, principally in the Murray Mallee and the central portions of Eyre Peninsula. This new activity arose from the Government's policy of taking the lead in promoting and encouraging settlement after the lean years of the 1880s and 1890s. The aims were to provide essential water supplies, with tanks and bores, and a transport network. This network of 'developmental railways' was constructed in advance of selection and settlement and was designed so that no farmer needed to haul his wheat more than about twelve miles to the railway, or to the coast in the case of Eyre Peninsula, or to the River Murray in the case of the Murray Mallee.[32] The lines were carefully located to avoid unproductive areas (e.g. the deep sands north and south of Pinnaroo) and halts were designated at approximately five-mile intervals, at most of which townships were surveyed (Fig. 16). Thus, two large areas of the State had a consciously planned transport-orientated pattern of township sites. Each township had a potential tributary area of approximately 125–150 square miles.

Since 1929 the Government has created only fourteen townships, the realization occurring at last that there were not only sufficient townships existing to cater for needs, but a super-abundance of them in the age of the automobile. The new towns were mainly in areas of intense horticulture, in the irrigation settlements of the Upper Murray such as Loveday, Cooltong, Ramco, and Winkie, and alongside the pastures of the lower Murray swamps at Jervois, or in areas particularly lacking in townships but settled since 1945, such as Pardana in the centre of the trace-element deficient lands of Kangaroo Island, Greenways and Padthaway in the Lower South-East, and Wanilla in Eyre Peninsula (Fig. 18).

Topography and Morphology of the Townships

The townships of South Australia, like any other group of urban centres have a set of geographical arrangements one with another, such as their spacing, their density, and their type and date of origin, all of which have been examined already. But in addition to these spatial arrangements there is another scale of areal consideration, which could be called the topographical and morphological, involving considerations of the site features of the towns and the internal character and variation of their plans. In examining these, the distinction between the 140 private townships and the 370 government townships is still basic and significant.

The private towns were surveyed wherever there was a possibility of an economic opportunity presenting itself to repay the cost of subdivision, and, ultimately to make a profit. The maximum returns could best be ensured in areas of potential agricultural prosperity, along main lines of roads, and particularly at road junctions, or in proximity to mineral deposits. Consequently, economic conditions (or at least the expectation of these) often predetermined the site of the town, which fact then had a direct bearing upon its morphological character, e.g., Noarlunga and Gawler.

In the government townships, however, the surveyors were armed with a complex predetermined plan that was applied to any suitable site—suitable usually meaning flat—and the morphology of the town reflected little of the physical qualities of the site. Even if the site chosen was varied, the plan tended to clothe it without being tailored to its contours. On the one hand, therefore, the site and shape characteristics of the private township are often entwined, and consequently are considered together. On the other hand, the site and shape characteristics of the government townships were by no means so inter-related, and they are considered separately.

The Site and Morphology of Private Townships[33]

The overwhelming majority of the private townships were located in the older surveyed and settled areas of the Mount Lofty Ranges and surrounding plains, and there were a few townships in the Lower South-East. They were surveyed wherever there was a possibility of economic success. The decisions that led to the layout of most of the townships are as obscure as those that led to the creation of the town itself. Although no plans of subdivisions needed to be kept before the 1857 legislation for registering land titles, it is clear from the examples of the townships that did succeed that the layout of most of them was uncompromisingly gridded. This arose, in part, from the fact that the private surveyors had to design the street plan within the strictly rectilinear pattern of prior rural subdivision laid out by the Government; survey before settlement being one of the distinguishing features of South Australian rural settlement. The grid pattern of the private townships also occurred because of the ease and accuracy obtained from working in straight lines and right angles, which required little training and ensured uniformity in road widths and allotment.

So widespread was the grid pattern in the private townships that it is difficult to find townships with either curving streets or any morphological variety. There are a few exceptions. The original part of Gawler (1839), with its axis of three connected squares laying along the top of a prominent interfluvial terrace between the North and South Para Rivers, had a roughly eliptical pattern of roads surrounding the axis at descending levels down the side of the terrace. The charm and originality of this design (strongly reminiscent as it is of North Adelaide) was rarely repeated elsewhere[34] (Fig. 89). Noarlunga (1839), or Horseshoe as it was once descriptively known, lay in the centre of an almost enclosed meander of the Onkaparinga River, and the pattern of streets was slightly curved to fit in with this topographical feature. The haphazard arrangement of miners' cottages and of roads leading to them, east of Moonta, is a refreshing relief from the monotony of the usual formal layout.[35]

Fig. 89. Gawler. Designed in 1839 from a plan by William Light. The core of the township is on a flat-topped interfluvial ridge between the North Para River (top) and South Para River (foreground). The rivers and their banks were designated as parklands which enclosed the town on three sides. The street system was based on three squares which were connected by Cowan street which ran along the top of the ridge. Parnell Square (on the right) is occupied by the Catholic church, Orleana Square by the Anglican church and Light Square (just off the left-hand margin) was to be occupied by the Presbyterian church, but it was never built. The main street of the town today is Murray street which runs along the top left of the photograph and is flanked by large buildings. Gawler was once a centre of flourishing agricultural-implements and building-work shops. They have all moved to Adelaide, and Adelaide itself is fast engulfing the once independent township.

On the whole the Government took little notice of, and did not wish to control the activity of the private town creators, something which was evident from its reluctance to record private subdivisions on the cadastral plans of the colony, even when they had become thriving townships. This reluctance to be involved was emphasized when in 1857 the townsfolk of Barton, a small township near Truro, complained that a John Fairey had fenced in the main street for three years; but the advice of the Commissioner of Crown Lands to the Surveyor-General who had to reply to the complaint was, 'Say that this is a private Township and the Government therefore cannot interfere'.[36] But the Government was not merely reluctant, but unable to interfere in these matters. It had no powers of control other than that of the Real Property Act of 1857 which required the deposition of a map of a proposed subdivision in the Office of the Registrar-General in order to facilitate the registration and conveyance of titles, deeds, and mortgages. In any case, after the Government had almost completely taken over secondary township creation after 1865 there was little room for private activity and hence little call for the control of subdivisional practices. Indeed, during the late nineteenth and most of the twentieth century the problem of most country townships has revolved around the embarrassing superfluity of allotments which they possess because of over-generous survey in the past, and the decline of their economic viability in an increasingly mobile society today.

The Sites of Government Townships

Unlike the private townships, the form of which was controlled by existing survey lines and fortuitous economic circumstances most government townships were created and surveyed as an integral part of the agricultural landscape. Therefore, in theory at least, they had a greater chance of being considered as whole units and sites and arranged to the best possible advantage in the newly settled areas. Sometimes, however, practice fell short of theory, and, for a variety of reasons, they were not the ideal communities it was hoped that they would be.

Generally speaking, the evidence is that good care was taken in the field to site the townships carefully. But at times there were problems. In some cases the township site might not have

been determined before the surrounding land had been surveyed and alienated. Therefore the best site had not been obtained and there was the difficulty of trying to fit the township
either in the spaces that remained unsold or within existing
sections. But, increasingly after 1869 the planning of the township
layout and its site was a part of the total planning of the hundred,
and this problem tended to disappear.

However, there was still one other major difficulty. The rigid
adherence by the Government surveyors to the predetermined
geometrical model militated against urban variety, interest, and
good planning. As in the case of the private townships, the surveyors generally selected the flattest site possible on which to
practise their routine. Meinig quotes the judgement which was
offered on township policy in the Northern Areas by the editor
of the *Jamestown Review*, who wrote sarcastically of what he
assumed were the instructions issued to the country surveyors by
the Lands Department:

> Avoid all sites that are naturally high and dry and possess
> natural facilities for easy drainage. If there be a gentle slope,
> sheltered by friendly upland, avoid that also; eschew any
> elements of the picturesque, and select rather the flattest, most
> uninteresting site possible; if a flat with a creek running through
> it and subject to overflow, by all means get on the lower bank
> of the creek and peg away. If a running creek be not available
> get in the way of a storm channel. A mangrove swamp with
> sinuous cozy channel is a combination of favourable conditions
> too good to be often hoped for, and if subject in addition, to
> direct tidal overflow, consider it perfection.[37]

He certainly had grounds for saying this, for many a town site
approximated to his parody of the surveyors' possible instructions
and the 'mangrove swamp with sinuous cozy channel' was all too
real a description of some of the minor ports along the coast (e.g.
Ports Broughton, Germain, Prime and Lorne). This did not matter
if the ports did not flourish, and many did not, but when a town
the size of Port Pirie turned out to be scarcely fifteen feet above
high water mark throughout most of its area; subject to tidal
inundations; practically impossible to drain of rainwater ac-

cumulation, and too expensive to sewer adequately because of the cost of pumping the effluent, then the result was disastrous.[38]

'A flat with a creek running through it and subject to overflow' was the very situation of Jamestown itself, and the situation of another new township planned for the hundred of Palmer, of which a reporter said :

'I can't commend the Government on the site chosen, for it is at the end of a creek and instead of the water running in one channel until it reaches Willochra, it spreads in one vast sheet, which will no doubt, in winter time be swamping the inhabitants out.'[39]

Indeed, it seemed to be a common failing for the surveyors to assess the land during the dry season and not appreciate the almost assured flooding during the winter months. Alongside Lake Albert, in the new town of Meningie, a surveyor had laid out allotments at low water. 'Any party buying would never for a moment think to find pegs out in the Lake as they are at present', commented a field surveyor later.[40]

The predilection for flat sites on which to survey the stereotyped township plan led to a further complication. Often the main street was placed on the level ground parallel to the base of the adjacent hills; consequently it was transformed into 'a sluggish drain fed by a whole set of new tributaries coursing down the straight streets of the slope'.[41] The winter results of such situations were enough to set another country newspaper editor at Pinnaroo a-speculating on the motives and instructions of the Lands Department and its surveyors

'Surely no officer sent out by Government ever blundered so capably! He must have been suffering from home-sickness and wanted to get through the jobs quickly, else, why in the name of all that is sacred did he select the spots he did for the towns of Lameroo and Pinnaroo . . . towns that are undoubtedly destined in the near future to take unto themselves large dimensions. Today the places are under water, and as the landscape is as flat as the proverbial pancake, there is absolutely no get-away for the superfluous fluid.'[42]

Two months later the place was still 'half land, half water'. There was the serious prospect of an outbreak of typhoid, and after more rain the townsfolk sent a telegram to the Treasurer. 'Two inches eleven points. Town submerged. Business stagnated. Will Government render assistance immediate drainage?' (Fig. 90). But no assistance and more rain the next year produced the same problem. 'Friday morning found the whole town in a frightful state of swamp.'[43] Eventually plans for the draining of the two towns were drawn up and expensive work completed.

Fig. 90. The mud bath of the main street of Pinnaroo, c. 1908.

Morphology of Government Townships

From the time Adelaide was created in 1837, the threefold pattern of town land, parkland and suburban land served as a model for 249 out of the 370 government townships. In most cases, the plan was applied unimaginatively to towns in a variety of environments ranging from the deserts of the interior to the high rainfall areas of the Mount Lofty Ranges and the Lower South-East, and even to the tropical coasts of the Northern Territory, which was under South Australian administration from 1863 to 1911. The basic elements of the design were copied with slight variations, and 'little Adelaide' was stamped on the countryside monotonously. The regularity and widespread distribution of such a distinctive urban morphological unit can have few counterparts in any other region of equal size.[44]

During the first twenty-eight years of township creation to 1864, forty-five towns were created, including Adelaide. Twenty-two had some parkland, and eleven had parkland on two sides or more, Wellington East, Bordertown, Blinman and Meningie, for example being completely surrounded. The continuing though intermittent provision of parklands during these twenty-eight years merely suggests that some country surveyors found the Adelaide design worth copying, either for its positive qualities or because of their lack of imagination. Colonel Light certainly had no influence on designs during this period, since he died in 1839, before any of the country towns had been surveyed. However, in that year, it is possible that Light as a surveyor in private practice, did design Gawler, twenty-five miles north of Adelaide. He gave it parklands on three sides, making it the only private town that displays true parkland features (see pp. 351–352).

From 1864 on, after G. W. Goyder, the Surveyor-General, had sent instructions to his staff on how the Northern Territory was to be surveyed, town design in South Australia changed greatly. Goyder provided a rough sketch of his ideal town plan for the surveyors' guidance and stipulated that roads should be laid out 'radiating in all available directions from the centre of population to the extent or confines of the land proposed to be sold'[45] (Fig. 91a). A letter sent a few days later by the Commissioner of Crown Lands and Immigration to the Government Resident in the Northern Territory amplified Goyder's instructions. It read, in part:

'As soon as the site of the principle town has been determined you should instruct the surveyors to lay it out as near as convenient in the form of a square, and subdivide it into 1,600 half acre lots, each measuring two chains by two and a half chains or there abouts, with streets at right angles to each other, round every eight allotments. A principal square should be reserved near the centre of the township, measuring six acres, and four smaller squares of three acres each should be arranged at equidistant intervals as in South Adelaide; and a reserve of land half a mile wide should be left all round the town for parklands, if possible.'

The model was adopted in South Australia; for a little later the Commissioner wrote to the Cabinet asking for authority 'to lay

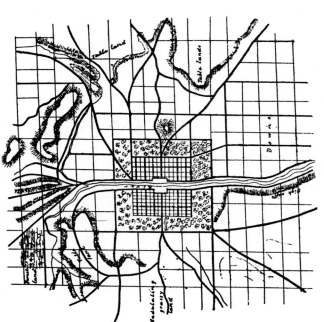

Fig. 91. (a, left) Goyder's ideal township, 1864. (b, right) An almost perfect replica of the ideal township, Maitland in Yorke Peninsula. Maitland was surveyed in 1872 with 101 acres of town lands, 129 acres of parklands and 580 acres of sub-urban lands. (By courtesy of Director of Lands S.A.)

FIG. 92 (a, left) Edithburgh on Yorke Peninsula was typical of many of the wheat exporting ports along the coast where the ideal plan was simply split in half to fit the new site. Surveyed in 1869, Edithburgh consisted of 168 acres of town land, 169 acres of parkland and 1,738 acres of suburban land. (b, right) Pinnaroo in the Murray Mallee, surveyed in 1904 was typical of the post-1900 townships in that the suburban lands were almost eliminated, the parkland greatly reduced and the railway penetrated the centre of the township, which was now split into two halves. (By courtesy of Director of Lands S.A.)

out in each hundred at least one government township of say 100 acres with parklands surrounding of say one third of a mile in depth' (Figs. 91 and 92). In the next five years eighteen towns were surveyed in South Australia, of which only one was without parklands and another had parklands on one side only; the remaining sixteen were either almost or entirely surrounded by parklands.

Thereafter government-surveyed townships became so numerous that it seems best to analyse the information by regions, particularly as certain parts of South Australia showed differences in the occurrence, distribution and form of their town patterns, depending on whether they were being settled when the parkland design was in or out of favour, or when minor variations of the design were in vogue. The progress of the surveys is summarized in Table XIX and their distribution of parkland and non-parkland townships is shown in Fig. 93. Both the table and map have been divided into six parts corresponding to six broad regions within the state; the older-settled regions of the Mount Lofty Ranges, together with the Central Hill Country and Kangaroo Island, the Northern Areas and Yorke Peninsula, the South-East, the Murray Mallee, Eyre Peninsula, and the rest or 'un-settled' part of South Australia, sometimes called descriptively, out-of-hundreds.

In all, there were only thirty-five government townships in the older settled regions of which fifteen had no parkland, six had small pieces of parkland adjoining and only fourteen were true parkland towns. Altogether, the parkland town was not a conspicuous feature of the landscape in this region, because there were so many private townships and so few government ones, because most of the government townships were designed before the general acceptance of the model in 1865, and because some of the townships which did have parklands, such as Anama, Hilltown, Hansborough and Euromina, never started as recognizable urban centres.

In the Northern Areas and Yorke Peninsula there was a total of 144 government townships. Eighteen were created before 1869, and, as has already been pointed out, some of them were associated with copper mining, smelting and transport, and others with the provision of staging-posts for the pastoral interior. Of

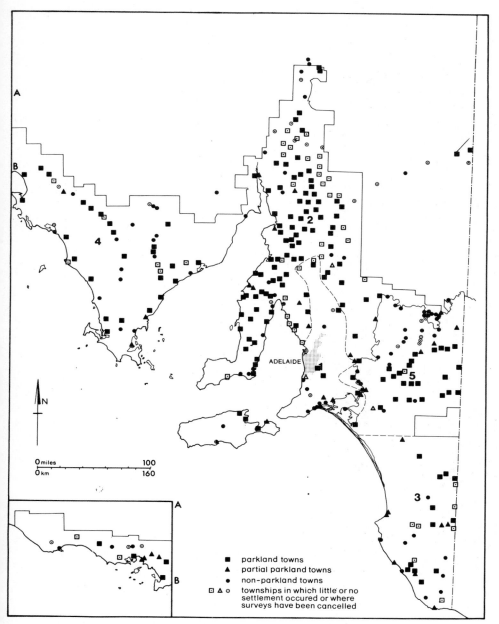

Fᴵɢ. 93. Parkland and non-parkland in government townships.

Table XIX

Parkland in South Australian Government Townships

NP, No parkland. PP, Partial parkland. FP, Full parkland

Date	Central Region			Northern Region			Southeastern Region			Eyre Peninsula			Murray Mallee			Out of Hundreds			Total
	NP	PP	FP	NP	PP	FP	NP	PP	FP	NP	PP	FP	NP	PP	FP	NP	PP	FP	
1836–1859	6	2	3	1	3	–	2	1	2	–	1	–	–	–	–	–	–	–	21
1860–1864	1	1	1	7	2	5	2	2	–	1	–	–	–	–	–	2	–	–	24
1865–1869	–	1	4	–	–	9	1	–	1	–	–	2	–	–	–	–	–	–	18
1870–1879	3	–	2	5	4	66	–	3	8	–	–	6	–	–	–	2	–	1	101
1880–1889	1	1	3	6	2	28	1	–	6	1	–	5	–	–	–	3	–	2	60
1890–1899	–	1	1	1	–	–	–	–	–	1	–	2	–	–	–	4	1	2	13
1900–1909	2	–	–	1	–	1	–	2	1	1	2	3	5	–	7	1	1	–	26
1910–1919	–	–	–	–	–	1	–	–	–	6	1	18	12	4	18	1	–	–	61
1920–1929	1	–	–	1	–	–	1	–	–	11	3	1	12	–	1	1	–	–	32
1930–1939	–	–	–	1	–	–	–	–	–	4	–	–	2	–	–	–	–	–	7
1940 and after	1	–	–	–	–	–	2	–	–	1	–	–	3	–	–	–	–	–	7
TOTAL	15	6	14	23	11	110	9	8	18	26	7	37	34	5	27	14	1	5	
GRAND TOTAL	35			144			35			70			66			20			370

Source: S.A. Lands Dept., township files.

these eighteen early townships only five could be classed as parkland towns.

But in 1869, when the Government opened up the whole of the northern wheatlands to credit selection, it embarked on an extensive and thorough programme of town creation in which the three elements of the model town were repeated incessantly and which left little room for private development. Nine towns were surveyed late in 1869 and 111 from 1870 through 1889; and of this total of 120, only eleven did not have parklands, and only six had partial parklands, making this the region with the greatest concentration of parkland towns in South Australia.

Each town was as near a copy of Goyder's ideal town as terrain and previously surveyed roads and boundary fence lines permitted (Fig. 91b). Communication was perhaps the only factor allowed to disrupt markedly this stereotyped design. The parkland town abutting the coast on one side was typical of sixteen minor ports exporting wheat and wool (Fig. 92a). Similarly, new towns built along railways, particularly after about 1880, often had railway lines and yards on one side instead of parkland. In towns surveyed before the laying of railways the rail lines were taken through an existing piece of parkland, as in Adelaide, Jamestown, Halbury, Farrell Flat, Crystal Brook, and Caltowie. By 1939, 144 townships had been surveyed in the Northern Areas, of which 110, or 76 per cent, were true parkland towns.

The South-East has a history of land settlement and town creation that partakes of the characteristics of both the older settled areas and the Northern Areas. In the areas of older settlement, parkland towns are few, but in the areas settled from 1869 through to 1889 under the same credit selection conditions as in the Northern Areas, eighteen townships were created, only one without parklands. These townships were concentrated in the reclaimed swamps near the coast, and carefully sited out of reach of the water, e.g. Millicent,[46] Hatherleigh, Rendelsham and Tantanoola, and there were others along the railway line linking Kingston, the northernmost of the three ports, to the inland agricultural centres of Naracoorte and Bordertown.

In Eyre Peninsula 70 government townships were surveyed and in the Murray Mallee a further 66. Most of those in Eyre Peninsula surveyed before 1900 were ports along the high rainfall western coast, and of these towns, 15 were parkland towns. But after 1900, the settlement of the interior of the Peninsula was by developmental railways, and this settlement was similar to, and contemporaneous with, that of the Murray Mallee. In all, 119 railway-oriented towns were surveyed of which 51 were full parkland towns, 12 had partial parklands and 56 had none (Fig. 926).

The final region lies outside the agricultural, or 'settled', area of the state. There are only twenty towns in this semi-arid and desert region. Most of them were associated with the transcontinental railways to Western Australia, to Alice Springs and the Northern Territory, and eastward to the mining centre of Broken Hill and New South Wales and were therefore post-1880 creations. The group of towns just beyond the northern extremity of the settled area were 'the pastoral townships', and the isolated settlement of Iron Knob in Eyre Peninsula is a present-day source of high-grade iron ore. Only five of the settlements display total parkland features : Cockburn (1886), Saltash (1891), and Mingary (1892) on the Broken Hill line; and Beltana (1873) and Marree (1883) on the northern line.

Decline of the Parkland Town

A thorough reading of local newspapers for the second half of the nineteenth century reveals that the morphology of the government townships came in for little overt criticism, other than of the size of the constituent elements of townlands, parklands and suburban lands. Certainly, the presence of the parklands for recreational and public uses was a much admired part of the design. Initially they provided space for railways to penetrate the centre of the town, space for showgrounds, and even race-courses, and later, when the leisure activities of the inhabitants became more varied, they provided space for bowling greens, swimming pools, playing fields, golf courses, camping grounds and even schools and hospitals. Unfortunately, the dedication of the land for public purposes could be construed in other ways, and could also include rubbish dumps, slaughter houses, and sewage treatment plants. This was not all loss to a rural community, however, but a considerable gain. Open space had little emotional, visual, and aesthetic appeal to a person living in a community of a few hundred in the midst of paddocks that stretched away as far as one could see; neurosis was a more likely result. The presence of the new facilities in close proximity to the town enriched the quality of life and expanded the spirit of community. Where the town did not grow large enough to fill its townlands, and the parkland was not given over to any specific use, the 'weed infested' parklands were ploughed and sown occasionally to wheat, the proceeds of the crop going to provide or maintain some work of community need or pride, like a swimming pool, hospital or hall. Where the parklands remained uncleared, as in the sandy drifting soils of the Murray Mallee, Eyre Peninsula and the Upper South-East, the trees acted as a shelter-belt and dust-trap for the urban community inside.

Despite these advantages, however, the parkland did appear to be a superfluous, even wasteful use of land in the midst of the open spaces of the country. The decline of the parkland town really dates from 1919, when the newly appointed town planner of South Australia, Charles C. Reade, produced a critical report on the subdivision of land in the Adelaide urban area, and on the design of country towns.[47] Reade criticized the 'parkland principle' on the ground that it augmented railway-crossing difficulties and led to blind alleys or back lanes and their inevitable accompaniment of bad housing. He also felt that there was no adequate zoning of activity within the town land. Towns that had been fortunate to grow were locked up by their parklands 'as completely as many of the European towns were once upon a time hemmed in by fortifications'. Reade did not, however, condemn the parkland towns outright but suggested that they should be 'so arranged that as time proceeds no physical dislocation will be enforced, but that there will be continuous growth and contact between the central and suburban areas'. Reade's criticism had an effect. In the decade before his report sixty-one towns were surveyed, thirty-seven with parklands and five with partial parklands (Table XIX); in the decade after his report thirty-two townships were surveyed, only two with parklands and three with partial parklands. Since that time, only open spaces and reserves have been provided, and the once distinctive element in South Australian towns has not been repeated.

Town lands and Suburban lands

Finally, there were the other two elements of the parkland design—the town lands and the suburban lands—which even at the time of their survey were considered large by some.[48] Tables XX and XXI show the sizes of the town lands and suburban lands in South Australian government townships and Fig. 94 shows the distribution of the combined size of these elements throughout the State.

Up to and including the decade 1870–1879 towns with centres of more than 60 acres constituted 72 per cent of the total (Table XX). But thereafter the number decreased. From 1880 on only 29 out of 206 townships, or 14 per cent, had centres of more than 60 acres; in the 1910s and 1920s the town surveyors showed a marked predilection for town centres of 33 acres. The large town centre was therefore common in areas settled before 1879, mainly in the Central and Northern Regions; the smaller centres were most marked in railway-focussed towns of the Murray Mallee and Eyre Peninsula.

However, the decreasing size of the town lands in the Murray Mallee and Eyre Peninsula, and their bisection by the railway produced some new problems which the Premier of South Australia commented upon at length, after a visit to the Murray Mallee in 1909;

'At Lameroo, for instance, the bank, the hotel, the newspaper office, and other important places are on one side of the line, while two churches, the institute, and butchers and bakers shops are on the other side. People doing business at several places have either to go a long way round to get through the gates, or else have to scramble through the railway fence which is protected by barbed wire. The latter course frequently leads to torn clothing and profane language. I am only expressing my own opinion in this matter, [he continued] but I hope that the officers of the Survey Department will see to it that in future surveys the townships should be all one side of the railway line'.

The criticism was strongly reiterated by the Railways Commissioner in 1912 because of the cost of providing crossings and

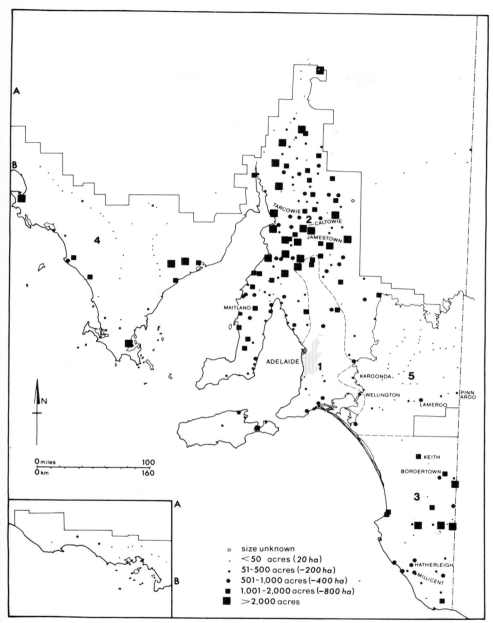

FIG. 94. Size of government townships.

Table XX

Town-Land Size in South Australian Government Townships (acres)

(50 acres = 32·375 ha)

Date	0–19	20–39	40–59	60–79	80–99	100–149	150+	Total
1836–1859	1	1	4	3	2	3	7	21
1860–1864	1	7	2	—	6	6	2	24
1865–1869	—	2	1	3	—	10	2	18
1870–1879	4	12	11	27	15	27	5	101
1880–1889	11	13	16	13	4	2	1	60
1890–1899	2	7	2	1	—	1	—	13
1900–1909	5	14	5	—	1	1	—	26
1910–1919	11	40	8	1	1	—	—	61
1920–1929	14	14	2	1	1	—	—	32
1930–1939	7	—	—	—	—	—	—	7
1940 and after	3	—	3	—	—	—	1	7
TOTAL	59	110	54	49	30	50	18	370

Source: S.A. Lands Dept., township files.

overhead pedestrian ways.[49] Indeed, only Coonalpyn, Avenue and Keith in the South-East, Kadina in northern Yorke Peninsula, Snowtown in the Lower North, and Pinnaroo, Lameroo, Marama, Karoonda and Wunkar in the Murray Mallee, all surveyed before 1912, were consciously planned in this way and after 1912 approximately 102 townships were surveyed on one side of the railway line only.

A trend similar to that in the town lands can be observed in the size of the suburban lands (Table XXI). Up to 1879, 88 out of 164 townships (54 per cent) had suburban lands of 500 acres or more; many were between four and six square miles in extent. Since 1880, only 27 out of 206 townships have had suburban lands of more than 500 acres, but what is more significant is that 150 towns have no suburban lands at all. Suburban land all but disappeared from towns created after 1889.

Both the size of the towns and the extent of their suburban lands were symbols of the spirit of optimism that swept through South Australia in the 1870s and early 1880s, when the Northern Region in particular and parts of the South-East and of Eyre Peninsula were first settled. For example, in the Northern Areas there were six towns over 4,000 acres in size, nineteen over 2,000 acres and few were under one square mile. Such a development seemed unreasonable in an area where the main product was wheat. Yet, Fig. 94 suggests that at least some judgement was exercised initially as far as the ports and a few of the inland centres were concerned and some attempt was made to vary size according to potential importance. This partial concept of a hierarchy of potential township size was inadequate in other areas, however, for example, within about a ten-mile radius of Caltowie there were five townships of over 2,500 acres in size, which, if each lot had been settled would have given individual townships of 10,000 people or more. It is possible that one such township would have succeeded and outstripped its rivals at that time, but there could be little hope that all would grow, let alone survive, at that high level. In retrospect it seems clear that much of this optimism was misplaced and unrealistic; it was impossible for some of the large towns to grow in competition with others sited close to them. Similarly, how could so many towns exist successfully on the edge of the dry, sunburned plains on the eastern and northern fringes of

Table XXI

Suburban Land Size in South Australian Government Townships (acres)

(250 acres = 101·171 ha; 1000 acres = 404·686 ha)

Date	None	1–124	125–249	250–499	500–999	1,000–1,999	2,000+	Total
1836–1859	8	7	—	1	3	1	1	21
1860–1864	12	1	1	1	5	3	1	24
1865–1869	1	—	—	4	3	6	4	18
1870–1879	11	10	6	13	24	20	17	101
1880–1889	14	6	6	10	13	7	4	60
1890–1899	11	—	—	—	2	—	—	13
1900–1909	22	1	1	1	1	—	—	26
1910–1919	59	2	—	—	—	—	—	61
1920–1929	30	2	—	—	—	—	—	32
1930–1939	7	—	—	—	—	—	—	7
1940 and after	7	—	—	—	—	—	—	7
TOTAL	182	29	14	30	51	37	27	370

Source: S.A. Lands Dept., township files.

the Central Hill Country and the Northern Region? Moreover, the whole concept of the suburban lands was open to question, since lots from half an acre to forty acres, useful perhaps for small holdings or market gardens, 'were suitable for the periphery of a metropolis but hardly for that of a country township in the midst of a mono-economy, large scale wheat region. After all, "suburban" presupposes an "urban" centre'[50] (Fig. 95).

The disposition of the suburban lands often left much to be desired. In Naracoorte, for example the vast area of 7,705 acres of suburban lands was separated from the town core by open rural sections, to say nothing of the fact that the parklands were between $1\frac{1}{2}$ and 2 miles distant from the town, to the south. Eventually, the absurdity of the arrangement was realized and the original parklands were resumed and converted into suburban lands and the new parklands were created adjacent to the township by resuming suburban lots and rural sections.[51] The layout of the suburban lands around Millicent was even more absurd, if that was possible, and they splayed over the swamps up to 7 miles distant.[52] Most of the suburban blocks in these and similar large towns were ultimately purchased by adjacent farmers and amalgamated into rural sections.

As Meinig points out, the desire for revenue was probably high in the Government's priorities, since it had to pay for public works, and would help to explain both the over-provision and over-large size of the towns, as well as the capricious variation of lot size and the ratio between town land and suburban land. Table XXII shows that, in all, the Government received £142,499 for 5,274 acres of town land, and £267,280 for 86,531 acres of suburban land between 1860 and 1889, which was not an inconsiderable addition to the Treasury. Compared with the proceeds from the sale of rural land, however, this amount was not so startling, for example, the total of £411,779 received from the sale of all urban land for the thirty years under consideration was barely half of the total of £1,051,059 received from the sale of rural land during the five year period, 1864–69 alone. It was strange that with the results of this sizable additional revenue the Government did not create subdivisions around Adelaide, which were left to the energies of the private speculator, who now had little possibility of profit in the country townships.

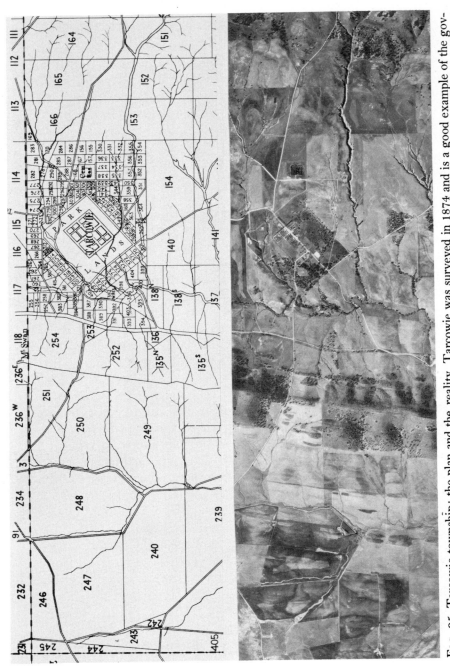

Fig. 95. Tarcowie township; the plan and the reality. Tarcowie was surveyed in 1874 and is a good example of the government township that never made it. The upper plan shows the generous provision of town lands, parklands and suburban lands in the original township. The photograph shows how the grid of town-land blocks is not filled by settlement and is now barely distinguishable from the parkland. The suburban land was long ago re-surveyed into rural sections. (By courtesy of the Director of Lands S.A.)

Table XXII

Sale of Town, Suburban and Rural Crown Land, 1860–1889

(1000 acres = 404·686 ha; 100,000 acres = 40468·6 ha)

	Town Lands			Suburban Lands			Rural Lands		
	Acres sold	Total paid (to nearest £)	Aver. per acre (to nearest shilling) £–s.	Acres sold	Total paid (to nearest £)	Aver. per acre (to nearest shilling) £–s.	Acres sold	Total paid (to nearest £)	Aver. per acre (to nearest shilling) £–s.
1860–64	688	2,678	38–18	—	—	—	517,702	625,089	1– 4
1865–69	397	7,887	20– 2	8,105	25,165	3– 2	709,203	1,051,059	2– 0
1870–74	930	15,893	20– 6	14,398	33,740	2– 7	155,600*	194,633	1– 5
1875–79	2,043	88,130	43– 3	41,018	131,380	3– 4	20,383	22,747	1– 2
1880–84	1,001	33,568	33–11	18,277	67,081	3–13	15,427	16,464	1– 1
1885–89	235	4,343	18–10	4,733	9,914	2– 2	41	186	4–11

*Credit selection was introduced late in 1869, therefore the total of sold land declines rapidly.

Source: S.A. Stat. Reg.

The severe droughts of 1881–84, (and later in 1896 and 1902) which plunged the colony into economic distress of varying degrees of severity, were sharp antidotes to the optimism that had been apparent in former years. Competition for urban land reached its peak during the period from 1874–79 when an average of £43-3s. was being paid for each acre,[53] but after those 'boom' years activity subsided rapidly, and the decade of the 1890s was one of question, re-assessment and change. In the settlement of the Murray Mallee and the Eyre Peninsula in the twentieth century, a more cautious and realistic approach can be detected in the proportions of land allotted to the three elements of the model and in the relationship of the size of the town to the agricultural potential of the land, though even in the dry northern fringes of these two regions, too many towns were surveyed, some of which were destined never to grow to even the modest size of a hamlet. However well planned South Australian settlement policy was, a certain amount of empirical testing of the quality of the land was inevitable. In the regions settled in the twentieth century, as in those settled in the nineteenth (though to a much smaller extent), this experimentation led to the creation of superfluous townships which look impressive on the cadastral map but are virtually absent from the landscape. Some suffered the fate of Howe, surveyed in 1887, about which a farmer, John Dee of Kainton, wrote to the Surveyor-General:

> 'Will you kindly inform me if the block of land known as the township of Howe in the hundred of Clinton can be leased from the government? If so I beg to offer the sum of £3 three pounds per year for three years with the right to clear and crop it. At present it is a nuisance [sic] to those alongside of it as it is a perfect harbour for rabbits and other vermin I live close to it and as my holding is small it would be a great benefit to me and I do not think it will ever be required for a township.'[54]

He was right, it was not required, since the townships of Price, and Clinton more than catered for the needs of the population, and he was allowed to lease it on the terms he wanted.

All in all, no better illustration of South Australian idealism, self-assurance, and centralized planning can be offered than the liberal provision of parkland towns and their widespread distribution in a variety of environments. The whole process of town creation was a nice blend of the doctrinaire and the theoretical with the opportune, which epitomizes much of the geography and history of South Australian settlement.

Sorting Out the Sites

The traveller to South Australia today cannot but be struck by the large number of townships that he encounters, but he must be struck, too, by the often dishevelled, unkempt, and straggling appearance of many of them. There are also many townships named on the map, but not to be seen on the ground. As it is now, so it was in the past, the fact is simply that there have always been too many townships in South Australia, and not all could possibly survive (Figs. 96a and b).

Private subdividers and the Government, but particularly the latter, marked out a scatter of potential sites over the settled parts of the colony. In the older settled areas of the Mount Lofty Ranges and surrounding areas, the towns were located in advantageous positions in the valleys and over much of the Northern Areas and the South-East there was a site in nearly every hundred. In the interior of Eyre Peninsula and in the Murray Mallee there was a site nearly every five miles along the railways, and along the coast line, ports were sprinkled with liberality. But towns do not grow just because they are created; they need a basis of support and trade, and unless they are located over mineral deposits, they are bound to their surrounding areas by commercial and social ties.

Therefore, the proliferation of sites was bound to cause some problems as each potential township competed for the custom of its neighbourhood, and, if it aspired to grow to anything greater than the minimum level of development, for the custom of the surrounding townships. Even if a township did succeed and attain a certain level of development, there was no guarantee that it would maintain it; new factors might enter into the support structure that would rob the town of its prosperity, and it could decline. 'Hansonia's Lament' (see Chapterhead) was an all too common occurrence. The question of town growth, and, by implication, that of town decline, therefore, is essentially dynamic,

FIG. 96a. Cadnia East township, 1872, an aspiring urban centre on the fringes of the Flinders Ranges.

FIG. 96b. Cadnia East township, 1972, a ghost town. All that remains is the ruin of the hotel, which is the substantial stone building in the left of Fig. 96a.

involving changing space relationships engendered by changing personal preferences, governmental policies or new technologies.

To catch the nature of these local relationships and the flavour of the times to which they relate is difficult. It is, perhaps, best done by reconstructing a series of hierarchies of the urban structure by listing the population and the important services offered by townships at specific and significant dates. This has been done for South Australia for 1855, 1865 and 1901, and for the Northern Areas for 1884.[55] These and other hierarchies would then be a series of 'stills' in the ever changing picture of central places and should provide a dynamic view of town–country relationships. Such a scheme, however, would be a major research undertaking and is beyond the immediate scope of this study, but even if such a scheme was undertaken, it is doubtful if it would be workable.[56] There are, for example, problems associated with the Australian census data, as it is difficult to know accurately the population of any urban area other than the corporate towns, and, in any case, population is a poor indicator of urban importance. The occupational structure of the population of the towns is almost impossible to assess in detail without a close study of the Rate Books, but these are available only when the town is incorporated. In nearly every case it is for the larger towns only, and never for the mass of smaller centres, that the information exists. Street directories are often misleading because they tend to record the residence rather than the work place of people, and hence the number of banks, pubs, local industries, retail outlets and services performed are difficult to assess. Sometimes the only guide is given by those firms which advertise. Thus, while the making of an array of population and services, as far as they are known, for any particular locality does sort-out urban centres into three or four recognizable, but general, levels of development for any past time, omissions and changes in the nature of sources make it difficult to compare one 'still' with another. One cannot make absolute comparisons, as the nature of the services which differentiate hierarchies change through time, and the 'stills' are not comparable. Another difficulty arises for which there is probably no ready answer, and that is that, although one may get an indication of the size of a town, one has no knowledge either of the size of the area tributary to it or of the number of people such an urban field contains, except by inference from the level of development of surrounding centres. Therefore, the conclusion is that satisfactory retrospective studies of central places are limited in their validity, and consequently, that in a series of past, central-place studies of this kind it is difficult to compare one with another.

If the patterns are difficult to assess accurately, at least some of the processes seem to have had a general and widespread applicability. In a horse and foot age, personal mobility was limited and the fairly regular spacing of townships, initiated mainly by the Government, usually did ensure a minimum trade area. Yet, it was evident that to subdivide a section and call it a town was not enough to engender the necessary support. Investment in some essential services then became a way of attracting buyers and eventually settlers. The advice to 'put up a public house and a blacksmith's shop, and a village will soon follow' was adopted in some new private subdivisions such as those in Normanville, Auburn, Watervale, Naracoorte, and Collinsfield.[57] If a school and a general store, and possibly places of worship were added, it was often enough to generate and attract trade from the surrounding rural areas. If at least some of these essential services could be obtained then the town had a chance of growing to about 100 people and achieving some permanence as a nodal centre. Yet, the precariousness of the support of a town can be gauged from the case of Stephenson on the outer fringes in the Northern Areas.

'This township is rather in decline for at one time it could boast of two stores, a blacksmith's shop and wine shanty, but one of our storekeepers has cleared [out] while the other only opens two days a week'.

Four months later the correspondent wrote :

'This town is in decline instead of going ahead as it ought to do . . . for it now only boasts of a blacksmith's shop and a schoolroom. Mr. Cottrell has shifted his store to the new township (Bruce) which makes it rather awkward for the settlers around, as they now have either to go to Bruce, which is six miles, or Quorn, which is ten miles to procure their stores.'[58]

In time, the township of Stephenson disappeared completely. Examples such as this, for small as well as for large towns, could be multiplied tediously from the files of local newspapers for any region, at any time.[59] Nevertheless, their full investigation through regional studies for past periods is needed before the full facts of causation and competition can be identified with certainty. We can be sure from Meinig's work in the Northern Areas and from abundant evidence from the South-East and Central Areas that this intangible factor of local initiative in attracting trade and industry was decisive in many circumstances. More tangible was the presence of a railway which, while not ensuring urban development, did give the township that possessed a line a clear start over one that did not. The see-saw battle between Terowie and Peterborough over the choice of the terminus for the Barrier Range line was repeated elsewhere.[60] In the Murray Mallee and Eyre Peninsula the railway was the very reason for the establishment of the pattern of townships.

In addition to railways, there was the whole range of government provided facilities that could quite markedly affect the stature of a town. A jetty, police station, post office, school and courthouses set the government town far ahead of the private town, if one existed. Occasionally this was not so, as in the case of the hybrid township of Naracoorte. The private township of Kincraig (1852) was so successful that the Government decided to lay-out a new township of Naracoorte of 103 acres north of Kincraig in the hope of capturing some of the revenue that was obviously changing hands through the sale of town lots. Thus, in 1859, a police station, post office, telegraph office and local court house were erected in 'the midst of a beggarly array of unoccupied allotments'.[61]

The residents of Kincraig had to walk between half and one mile to collect and post their letters, and it was not until after the mid 1860s, when the greater part of Naracoorte was still unsold and unsettled, and repeated petitions were presented to the Government that it reluctantly moved the post office to Kincraig.

Another important factor in town success was simply the chance of being the first settlement to be surveyed. The principle of initial advantage was borne out time and again, especially in some of the pastoral townships and ports created before 1865, and in those townships and ports created in the Agricultural Areas in the North and the South-East, such as Edithburgh in Troughbridge

Agricultural Area, Georgetown in Gulnare, and Millicent in Mayurra, to mention but a few. The success of these townships can sometimes be measured by the official cancellation of adjacent surveys which barely sold a block of land, although in the Northern Areas the fact that settlement had penetrated the low rainfall margins of the region had a great effect in causing town failure. Thus, Amyton, Stephenson, Chapmantown, Craddock and Dawlish in the Northern Areas have been wiped off the cadastral map, as have Cotton in the Mount Lofty Ranges, Bedford near the Murray Jessie and Custon in the South-East, Yangara and Forns in Eyre Peninsula, and Allen, Yinkanie and Wappilka in the Murray Mallee. At least treble that number of townships could similarly be eliminated today if a thorough tidying-up of books of the Lands Department was undertaken.

Obviously, past urban arrangements are inefficient by present behavioural and economic patterns and many of the townships live uncomfortably within their standardized and sometimes ungainly anatomy and arrangements of the past. The township sites are being sorted out mercilessly by the motor car and by the social and economic changes which it brings. Motor car ownership throughout South Australia is at a level of 2·69 persons per vehicle, and the ratio is much less than that in some rural areas. This high degree of personal mobility, coupled with an ever extending network of all-weather roads is leading to the centralization of facilities in major townships and the by-passing of the smaller townships as the retail and social attractions of the former get progressively greater. The core facilities of many small townships are a general-store/post office, with possibly a garage, and when it is known that these can exist on the custom of between fifteen and twenty families, then it is clear why the loss of only a few people is enough to cause the store to be closed down and the township to die.

The loss of customers occurs in many ways other than by the relative attraction of more distant centres. For example, the trend to greater farm mechanization means that one man can handle larger holdings than before, and so the owners of small holdings sell out to neighbours and leave their local district (Fig. 19). This voluntary trend towards depopulation is paralleled by governmentally induced action in the re-organization of railways and schools. For example, in the Murray Mallee district to the south and east of the River Murray, there were 75 loading sites for bagged wheat in 1951, which gave a lot of local employment. Twenty years later the number of sites had been reduced to 12, but 24 large bulk handling storages had been built instead, and nearly all activity was being focussed on these sites with silos, as farmers had invested heavily in the equipment needed for the bulk handling of grain. The townships with the silos tend to be growing, or at least their decline has been halted (Fig. 97).

Fig. 97. Lock, 95 miles north of Port Lincoln on Eyre Peninsula. This township was surveyed in 1918. Its future seems reasonably assured because of the Area School and the bulk handling facilities and silos for grain, both of which bring much local trade.

The re-organization of rural school has probably had an even greater effect on townships than has the re-organization of the handling of grain. Many one-teacher schools have been closed on account of low attendance, inefficiency in the employment of scarce staff and the lack of opportunities for children of widely differing ages and abilities in such establishments. They have been replaced by new well-equipped Area Schools or High Schools in the large urban centres to which the children of all ages from a wide area are taken by school bus service. Many shopkeepers saw this trend as the doom of their business maintaining, rightly, that the town in which the children went to school was the town which the parents identified as 'their' town, and in which they would do much of their shopping.

At the time of writing an article appeared in the *South Australian Advertiser* concerning the closure of Pine Point school on Yorke Peninsula, one of twenty-three schools in South Australia to be closed during 1972. A town spokesman said

'If the school is closed it will make Pine Point a ghost town, I have seen it happen in other places, The townspeople feel very strongly about the closure. Many of them have gone to live there because their children can attend the local school. But they don't like the idea of their young children having to travel away from the town to go to school. The town's future is threatened.'[62]

The school was closed in December 1971, and already trade has been diverted from the two local stores to the larger centre of Ardrossan, eleven miles away, which has the Area School and the grain silos.

Anyone who travels through the extensively-farmed wheat-growing areas of South Australia today, and who cares to pause and look, can see the results of these trends.

On the one hand there are the signs of decay in boarded-up shop-fronts, often ancient in design, broken windows, unkempt streets and pavements, and even some ruins. There rarely seem to be people about in these smaller towns which are encountered at roughly 10–15 mile intervals. On the other hand, there are the much larger towns at much greater distances apart.[63] New brick buildings with large shop windows display a moderate range of goods and indicate a moderate prosperity. The main street is full of cars and full of bustle in the late afternoon, when many parents drive into town to pick up their children from school, do some shopping, and meet friends and neighbours. The scene betokens a population captured from some near and starved townships, but now feeding the larger centre and keeping it alive.

8. Notes

1. D. W. Meinig, *On the margins of the good earth: the South Australian wheat frontier, 1869–1884* (1962), 166.

2. W. Bate, 'The urban sprinkle: Country towns and Australian regional history', *Austr. Econ. Hist. Rev.*, X (1970), 204–17.

3. D. N. Jeans, 'Territorial divisions and the location of towns in New South Wales, 1826–1842', *Austr. Geogr.*, X (1967), 243;
   Idem., 'Town planning in New South Wales, 1829–1842', *Aust. Planning Institute Journ.*, III (1965), 191.

4. M. Williams, 'Delimiting the spread of settlement', *Econ. Geog.*, XLII (1966), 336.

5. For example see E. Dick, *The lure of the land* (1970), Ch. XVI, 'Town building on the public lands'.

6. In 1840, Governor Gipps of Victoria wrote to the Secretary of State for the Colonies and said that in South Australia 'the formation of all minor towns is to be left to private enterprise, and this is a return to the natural order of things and to the way in which most towns on the old world have been formed'. Mitchell Library, 1223, p. 1007.

7. See F. Duval's enquiry as to whether or not the Government was going to survey parklands and suburban blocks around Port Augusta, and Beddome's request concerning Goolwa. SGO, 612/1856 (in); and 575/1856 (in). Both requests were rejected.

8. Anon., *Secondary Towns Association formed for the purchasing of one or more Special Surveys or surveys of land in South Australia for the sites of secondary towns* (1847).

9. For collections of subdivisional plans see S. A. Archives, and the Mitchell Library, Collection D 262, plans from 1860 to 1905. Plans did not have to be deposited in the Lands Titles Office before 1857.

10. S. Sidney, *The Three Colonies of Australia: New South Wales, Victoria, and South Australia* (1852), 204.

11. M. Williams, 'Two studies in the historical geography of South Australia', in *Studies in Australian Geography*, ed. G. H. Dury and M. I. Logan (1968), 71–98.

12. SGO, 89/1861 (out). 'Many persons are desirous to purchase land and build but are prevented so by the exorbitant price demanded for allotments in the Private Township'.

13. SGO, 1835/1860 (out), the case of the new township of St Vincent, near Tungkillo.

14. SGO, 1444/1860 (in). The actual instructions for laying out the new port of Pine Creek are contained in SGO, 82/1861 (out).

15. SGO, 436/1854 (out).

16. SGO, 232/1859 (in).

17. SGO, 1550/1859 (out). The proposed township of Overland Corner was not surveyed for the same reasons—that the land would not sell and that the population was already concentrated at Blanchetown, 'The erection there, I believe, to be one Public House, and I think a Township at Overland Corner would share the same fate'. SGO, 2145/1859 (out).

18. SGO, 1820/1859.

19. SGO, 2235/1859 (out); and 30/1860 (in).

20. SGO, 1270/1860 (out).

21. SGO, 1591/1860 (out);
for the suggested surveys see SGO, 391/1863 (out); 158/1862 (out); and 75/1863 (out). For the details of some of the successful surveys see SGO, 1699/1860 (out).

22. SGO, 1018/1860 (in).

23. SGO, 1560/1860 (in). The second page of this letter is missing. Black is the pastoralist who figures so largely in M. L. Kiddle, *Men of Yesterday* (1961); J. M. Powell, *The Public Lands of Australia Felix* (1970), 133–142. Black was a notorious manipulator of land.

24. SGO, 386/1867 (in); and 1076/1866 (in).

25. See CLO, 712 (or 812?)/1865 (out); 846–1865 (in).

26. C. B. Fisher, who owned the Hill River estate tried, unsuccessfully, to alter the location of Hilltown further to the south-west. CLO, 2581/1865 (in).

27. *SAPD* (H.A.) (1868–69), col. 1020.

28. *Border Watch* (8 April 1867).

29. D. W. Meinig, op. cit., 173.

30. *Yorke Peninsula Advertiser* (28 Jan. 1879). The town was never surveyed. Docket between SGO, 1929 and 1965/1872 (in), A. Maclean and H. Inglis to S.G. (24 August) and memos.

31. For other examples see *Yorke Peninsula Advertiser* (5 July 1878); SGO, 1781/1877 (in).

32. *SAPP*, 33 (1912), vii, and 72 (1912), i, for the Murray Mallee; and *SAPP*, 51 (1911), for Eyre Peninsula.

33. For a fuller treatment of the private towns see M. Williams, 'Early town plans in South Australia', *Aust. Planning Institute Journ.* (1966), 45.

34. For a detailed study of Gawler see M. Williams, 'Gawler: the changing geography of a South Australian country town', *Aust. Geogr.*, IX (1964), 195. In April 1839 Col. William Light wrote in his diary, 'I find myself applied to by many parties to survey, plan towns etc. I have refused all but the town of Gawler which I have just planned'.

35. For an aerial view of these see M. Williams (ed.), *South Australia from the air* (1969), 54–55.

36. SGO, 313/1857 (in).

37. *Jamestown Review* (26 Sept. 1878), quoted in D. W. Meinig, op. cit., 182.

38. An article in the *Advertiser* (21 Sept. 1878), talked of the 'blunders' at Port Pirie which presented some of the 'most difficult conditions imaginable for the decent building of a town'. For details of later flooding see SGO, 1449/1889 (in).

39. *Yorke Peninsula Advertiser* (28 Jan. 1879).

40. SGO, 386/1866 (in).

41. D. W. Meinig, op. cit., 182.

42. *Pinnaroo and Country News* (10 July 1908).

43. *Pinnaroo and Country News* (4 and 11 Sept. 1908; 20 August 1909).

44. See M. Williams, 'The Parkland Towns of Australia and New Zealand', *Geog. Rev.*, LVI (1966), 67.

45. *SAPP*, 36 (1864).

46. For photographs and a description of the site qualities of Millicent see M. Williams (ed.), *South Australia from the air* (1969), 58–59.

47. *SAPP*, 63 (1919), 20–21.

48. *S.A. Advertiser* (21 Sept. 1878).

49. *Pinnaroo and Country News* (30 July 1909; 19 April 1912).

50. D. W. Meinig, op. cit. 175–179.

51. See M. Williams (ed.), *South Australia from the air* (1969), 50–51.

52. SGO, 2160/1873 (in);

53. The peak average annual price per acre of town land was £80 during 1878. For comments on town size and revenue considerations see *S.A. Advertiser* (21 Sept. 1878).

54. SGO, 342/1902 (in).

55. For 1855 see M. Williams, 'Two studies in the historical geography of South Australia', in *Studies in Australian Geography*, (ed.) G. H. Dury and M. I. Logan, (1968), 71–98;
For 1865 and 1901, M. Williams, unpublished research;
For 1884, D. W. Meinig, op. cit. 197–201.

56. For an interesting attempt to do this see J. H. Brush and H. L. Gauthier, 'Service centres and consumer trips: Studies on the Philadelphia Metropolitan fringe', *University of Chicago, Department of Geography, Research Paper, No. 113* (1968), particularly pp. 18–63.

57. *S.A. Register* (16 April, 15 July 1851); and *Northern Argus* (25 May 1875).

58. *Yorke Peninsula Advertiser* (8 March and 26 July 1881, respectively).

59. For one such micro-study, see K. W. Thomson, 'Urban settlement and the wheat frontier in the Flinders Ranges, South Australia', *Proc. Roy. Geog. Soc., S.A.*, LX (1958–9), 25.

60. D. W. Meinig, op. cit., 195.

61. E. Ward, *The South-Eastern district of South Australia* (1869), 36.

62. *S.A. Advertiser* (25 Sept. 1971). Pine Point had 13 functional units in 1971, one of which is the school. It is vulnerable. In *Education in South Australia: Report of the Committee of Enquiry into Education in South Australia, 1969–1970* (1971), (The Karmel Report), it was recommended that all schools with an average annual attendance below 8 should be closed and it doubted seriously the wisdom of maintaining schools of slightly higher attendance, pp. 203–209.

63. For an examination of 'current' (1965–66) hierarchical arrangements throughout South Australia, see P. J. Smailes, 'Some aspects of the South Australian urban system', *Aust. Geog.*, XI (1969), 29.

9
The Making of Adelaide

'Let it be admitted of colonial cities that they are strictly modern collections of shops, warehouses, and dwelling houses, comfortable but mostly commonplace, and without the art treasures, the historical associations and the architectural grandeur of the finer towns of Europe.' W. Pember Reeves, *State experiments in Australia and New Zealand*, Vol. I (1902), 37.

'Australia is the small house'. R. Boyd, *Australia's home* (1961), Preface.

So far, the rural scene has been almost our only concern; even the account of the building of towns was intimately connected with rural events, the creation of the townships being largely a result of rural expansion, and their growth or decline being largely a response to rural prosperity and change. But the most intense and most dynamic of man's visual creations has been the making of the capital city, Adelaide, which even now covers less than one third of one per cent of the settled area of the State but contains over 69 per cent of the total population.

The importance of the topic of Adelaide in the making of the South Australian landscape cannot be denied, but the method, depth and emphasis of the treatment of that topic are hard to suggest; the field is there but the focus is hard to define.[1] That cities grow outwards and cover the rural landscape, and that they change internally are obvious and important facts, but, that having been said, an historical-geographical account of a large urban area immediately encounters the twin difficulties of describing the patterns produced by the swarming population of the urban area, and of defining the processes, both internal and external, that create, change and even at times extinguish those patterns. What are the forces that bring about changes in the distributions, densities and actions of the complex amalgam of many thousands of people on one small spot of the earth's surface, each person with individual background, occupation, motivations, tastes and desires, yet each inextricably involved with many others by economic and social ties of work, residence, entertainment and travel? The problem is even greater than that, however, for, if we agree that each and every age in a region can have its own particular geography, the same, therefore, applies to each age in the city; and, if each geography is amenable to techniques such as social area and trend surface analysis and other devices which are being used in the geographical examination of contemporary urban areas, then we are forced to concede that logically the geographical account of an urban area through time is exceedingly long and complex.[2] Such an account would probably require a book to itself, each chapter isolating one aspect of the urban area's emerging and changing gross pattern or inner detail; analogous and parallel, perhaps, to the chapters that have gone before which isolate, one at a time, an aspect of man's fashioning of the rural landscape.

But such a treatment is beyond the scope of this work, and we must be content with something less. If the making of the landscape is the starting point and aim of this inquiry, then an account of the patterns of growth and internal change in the material (and, to a lesser extent, social) landscape of Adelaide, and of some of the processes which produced those patterns, is necessary. In particular, there is the consideration of Adelaide's unique morphology. It was a physical plan that was such a marked feature of the town's early establishment and was also a lasting influence on its future pattern. Then there is the question of the effects of services on the emerging urban area, particularly of public transport and the provision of water and the disposal of sewage. The detail of the street pattern, the method of subdivision and the style of the buildings are a fitting conclusion. Embedded and entwined in all of these themes is the social and economic regionalization of areas, first in the Central Business District and then within each suburb, the origins of this regionalization often going back a long way. Throughout, the emphasis is on the origins and development of the urban landscape, and, apart from vital population statistics little attention is given to the demographic and social characteristics of the population, not because they are unimportant but because they belong rightly to some other study of urban society in the past.

The First Years

One of the most distinctive aspects of the landscape of Adelaide is the morphology of its original and central part. The threefold urban pattern has no real counterpart anywhere else in the world. It consists of a core of 'town lands', for business and commerce, called the City[3] (split into North and South Adelaide by the River Torrens), a surrounding belt of parklands reserved for public uses, and a peripheral zone of 'suburban lands' beyond, which lead eventually into the rural sections. The entire plan was a mould into which the plastic life of the new urban area was poured, and one of its more lasting contributions was to predispose its inhabitants into thinking of a two-part urban structure—a business core and a suburban periphery (Fig. 98).

The significance of the Adelaide plan lies not only in its unique character and formalization of functional zones, but also in its use as a model for over two hundred smaller towns and villages in South Australia, and for several towns larger than these in New Zealand. In addition, it may have contributed to the idea of 'green belts' which has been applied, and is being applied, with varying degrees of success to many of the world's largest cities.[4]

'The Fancied Metropolis'

The origins of the distinctive features of the Adelaide plan surveyed by Colonel William Light in 1837 are obscure. He left no record of either the sources of his own inspiration or of directions from any one else. It is possible to find other town plans which look similar to that of Adelaide in one respect or another, but it is difficult to trace and document with certainty the influences which these antecedents may have had on the Adelaide design.

An added problem is to know who it was that was influenced; the Commissioners who employed Light, or Light himself? There certainly is nothing in Light's orders for laying out Adelaide to suggest that he was instructed to design such a town; he was

FIG. 98. The city of Adelaide looking south across North Adelaide in the foreground, the intervening belt of parklands either side of the River Torrens, and south Adelaide (or the 'City') with its five squares. Around the whole is the encircling ring of parklands and beyond, to the south, the pre-urban cadastre of major roads separating each pair of 134-acre sections, provides a framework for the grid of suburban streets that stretches to the edge of the Mt Lofty escarpment.

instructed merely 'to make the streets of ample width, arranging them with reference to convenience, beauty and salubrity; and making the necessary reserves, for squares, public walks and quays'.[5] However, one may suppose that as both the Commissioners and Light were engaged in founding a new colony, they would have tried to acquaint themselves with similar schemes elsewhere in the world. North America, in particular, was an obvious place to look for parallels and precedents. There were many examples of new and experimental urban forms in existence before the creation of South Australia in 1836 both in the United

States, which was being settled by diverse groups of migrants, and in Upper Canada, which attracted the British after the 1776 War of Independence.

Of the visual elements of the plan, the grid-pattern of the streets was not original. It could have been based on towns created anywhere in the world at any time in history.[6] The disposition of the five squares in South Adelaide has no such obvious precedent other than, perhaps, William Penn's plan of Philadelphia, surveyed in 1682. It, in turn, was probably influenced by an earlier plan of Newcourt's for the rebuilding of London after the Great Fire in 1666.[7] The parklands, and the division of land into lots of different sizes, however, are a more interesting and distinctive feature of the plan, and the possible origins of these are now traced in more detail.

In 1717, Sir Robert Montgomery was granted land between the Altamaha and Savannah rivers in Georgia, U.S.A., so that he could establish a new settlement to be called the Margravate of Azilia. A plan shows that the whole settlement was to consist of approximately 400 square miles encompassed by fortifications. In the centre was the town, surrounded by a park-like belt—'a large void of space, which will be useful for a thousand purposes, and amongst the rest as being airy and affording a fine prospect of the town on drawing near to it'. Around the parkland was a symmetrical but complex arrangement of 116 one mile-square estates 'for the gentry', and 'four great parks, or rather forests' which were to be the commons for stock-breeding. Beyond these a belt of land two miles wide was reserved for freeholders, and there was an outer ring of land, one mile wide, consisting of ground belonging to the Margraves which was to be cultivated by the defenders of the fortifications. Montgomery's planned settlement came to nothing but in 1732 General J. E. Oglethorpe led a party to the same area and during the next year started laying out the town of Savannah. The plan of Savannah was not as grandiose as that of the Margravate, and consisted of a grid of roads dividing the land into a series of urban units (wards) with forty lots grouped around a square. Around all of these was an irregularly shaped common, and beyond that again 5-acre garden lots and farms of forty-five acres.[8]

Even stronger links than existed between Montgomery's Azilia and Oglethorpe's Savannah can be proved to have existed between Savannah and Granville Sharp's plan for a new township unit which was contained in his tract *A general plan for laying out towns and townships on the new-acquired lands in the East Indies, America, and Elsewhere*, first published in 1794 and reprinted in 1804. Sharp was a complex man of many parts and his interest in land subdivision is shown in another pamphlet written in 1794 entitled *Account of the Ancient Division of the English nation into Hundreds and Tythings*.[9] But he was better known as a biblical scholar, anti-slavery advocate and a prolific pamphleteer. His anti-slavery campaign culminated in his success in a court judgement in 1772 (the Sommersett case) which ruled that any slave who landed in Britain was immediately free. He followed this up with active participation in the founding of the Colony of Sierra Leone, in 1786, for freed slaves. Sharp's success had brought him into contact with Oglethorpe, who attempted to involve him in his campaign against the press-gang system.[10] They corresponded, and Sharp mentions in one letter that he had read the accounts of the Georgia colony. As Reps puts it, 'the strength of their friendship is indicated by Sharp's appointment as trustee and executor under the will of Oglethorpe's widow'.[11]

Sharp, therefore, was probably aware of Azilia and Savannah. His ideal plan shows a perfectly gridded town and countryside, the town with 172 lots surrounded by a strip of 'common land round the town of 330 feet wide'. Beyond this were $2\frac{1}{2}$-acre sections for gardens and small farms, and further out again were 10-acre sections for larger holdings and provision for 40-acre farms beyond that. In addition to the idea of a strip of common it is interesting to note that Sharp had also arrived at the idea of the size of surveyed lots conforming to the tendency for the land use to become more intense with proximity to the marker, and therefore preceded, by nearly forty years, J. H. von Thunen's theoretical statement of this arrangement of land-use density, published in 1826. Such arrangements were common in the later designs of country towns in South Australia, and also at an earlier date around Melbourne, with blocks of 25, 80, 160 and 320 acres[12] (Fig. 99).

Sharp's theoretical township nearly had a practical application in Upper Canada. Lord Dorchester, Governor of the Canadas

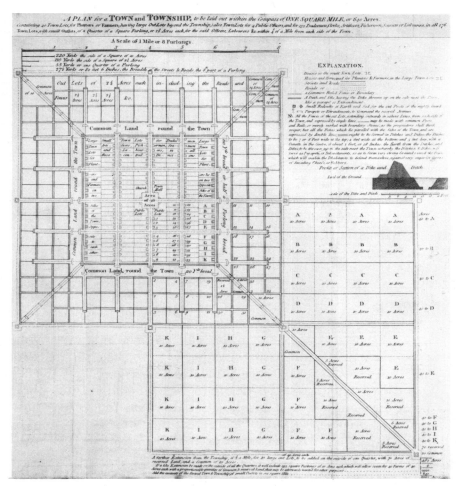

FIG. 99. The plan of Granville Sharp's ideal township, 1794.

between 1786 and 1796, directed that townships (North American connotation), were to be laid out measuring nine miles by twelve if abutting a navigable river or the coast, and ten miles square if inland. The urban core of the townships was to be a mile square divided into acre lots and like Sharp's model, surrounded by a town park. Both town–core and park were to be located in the middle of an inland township or on the water side of a 'river' township. These township plans of 1789 and 1790 are reproduced in the *Reports of the Department of Archives for the Province of Ontario,* and Adelaide resembles them closely.[13]

But the models were not implemented when the areas were eventually settled. In many cases, the theoretical plans were found impossible to implement owing to reasons of topography and to the fact that the land set aside had already been occupied. Toronto (York) was a case in point. The 'Government Park' is now occupied by a few cemeteries and industrial concerns.[14] Nevertheless, it is not inconceivable that Wakefield knew of these plans since he freely acknowledges his interest in the idea of non-pauper settlement in Upper Canada, and his debt to Robert Gourlay's *Statistical Account of Upper Canada,* printed in 1822.[15]

There is one more link in this chain of likely influences and ideas. In 1830 there was printed *The Friend of Australia,* written by a T. J. Maslen, who has been identified subsequently as Allen Francis Gardiner, a naval officer and missionary, particularly active in Natal and Chile.[16] Gardiner's ideal town was to be surrounded by parkland :

> 'All the entrances through every town should be through a park, that is to say, a belt of park of about a mile or two in diameter should entirely surround every town, save and excepting such sides as are washed by a river or a lake. This would greatly contribute to the health of the inhabitants in more ways than one, as well as pleasure; it would render the surrounding prospect beautiful and give a magnificent appearance to the town from whatever quarter viewed.'

The similarity of this description to that of the park around Montgomery's Azilia of 1717 is striking. It is difficult to say, however, to what extent this book, written at a time when interest was growing in the systematic colonization of South Australia, influenced contemporary ideas.

The search for an eighteenth or early nineteenth century colonial precedent for Adelaide's plan should not, in any case allow one to forget that the settlement of South Australia was formulated and planned within a particular social, economic and political context—that of early nineteenth century Britain. After the end of the Napoleonic Wars in 1815, the termination of war contracts caused unemployment among the industrial population of Britain for the next decade and a half. One of the many remedies suggested for its alleviation was assisted overseas migration of the unemployed and underfed, e.g. to South Australia. The early decades of the nineteenth century were also the age of the Industrial Revolution. In many places living conditions were appalling, particularly after 1820, when high prices led to efforts to reduce building costs by the use of materials of poor quality and in insufficient quantity, by the condoning of inferior workmanship, and by the cramming of as many houses on as little land as possible. It was then that the word 'slum'[17] and the conditions it connotes were born.

One of the first persons to recognise the deleterious effects of these conditions on health and character was Robert Owen. In the early years of the nineteenth century he had set up a model factory and community settlement at New Lanark, Scotland, and in the light of his practical experience there he put forward in 1817 a plan to employ Britain's surplus population in self-supporting, co-operative communities. Each community was intended to house about 1200 people and was to take the form of a large quadrangle, three sides to be occupied by four-room flats, and the fourth side by public rooms, schools, laundry, infirmary, and so on. The space inside the quadrangle was to be laid out in gardens and playgrounds. Other gardens surrounded the quadrangle, and beyond them lay the factories and workshops. This was probably the first attempt to 'zone' a settlement, and to provide open spaces, and Robert Owen must therefore be regarded as the originator of one of the fundamental town-planning concepts.[18]

As with the earlier plans of Oglethorpe, Sharp and Gardiner, it is difficult, if not impossible to assess the influence which Owen's plan had on any design of Adelaide. Yet it is also impossible to believe that current ideas were ignored completely, especially when the search for the ideal form of settlement, promoting the health and happiness of the greatest number, was an integral part of the search for the better society that preoccupied the educational, political and economic thinkers of the time. This is true particularly when it is realized that systematic colonization, and consequently the settlement of South Australia, arose out of such a movement; there was hardly a man among the colony's founders who was not connected with the Philosophical Radicals and in the forefront of some reformist movement in Britain in the early nineteenth century. The inter-connection of personalities is significant. Jeremy Bentham, Utilitarian philosopher, was a business partner of Owen's (1813–29) and a prominent member of the National Colonisation Society for South Australia.[19] Colonel Robert Torrens, economist, was a member of the Committee of Inquiry that looked into Owen's 'Plan for Villages of Co-operation' in 1819. He became chairman of the National Colonisation Society in 1835 and was the originator of the Torrens system of land registration in South Australia. Owen was a friend of Robert Gouger, another prominent member of the Society.[20]

Who, then, influenced whom? Light's instructions were signed by Rowland Hill (later inventor of the postage stamp), then secretary to the Commissioners for South Australia. Hill's brother, Matthew Davenport Hill, had charge of the Bill for the settlement of South Australia and saw it through Parliament, He is the one person for whom a definite claim has been made as the originator of the parkland town; it has been said that he suggested the idea to his brother, who presumably passed it on to Light. This claim was made by Catherine Spence who visited the two Hill brothers in 1865 and she recounted the following :

'When I visited Sir Rowland Hill he was recognised as the great post office reformer. To me he was also one of the founders of our province, and one of the first pioneers of quota representation. When I met Matthew Davenport Hill, I respected him, because he tried to keep delinquent boys out of gaol, and promote the establishment of reform schools; but I was also grateful to him for suggesting to his brother the parklands which surround Adelaide and give us both beauty and health. To Col. Light, who laid out the city so well, we owe the many open spaces and squares, but he did not originate the idea of parklands.'[21]

There is some contemporary support for the claims of the Hill brothers. F. R. Nixon, an early settler, wrote in 1838 '. . . the fancied metropolis has now become a real one . . . and now really does assume something of the look of Mr Rowland Hill's fine map, which was published long before the place had any other existence than in his own brain . . .'[22] B. T. Finniss, Light's friend and second-in-command of surveying, wrote in a letter in 1836, 'The town as originally designed in England, consists of 1000 acre Sections'.[23] Later, Finniss wrote in his diary 'the town was originally designed in England and a plan was shown to intending immigrants by Mr. Rowland Hill. This gave the impression, quite wrongly, that there would be some sort of settled spot where they could go on arrival . . .'[24] But whether it was Hill or not is another matter. Certainly, Matthew Davenport Hill was a close acquaintance of Jeremy Bentham, and as a prominent radical, engaged in prison reform, came into contact with Wakefield.[25]

Against these claims one can point out that Hill was an awkward and flamboyant man who quarrelled with Light.[26] Anthony Trollope, who worked under Hill in the Post Office said 'With him I never had any sympathy, nor he with me—In figures and facts he was most accurate but I never came across any one who so little understood the ways of men—unless it was his brother Frederic'.[27] If Hill did design a distinctive plan for Adelaide it seems strange that he did not claim the credit for it, and that nothing was specified in his instructions to Light.

Finally, we are left with Light, a sensitive, courteous, and intelligent man who displayed remarkable foresight and judgement in selecting the general situation of the main settlement and the site on which Adelaide now stands. Even if he was not the creator of the parkland design—and most of the evidence points to the fact that he was not—at least he did not attempt to change it. Rightly or wrongly, his name is indissolubly linked with the most magnificent treatment of parkland town anywhere in the world.

Light's Vision

The Commissioners for colonization gave Light the almost impossible task of exploring all the coasts of South Australia and selecting the site for the first settlement within about two months. With considerable geographical skill he limited his search to five principal locations, the southern part of Eyre Peninsula, Kangaroo Island, Encounter Bay, the mouth of the River Murray and the east coast of St Vincent Gulf. He rejected the first four locations for various sound reasons; inaccessibility, restricted hinterlands, poor soils and vegetation, limited water supplies, and inadequate harbour facilities. His preference was for the east coast of St

Vincent Gulf which looked 'more like land in the possession of persons of property rather than that left to the course of nature'. Once the entrance to the Port River was discovered he was sure of his choice, and thought that he would 'only be losing time' if he looked elsewhere.[28] His choice of the east coast of St Vincent Gulf was excellent for it was as central a point to the areas to be settled as any could be.

Light's next task was to decide upon the site for the capital. If, as the previous discussion suggests, he was given a pre-conceived plan which he had to lay out, then he had to find a suitable site of nearly 5 square miles in extent to accommodate the 1000 acres of town lots and the 2000 acres of parklands. The Port was the logical place but the surrounding land was either mangrove swamp or loose sand, and no fresh water was available. Instead, Light chose slightly elevated ground, on either side of the River Torrens, about six miles inland, in the centre of the plain. He wrote:

'The steps taken to ascertain the capabilities of the country now under survey are the result of my own observations, which in comparison with all other parts of this coast are so superior, the soil so good, the plain in the immediate neighbour-hood so extensive and the proximity of a plentiful supply of excellent fresh water all the year round, the probability also of one of the plains in the immediate neighbourhood extending as far as the Murray River or very near to it . . . the excellent sheep walks in the neighbourhood and the easy communication with the harbour over a dead flat of about six miles, and also the beauty of the country; these objects, in my mind could admit of no doubt of its capabilities for a capital.'[29]

Light drew a map of the plains which sums up many of the factors involved in his choice (Fig. 100).

Light's decision to locate the capital so far from the port was the target of bitter criticism. Governor Hindmarsh thought that it could never become a commercial centre and would at best 'be nothing more than the inland town of a fertile but very limited district'.[30] At least three serious attempts were made within the first few years to shift the site of the capital to either Port Adelaide or the Murray mouth, but investment was already so great, the

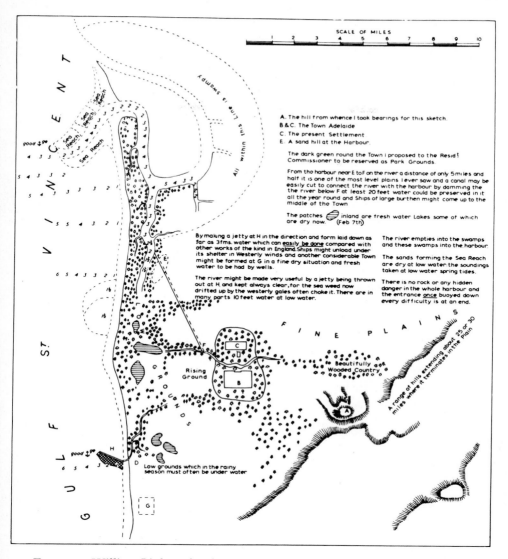

FIG. 100. William Light's sketch and assessment of the qualities of the site of Adelaide, Feb. 7th 1837. (Redrawn from the original survey by J. H. Bird, 1968.) There are three errors on the map. 1. The note 'A range of hills extending about 25 or 30 miles where it terminates in the Plain' is incorrect. The range continues northwards to the Central Hill Country. 2. The site of the port near E was moved a little down-stream because of the difficulty in crossing the mangrove swamp. 3. The canal between the city and the port (E–F) was never excavated, although a space for it does exist in the centre of the present-day Port Road. It was a move to allay the fears of those who wanted the city to be nearer to the port.

impetus of initial advantages so forceful, and the alternative sites so unsuitable, that nothing was done.[31] At the height of the controversy Light died, harried by his enemies and detractors, but his remarkable vision and grasp of locational realities was displayed once more in his Journal, in which he wrote just before he died :

> 'The reasons that led me to fix Adelaide where it is I do not expect to be generally understood or calmly judged of at present. My enemies, however, have done me the good service of fixing the whole of the responsibility upon me. I am perfectly willing to bear it; and I leave it to posterity, and not to them, to decide whether I am entitled to praise or to blame.'[32]

Light's friend B. T. Finniss, was staunchly loyal :

> 'After all what is six miles over a dead flat? Is it not absurd for persons who have witnessed in England the power of science to shorten distances to be frightened at six miles. What indeed will be the effect of this distance, it will put the first settlers at some expense to get their goods removed, but in the process of time as the population and wealth increases, Adelaide will approach nearer the Harbour, then six miles will become a vast suburb studded with shops and warehouses.'[33]

His was a lone voice at the time, but he was prophetic in his vision of what might happen eventually, and perceptive in his assessment of the effect of the changing technology of transport on the traditional urban form of the 'walking city'.

The Suburban Nodes

The 1040 acres of land in Adelaide were surveyed between 11 January and 10 March in 1837. The holders of the 437 Preliminary Land Orders selected their town acres by lot, and the remainder of the acres were sold at auction for prices which varied between £2-4s.-0d. and £14-4s.-0d.[34] However, after the town acres were bought no one could establish himself on the rural land which was not surveyed for another two years. In the meantime the enforced idleness led to excessive speculation in Adelaide which formed 'the great *rogue-et-noir* table of the early colonists',[35] and late in 1839 acre lots were changing hands for between £300 and

£2000, this speculation being made possible by the constant arrival of new settlers with supplies of cash and negotiable assets.[36]

The abundance of land in the City and the high price paid for it had two effects: first it caused the City acres to remain as vacant land, and, secondly, it forced out the labourers and lesser paid workers who could not afford the prices asked and who bought cheaper land on the outer parkland fringes. The abundance of land not built upon in the City was a topic which attracted attention continually. After looking at the plan of Adelaide, Horton said that it had 'an elegance and vastness' about it, but that viewed on the spot the town was like many other works of art and imagination; 'it recalls the picture very slightly'. The streets were not defined and the squares were so large that 'a cab would almost be required to get across them'.[37] Indeed, streets, blocks and squares were indistinguishable; tree-felling went on incessantly and it was not until the end of 1840 that all the streets were clear of timber.[38] The only construction was along, and in the vicinity of, the line of Hindley and Rundle Streets with odd pockets elsewhere. This is shown on the Kingston Map of Adelaide completed in 1841 which depicted every building and its material of construction, and was, as one settler said, 'one of the most faithful pictures of our city that could be given'.[39]

The need for suburban subdivisions and rural service centres, once the plains were thrown open to settlement in 1840, led to speculative buying and subdivision of rural sections within a radius of four to five miles around Adelaide. About thirty 'villages' were created. Writing in 1843, Bennett observed that it was a favourite scheme of the speculatively-minded to lay out a rural section of land in half acre blocks as a township and to sell these 'minute' portions to labourers, mechanics, etc. 'In this manner', he continued, 'almost every district boasts its township, although in most cases the site is discernible only by the board containing its name, or the name of some of the streets, with the pegs which mark the boundaries of the "lots".'

On the immediate north-westerly outer edge of the parklands were the new suburbs of Hindmarsh, Bowden and Prospect. These suburbs were inhabited mainly by persons assisting in the carrying trade between Port Adelaide and Adelaide, and by brickmakers, and labourers, 'who have houses of their own [and] rear a few pigs and poultry'. The houses were practical and comfortable, although 'little taste' was displayed. Thebarton, to the west of Adelaide, was an industrial suburb with tanneries, numerous brickworks and small workshops, inhabited mainly by labourers and mechanics who were attracted by the cheap freehold blocks near the City.[40]

The process of suburban differentiation was already at work. Walkerville, north-east of the City, was regarded as a superior area for businessmen and merchants, having 'many genteel residences and beautiful gardens and altogether decidedly more aristocratic and English'. Walkerville's 'neat and snug looking cottages' and large substantial brick houses, which seemed as though they had been 'built for future generations', had an air of comfort and prosperity. The high class nature of the suburb was reflected in the cost of land, its acre blocks selling for as much as £120, compared with the highest price of £80 in Hindmarsh, £75 in Bowden and £20 in Prospect.

Not suburban to Adelaide but a distant urban adjunct of it, was Port Adelaide. It had 472 inhabitants by 1840 and its population was said to be increasing rapidly. The marine character of the town was reflected in the occupations of its inhabitants, who consisted of 'ships' carpenters, fishermen, boatmen, and ships' chandlers, three or four publicans, several shipping agents, the men employed in the harbour and customs' department, a couple of butchers, a sailmaker, a blacksmith, etc.' Albert Town (now Alberton) was situated on the firm ground on the Adelaide side of the swamp, functioning basically as a residential suburb of the Port.

Somewhere intermediate in character between these suburbs and the rural villages were Unley and Goodwood on the southern edge of the parklands.

Of the more truly rural centres, Islington and Klemzig were probably the largest. Klemzig, was a village of German migrants, its orderly arrangement of houses, roads and gardens betokening a co-operative and communal settlement. There was, said Bennett 'nothing English here—even from the picturesque kirk down to the pony cart, all is different'. In addition to these villages, many other newly emergent settlements dotted the plains. Most of these were rudimentary service centres and contained 'at least a few houses, the residences probably of a carpenter, a blacksmith and shoe maker', the indispensable hotel, and, later, the general store. Edwardstown, for example, was divided into acre allotments on which lived eight families; Cowandilla had eight or nine pisé (mud) houses and a brickworks, and New Richmond had three dwellings and two or three more in the course of construction. These nodes, and many others, were to be of permanent significance, for they were tied to the City centre by main roads and they attracted early suburban settlers.

The Emergence of Patterns and Processes

The close observation which accompanied the establishment of the new settlement of Adelaide declined after the early 1840s when the success of the venture seemed assured. Admittedly, the scene became more complex to describe as the urban area grew larger and the number of inhabitants increased, and to indulge in the detail of individual house, person, or settlement as had been common before would have resulted in a morass of mind-befogging detail. Nevertheless, it does seem as though the experiment of establishing a large city before its hinterland was colonized had called for special comment, and now it was over as the farmers fanned out over the plains. Some, of course, of those did write, such as Wilkinson in 1848, Sidney in 1852 and Sinnett in 1862, but the essence of the spatial, functional and demographic changes that were taking place as the city grew eluded them. They seemed preoccupied with the new churches and public buildings—the objects of civic pride, the marks of civilization, and the most obvious symbols of change and prosperity—they could not comprehend the jostle of streets and houses forming around them; the new social map and material landscape being drawn on the Adelaide Plains bewildered them, even if they thought about it.

The commercial advantage of Adelaide and its port, reinforced by its administrative control was unchallenged. The self-perpetuating mechanism of initial advantage of the existing site (even with the division between the Port and the City) which had been appreciated only after a few years of settlement was even more in evidence after 1840, and was compounded every year.[41] Immigration (net increase, 88,696) boosted the population numbers and accounted for over two-thirds of the total population increase between 1841 and 1861, and of the shiploads of assisted and un-assisted migrants who disembarked at Port Adelaide the majority stayed in the Adelaide area. The demand for supplies increased and the growing network of roads, which was part of the expanding rural survey programme after 1840 steadily enlarged the area accessible to Adelaide for trading purposes,[42] while the area under cultivation increased rapidly to become the greatest in Australia (see Table XXIII).

Table XXIII

South Australia 1841–61

(1000 acres = 404·686 ha)

Date of census	Total population	Population Adelaide urban area	Thousands/ acres cultivated	No. of farms
1843	17,196	6,107	18·9	N.A.
1846	25,893	c. 9,000	26.2	1,714
1851	66,538	c. 15,000	64·7	2,821
1855	97,387	c. 28,000	129·7	5,321
1861	130,627	35,380	428·8	7,090

Source: S.A. Stat. Reg.; and S.A. Almanacs.

There were three ways in which the change in the size of Adelaide manifested itself. They were :
1. the increasing complexity of occupations and life;
2. suburban growth and differentiation;
3. the development of functional zones within the central City area.

These changes constituted the patterns and processes which emerged and which were to have enduring significance throughout the nineteenth and early twentieth centuries. Admittedly some of the locational decisions made and preferences expressed during the very first years of settlement up to 1840 were basic to the sub-sequent lineaments of urban growth and structure, but the seeds sown then really flourished during the two following decades.

Complexity

Late in 1839 a colonist wrote about what he saw in this new, raw
and unsophisticated settlement; it was a pioneer settlement:

> 'Adelaide presented a strange sight. Houses were built of every
> kind of material from the humble mud hut, to the neat brick
> building with plaster of Paris front wall, a few trees in one
> place and stumps in another, or the fallen trunk across the
> intended pathway, all showing that the hand of civilizing man
> is busy there while the native is to be seen wandering about . . .
> looking with wonder at the change in the land of their [*sic*]
> fathers . . .'[43]

Just ten years later Chauncey said:

> 'The population of the town is now supposed to be about
> 10,000; many of the streets exhibit as much bustle and activity
> as is to be observed in many an English city of double or treble
> that size . . .'[44]

There were 'handsome edifices belonging to the merchants' and
'numerous assemblages of shops filled up in every respect as in an
English town'. Adelaide had come a long way in ten years. By
1872, Trollope saw '60,000 people in a new city, with more than
all the appliances of humanity belonging to four times the number
in old cities'.[45]

But the detailed descriptions that were given must be abandoned
for the generalization and abstraction of the statistic, for the
occupational characteristics of the population are a good guide to
the increasing complexity of urban life. Three early censuses are
considered; 1845, 1855 and 1865—the first census had eight
categories of occupations, the second had 35 categories and the
third had 64 categories.

The 1845 census lacked detail and it covered an area that was
larger than the urban area.[46] However, some of the general
impression gained from its undoubtedly crude statistics are that
gardeners (probably small-scale farmers) made up 31 per cent of
the working population, and that the next largest group was
'mechanics and artisans' (25 per cent), most of whom must have
been engaged in building trades. Merchants and shopkeepers

accounted for 9 per cent, which is not unexpected considering the many accounts of the retail establishments in the City, and professional and government employees constituted 13 per cent. There was the almost inevitable nineteenth-century category of domestic service which was 19 per cent of all employment. It was a city of merchants, builders, and government officials, with a large sprinkling of farmers and domestic servants.

The tangled statistics of the 1855 and 1865 censuses have been enravelled to make, as far as it is possible, two sets of 12 comparable categories covering the same areas[47] (Table XXIV). Four major trends can be observed in the occupational structure of the urban area during these ten years. First, as the suburban houses spread and the urban character of the settlement was more firmly stamped on the ground the number of farmers and their labourers dropped to about one-third, from 1,979 to 769, and so did the other primary producers, the miners, sawyers and splitters and shepherds. Secondly, the task of building the town continued unabated and employment in construction increased slightly. It was the single largest group of workers in 1855, other than farmers and domestics. Thirdly, the number of people engaged in manufacturing increased nearly four-fold as the demand for locally produced goods rose with the burgeoning urban (and rural) population. They now accounted for 12·9 per cent of the workforce instead of 5·3 per cent ten years before. Whatever the household needed and the shops wished to store was now manufactured in Adelaide rather than imported. The growth was largest in the metal, wood working and clothing trades; it was essentially a development of craft industries, but there is a hint that the scale of manufacturing and business was increasing because of the rise from 287 to 1,403 in the unspecified class, which consisted mainly of labourers by 1865, and also by the rise in the number of clerks in the government, professional and clerks group. Finally, all service industries increased spectacularly. Trading and commerce more than doubled, clothing doubled, transport doubled and food preparation soared seven-fold as less and less people engaged in subsistence and became increasingly drawn into the new urban style of living. Domestic help stayed relatively stable.

This pattern of change and increasing complexity was consistent

Table XXIV

Occupations of the Population of the Adelaide Urban Area, 1855 and 1865

Occupation	1855 Number	1855 % of Workforce	1865 Number	1865 % of Workforce
PRIMARY INDUSTRY—Farmers, graziers, stockmen, shepherds, horticulturists and labourers	1979	21·3	769	5·8
OTHER PRIMARY INDUSTRY—miners, mine operators, sawyers	205	2·2	152	1·2
BUILDING TRADES—masons, bricklayers, slaters, carpenters etc.	1254	13·5	1393	10·6
MANUFACTURING TRADES—smiths, founders, printers, coachmakers, implement makers, cabinetmakers	496	5·3	1740	12·9
MERCHANTS, SHOPKEEPERS—commercial employees	820	8·8	1832	13·9
CLOTHING TRADES—shoemakers, tailors, dressers, hatters	523	5·6	1055	8·0
TRANSPORTATION TRADES—carriers, porters, sailors	467	5·0	808	6·1
FOOD TRADES—bakers, millers, butchers, greengrocers	91	1·0	622	4·7
INN KEEPERS	175	1·9	264	2·0
PROFESSIONAL AND GOVERNMENT WORKERS—clergy, lawyers, doctors, teachers, engineers, judicial, military officers	789	8·6	1054	8·0
DOMESTIC SERVANTS	2194	23·6	2115	16·0
MISCELLANEOUS PURSUITS	287	3·1	1403	10·6
TOTAL	9299	99·9	13,207	99·8
DEPENDENTS	24,290		28,905	
TOTAL	33,579		42,112	

Source: *S.APP*, 19 (1855/56), and 19 (1865).

with all we know of the process of urbanization. It was reflected in the landscape in the growth of suburbs and in the segregation of activities in the City area.

Suburban Growth and Differentiation

The extent of suburban growth over such a wide area and at such an early period was remarkable, and probably arose from two aspects of the original plan and site of Adelaide : the parkland belt and the divorce of the port from the City. By 1857 the prospect of a dispersed urban area seemed accepted, as the developments which had already occurred could continue unhindered over the flat plains which surrounded Adelaide in all directions and which afforded 'ample scope . . . for laying out suburban townships'.[48]

Speculation in suburban blocks, particularly in South Adelaide continued to be active during the late 1840s and early 1850s and many people were 'hopeful, active, . . . dealing with each other and with each party of newly arrived emigrants'.[49] An acre block in Hindley Street sold for £1,800 in 1848, and some were 'worth upwards of £2000 to £2849 generally', but elsewhere speculation had forced prices so high that many people could neither afford to build on their sections nor to sell them. As late as 1860 there were still 221 empty acre sections out of a total of 700 in the City, and they constituted the 'voids' south of Flinders and Franklin Streets. Consequently the City was still far from filled with houses, and in some places it looked as though the houses that were built were scattered 'in a vast park of 1130 acres'; and it was said in 1860 that the City's population of about 18,000 was dispersed over an area 'that could contain the inhabitants of any large European City'.[50] It was a new concept of an urban area.

It seems likely that the maintenance of such high land prices over a large area of the City was due to the encircling belt of parklands which acted as an insulating barrier to a gradual diminution of land values with distance from the centre. Hence, the growth of suburban housing and of industries using extensive amounts of land was far more likely to occur on the outer edges of the parkland belt where land prices dropped dramatically. Suburban growth at this stage was not a response to overcrowding in the City leading to competition for land use and to repeated subdivision, causing a flight of people to segregated suburban areas.

Secondly, growth continued around all the existing nodes, but particularly along the six miles of the Port Adelaide–Hindmarsh–City axis at many intermediate points such as Alberton, Cheltenham and Woodville. In 1848, Wilkinson described this 'bustling road' as being 'full of oxen drawing the produce of the country to the port or bringing up British merchandise to the stores in town'. In a survey of traffic on the road made as a preliminary to the abortive attempt to lay a railway in 1849, 1,553 horse drays, 276 bullock drays, 1,288 lighter vehicles, 6,204 passengers, 144 horse-riders and 737 pedestrians were counted at a mid-point during twelve working days. This was calculated to be the equivalent of 40,000 tons of freight and over 300,000 passengers annually.[51]

The linear growth of the urban area along the Port Adelaide–Hindmarsh–Hindley/Rundle Street axis was continued eastwards with the major suburban expansion of the Kensington-Norwood area. As far back as 1838 Kensington had been subdivided into 114 acre-blocks and was advertised as suitable for 'the working classes and small capitalists . . . who wish for a comfortable retreat within a short distance from their employment.'[52] The blocks were re-advertised a year later as being for 'the wealthy and industrious', and the adjacent section to the south was laid out as Marryatville, the two subdivisions being described as 'a growing village, boasting a store, hotel, butcher, shoemaker, and wanting only a carpenter to complete its independence from Adelaide'. But the ideal of a rural retreat, with social and economic independence and a sense of community was not to last for long, since the nearness and relatively low price of this attractive, forested, and well-watered land to the east of the City made it 'extremely eligible for villa residences' and encouraged the middle classes to build a new residential environment, the modern suburb. By 1847 the four 134-acre sections that lay between Kensington and the City were subdivided and Norwood, the new suburb, grew so rapidly that a corporation was formed in 1853; by 1855 the population reached 2,553 and was 3386 by 1861 which made it the most populous area outside of the City.[53] (For the location of some of these suburbs see Fig. 111.)

These qualitative accounts of the different suburbs of Adelaide can be given some quantitative support for the first time in 1861 when the census recorded the number of houses, and the type of building material and number of rooms in each, in Adelaide and the surrounding areas.[54] Generally speaking, in South Australia there was a progression from the use of less durable to more durable building materials with the passage of time.

> We read of the iron age, the stone age, etc., of old and similarly we might speak of the mud age, the brick age and the stone age in referring to the residential portion of Kensington, for while the early habitations were mostly constructed of the first-named material, there came a period when brick making was extensively carried on resulting in their use for the erection of most of the houses of that time. Later, when the Glen Osmond and other quarries were opened stone building came into fashion and remains so to the present day.[55]

This was an experience common to all suburbs built during the nineteenth century, and social pressures were (and still are) great to build in stone and brick rather than in wood; solid houses were equated with solid citizens, and the high percentage of stone and brick buildings is a distinctive mark of South Australia compared with all other states, even today. Hence, in 1861, the type of building material was an important indicator of the socio–economic level of portions of the urban community.

Of the 4,352 houses in the City (Table XXV) 94·8 per cent were built of durable materials such as concrete, but overwhelmingly of brick and stone, the remainder consisting of 184 wooden dwellings and only 28 mud, canvas or slab huts. There was little difference in the proportion between North and South Adelaide. This high proportion of solid durable building material was matched by superior suburbs, such as Kensington–Norwood (96·5 per cent) and Walkerville (84·0 per cent) and the fashionable seaside resort of Glenelg (97·4 per cent) although the sister resort of Brighton had only 77·1 per cent of solid buildings. In the only slightly urban District Council areas of Burnside and Mitcham to the east and south-east of Adelaide the proportions were 85·8 and 75·8 per cent respectively. In the suburbs said to be more working–class the proportion dropped markedly. In Port Adelaide and the adjacent Portland estate only 43 per cent of the houses were of brick and stone and 57 per cent of wood, and in Alberton and Queenstown only two-thirds of the houses were of durable

Table XXV

Construction Materials of Dwellings : Adelaide Area, 1861

	Total Dwellings	Solid Construction			Non-solid Construction				Cultivated Land in Council Area
		Brick and Stone	Concrete	% Solid Construction	Iron	Wood	Mud and Canvas	Not Stated	
URBAN									
S. Adelaide	3,528	3,185	149	94·5	4	163	13	14	
N. Adelaide	824	757	28	95·2	—	21	15	3	
Total City	4,352	3,942	177	94·6	4	184	28	17	
Kensington and Norwood	825	639	156	96·5		20	9	—	
Walkerville	163	128	9	84·0		3	23	181	483
Hindmarsh	952	623	133	79·4		14	1	—	
Port Adelaide	662	283	2	43·0		372	—	—	
Alberton and Queenstown	314	175	35	66·9		94	9	—	
Glenelg	154	133	17	97·4		4	—	—	32
Brighton	92	60	11	77·1	1	1	20	—	
SEMI-URBAN									
Burnside	261	203	21	85·8		19	18	—	2,071
Mitcham	741	512	51	75·8	1	73	—	—	6,320

Source: S.A. Stat. Reg., (1861).

materials. The 79·4 per cent for Hindmarsh is surprisingly high, but when all other evidence is put together one suspects that the 181, or 19·0 per cent, of the houses in the area for which there is no information on building materials were most likely to be either of wood or of mud.

One other 'objective' means of establishing the varying residential characteristics of the suburbs is the size of the dwellings. On the assumption that 1 to 4 rooms constitute a poor to average house, 5 or 6 rooms a better than average house, and over 6 rooms a large house characteristic of superior suburbs with people able to afford domestic help,[56] then Table XXVI shows that the highest proportion of small houses was in those very suburbs that had the least number of houses built of durable materials, for example, 85·3 and 79·2 per cent of the houses of Port Adelaide,

Table XXVI
Size of Dwellings by Number of rooms : Adelaide Area, 1861

	Number of rooms				Number of rooms as percentage of total		
	1–4	5–6	+6	N.S.	1–4	5–6	+6
URBAN							
S. Adelaide	2,671	446	331	80	75·7	12·6	9·4
N. Adelaide	515	147	111	51	62·5	17·8	13·5
Total City	3,186	593	442	131	73·2	13·6	10·2
Kensington and Norwood	557	163	101	4	67·5	19·7	12·2
Walkerville	115	22	26	—	70·6	13·5	15·9
Hindmarsh	605	102	64	181	63·6	10·7	6·7
Port Adelaide	565	44	53	—	85·3	6·6	8·0
Alberton and Queenstown	249	44	19	2	79·2	14·0	6·0
Glenelg	86	25	38	5	55·8	16·2	24·7
Brighton	51	20	18	3	55·4	21·7	19·5
SEMI–URBAN							
Burnside	157	43	58	3	60·2	16·5	22·2
Mitcham	516	100	118	7	69·6	13·4	15·9

Source: S.A. Stat. Reg. (1861).

and Alberton–Queenstown respectively had four rooms or fewer. The figure for Hindmarsh (60·2 per cent) is suspect because of the large number of houses (19·0 per cent) for which the size was not stated, but its number of small houses was probably near to that of Port Adelaide. At the other end of the scale, 13·5 per cent of North Adelaide's houses had over 6 rooms, and the percentages for Glenelg, Brighton and Walkerville were 24·7, 22·2 and 15·9 respectively. These measures could be repeated for later censuses.

Internal City Differentiation

The other recognizable change taking place within Adelaide during the 1850s was the internal differentiation of functions which has persisted up to the present. In 1841 Bennett said that the City contained about two hundred stores, shops and warehouses, the majority of which were concentrated in Hindley, Rundle, Grenfell and Currie Streets, which were 'fast assuming the appearance of thickly populated thoroughfares . . . possessing many shops and warehouses equal to those of any country town in the North Country, either as regards appearance, or the variety and quality of goods for sale'.[57] By 1848, the concentration was most marked in Hindley Street which was the 'principal place of business'. Here was to be seen and heard 'all the bustle of a flourishing town', as pedestrians, carriages and drays heavily laden with produce clogged the street.[58] However, a locational shift was imminent; although Hindley Street continued to be one of the 'most thickly populated and active streets', at some time between 1852 and 1860 the current of trade deserted it and flowed eastwards into Rundle Street and its tributary thoroughfares, a feature that has remained ever since, so that Rundle Street has a concentration of major retail stores that is unique in Australian capital cities. Perhaps it was the growth of the suburb of Kensington–Norwood to the east of Rundle Street, and the superior spending power of its inhabitants, many of whom worked in City offices and stores that caused the shift, but it is impossible to be certain. Whatever the cause, the concentration of business generally within the Hindley–Rundle Street axis was so great that by 1862 it was said that a tradesman might as well 'retire into the bush as open a shop in any one of the back localities'.[59] Wholesale warehouses and stores ringed the retail stores (Figs. 101 and 102).

FIG. 101. Rundle Street, looking east, 1845. (Watercolour by T. S. Gill.)

FIG. 102. Rundle Street looking east, 1911.

The other main street, the broad expanse of King William Street, was busy but undistinguished by any localization of functions in 1848. By 1860 it had acquired a distinctive character, for it was becoming lined with banks and finance and business houses, and at the Rundle Street–Hindley Street intersection, it was 'elegantly shoppy'. North Terrace was always distinguished by its solid public buildings, such as Government House, the Parliament buildings and the Railway Station, and its eastern section was already being patronized by medical men. Other governmental administrative offices, such as the Lands Department and Lands Titles Office, as well as the Law Courts, were divorced from the executive core and surrounded Victoria Square about half a mile south of North Terrace. Beyond them lay many small houses, miscellaneous industries and markets (Fig. 103).

FIG. 103. The generous planning and open space of Adelaide. Victoria Square looking south from the Post Office sometime between 1883 and 1894. The Law Courts faced the square.

Apart from these localities, the rest of South Adelaide was a muddle and a hotch-potch:

'The impressions a stranger forms of Adelaide at first sight depend chiefly upon his previous conceptions and expectations . . . if he looks for the beauty and regularity of a first class English Street—he will be disappointed. It is only here and there that capitalists have raised rows of uniform and contiguous buildings. For the most part every man has built on his land according to his means, to suit his own purpose, and to satisfy his own taste—or illustrate his want of it—as the case may be. Accordingly handsome houses and shops are flanked by small, rickety edifices, that look incongruous and out of place'.[60]

Rising land values were beginning to sort out this kind of mixture within the City and the owner of the shabby little dwelling or place of business on a good site discovered that he could profit by selling the land to a more affluent businessman or resident, and move on elsewhere.

A Century of Suburbs

The hints of the changing spatial characteristics of the landscape of Adelaide as it grew in size during the last years of the 1850s are confirmed increasingly during the next decades. Contemporary observers of the time seemed unaware of the processes taking place and of the patterns being produced, particularly the sprawl of the suburbs which was burying a familiar landscape under a network of roads and a mass of individual houses. Admittedly, the lack of comprehension of what was going on was not unique to that age; it afflicts us today. The causes of urban growth are hard to grasp and the sequence of events is even harder to disentangle; cause and effect are a constant problem of interpretation. The multitude of decisions and actions in the popular movement of block buying and house building crept by unnoticed. These two activities of the suburbanite are almost analagous to woodland clearing by the farmer, which individually was unrecorded and insignificant, but which *in toto* constituted a radical transformation of the landscape. The development of large housing estates for which records were kept, as in London, is seldom present in the Australian context and certainly not in Adelaide at this time.[61]

Therefore, the largely repetitious story of the suburbs must be told by looking at the patterns that were the outcome of individual decisions, such as the total amount of land subdivided, the expansion of the built-up area, and also by looking at the extension of services such as water supply, sewerage, tramway tracks and railways, which usually lagged behind suburban growth but did integrate the thousands of individual actions and were common to all areas. The map and the statistic become the means of comprehending the changing visual and human scale of the city during this century of suburbs after about 1861.

Currents of Change and Patterns of Growth

The suburban growth of Adelaide was not steady, there were boom years and there were quiet years. Some of these fluctuations are reflected in the patterns of growth in the maps of the subdivision of land for urban purposes (Fig. 104) and by the maps of the expansion of the built-up area (Fig. 105). It is worth examining these years to see what currents of change were running through the economy and life in South Australia, although the task is difficult because the sweep of a hundred years from 1861 to 1961 is vast and the changes in the urban area of Adelaide numerous and complex. Between 1861 and 1961 there were fourteen census returns each of which provide a mass of information which awaits analysis.

Before 1901

During the nineteenth century the most obvious indication of change was the growth of the population from 35,380 in 1861 to 141,403 in 1901, an increase of almost exactly 400 per cent, approximately double that of the non-metropolitan population during the same years (See Table XXVII). Because Adelaide's population grew more quickly than that of the rest of the colony its share of the total population increased from 27·1 per cent in 1861 to 42·2 per cent in 1901.

The rapid growth of Adelaide during these years was not unique amongst Australian capital cities; Melbourne and Sydney grew even faster at times, and centralization was a common experience of all capitals. These twin phenomena of growth and centralization require some explanation.

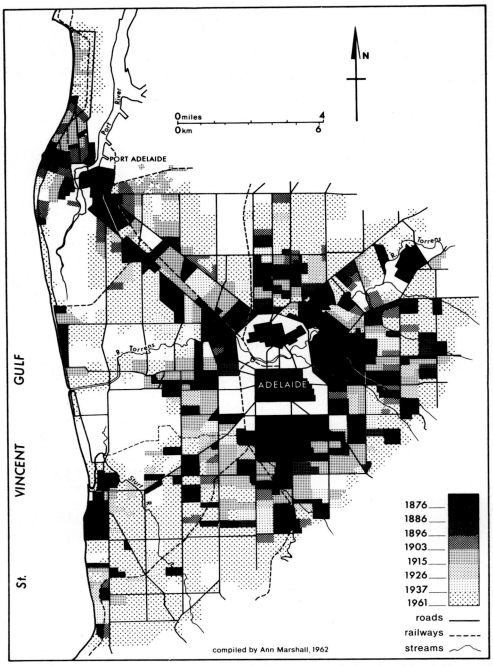

Fıg. 104. The subdivision of the Adelaide Plains, 1836–1961. (After Ann Marshall, 1962.)

Fıg. 105 (opposite). The growth of the Adelaide urban area, 1880, 1919, 1939 and 1965. Black indicates built-up areas, stipple indicates reserves (parks, public services etc.). (After *Metropolitan Adelaide Report*, 1962; and Williams, 1966.)

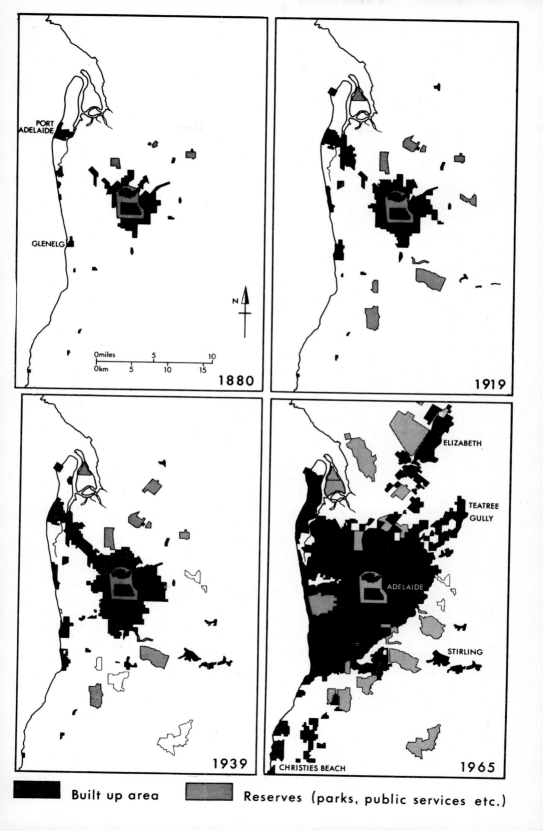

PORT ADELAIDE

GLENELG

N

0miles 5 10
0km 5 10 15

1880

1919

ELIZABETH

TEATREE GULLY

ADELAIDE

STIRLING

CHRISTIES BEACH

1939

1965

■ Built up area   ▨ Reserves (parks, public services etc.)

Table XXVII

The Population of the Adelaide Urban Area and South Australia,
1861–1901

	1861	1871	1881	1891	1901
City Adelaide	18,303	27,208	38,479	37,837	39,240
Suburbs	17,077	23,895	53,332	79,343	102,163
TOTAL ADELAIDE URBAN	35,380	51,103	91,811	117,184	141,403
TOTAL SOUTH AUSTRALIA	130,627	188,817	282,873	319,804	359,074
Adelaide as % of S. Australia	27.1	27.0	32.5	36.5	39.3

Source: The figures for Adelaide's suburbs are based on McCarty, *Aust. Econ.
Hist. Rev.*, X (1970), 132; those for the State on the *S.A. Stat. Reg.*
Undoubtedly McCarty's calculations give a more accurate view of the
truly urban population because the surrounding District Councils included many rural people. The official calculations for Adelaide's
population in 1861 and 1901 for example, are 44,857 and 163,430
respectively. However, McCarty has not carried his calculations beyond
1911 and therefore, they cannot be used for this century (see Table
XXX). Another real problem is that it is impossible to know which
individuals of the population in the more rural portions of the District
Councils have been deleted by McCarty, and the moment one wishes to
look at other attributes of the population (e.g. occupations, birth
place, age, etc.) one must revert to the entire census returns, bearing in
mind the semi-rural nature of some of the census districts.

All Australian capital cities, except for Sydney, were nineteenth-
century creations, and Adelaide, Melbourne and Perth were the
products of the second quarter of the nineteenth century when
technological, social and political changes and advances enabled
major towns to consolidate their hold on their tributary areas in a
way they had never been able to before. There had been a short
period of almost subsistence agriculture in South Australia up to
about 1855, but from then on the farmer and grazier became

increasingly market-orientated, particularly towards the overseas market, producing all their crop or fleece for cash and buying all else they wanted. The *per capita* value of exports by the late nineteenth century was the second highest in Australia and certainly one of the highest in the world (Table XXVIII) and it emphasizes the orientation of economic life in South Australia, which was focused on its major port. But as Table XXVIII shows, there was another side to this commercial emphasis, that of imports. Despite the large number of country towns in South Australia, few rose to be anything more than small service centres in areas of sparse rural population. They had no basis for sustained growth and constituted no intervening opportunity to a highly mobile and commercially minded farming community which gravitated easily and frequently to Adelaide for anything other than day-to-day goods. Many of the goods the rural population wanted were manufactured from overseas, and they were to be found in the stores and warehouses of the major port and settlement of the colony.

Of course, the indented coast of South Australia did allow the development of a distinctive pattern of regional ports, each served by a short feeder railway, and there was a host of smaller ports. But the effectiveness of the former was largely destroyed by

Table XXVIII

South Australia and United Kingdom:
Per Capita Value of Imports and Exports, 1860–1900 (To nearest £)

	South Australia		United Kingdom	
	IMP	EX	IMP	EX
1860	13	14	8	4
1870	12	13	11	7
1880	21	21	11	7
1890	26	28	11	7
1900	22	22	13	7

Sources: B. R. Mitchell, *Abstract of British historical statistics* (1962), 283; *S.A. Stat. Reg.*; and D. J. Gordon, *The Central State* (1903), 36.

a deliberate policy of railway centralization which was largely complete by 1880 (Fig. 14 and pp. 44–45), and the complex system of coastal shipping from the small ports which flourished in the sheltered water of the Gulfs was focused on Port Adelaide, which tied the ports and their hinterlands to Adelaide. Therefore, Adelaide's central position within the settled parts of South Australia was enhanced steadily by the centralization of transport networks and commercial activity. It was a great stimulus to growth.

Adelaide's supremacy as a commercial and financial centre, coupled with its existence as a political and administrative centre, made its dominance overwhelming. Continued urbanization and a concentrated and growing market, extended because of the links to all parts of the colony by rail and ship, encouraged industrial activity, which was the reverse sequence of events when it is compared with that of European cities. During these decades manufacturing was probably the fastest growing segment of the Australian economy, and this was substantially true for South Australia. Distance from competitors within Australia and the wider world paradoxically protected manufacturing.[62] Manufacturing was evidence of a new era of life in the town and of a new set of relationships. Clearly, small workshops had existed from the very beginning of settlement and had grown with the expansion of the population, but the impression given by the admittedly very unsatisfactory statistics of factories during the nineteenth century, is that the 1870s and 1880s saw a great increase in the number of establishments and workers in secondary activities, stimulated by the demand for materials, equipment and consumer goods.[63] Moreover, the scale of operations, as indicated by the number of workers per factory had increased (Table XXIX).

The pace of the change in the size of Adelaide was not even; there were many fluctuations, most of which were related to the rural economy, for, after all, Adelaide to begin with was really an enlarged service centre for all the country areas. Many different indices can be used to show fluctuating activity, but two seem particularly relevant: net migration and the number of rooms added per annum, both for the colony as a whole up to 1901, after which they change (Fig. 106). In the absence of precise figures for Adelaide, one must assume that Adelaide accounted for an

Table XXIX

Factories in South Australia, 1877–1904

	No. of factories	People employed	Horsepower used
1877	397	6,313	1,455
1881	771	11,291	2,519
1885	640	9,002	2,856
1891	915	13,480	4,969
1896	757	12,664	5,169
1899	820	14,997	11,501
1904	853	17,697	11,991

Source: S.A. Stat. Reg. (Note, mills are excluded from these figures.)

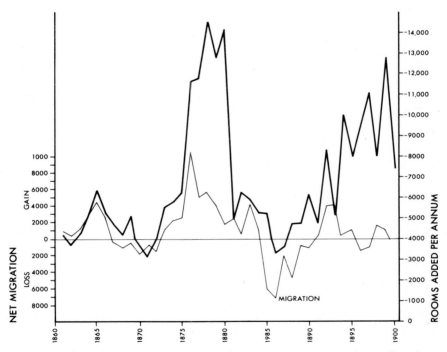

Fig. 106. Immigration and number of rooms added, 1862–1900. Based on *S.A. Stat. Reg.* and Butlin, (1962).

increasing proportion of the rooms added, in accordance with its constantly increasing proportion of the total population throughout the nineteenth century.[64]

The general relationship between the two indices is clear. The steady progress of the early 1860s changed after 1865 to one of decline because of disease in wheat, drought, and a general slowing of rural expansion. It took nearly ten years to get back to the situation of 1865. The cumulative measures of liberalizing the land laws in 1869, an extensive programme of public works in railways, jetties and road building, and favourable prices for farm produce resulted in a spectacular building boom from about 1875 to 1882. This was a period of massive subdivisional activity in Adelaide, particularly in the southern and eastern suburbs (Fig. 104). 'A mania for land speculation . . . swept over the community' wrote an observer. Sections were purchased 'for fancy prices, surveyed as townships and offered for sale, to the enrichment of some but the impoverishment of many more'.[65] Another said :

> 'Business sites rose 120 per cent in value, and good residence sites 100 per cent. New townships were laid out on the Adelaide Plains and on the sea board and syndicates purchased land here and there with the idea of cutting it up into residential lots . . . By 1882–3 had come the re-action and the vain regrets.'[66]

Drought and over-expansion of settlement in the Northern Areas led to a rapid decline in spending power, and many industries in Adelaide engaged in the manufacture of agricultural machinery, fertilizer, harness and saddlery goods, and milling, felt the effect. The 1880s were years of steadily worsening depression that reached its low point around 1885–86. Subdivision stopped. Emigration from the colony was running at between 6,000 and 7,000 per annum, many of these workers going to find work in the building and construction trades of booming Melbourne. The depression in South Australia was about ten years ahead of that in the eastern colonies, and, if the 1880s could be called the decade of 'Marvellous Melbourne' in Victoria, those years in South Australia were the decade of 'Adelaide in Adversity'.

The late 1880s and early 1890s saw a quickening of the economic conditions but little true prosperity since the rest of Australia and

the world generally were in the throes of economic recession.
There was barely any subdivision and the rate of house construction fluctuated wildly year by year, but in general it increased
slowly, which, when compared with the very low level of immigration, suggests that it was the natural increase of the
population, accompanied by a steadily declining death-rate, that
was creating a demand for housing. The urban area had acquired
its own momentum now, born of initial advantage and a policy of
centralization.

After 1901

By the turn of the century the vast amount of land subdivided
during previous years but not built upon, controlled, to a certain
extent, the physical expansion of the city, and the city grew in a
roughly circular fashion with one urban arm reaching out north
westerly to Port Adelaide (Fig. 105). For the first forty years
of the century earlier processes continued to operate and common
patterns to be elaborated, admittedly sometimes different in
pace and scale compared with those during the nineteenth century,
but still essentially the same. The twin features of centralization
and suburban sprawl continued unabated. The colonization
of new rural areas, particularly in the Murray Mallee the railway system of which was centred on Adelaide, was an added
reason for growth. The population of the Adelaide urban area
more than doubled from 163,000 in 1901 to 350,000 in 1941,
(Table XXX) and the rate of housing construction showed two
boom periods, one from about 1910 to 1914, after which war-time
conditions caused a diversion of men and materials from private
construction, and the other from 1921 to 1930. From then on the
Depression wrought havoc with the economy.

The continued growth and essential stability of the metropolitan
society of Adelaide throughout the early twentieth century were
based on patterns and events similar to those that had been in
operation during the later part of the nineteenth century. This was
all the more marked because of the revolutionary changes which
occurred during the years that followed, especially in the extent of
the urban area between 1939 and 1965 (Fig. 105).

The Second World War proved to be a great divide in the
fortunes of South Australia, and particularly for Adelaide where

Table XXX

Population of Adelaide Urban Area and South Australia, 1901–71

(to nearest '000)

	1901	1911	1921	1931	1941	1951	1961	1971
Adelaide urban area	163	199	260	313	350	447	590	809
South Australia	359	419	502	581	606	744	977	1,173
Adelaide as % of South Australia	45·4	47·5	51·8	53·9	57·6	60·1	60·4	67·0

Source: S.A. Stat. Reg.

most of the subsequent changes took place. The pre-war policy of encouraging the diversification of employment in a predominantly rural community was intensified under the impetus of war-time conditions. Munition and armament factories were established which became the basis later of peace-time electrical and electronic industries (and even rocketry with the establishment of the Weapons Research Establishment), and of the manufacture of many consumer durables, particularly refrigerators and motor cars. The number of people employed in factories increased by nearly 170 per cent between 1939 and 1965, most of them in Adelaide, which was a rate of growth above the national average and second only to that of Victoria.

Post-war migration at an average annual rate of about 11,600 between 1946 and 1966 not only added greatly to the population, so that yet again it more than doubled from 350,000 in 1941 to 733,000 in 1966, but it had a marked effect upon the composition of the population. Before 1940 one could safely say that Adelaide had a homogeneous population which was about 98 per cent Australian or British, born with a small German element; any suburban segregation was basically socio-economic. Now, however, substantial Italian, Greek and Yugoslav concentrations have given a new element to residential differences in the inner ring of older suburbs, and, incidentally, have given these areas a new lease of life with the careful refurbishing of older dwellings.

Over and above all these deliberate political and economic changes there occurred a technological change, the advent of

universal car ownership. Whereas there were 6·52 persons per
motor vehicle in 1940, the number had dwindled to 2·69 persons in
1966, the lowest in Australia. The effect of the general availability
of the car and truck has been to liberate a large part of the work
force so that it no longer depends upon public transport (Fig. 107),
and it has helped industry to spread away from the Port and the
railways. The spatial effects have been to enlarge the city area
and to scatter its land-use patterns; dispersal and dynamicism are
the features of the new metropolitan society.

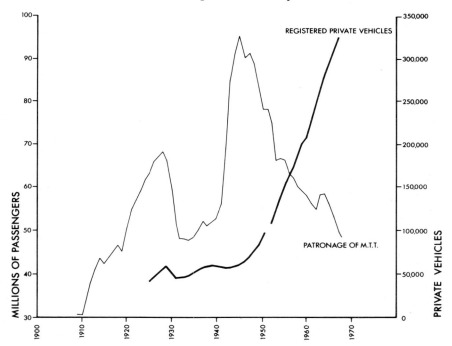

FIG. 107. Public transport patronage and car ownership, 1910–1968. (*S.A.
Stat. Reg.*)

Finally, the formation of the South Australian Housing Trust
in 1936 to construct housing for workers (for rental but primarily
for purchase), at the lowest cost possible compatible with the
ideals of the detached dwelling and the compromise, the double
dwelling, have had a marked effect upon suburban growth patterns
and forms. Large areas of land have been acquired and about

68,000 dwellings constructed, three-quarters of them in the metropolitan area. The activities of the Trust have varied from initially small estates of a few score houses to complete suburbs as at Enfield, Ingle Farm and Seacombe Gardens, and to completely new satellite centres, such as Elizabeth, north of Adelaide begun in 1954 and now having a population of over 50,000, and Christies Beach, south of Adelaide, begun in 1961 and already with a population approaching 6,000. The constrictions of the coast and scarp of the Ranges go a long way towards explaining the north-south extent of Adelaide's growth during recent years, but the activities of the Trust have been paramount in promoting and encouraging that trend towards creating one of the world's first truly linear cities.[67]

The Pattern of Services

As the urban area splayed out over the plains for about two miles in all directions, and up to six miles towards the early nuclei of the Port and Glenelg, the need arose for a network of supporting services to bind together the mass of individual houses in the suburbs so as to enable them to function coherently as part of the larger urban area to which they belonged. The provision of services was largely a matter of public expenditure, and, as such, tended to lag behind the suburban sprawl. Water supply and sewerage were good examples of this, and to a certain extent public transport lagged too, but in time the developing network of railways and street tramways exerted a powerful influence upon the pace and direction of suburban growth.

Water Supply

The supply of water, that essential prerequisite of urban living for which there is no substitute, always loomed large in the South Australian mind. Even before settlement actually began the question of water supply had exerted a locational influence; Light had rejected Port Adelaide as the site for the main settlement because of its brackish underground water supply. Further inland, however, the thick colluvial deposits of the plains as they sloped gently eastwards up to the scarp foot of the Mount Lofty Ranges held abundant water at various depths, and the River Torrens and streams running off the western edge of the Ranges were also utilized; all of which goes a long way to explain the numerous 'villages' located between Adelaide and the Ranges.

By the late 1840s Adelaide's population had risen to about 20,000 and the demand for a supply of water more regular than that obtained from wells and rainwater tanks brought into being a host of water-carriers who carted the water from the Torrens to individual houses at a charge of between 1s.-6d. and 3 shillings for 50 gallons, depending upon the distances of delivery within the City area. But even a rationalization of the system with the creation of two water carrying companies in 1850 could not keep pace with the growth of population and the demand for water, and five years later investigations were undertaken to utilize the creeks east of the City. The damming of these creeks would have had the advantage of allowing the gravitational discharge of piped water to the new eastern suburbs which lay between 200 and 600 feet above sea level, but the creek catchments were too restricted to supply a demand that was estimated to be about 27 gallons per head per day for about 30,000 persons. Accordingly, the River Torrens, which rose in the centre of Ranges, was the obvious source; a weir was constructed across the river where it emerged from the Ranges in the Torrens Gorge and the water was diverted to a new reservoir at Thorndon Park, which was capable of holding 150 million gallons (Fig. 108). A pipeline was laid to Adelaide and water reticulated to the houses at a cost of 1s.-9d. per 1000 gallons, which compared favourably with the minimum cost of 30 shillings per 1000 gallons for carting, but even that was considered to be higher than it needed to be because of the 'unnecessary size of the town' which required the laying of an excessive length of piping in relation to the population served.[68]

The effect of piped water on urban growth is hard to ascertain. For Adelaide the main benefits were said to be 'immunity from fire, the lowering of rates of insurance and greatly increased facilities for watering the streets', presumably to reduce the dust during the summer months. There was no evidence, at this stage, that the provision of piped water became a positive attraction to new building and boosted suburban development. Nevertheless, existing settlements wanted piped water and the inquiry into the extension of supplies to Port Adelaide suggested that it would

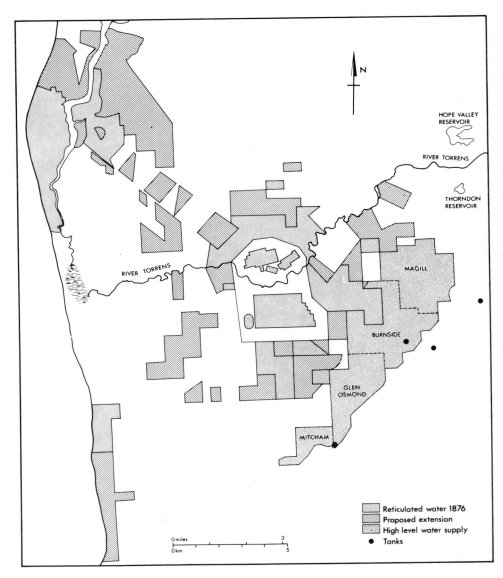

FIG. 108. Adelaide water supply, 1876, and proposed extensions. Based on
SAPP, 238 (1877).

'have the effect of increasing manufactories' there, as well as being an encouragement for 'the working people to keep clean'.[69]

By 1866 Port Adelaide, which was previously supplied by wells and water carted from Adelaide, was connected to the system, which meant that water now reached the houses of about 25,000 people. But continued growth, particularly in the eastern suburbs of Kensington and Norwood, could not be overlooked and it was forecast that

> '. . . the question of increased storage accommodation to supply the City and the various suburban villages must ere long occupy the attention of the government.'

Not only was the number of houses connected to the system increasing continuously with population growth, but so was the *per capita* consumption of water, which had risen to 32 gallons per day. Previously it was thought that not much waste of water would occur because there was no drainage or sewerage system, but the very availability and cheapness of the water made the irrigation of gardens and vegetable plots more popular, and meters were installed in order 'to correct the evil to some extent'.[70]

Consideration was given, only fleetingly at this time, to piping supplies from the River Murray,[71] but finally the more obvious and nearer solution of constructing a new reservoir on the River Torrens was undertaken, and Hope Valley reservoir (capacity 765 million gallons) was completed by 1871 as a 'suburban reservoir', while Thorndon Park still served Adelaide and Port Adelaide.[72] Thirty-one miles of suburban mains were laid to the inner ring of suburbs of Kensington, Norwood, Stepney, Kent Town, Hackney, Walkerville, Medindie, Bowden, Brompton, Hindmarsh, Goodwood, Unley, Unley Park and Fullarton, as well as to Glanville, Semaphore and the Portland Estate near Port Adelaide. Year by year, as the building boom got under way, the *Public Works Report* listed the new suburbs as they were connected to the system, and in 1874 a main was laid for six miles southwest across the plains to Glenelg. The extent of the water-supply system in the Adelaide Plains by 1877 is depicted in Fig. 108, which shows the areas that were serviced, and the areas in which suburban growth was expected and in which it was proposed to extend the service. There were also some subdivisions too far, too isolated or too difficult to be worth connecting, the majority of these being above the level of the Torrens weir and located in the eastern foothills running from Magill in the north-west through Burnside, Glen Osmond and Mitcham to the south-west.[73]

During the 1880s, the proposed areas of extension were slowly connected (and there is some evidence to suggest that the publication of the 1877 plan may have promoted subdivisional activity), and small reservoirs and storage tanks tapping local supplies at Horsnell's Creek, Second Creek, Brownhill Creek and First Creek were established in the foothills and a pumping station built at Magill to pump Hope Valley water up to this new inter-connected system during the summer. Over 240 miles of mains had been laid and 72,000 people connected by 1880. But there were problems which the Chief Engineer could foresee :

'Although the storage is sufficient for the immediate wants of the city it is important to bear in mind that improved drainage means also increased water supply, and as in a short space of time it is to be hoped that the whole of the city and suburbs will be experiencing the benefits of deep drainage it is highly necessary that immediate steps should be taken to select sites available for further storage.'

This far-sighted view was not heeded during the slackening of building activity during the depression of the 1880s, and it was felt by 1887 that the system was 'a complete work' needing little extension.[74] But, as building got under way again the slow but steady suburban expansion after about 1888 hastened the search for a new source, and by 1892 work began on the Happy Valley reservoir on the Onkaparinga River south of Adelaide, so that by 1897 the reservoir was supplying all the southern and western suburbs of Adelaide. With a capacity about four times that of Hope Valley it was predicted confidently that the Happy Valley reservoir would 'place Adelaide and the suburbs beyond all fear of water failure for many years'.[75]

Sewage disposal

A system of sewage disposal which relied upon cess-pits, night-soil removal, the emptying of effluent into the Torrens and into the surrounding ring of parklands was probably tolerable when Adelaide's population was about 18,000 and that of its suburbs and surrounding scattered settlements about 17,000. But scares of cholera and typhoid, and the well-attested fact that these were water-borne diseases hastened investigations by the City Council into a system of 'deep drainage' in 1865, 1871 and 1875.[76] All plans, however, were abandoned because of friction and disagreement between the Colonial Government and the Council on aspects of raising funds and the repayment of loans through rates.

Finally, in 1878, when Adelaide's population was approaching 80,000 and the built-up area was getting to be a continuous ring one mile deep around the parklands, provision was made to sewer all the suburbs. Once the plan was accepted and the financial problems overcome, the only question that needed a decision was that of the method of disposal. Because of the lack of tidal action in the Gulf, disposal of effluent into the sea was not a practical solution, and the authorities were forced to construct a complex and expensive sewerage farm at Islington, north of Adelaide. By 1882, the first 207 houses were connected; by 1883 the 6500 houses within the City; by 1888 the north-eastern suburbs of Hackney, St Peters and Stepney; by 1891 the eastern suburbs of Norwood, Kensington, Parkside and Eastwood; and by 1896 the southern suburbs of Goodwood, Unley and Hyde Park. This list could be extended endlessly, but suffice to say that by 1896, 15,062 houses were connected and that by 1901, 19,001 houses, which was approximately two-thirds of all the houses in the built-up area. By the turn of the century good sanitation was an established adjunct of the average suburban house.

The remarkable things about water supply and sewage disposal in Adelaide, compared with all other cities in Australia, were the earliness of their installation and the ease with which they were extended subsequently. Investigations into the causes of earliness would entail a detailed comparison with each other city, which is beyond the scope of this study, but it is true to say that once established they were so popular that there was overwhelming public support for their extension. In fact they were unquestioned facets of suburban growth. Topographically, there were only a few places on the gently sloping plains that were difficult to sewer gravitationally, such as parts of Brompton and Hindmarsh, and the early provision of piped water made it all the easier. An important factor in earliness and ease was the centralization of control of these essential services. This stemmed from a decision by the government in 1870 that the control of all waterworks in Adelaide and Port Adelaide should not be vested in those individual corporations but in semi-governmental instrumentalities. Responsibility passed first to the Commissioner of Public Works in 1876 and then to the Hydraulic Engineer's Department, so that by 1882 the government, through its statutory bodies, could extend new works as suburban growth demanded, without seeking Parliamentary approval each time. In 1888 all sanitation was administered by the Sanitary Engineer. Finally, both water and sanitation came under the control of the Engineering and Water Supply Department where they have remained ever since. Thus, from an early date, these two utilities were thought of as a combined operation under semi-government control and this avoided the problems of fragmentation and dispute between councils that happened, for example in Melbourne.[77]

As fast as the new houses spread in the suburban blocks the public authorities provided essential facilities which later included gas and electricity; in a way, there was an undeclared partnership between the individual private house builder and the larger public authority to propagate the new environment of the suburbs.

Transport: Railways

Once established, the unseen services underground were regarded as so essential, so indisputable that they aroused little debate except as to where and when they would be extended to catch up or keep pace with the ever-expanding urban area. However, the services above ground, particularly transport, were a different matter because a variety of alternatives existed—foot, horse, train and tramway—and because transport facilities did affect the expansion of the urban area.

Public transport only becomes necessary when a city grows beyond the distance which people are prepared to walk regularly to work, which is commonly taken to be a radius of about 2 to 2·5 miles from the city centre.[78] Adelaide certainly did not reach that stage until about 1880 when horse-drawn street trams flourished and altered the face of the townscape, and even then they could possibly have been regarded as premature were it not for the fact that the encircling belt of parklands added another half mile to every journey from a suburb to the City centre. But Adelaide did have two far flung agglomerations of population, six miles from the centre, at Glenelg and at Port Adelaide, to which railways were laid at an early stage.

In 1861 Port Adelaide, as well as being the major port of South Australia, was also an important commercial and industrial centre. It had a population of 3176, which rose to 14,000 in 1881 and 20,000 by 1901. A railway between the Port and Adelaide seemed an unquestionable necessity from both the passenger and freight point or view, and after many false starts a line was completed in 1865, together with the first part of the northern line to Salisbury, which eventually linked Gawler and the copper mines of Kapunda to Adelaide (Fig. 109).

Glenelg was the other focus of attention. An early attempt in 1870 to lay a street railway between Adelaide and the resort came to nothing,[79] but by the late 1870s, the settlement had grown large enough to attract railway promoters, and in 1873 the Adelaide, Glenelg and Suburban Railway was opened, between Victoria Square and Glenelg, with the hope that it would be extended later on southwards to Marino and eastwards to the fast growing middle-class suburbs east of Adelaide at Kensington and Norwood.[80] The users of the railway were varied. The line was constructed primarily to cater for day trippers and the holiday trade : the demand by the urban population for sea bathing and cool sea breezes during the long hot summer months was thought to be 'capable of almost infinite extension'. There were also people who had retired to the coast and desired the occasional journey to the City and there were the grand holiday houses of the richer people, both from the City and country districts, who felt 'these advantages [breezes, bathing and now transport] preponderate so much over those that are offered by the hills' up till then the summer retreat of the well-to-do.[81] There were also, at this time a few businessmen who commuted to the City. The railway was given an added importance and more custom when it was decided to land the overseas mail at the Glenelg Jetty after 1874 instead of at Port Adelaide.

Complaints that the railway company exercised 'vexatious,

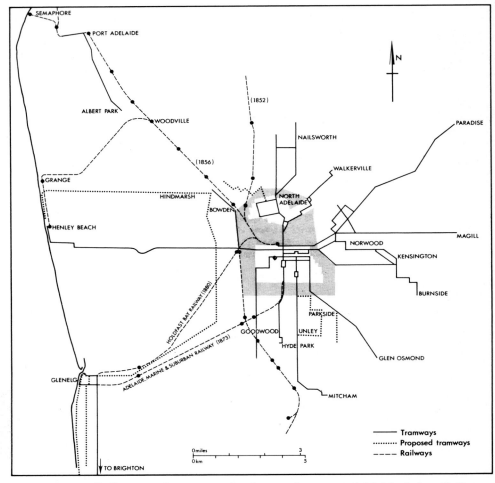

FIG. 109. Railways and tramways in nineteenth-century Adelaide (after C. S. Kingsborough).

monopolistic tendencies', particularly in its strange disregard for the custom of the race-goers to the Morphettville Racecourse, about half-way along the line, led to a sustained campaign to provide an alternative means of transport to the coast. The Hold-fast Bay railway from North Terrace to Glenelg was proposed; the Bill was passed, and the railway laid and opened in May 1880. Obviously, economic considerations had not weighed heavily with the promoters, and the over-provision of service resulted in competition, less revenue and the eventual amalgamation of the two companies eighteen months later. A new railway along the coast from Glenelg to Brighton and Marino was similarly constructed with little regard for revenue and opened in 1879, but closed the next year.[82]

But what effect did all this activity have on urban expansion? It was thought that generally 'where-ever you put a railway population follows',[83] and the promoters of the Holdfast Bay railway were hopeful that new townships were going to grow up at Hilton, Cowandilla, Richmond and other stops along the line. Land values tended to go up in the vicinity of intermediate stations but not at the terminals of the Adelaide, Glenelg and Suburban Railway which ran along King William Street in Adelaide and Jetty Road in Glenelg; not all citizens liked 'to be shaken in their beds by the passage of railway trains'. Nevertheless, generally speaking, it was thought that land values had trebled around Glenelg after the line had been laid,[84] and that soon villa residences would line the whole of the railway. The abortive plans to extend the railway along the coast in 1876 led to much speculative land-dealing in the southern margins of Glenelg.

The only ready measure available of the effect of the railway is that the population of Glenelg and Brighton rose from 708 in 1861, to 1342 in 1871, and to 3495 in 1881, and then to 5,029 in 1901.

The success of the Glenelg line in promoting suburban growth led to the plan to construct a line from Woodville (about half-way along the Adelaide–Port Adelaide line) to Grange on the coast. The promoters had already bought 400 acres at Grange, part of which was laid out as Grange township, and they contemplated subdividing the remainder when the line was completed. They had also constructed a jetty and levelled sandhills for a public area on the foreshore. But the line was not constructed until 1893, and it seemed as though the Government was not prepared to sanction a speculative railway ahead of existing population; in any case the scheme smacked of jobbery. Similarly, early plans to lay a line to Semaphore in 1869 and again in 1874 were not allowed, the lines finally being constructed in 1891 to serve the Semaphore and Largs forts and the jetties at which larger ocean-going vessels docked, which could not enter Port Adelaide.[85]

One other scene of activity and plans was towards the east of Adelaide where there were many schemes to penetrate the various gullies of the Ranges and get across the hills to Nairne to eventually join up with Melbourne. This line was not completed until 1883, when it had the effect of linking Mitcham with the City and also opening up the summer retreat areas of Blackwood, Aldgate and Mount Lofty.

The pattern of railways created around Adelaide nowhere approached the complexity of that of either Sydney or Melbourne. Although Adelaide was situated in the middle of a plain the topographical constraints of the sea and the Ranges did limit the radial development of lines, and eventually the Northern line and the line over the Ranges were the two entries for all other lines to the Adelaide–Port Adelaide urban area.

Transport: Tramways

Railway construction for truly suburban needs was never important in Adelaide, with the exception of the Glenelg railway, but what Adelaide lacked in railways it made up for in tramways which filled up the gaps in the transport network (Fig. 110). This was reasonable; tramways were more versatile, the capital and running

F I G. 110. Electric and horse-drawn tramways, junction of Ward and O'Connell Streets, North Adelaide, 1909.

costs were low compared with those of railways, and they were easy to construct on the almost level land and wide streets of Adelaide and its surrounding areas. For investors their profitability was high. The new tramways can be seen as a response to the emerging suburbs of the late 1870s and the desire for versatile, smooth-running, short-haul transport to the City centre by the well-to-do, and also by the working man who could not afford City prices and was separated from his place of work by the parklands. But tramways can also be seen as promoters of suburban development, especially after 1882, when it was said that the people 'had got educated to the tramways now'.[86] They enabled suburban divisions to proceed within a radius of about four miles of the City centre, extended the city beyond the radius of walking and perpetrated and increased the segregation of the urban area. There had, of course, been some horse-drawn buses plying between Adelaide and North Adelaide, and between Adelaide and Kensington, but they were not a reliable form of transport and must have been rather like Mr Whittaker's buses from Payneham which were later described as being

'. . . a very uncertain means of conveyance as he pleases himself as to the time he runs. On holiday times if he thinks he can do better elsewhere he does so. In fact he just goes where and when he pleases.'[87]

It was not a satisfactory basis for intra-urban transport and a regular journey to work.

The real beginnings of tramway development came with the promotional activities of W. C. Buik, a Rundle Street retailer and resident of Norwood. He visited the United States in 1875 and came back convinced of the utility of tramways, and proposed the Adelaide and Suburban Company with lines between Kensington–Norwood and Rundle Street. A Bill was introduced into Parliament in October 1875, and after many legal wrangles and delays the line was finally opened in June 1878, with Buik as the Chairman of the Company.[88] Within the first six months of operation the line carried 405,763 passengers, or about 15,000 persons a week, and the success of the venture encouraged the Company to extend its lines to North Adelaide in 1879, and led to the formation and opening of the Adelaide–Unley–Mitcham line of 5 miles in

February 1879; the Port Adelaide–Alberton line of $2\frac{1}{4}$ miles in May 1879; the Adelaide–Hindmarsh line of $3\frac{1}{2}$ miles in 1880; followed by the Adelaide–Parkside and Adelaide–Goodwood lines in 1881[89] (Fig. 109). These developments in Adelaide were early in comparison with those in other cities in Australia, and the lines certainly served a much smaller population, a point which was not lost on some promoters. 'There is no city so small as Adelaide that I am aware of that has them'. They were only found in 'the big cities such as San Francisco, Chicago, New York, Salt Lake'.[90]

The reasons for these comparisons are not part of this study, but the tramways were so successful that another bout of expansion occurred; the Adelaide and Suburban extended its lines to Walkerville, the Adelaide–Hindmarsh Company constructed a long line to Henley Beach in 1881. During 1882, lines were constructed from Adelaide to Prospect and Nailsworth, north of the City; from Adelaide to Hyde Park in the south; along the coast between Glenelg, Somerton and Brighton; and the Adelaide and Suburban Company built two more lines that stretched eastwards to terminate at Magill and Burnside at the foot of the hills, near which were Morialta Falls and Waterfall Gully, two scenic attractions and popular picnic spots which fulfilled the requirements of a new and emerging institution, the Sunday outing.[91] Another new line extended about six miles to the north-east through Payneham to Paradise.[92] In the United States only New Orleans had its street car that went to Desire; in Australia only Adelaide had its tramway to Paradise.

Generally, opinion was in favour of the tramways, which were regarded as a public benefit. The Government offered no real opposition as it had to the suburban railway lines, although it did subject each scheme to a minute scrutiny by a Select Committee of both Houses and did reject a few proposals. Surprisingly, however, despite the days of inquiry (and hundreds of pages of evidence) these Committees gave little thought to the areas to be served by the tramways or the possible patronage of the lines. The inquiries concentrated more on the technical and safety problems of laying tramlines in the roadways, the problems of road maintenance, and the inconvenience that the lines and the frequent trams would cause to other road users and to businesses alongside the roads, particularly those within the City of Adelaide. Paradoxically, the City Council showed a very hostile attitude to the companies which were providing the City with business and customers, because it wanted to control the operations of the companies within the City area. But as the lines proliferated and Adelaide became 'a honeycomb of tramways',[93] a greater concern began to be expressed by the Government and the companies alike about the economic working of the lines, particularly as the 1880s progressed and Adelaide and the rest of the Colony entered a period of depression, which caused a decline in traffic. The increasing popularity of bicycles contributed to the decline. Between 1884 and 1887 four companies were wound up.[94]

The questions of for whom the lines were catering and what effect they were having on suburban growth were barely asked by anyone. In many cases the 'benefits were more prospective than actual' and lines were laid in the hope of encouraging building development and hence patronage. For example, the new line from Port Adelaide to Albert Park was supposed to be for 'the working people' of Port Adelaide who could not afford the high prices asked for the few remaining blocks in the Port Adelaide area and who had to buy land further to the south-east along the Port Road. Building costs had also risen because the Corporation had decided to ban the construction of timber houses in its area. Therefore high rents increased the travelling distance.

> 'You see numbers of them travelling [by foot] in the heat of the day backwards and forwards to their meals—having perhaps ten minutes at home. They would derive great benefit from the tramway.'

But the promoters were also thinking of the potential increase in the population that would occur once the line was built : 'it would make an opening for many wealthy people who would take land there and build if they could get backwards and forwards by tramway', and already several sections had been divided between Alberton and Albert Park and new houses were being built 'in all directions'.[95]

Some promoters pinned their faith on the increased leisure time of the working people. There were only twenty houses at Henley Beach when the Adelaide–Hindmarsh Company built its line to the coast, and it hoped to have 'the eight-hour people who leave work at half past four every day and will avail themselves of the line to get to the sea in the summer time.'[96]

But the greatest profits were to be had if one owned land or houses alongside the projected routes. It was known that land values in Kensington and Norwood had risen by between 200 and 300 per cent after the tramway had been laid, and it was generally acknowledged that tramways had 'the effect of increasing the value of land in the suburbs'.[97] In some cases it seemed that tramway schemes were 'brought forward not to benefit the public so much as to benefit certain holders along the route', as seems to have been the case in the abortive proposal to lay a line from Adelaide along the Bay Road and then down South Road to Edwardstown, along which route there was scarcely any population.[98]

The new suburbs south of Adelaide were probably the most promising territory for the speculative tramway builder. Initially Parkside, Eastwood, Unley, Malvern and Goodwood were, generally speaking, working-class suburbs on the edge of the parklands where there were 'scarcely two people in a hundred, . . . who have their own vehicles'. Cottages were 'spreading rapidly' and most of the population worked in the City and needed transport. It was established that people were prepared to walk about half a mile to a tramway and by 1882 four lines penetrated this area. The attraction of these suburbs was such that even during the depression years house building went on in Malvern, which was very popular and the patronage of the lines increased steadily (Table XXXI). The character of the suburbs began to change with the impact of the tramways. By 1896, when the duplication of the Parkside line was contemplated, one of the directors was asked:

'Can you give us any idea to which class the population there belongs?—Well, what is commonly termed the middle class if you will allow me to use the expression. Of course men who want to put up a £5000 or £10,000 house would not be likely to erect it at Parkside but would most likely go further up into the hills districts.'[99]

In contrast the more solidly working class districts of Hindmarsh, Bowden, Brompton and Ovingham to the north-west of

Table XXXI

Patronage of some Suburban Tramways

	Adelaide and Suburban	Unley and Mitcham	Hindmarsh	Parkside	Hyde Park	Goodwood and Paradise
1879–80	2,354,649	c.211,600	c.500,000	648,537[1]	c.200,000[2]	?
1891	4,886,147	733,063	726,362	780,345	326,589	c.750,000
1896	5,267,838	948,930	842,418	836,116	420,727	c.950,000
1901	5,539,211	1,229,335	909,568	938,877	464,622	c.1,258,000

Source: Half-yearly reports of companies, *S.A. Register.*

1. Sept. 1882–83.
2. Sept. 1883–84.

Adelaide were badly served by tramways. Employment was local and this generated little traffic, and there was not the potential within these suburbs, for middle-class housing development which the promoters were realising increasingly was the key to the profitability of tramways; nevertheless traffic on the Hindmarsh line increased modestly (Table XXXI).

'A decent, orderly, progressive civilization'

After 1900, the provision of services was so taken for granted as a matter of health, convenience and amenity in the suburbs that the narrative of their growth and spread is repetitive. Had they lagged behind or raced ahead of the suburban sprawl then they would have created patterns different in their timing and extent from those shown in Fig. 105. But as it was, sewerage and water supply just did a little better than keep up with suburban sprawl, so that all new houses were connected and the back-log of old ones was catered for. State instrumentalities regarded as imperative the provision of these services to as many areas as possible, regardless of their socio-economic standing or administrative location, as they did with such things as schools, and as private companies did with electricity and gas. Uniform prices (although based upon rateable values) was another feature of the metropolitan services of water and sanitation which simplified their distribution and contributed to their uniting effect. Each man's private castle became linked increasingly to all others by tramway rails on the ground, a tangle of wires above the ground, and a mass of pipes below the ground.

Transport was slightly different, and it did lag when the electrification of the tramways was delayed; after being first in the field of urban transport in Australia, Adelaide fell behind badly. The 'antiquated tramcar and its overworked slave' were a sight that drove many Adelaide citizens to indignation, and increasingly they complained about the companies and campaigned for the public control of the transport system. Schemes for electrification failed between 1899 and 1901, again because of feuds between the City Council and surrounding councils. Finally in 1906 the companies were bought out for £280,000 and the Municipal Tramways Trust was set up to administer the system as a whole.

Electrification followed quickly. Public good had triumphed over private interests. By 1925, the M.T.T. had introduced motor buses and networks of routes were created between half and one mile apart radiating out from the City centre to the suburbs.

Indeed, patterns had been set and a sort of society created that was to endure for decades. Writing in 1902 Pember Reeves compared the unpleasantness of some European cities with the urban products of Australia which 'however unnatural on paper are not disagreeable to the eye or unwholesome to the lungs'. In particular,

'Adelaide's 160,000 inhabitants are scattered about an expanse twenty miles across. Trees, grass, flowers, and, except in a few central blocks vegetable gardens and orchards meet the eye almost everywhere in the average colonial municipal district. Fresh air, good water, good food and plenty of it, reasonable hours of labour, good pay (as a rule) plenty of time for recreation,—these things explain why large urban populations do not entail physical or moral degeneracy and why you have towns with a death rate as low as 11 in the thousand . . .'

The social landscapes of the city were different from those of its European counterparts. They were

'hives of workers, with no idle classes of dilettante or mere pleasure seekers, and hardly a millionaire. They show what communities of busy people, seldom very rich, as seldom miserably poor, can do in the way of organising a decent, orderly, progressive civilization.'[100]

Reeves's description was substantially correct, and the citizens of Adelaide were enjoying what must have been one of the highest standards of living in the world at the time, which was reflected in the continued expansion of the individual houses in the suburbs each of which was a re-creation of the rural ideal of privacy in a natural surrounding.

Streets, Subdivisions and Styles

This chapter on the making of Adelaide began with an examination of the characteristics and origins of the distinctive core of the urban area, its town lands and surrounding belt of parklands. But that was only a small part of the new landscape that spread out over the plains, engulfed the suburban cores of the rural settlements, and eventually lapped and spread beyond the constricting edges of the hills. That century of creation of mainly residential structures has left many marks on the landscape. There is the pattern of the streets and the style of the houses and there is the less obvious vestiges left by the intricacies of land ownership which affect the pattern of land subdivision. Visible or invisible, however, all added up to a landscape that was supremely artificial and man-made.

But streets, subdivisions and styles are something more than the end-products of suburban growth; in a sense they are the unifying themes in the midst of the thousands of individual block-buying and house-building actions during that long century. Just because the actions and decisions were so numerous and so individual, pre-urban patterns of roads and preconceived ideas of style and the desirable mode of living subdued the individuality of lay-out and building, and formed a framework for uniformity. The result was, as Warner has suggested in his study of Boston, 'a kind of regulation without laws'.[101]

Streets

The methodical rural subdivision of the Adelaide Plains into a grid of roads surrounding groups of 80-acre and 134-acre sections, with major diagonal roads from the City to the Port, Glenelg and the River Torrens, formed a framework for all later subdivisional activity (see pp. 67–71 and Fig. 22). Most of the rural roads were one chain (66 feet) wide, but have been widened subsequently; the Bay road to Glenelg was two chains (132 feet) wide and the Port Road was $3\frac{1}{2}$ chains (231 feet) wide, the land in the centre of the road originally being set aside for a canal between the Port and the City. All these country roads, except for a few along the base of the hills scarp, have become ossified in the landscape as the major traffic arteries of the greater Adelaide metropolitan area. The effect of these roads in later subdivisional activity is shown in Fig. 111. With few exceptions, the pre-urban survey system had determined the overwhelmingly north-south and east-west orientation of the suburban road system, and the variations at approximately 45° along the Port Road and the upper portion of the River Torrens. The point is simple and needs little elaboration, but it is basic to the interpretation of subsequent changes on the Adelaide Plain.

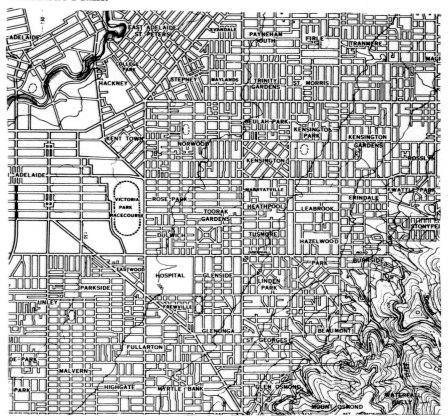

Fig. 111. The patterns of subdivision and roads in the eastern and southern suburbs of Adelaide (Scale I : 63360. By courtesy of Director of Dept. of National Mapping, Canberra).

Subdivisions

The repetitive geometry of the rectangle of the main country roads was repeated on a smaller scale with every 80-acre or 134-acre section, nearly all of which were single holdings. This finer mesh of cadastral lines had its effect upon subdivisional patterns, for the desire to convert the land from rural to urban uses usually took place within the confines of a set of property boundaries. In many ways, the street pattern of suburban Adelaide can be looked at as a palimpsest on which is marked the lines of the rural cadaster at the time at which subdivision occurred.

To the east and the south of the City the 134-acre sections have left an indelible imprint on the subdivisional pattern, each section having its own particular grid pattern of roads (Fig. 111), largely unrelated to the pattern of the adjoining section except by the pre-urban roads (which ran mainly north–south), and also by the new section boundary roads which ran mainly east–west in a continuous line. Most of these section boundary roads were not more than 66 feet wide, but a few were much wider. Norwood Parade, for example, surveyed in 1847, ran down the middle of four adjacent 134-acre sections that were subdivided contemporaneously, and it is 99 feet wide. Osmond Terrace, which bisected those same four sections in a north-south direction was 132 feet wide.

The 80-acre sections to the north, west, and south-west of the City also exercised an influence on the subdivisional pattern. They were smaller units than the 134-acre sections and therefore less likely to be subdivided with an individual and distinctive plan. The tendency was to subdivide them with a simple grid, and the lines of the grid of one subdivision within a section often coincided with an adjacent one, but sometimes were discontinuous because of the different ownership boundaries, and therefore the timing and type of subdivision.

All of this, of course, presupposes that subdivision took place within whole sections, which was true at an earlier stage and where large 'country' estates were established, particularly in the 134-acre sections in the eastern and south-eastern plains that rose gently towards the hills. But as time progressed there was a tendency for more intensive rural land use on the urban fringe, which caused a fragmentation and division of holdings, into smaller ownership units. In any case, the limited capital of many of the suburban developers enabled them to buy only small pieces of larger holdings which encouraged the owners to yield only small portions from time to time. Consequently, a much more complex pattern of suburban subdivision occurred eventually; but, even so, in comparison with European cities and those on the eastern seaboard of the United States, the land had changed hands fewer times and the complications of ownership were much less, especially as, whatever the size of the parcel of land held, its boundaries would be in straight lines and at right angles.[102] Just one of the many possible examples of complications to street patterns caused by ownership boundaries is shown in Figs. 112a and b. It concerns 120 acres in the suburb of Marleston, immediately south-west of the City. In about 1918 the land was held by ten people. *A* had already subdivided his land and had got 61 blocks out of it, and *J* had got 4 long blocks out of his small holding. *B* wanted to subdivide his section and get 17 blocks out of it by driving a 40 foot wide road north-south through the western side of his land, reserving a 10 foot strip of land between the road and *C*'s boundary to prevent *C* getting access to his street. *C* then wanted to subdivide his section by running a single road down the middle of his land, and, in retaliation would not agree to a suggestion that *B*'s road be increased in width from 40 to 60 feet so that it could be a main road to the railway station for *F*'s intended new subdivision of 114 blocks. *F*'s subdivision left much to be desired as he was not prepared to sacrifice the revenue from one block to provide access westwards across the railway, but, paradoxically, so implanted was the idea of a grid that he was not prepared to subdivide the large corner blocks diagonally. *G*, *H*, and *I* did not wish to subdivide at this stage, neither did *E*, but *D*, who did, had no access to any streets. This was a case where the conflicting interests of owners not only were inimical to good and reasonable planning but were actually detrimental to the simple process of subdivision. Eventually, the issue was resolved under the new powers granted to the Town Planner in 1919, and the resultant plan (Fig. 112b) was approved by all parties. However, a big factor in the compromise was the fact that the State Bank agreed to purchase *D*'s land for housing ex-soldiers, which gave the whole subdivision a good start.

The reason behind each subdivisional pattern within the ownership boundaries is largely lost, although the patterns of land ownership do give some clues. An account of the subdivision of Walkerville in 1838 illustrates the haphazard nature of some plans. Mann recalls the following :

'. . . a friend of mine . . . asked me to accompany him to a public meeting of the subscribers to a new township, which

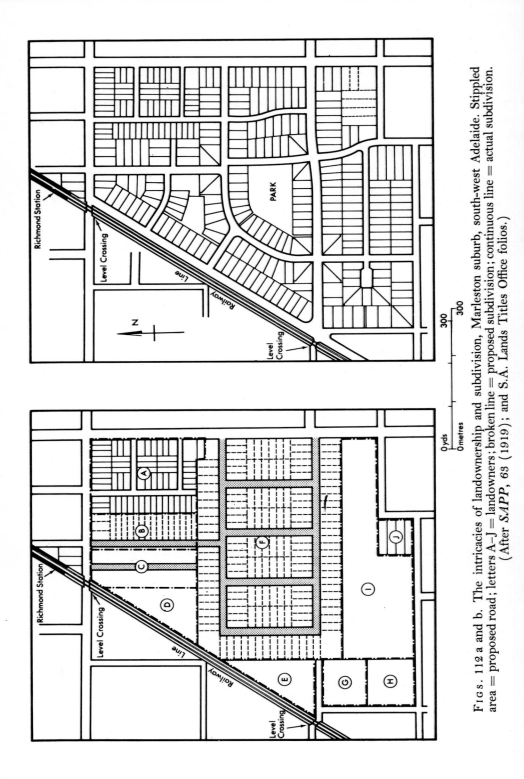

FIGS. 112 a and b. The intricacies of landownership and subdivision, Marleston suburb, south-west Adelaide. Stippled area = landowners; broken line = proposed subdivision; continuous line = actual subdivision. letters A–J = landowners; broken line = proposed subdivision; continuous line = actual subdivision. (After *SAPP*, 63 (1919); and S.A. Lands Titles Office folios.)

was in progress about three miles from the city. . . . The subscriptions for the purchase of the site of the new village was [sic] to be paid up at this meeting; and my friend, being the Treasurer, made a short speech on the object of the meeting and commenced collecting, at the same time calling for "money which had been previously subscribed". A person . . . stated that the town was not named, or laid out yet as streets, terraces, or squares. Another near him said he would remedy that deficiency; and, calling for a pair of compasses, which were supplied by a carpenter who was present, he procured a ruler and a sheet of paper, and in less than ten minutes had covered it with the dimensions of the required streets. . . .'103

The arbitrariness of the subdivision must have been repeated in many other early suburbs, and as no plan had to be kept, confusion over the dimensions, directions and ownership of blocks arose. In 1853, the suggestion was made that the Government should keep an accurate plan in the Lands Titles Office of all private townships with a view to protecting purchasers. It had been found that the suburban subdivisions of Hindmarsh, Brompton, Bowden, Beverly, York, Kilkenny, Woodville and Cheltenham, all situated between Adelaide and Port Adelaide, had no official and registered plans, even though title deeds were issued with reference to the plans, and that half the width of the road was sometimes being sold with an allotment. 'The probable evil of this loose, if not *tricky* manner of subdividing and selling land to a future generation' was obvious and needed attention. Yet, the Surveyor-General, while sympathetic to the suggestion for reform, could not get official approval for the move.104

However, the problem of registering land titles began to be more pressing during the next few years, not only in the city but also in the country, and in 1857 the relatively simple and orderly Torrens system of registering land titles was begun. It required amongst other things, that any subdivider of land should,

'for the purpose of selling the same in allotments as a township to deposit with the Registrar General a map of such township provided that such map shall be on a scale of not less than one inch to one chain and shall exhibit distinctly delineated all roads, streets, passages, thoroughfares, squares or reserves appropriated or set apart for public use and also all allotments into which the said land may be divided marked with distinct numbers or symbols, and the person depositing such map shall sign the same and shall certify the accuracy thereof by declaration before the Registrar General or the Justice of the Peace.'[105]

The wording of these requirements over subdivision remained unchanged for seventy years, except that in 1861 it was specified that no plan could be made unless by a licensed surveyor, and that in 1917 it was stipulated that no property could be re-subdivided once the plan had been deposited in the Lands Titles Office and that no intervening strip of 10 feet or less could be left alongside a subdivision in order to prevent access.[106]

The registration of land titles and the accurate survey of blocks, became, therefore, additional reasons to those of the pre-urban cadaster and street plan for adopting a methodical subdivisional pattern. In each development a grid of streets was laid out in such a way that a series of rectangular blocks was created, each with a street frontage on its narrowest side. In the absence of any regulations about either allotment size or frontage length this arrangement established a standard of uniformity, and it was also versatile and cheap. Its versatility lay in the fact that blocks could be amalgamated or re-subdivided according to any need that arose. In Norwood, for example, the earliest subdivision was in blocks of 15 acres, but as the demand for housing sites increased these were cut up into smaller blocks of $7\frac{1}{2}$, 5 and $2\frac{1}{2}$ acres, and then into smaller blocks again during the 1880s. But a more common situation was the one in the new suburbs which were largely created, and certainly served, by the tramways. Here large tracts of land were opened up to small investors, and small parcels of land were made available in various combinations to suit individual purchasers.[107]

The cheapness of the rectangular block system lay in the reduction of the number of feet of services which the developer had to provide. The narrower he could make the frontage and the deeper the block relatively then the greater his profit, particularly after 1870 and 1880 when piped water and sewerage respectively had to be added to the cost of necessary road works.[108] As these utilities tended to run down the main roads, right-angle connections were the cheapest and easiest. Added to all this was the desire for the detached house amongst all classes of people which became so strong that few terrace houses were constructed after about 1880. Implicit in the ideal of the detached house were the requirements of air, space, privacy and amenities and a separate frontage on to a well-made road; for back lanes or alleys were forbidden—they encouraged bad housing and in time became associated with 'overcrowding, disease and crime'.[109] Thus, the rectangular block had the support of moral considerations. By placing the house in the centre of the block all the minimum requirements could be achieved, and they could be regarded as the minimum standards which the middle classes and aspiring working classes held. When popular taste dictated homogeneous building styles, perpetuated in solid stone, the result was a uniform frontage that today we look at and call 'monotonous suburbs'. As far as can be made out the builders welcomed these trends, for most were very small-scale operators, and building a standardized, uniform house, with perhaps a few embellishments and twirls here and there, kept down costs and ensured a sale because of its popularity. Row houses and multiple-storey dwellings were rarely contemplated; the preference was for the detached house in its own block, which was a reflection of the low prices of land, high wages and good urban transport. All in all, the self regulating mechanism of common desires and common styles worked well, although there were a few cases where unscrupulous subdividers in the inner, older suburbs attempted to cram too many houses into re-subdivided blocks. Too late to affect these events, but at least setting a minimum requirement in the Statute Book, was the Building Act of 1935 which stipulated that a block should not have less than a 30 foot frontage and not be less than 3960 square feet (30 ft. × 132 ft.), and that the house on it should not be less than 500 square feet in floor area.[110]

But gridded streets and rectangular blocks with narrow frontages to streets were not absolutely necessary for the maintenance of popular standards which became the norm. During the years immediately after the First World War, the impact of the British garden city and suburb hit Adelaide, and there are a few examples of winding streets and irregularly shaped blocks which add a welcome variety to the chequer-board landscape of the suburbs.

The suggestions of C. Reade, the Town Planner for Marleston were a move in this direction, but his plan for Gallipoli Garden Village (afterwards named Allenby Gardens) consisting of 120 acres along the Port Road showed that besides being aesthetically more pleasing than the suggested grid of streets which it replaced, it was more practical, taking into account, as it did, the new mode of transport, the car, by attempting to segregate the major traffic roads from the essentially pedestrian roads. Moreover, Reade's plan was more profitable than a strictly gridded system of sub-division, as it increased the number of blocks that could be sold from 315 to 352 and the number of rateable feet of frontage from 20,591 to 22,294.

Other plans, such as the one for Linden Park (Fig. 111), and Reade's own massive conception of Colonel Light Gardens, which he designed for ex-service men, were other signs of the trend away from the grid. But the trend was only temporary and limited. The great majority of private subdivisions in the 20s and 30s, as well as most of those in the plains south and south-west of Adelaide after the Second World War, reverted to the grid. It was a traditional and popular method which made subdivisional profits easier and more assured.

The really great change came with the formation of the South Australian Housing Trust in 1936, which was empowered to build low cost houses, not primarily for the poor but for the essential workers needed for the industries which it was hoped would be attracted to South Australia under the new policy of diversification and industrialization. The policy of the Trust was to buy large areas of land cheaply and so overcome the inflated prices of the speculators, and to build houses fairly uniform but substantial, at the lowest price possible. Large areas were bought in Enfield, Hillcrest and Clearview, for example, and planned on a pattern different from that of the usual subdivisions, but all of these variations still took place within the framework of the major pre-urban roads.

The greatest experiments were yet to come. In 1948 the Trust purchased over 500 acres for a satellite town seventeen miles north of Adelaide. Elizabeth was planned as a series of eleven neighbourhood units around a new town centre, the inspiration being the 'New Towns' in Britain. The pattern was totally different from all that had gone before (Fig. 113). Strangely, the Trust seemed to fall short of its ideals with the new satellite suburb (for it was not a town) created in 1960 at Christies Beach south of Adelaide. It was merely a variation on the more imaginative of private designs.

Since then, private builders have adopted the Trust's policy to a greater or lesser degree depending on the scale of the enterprise. They buy large tracts of land and sell ready-built houses on blocks with all services and amenities provided instead of just selling the land and allowing the purchaser to engage a builder. Generally, the public are not content with straight lines and right angles,

FIG. 113. Elizabeth, looking south towards the town centre (to the right of the curve of the major highway). Elizabeth is a satellite town about 15 miles north of Adelaide. It has been built by the S.A. Housing Trust and now has a population of over 40,000. It consists of a series of neighbourhood units each grouped around a primary school and local shops. Although Elizabeth has its own employment opportunities many of its inhabitants work in Adelaide and the satellite settlement is fast being grafted onto the larger Adelaide urban area.

particularly where subdivision is creeping out of the dull monotony of the plains and on to the lower foothills of the scarp, and the undulating vales to the south of the plains. But again, all schemes are contained within the constraints of 320 acre squares of rural roads. It is an indelible pattern.

Styles

Although there were rows of single-storeyed 'cottages' in the older parts of the City and of Port Adelaide, this mode of living and style of architecture barely spread outside these core areas of early settlement. By 1861, the ideal of individual house ownership in a fenced block of land, divided off from neighbours was popularly accepted by poor as well as rich on the grounds of health, sanitation and privacy. As the century progressed, it became 'as inevitable and unquestionable a goal of the average Australian as marriage', and was one of the visible signs of the high standard of living achieved in the continent.[111]

Figures are hard to come by on the extent of home ownership during the nineteenth century. It could have been as high as 60 per cent at one point during the late 1870s but would probably have dropped during the depression of the 1880s; certainly by 1911 it was almost exactly 50 per cent of all houses and was 74 per cent by 1966.

Rows of town houses for wealthy city dwellers were hardly ever erected in Adelaide. Not only had the age of large town row houses passed by the 1860s, but the need for them was simply not there. There was ample room in North Adelaide and in East and South Terraces in South Adelaide for large double-storeyed detached houses situated in mini-landscaped estates, sometimes of an acre in size. When all these blocks were filled up there were the adjacent areas across the parklands in Medindie and Walkerville. It is true that had Adelaide grown large before tramways came into existence, and when walking was the main form of transport, then one would have seen a greater density of houses. But Adelaide did not. In one sense, therefore, there was no essential distinction between the architecture of the City centre and that of the suburb, the two differed only in size and in ornament. Close living never succeeded in Adelaide; there was no solid expanse of building except in the offices, shops and showrooms of the Central

Business District where face to face relationships were important, and nearly every one achieved his ideal of what he thought of as a semi-rural retreat on his own block of land.

The trend had one important effect—uniformity, for as with the streets and the subdivisions there was a basic sameness about the suburban houses that subdued the mass of individual decisions and tastes. The small-scale builders (and they seemed to constitute the majority of the builders) sought security for their effort and their money, and possibly a quick turnover to meet short-term loans, by following the popular style of the time. Hence street after street within a suburb, and suburb after suburb throughout Adelaide copied one another; as each man's private castle looked reassuringly like the private castle next door. The sameness of the style could not be hidden. The roof lines were often major features of the styles, and, because of the almost universal single storey, they struck the eye. In any case, because of the rectangular sub-division of blocks, all houses had a street front façade, whatever was at the back. The overwhelming use of stone and brick cut down the amount of embellishment possible and made subsequent alterations to the façade difficult. There emerged typically Adelaideian styles of houses, which were different in many ways from contemporary styles in the Eastern States. They are an enduring monument to this century of suburban building.

The essential sameness of the houses was a function not only of the style but also of the floor plan. There were two basic floor plans for the average house, the elongated row cottage of three or four rooms set on a narrow strip of land, each room behind the other; and the symmetrically-fronted house on the wide block. The first was not very common; it was difficult to get light into the middle rooms, and, as standards rose and bathrooms, laundries and lavatories became essential, the basic problems of the design became more and more apparent. There was a limit to the numbers of 'lean-to's' that could be tacked on to the end of a house, and since the design could not evolve with the increasing expectations of the population it generally went out of existence (Fig. 114).

In contrast, the double fronted, usually four room, house set on a wider block was capable of great modification. Two rooms were added to the back without any loss of light and during the 1860s and 1870s as the average house size increased, these additional

Fig. 114. Row cottages, pre 1860. North Unley.

Fig. 115. Blue-stone 'Georgian' villas, c. 1860z70. North Unley.

rooms were accompanied by a wide five foot passage cut down the middle of the house. The lounge and main bedroom were on either side of the passage and facing the road, with two other bedrooms behind and the fourth bedroom and kitchen at the back. The lavatory was in the back yard, but, with the extension of plumbing and sanitation, became attached to the back of the house during the late 1880s, sometimes with a laundry and bathroom.

Some evidence of these changes can be gleaned from information on average house sizes in South Australia. They rose from 3·25 rooms in 1861 to 4·70 rooms in 1901 and to 5·46 rooms in 1966, which was consistently about a room less than in other states, because, it is suggested, of the more expensive brick and stone construction.[112]

The typical house of the years after 1860 to about the late 1880s is shown in Fig. 115.[113] It usually had a front of locally quarried blue-stone but sides of brick, the front sheathed in a corrugated iron concave verandah, sometimes embellished with delicate cast iron work. One innovation during the 1890s was for the front lounge to be extended forward slightly into a bay window and the verandah consequently reduced by about a third. In both cases the roof was of corrugated iron, with relatively steep but short slopes on front and sides, but more gently sloping at the back.

The bay window style led ultimately to the 'villa front' house built by the thousands between 1890 and about 1905, with its projecting gable and a pair of box frame windows usually with shutters (Fig. 116). The verandah was reversed and now became convex or 'bull nosed', and cast iron work became more ornamental. One elaborate variation of this style was the 'gentleman's return verandah' in which one room at the side projected out a few feet and the verandah carried around the side of the house to it. But these were mere details, the building materials, the roof construction and the room numbers and arrangements were unchanged and the basic uniformity of the streets continued.

The 'villa front' faded out as the 'art nouveau' style came in and flourished during the building boom from about 1900 to the beginning of the First World War, and a little after in a modified form (Fig. 117). The roof line now changed radically. It became a 'hipped' roof with a small half gable, most roofs were constructed of corrugated iron, although terra cotta tiles began to make

FIG. 116. The Villa front house, *c.* 1890–1900. North Unley.

FIG. 117. 'Art Nouveau'—gables and gargoyles, *c.* 1900. North Adelaide.

inroads, and chimney pots replaced the attractive white painted stucco brick chimneys of the past. In some houses the floor plan changed slightly with the introduction of an L-shaped interior passage, with the front door at the end of a return verandah which stretched around two sides of the house. Wooden trellising and fretwork replaced cast iron. The emphasis was on the quaint and the picturesque, and on flowing lines and curves; there were few Australian plants in the garden for they were hardly an 'improvement' in real estate terms.

The War produced another break in the stylistic traditions, and as the 1920s got under way the bungalow dominated the suburban building scene until the depression years of the mid 1930s. The bungalow is commonly thought to have been a builder's importation from the United States, and was regarded as an 'informal' type of house after the quaintness of the previous years. Its squat and heavy appearance was the result of the low wide gable and wide front verandah that were supported by massive stone or brick pillars, sometimes five feet across at the bottom and tapering inwards at the top (Fig. 118). In larger editions of the house the passage-way ran across the block and the rooms faced either the back or the front, and not the side. This gave a 'triple fronted house' which demanded a wider block of land, and, with the advent of the motor car, a side drive and car-port or garage were essential. Hence subdividers tended to produce square rather than deep blocks with narrow frontages. The other major feature of this house was that bathroom and lavatory were now definitely incorporated under the roof as hot water systems and modern living became universally accepted. The roof was usually of corrugated iron, and the façade built from buff coloured freestone. Lawns increased in popularity and flower beds declined, and native trees were planted. It was one of the best ways to achieve informality and naturalness.

So overwhelming was the success of the bungalow style that it held sway for about twenty years. During the 1930s, when sales were lagging and returns not so assured, builders began to experiment with variations. One was the Tudor style, with steep (60 degree) corrugated iron roofs, although now often in terra cotta tiles, high pointed gables, and twisted brick chimneys (Fig. 119). The other variation was the Spanish mission with its veneer

FIG. 118. The Bungalow. *c.* 1920. Free stone front and brick behind, Malvern.

FIG. 119. The Tudor variation of the Bungalow, 1934. Burnside.

of white stucco, its pre-cast twisted pillars that looked as though they should have been on the top of an iced cake and with a few curved gable ends and trimmings of Cordoba tiles here and there (Fig. 120). Both Tudor and Spanish mission houses with double and triple fronts of stone but the basic floor plan of six or seven rooms

FIG. 120. The Spanish Mission variation of the Bungalow, late edition *c*. 1950. Hazelwood Park.

FIG. 121. Post Second World War, *c*. 1955. Hazelwood Park.

remained the same as in the bungalow, the only addition being the garage, sometimes incorporated within the house.

The period of austerity after the Second World War produced a simple brick, hipped-roofed house with a concrete porch and standard steel framed windows. The floor plan was slightly different with an L-shaped living-dining room as the focal point of the house (Fig. 121). Once building restrictions were relaxed the standard house became larger and triple-fronted; and the feature of the early sixties was the veneer of vividly coloured Basket Range stone over the façade with tuck pointed cement joints. The subsequent years have witnessed a progression of styles, with 'Georgian' and 'Colonial' as the dominant themes and 'Mediterranean' during the 1970s. But, on the whole, the majority of houses still retain the same internal plan, and are situated on the same kind of block.

Since the 1960s a much greater variety of house design makes it more difficult to be definite about predominant designs and styles. The increasing affluence of Australians has led to more architecturally-designed houses and even the large scale developers have succumbed to variety with professionally designed houses in the large estates. In the past however, the majority of houses were erected by what one can call the amateur builder who built only a few houses at a time and did not have the capital to experiment with styles. Architects were rarely employed except amongst the rich, but in time any new style passed down slowly through the various income groups, losing its space, its original cohesion as a living unit and its visual effect as an architectural design as each successive filter of the socio economic strata took a little bit away and reduced it to its bare essentials. Eventually there remained a house, the façade of which might have changed but which in its basic essentials was little different from its shrunken predecessors. One land plan of streets and subdivisions, and a few basic floor plans with different trimmings, predominated.

Individually the houses that resulted from this paring down of styles leave much to be desired aesthetically, but collectively they represent the greatest achievement of urban Australia for its inhabitants. Anyone who walks through the streets and suburbs of Adelaide today can see on every side the overwhelming visual impact of these styles, created during that long century of suburbs.

9. Notes

1. Whilst contemporary urbanism in all its facets has an enormous and ever expanding literature that defies even summary citation, interest in the historical development of the city has been relatively neglected until the last decade, which is another example of Western society's distorted view of its past and the preference for the rural ideal. General and wide-ranging works which attempt to define the methodology and content of cities in the past are:

   O. Handlin and J. Burchard, *The historian and the city* (1963);
   H. J. Dyos, (ed.) *The study of urban history* (1968).
   Locally, N. D. Harper's 'The rural and urban frontiers', *Historical Studies, Australia and New Zealand*, Vol. X (1963), 401, was an early but neglected plea for a more balanced view.
   N. G. Butlin, *Investment in Australian economic development, 1861–1900* (1964) has much relevant material, but it relates mainly to the eastern colonies of N.S.W., Victoria and Queensland.
   Since then there have appeared S. Glynn, *Urbanisation in Australian history* (1970), and 'Urbanization in Australia', a special issue of *Australian Economic History Review*, Vol. X (1970), 107–225.

2. For example, P. G. Goheen, 'Victorian Toronto, 1850–1900: Pattern and Process of Growth', *Department of Geography, Research Paper, No. 127*, Chicago (1970);
   D. Ward, *Cities and immigrants: A geography of change in nineteenth century cities* (1971);
   S. Thernstrom and R. Sinnett (eds.) *Nineteenth century cities: essays in the new urban history* (1969).

3. Throughout this chapter, 'City' means the area within the parklands of Adelaide, and 'city' means the larger urban area.

4. For example see F. Osborn, *Green-belt cities* (1946);
   D. Thomas, *London's green belt* (1970);
   A. Faludi, 'Der Wiener Wald—und Wiesengürtel und der Ursprung der "green belt" Idee', *Raumforschung und Raumordnung*, V (1967), 193–206.

5. Quoted in J. Stephens, *The land of promise* (1839), 97.

6. See D. Stanislawski, 'The origin and spread of the grid-pattern town', *Geogr. Rev.*, XXXVI (1946), 105.

7. For plans of Philadelphia and Newcourt's London, see J. W. Reps, *The making of urban America* (1965), Figs. 91 and 97.

8. Quoted in J. W. Reps, 'Town planning in colonial Georgia', *Town Planning Rev.*, XXX (1959–60), 273–85.

9. Unfortunately, the only known copy of Sharp's pamphlet on *Hundreds and*

Tythings was in the British Museum and it was destroyed by fire during the Blitz of 1941. We have no way of knowing its contents.

10. *Dictionary of National Biography*, LI (1897).

11. J. W. Reps, 'The green belt concept' *Town and Country Planning*, XXVIII (1960), 246–50.

12. See D. N. Jeans, 'Crown land sales and the accommodation of the small settler in New South Wales, 1825–1842'. *Historical Studies: Australia and New Zealand*, XII (1966), 205–12;
J. M. Powell, *The public lands of Australia Felix* (1970), 38–40.

13. *Third Report*, (1905) pp. lxxxii–lxxxiii and c–ciii; and *16th Report* (1920), 26–31.
Lillian F. Gates, *Land Policies of Upper Canada*, (1968), 27 comments on these plans.

14. Personal communication, with Mr David Russell, Ontario Department of Archives (11th June 1971) and evidence contained in R. G. I. Crown Lands Department, Report of the Surveyor-General, 1799–1802, A-II-I, Vol. 2.

15. R. F. Gourlay, *A General Introduction to Statistical Accounts of Upper Canada* (1822), particularly Vol. I.

16. (T. J. Maslen), A. F. Gardiner, *The friend of Australia; or, a plan for exploring the interior, and for carrying on a survey of the whole continent of Australia* (1830). On p. 263 Maslen described himself as 'a retired officer of the Hon. East India Company's service' and admits that he has never been to Australia but feels well qualified to write about it because it must resemble India, which he knows well. Maslen's 'Plan of a Town for Australia' is on Plate 4. It does not show the parkland 'for want of room', but the parkland is described on p. 426.

17. G. W. Hoskins, *The making of the English Landscape* (1955), 172–3.

18. Robert Owen, *A New View of Society . . .: Mr. Owen's Report to the Committee of the Association for the Relief of the Manufacturing and Labouring Poor* (1817). Owen's proposal was repeated and elaborated in 1821. The British and Foreign Philanthropic Society was founded in the following year and raised £50,000 to establish a model. 'Village of Co-operation' Robert Owen: *Report to the County of Lanark for a Plan for Relieving Public Distress . . .* (1821). Nothing was done, however, and Owen lost interest in the scheme, diverting his energy into attempts to establish communal colonies in Ireland and, later, at New Harmony, Indiana; Yellow Springs, Ohio; and Mashoba, Tennessee.

19. See D. Pike, 'The utopian dreams of Adelaide's founders', *Proc. Royal Geogr. Soc. S.A.*, LIII, (1951–52), 65–77, for the important part Bentham took in the formulation of Wakefield's ideas.

20. F. Podmore, *Robert Owen: A biography* (1923) is the 'standard' biography of Owen and a valuable source of information on these connections.

21. Catherine H. Spence : *Autobiography* (1910), 37. For supporting statements see Miss C. E. Clark's reminiscences in *S.A.A.* 1045/ p. 112.
22. *Adelaide Magazine*, Vol. I, no. 4 (1838), 112.
23. S.A.A., 1054 (M), Diary of Boyle Travers Finniss. Letter to unknown person written between 21 March and 11 April 1836.
24. B. T. Finniss, Diary (March 1837). Quoted in *The Advertiser* (2 Sept. 1936).
25. *Dictionary of National Biography*, XXVI (1891).
26. *South Australian* (7 July 1838).
27. A. Trollope, *An Autobiography*, Vol. I (1883), 177.
28. W. Light, *A Brief Journal of William Light* (1839), 24.
29. W. Light, *A Brief Journal*, p. 14. Light was incorrect in his assumption about the plains reaching the Murray.
    For an evaluation of the site characteristics of the Port, see J. Bird, 'The foundation of Australian seaport capitals', *Econ. Geog.* XXXXI (1965), 283–99.
30. S.A.A., 1105/15, p. 23. Hindmarsh to Colonial Office. (n.d.).
31. Light recounted a walk with Governor Hindmarsh to inspect a new site for Adelaide two miles further west towards the sea, but when they arrived there they found the whole area flooded. W. Light, *A Brief Journal* (1839), 64–5.
32. W. Light, *A Brief Journal* (1839). Preface.
33. S.A.A. 1054 (M), The Diary of B. T. Finniss.
34. S.A.A. 449/9, and map of sections sold in Map Cabinet of the Council Room of the Royal Geographical Society of South Australia, North Terrace.
    See also W. Oldham, 'How Adelaide was bought and sold', *Proc. Roy. Geog. Soc., S.A.,* XXXXV (1944), 15–23.
35. S. Sidney, *The Three Colonies of Australia* (1852), 204.
36. D. Pike, *Paradise of Dissent*, 177.
37. J. Horton, *Six months in South Australia* (1838), 31.
    For similar comments on getting lost in the 'wilds' of Adelaide, see J. Mann, *Six years' residence in the Australian provinces . . .* (1839), 273.
38. J. F. Bennett, *South Australian Almanac* (1841), 94.
39. For a description and evaluation of the map, see M. Williams 'Early morphological maps of Australian towns', *Geogr. Journ.* CXXX (1964), 309–310.
40. This and the following paragraphs are based on:
    J. F. Bennett, *An historical and descriptive account of South Australia, founded upon the experience of three years' residence in that Colony* (1843), 132;
    Idem., 'Villages round Adelaide' and 'A ride through South Australia', *South Australian Magazine*, I (1841), 187 and 343.

Some of the data on the population and facilities of the new suburban nodes are taken from Papers Relative to South Australia, *British Parliamentary Papers*, No. 505 (1843), 70–101.

For a detailed analysis of these data see M. Williams 'Two studies in the Historical Geography of South Australia', in *Studies in Australian Geography*, ed. G. H. Drury and M. I. Logan (1968), 71–98.

41. For the working of this cumulative and circular causation in North America see A. Pred, 'Industrialization, initial advantage, and American metropolitan growth', *Geogr. Rev.* LV (1965), 158–85.

42. In 1862, F. Sinnett in his *Account of the colony of South Australia*, 11, said that during the previous decade 'roads have been improved and bridges formed, so as quite to change the character of inland travelling for hundreds of miles from Adelaide'.

43. A Russell, *A tour through the Australian Colonies in 1839* (1840), 61–2.

44. W. S. Chauncey, *A Guide to South Australia* (1849), 61.

45. P. D. Edwards and R. B. Joyce (eds), *Australian by Anthony Trollope* (1967).

46. Printed in J. Allen (ed.), *S.A. Almanac, 1845,*

47. The districts taken to represent the urban area in 1855 include some semi-rural areas in order that the expanded urban area of 1865 could be accommodated within the same spatial limits. The censuses are printed in *SAPP*, 19 (1855/56), and 19 (1865).

48. *South Australian Almanac* (1857), 29.

49. S. Sidney, *The three colonies of Australia* (1852), 199.

50. W. S. Chauncey, *A guide to South Australia* (1849), 62; R. Harrison, *Colonial Sketches* (1862), 32.

51. For the survey on the Port Road see *S.A. Govt. Gazette* (1 March 1849). For the subsequent history of the line, see D. Pike, *Paradise of Dissent* (1957), 345–7.

52. *S.A. Gazette and Col Reg.* (20 Oct. 1838).

53. See *S.A. Register* (5 Jan. 1848); for other information, see G. W. Gooden and T. L. Moore, *Fifty years' history of the town of Kensington and Norwood* (1903); and M. A. Blackburn, *The history of Kensington and Norwood* (1954).

54. The censuses before 1861 are not of much help. The types of information sought are not available and the census of 1844 is not comparable with that of 1855, which in turn is not comparable with those of later years, 1861, 1866, 1871, 1876 and 1881. There was a return of the number of houses, roofing materials, building materials and number of floors in April 1860 for Municipal Councils, but as it does not deal with District areas and is so near to the 1861 census, it has not been used.

55. G. W. Gooden and T. L. Moore, op. cit., 7.

56. For some precedents for these assumptions, see G. Davison, 'Public utilities and the expansion of Melbourne in the 1880s', *Aust. Econ. Hist. Rev.* X (1970), 169–89.

57. J. F. Bennett, *South Australian Almanac* (1841), 94.

58. G. B. Wilkinson, *The working man's handbook* (1849), 47–8; F. Sinnett, *Account of the Colony of South Australia* (1862), 51. For corroborative evidence of the early importance of Hindley Street, see S.A.A., 1045/ pp. 111–2, Miss Caroline Emily Clark's first experiences in South Australia, *ca.* 1850, and the fact that when F. R. Nixon engraved various scenes of Adelaide in 1848, he depicted Hindley Street but not Rundle Street.

59. R. Harrison, *Colonial sketches* (1862), 32.

60. F. Sinnett, op. cit., 52.

61. For London, see H. C. Prince, 'North West London, 1814–1863 and 1864–1914', in *Greater London*, ed. J. T. Coppock and H. C. Prince (1964), 80–141. also J. H. Johnson, 'The suburban expansion of housing in London, 1918–1939', op. cit. 142–66. Another interesting study is D. A. Reeder, 'A theatre of suburbs : some patterns of development in west London, 1801–1911' in *The Study of Urban History*, ed. H. J. Dyos (1968). For the experience in Australia, see D. A. L. Saunders, 'Three factors behind the form of Melbourne's nineteenth century suburbs', in *Urban Re-development in Australia*, ed. P. N. Troy (1966), 1–18.

62. N. G. Butlin, *Investment in Australian economic development, 1861–1900* (1964), 181–4.

63. The basis of collection changes constantly, particularly before 1877 and between 1899 and 1904, hence the choice of years in Table XXIX.

64. Based on N. G. Butlin, *Australian Domestic Product, Investment and Foreign borrowing, 1861–1938/39* (1962), Table 152. The figures for rooms added must be treated with caution and are, says Butlin, 'much the weakest of our residential calculations of states'. Nevertheless, the major trends seem to be confirmed by other evidence.

65. H. T. Burgess (ed.) *The Cyclopedia of South Australia* (1903), Vol. 2, 496.

66. J. J. Pascoe, *History of Adelaide and vicinity* (1901), 178.

67. For an excellent account of the formation of the Trust, and of the subsequent growth and probable future shape of Adelaide, see H. Stretton, *Ideas for Australian cities* (1970), particularly pp. 141–96. For expansion south of Adelaide see T. C. Griffin 'The evolution and duplication of a pattern of urban growth', *Economic Geography* XXXXI (1965), 133–56.

68. F. Sinnett, op. cit., 52.

69. See *SAPP*, 25 (1863); and 72 (1863), qu. 624. Except for specific quotations and references, this and the following pages on water supply

and sewerage are based on the annual reports of the Commissioner of Public Works (usually printed as *SAPP*, 29 from 1880 onwards) and major commissions of enquiry.

70. *SAPP*, 25 (1862); and 40 (1866–67).
71. *SAPP*, 17 (1869–70).
72. *SAPP*, 37 (1872).
73. *SAPP*, 238 (1877).
74. *SAPP*, 29A (1880); 29 (1883); and 29 (1887).
75. *SAPP*, 29 (1896).
76. The 1865 investigation gave rise to a competition for the best essay on Adelaide's proposed sanitation system. The essays by R. G. Thomas, C. T. Hargreaves and J. McGregor make interesting reading and provided many insights into contemporary Adelaide. For the actual works see *SAPP*, 63 (1878), and 70 (1879); and for the reasons behind the failures of the various proposals, see T. Worsnop, *History of the City of Adelaide* (1878), 269, 340 and 345–46.
77. Compare G. Davison, 'Public utilities and the expansion of Melbourne in the 1880s', *Aust. Econ. Hist. Rev.*, X (1970), 182–3.
78. S. B. Warner, *Streetcar Suburbs: the process of growth in Boston, 1870–1900* (1962), 2.
79. *SAPP*, 206 (1870/71).
80. *SAPP*, 166 (1869/70) and 106 (1871).
81. *SAPP*, 153 (1876).
82. *SAPP*, 201 (1880);
    see also W. H. Jeanes, *Glenelg: Birthplace of South Australia* (1955), 194, 201–2.
83. *SAPP*, 105 (1876), qu. 61.
84. *SAPP*, 153 (1876), qu. 515.
    J. P. Stow, *South Australia* (1884), 118, said, 'since the opening of the first of these lines, the value of land at Glenelg has risen enormously, and the population greatly'.
85. See *SAPP*, 209 (1869/70); and 82, 96, 164, 216 (1874).
86. *SAPP*, 47A (1882), qu. 1343.
87. *SAPP*, 123 (1889), qu. 125.
88. For the early history of the tramways, see P. Kannis, 'Tramways in Adelaide; 1876–1907'. Unpublished B.A. Hons. thesis, University of Adelaide (1965) 1–29.
    Proposals for tramways had been put forward as early as 1871, see *SAPP*, 206 (1870–71) but the size of Adelaide was not sufficient to warrant investment and construction at that time.
89. See respectively *SAPP* 49 (1876); 189 (1877); 201 (1877); 200 (1877); 119 (1881); and 155 (1881).

90. *SAPP*, 210 (1877), qu. 283.

91. *SAPP*, 128 (1881); 95 (1881); and 45 (1882).

92. The Adelaide–Ovingham line was approved but never constructed and the Glenelg–Marino line so clearly duplicated the Glenelg–Brighton tramway and the Glenelg–Marino railway that only a portion of it was built.

93. *SAPP*, 210 (1877).

94. The Glenelg–Brighton; Adelaide–Nailsworth; Adelaide–Paradise; and Glenelg–Marino.

95. *SAPP*, 205 (1877), qu. 106–109, 122–23, and 167–185.

96. *SAPP*, 128 (1881), qu. 234 and 250.

97. *S.A. Register* (13 February 1879 and 30 May 1883).

98. *SAPD* (L.C.) (13 June 1888), 81 and *S.A. Register* (11 Sept. 1883). Nevertheless, despite these few examples, there was nothing in Adelaide to compare with the blatant jobbery in Melbourne. See M. Cannon, *The land-boomers* (1966), 39–40.

99. *SAPP*, 42 (1883–4), qu. 815 and 719; 134 (1891), qu. 49; and 71 (1896), qu. 43.

100. W. Pember Reeves, *State Experiments in Australia and New Zealand* (1902) Vol. I, 36–37.

101. S. B. Warner, *Streetcar suburbs* (1962), 117.

102. Probably the first person to point to the influence of the rural pattern of roads on the urban landscape was W. G. Hoskins, in his investigation into the effect of fields and roads on urban conditions in Nottingham, in *The Making of the English Landscape* (1955), 218–23.
An influential study by a geographer was D. Ward, 'The pre-urban cadaster and the urban pattern of Leeds', *Ann. Assoc. Amer. Geogr.*, LII (1962), 150–66;
there is also R. J. Johnston's, 'An outline of the development of Melbourne's street pattern', *Aust. Geogr.* X (1968), 453–65.

103. W. Mann, *Six years' residence in the Australian Provinces* (1839), 278–79.

104. SGO. 224/1853 (in); 192/1853 (out). Nevertheless, from here on private subdividers were playing safe and plans were being sent to the Surveyor-General for approval.

105. *Act*, 15/1857–58. An act to simplify the laws relating to the transfer and encumbrance of freehold and other interests in land (The Torrens Land Act).

106. *Act*, 22/1861. Real Property Act; and *Act*, 1304/1917 Control of subdivision of land act. Under this act no subdivision was approved unless the newly appointed Town Planner was satisfied with it.

107. For detailed examples of the characteristics of suburban development by small-scale buyers and builders, see D. A. L. Saunders in *Urban Redevelopment in Australia*, ed. P. N. Troy (1966), 1–18.

108. Under the Municipal Corporations Act (*Act* 497/1890) the cost of new streets was the exclusive expense of the owners, but it does appear that any subdivider within a District Council area could pass on to the District Council half the cost of laying out a new township. See *Act* 419/1887.

109. *SAPP*, 63 (1919), 32. Since the Municipal Corporations Act of 1880 (*Act* 190/1880) all new streets had to be at least 40 feet wide but the Act did allow the maintenance of prior streets of not less than twenty feet, the absolute minimum.

110. *Act* 1923/1935, Building Act.

111. R. Boyd, *Australia's home: its origins, builders, and occupiers* (1952), preface.

112. N. G. Butlin, *Investment in Australian economic development, 1861–1901* (1964), 222–23.

113. This impressionistic sketch of the visual characteristics of styles is based primarily on what can be seen by walking along the streets of suburbs, and a random sample of builders' advertisements from Adelaide daily newspapers. Helpful guides are R. Boyd's *Australia's home* and a series of articles in the *Advertiser* (11, 18, 25 June 1958).

10
The Fabric of the Landscape

A major aim of this book has been to introduce students and interested readers to the historical geography of a sizeable portion of the Australian continent and to the richness of the local scene. The work started as a personal inquiry into the reasons for what could be seen and if in answering some of the questions satisfactorily it has been possible to heighten the understanding and appreciation of others concerning the antecedents of the landscape and the reasons for the changes and adjustments that have taken, and still are taking place then they will have shared, however little, in that excitement that comes from knowing a place. The greatest satisfaction, however, comes from visiting the places, which is merely to say that words, maps and photographs are only substitutes for seeing the features themselves.

It is not necessary for a landscape to be hundreds or thousands of years old, with relict features ossifying previous arrangements and hinting at previous activities, to be worthy of study. The simplicity and obvious recency of the man-made landscape in South Australia are not an impediment to its serious study. On the contrary, they are probably the major attractions in the task of interpreting the visual scene. The lack of successive layers of occupance simplifies investigation and the abundance of literary and map evidence that accompanied settlement facilitates explanation.

Every landscape settled by man becomes a blend of the natural and the human and it is the historical geographer's special task to elucidate the changes and understand the new arrangements.

If one regards a landscape as a fabric made by man then we can say that an attempt has been made here to analyse the material of its construction and the patterns of its design. To do that we have provided a weft of cross threads in the account of the spread of settlement into which the threads of the warp of the activities of change have been woven. But the ends of the threads cannot be left hanging loosely, and it would seem appropriate to look back over the detail of these activities to see which themes and questions are worth probing and asking, to tie together the threads of that rich and complicated fabric. Where does South Australia stand now in relation to its history of expansion, thrust and change; what activities have ceased to be important and which are accelerating in their impact; what has been achieved over 130 years and what has been lost; and what are some of the institutions and characteristics of the society that has been scrutinized, for the landscape is a reflection, in part, of the society which produces it?

Limits and Phases

D. J. Gordon's remark in 1906 that 'growth is sometimes checked, but movement is ever outward'[1] was typical of his unbounded optimism about the future of South Australia, nevertheless, up till then, and certainly for the next three decades, his judgement was correct—there were always new lands to fill. After that, however, the limits of successful farming had been set and there was no more good land left to be settled. The exact limits of farming were more or less known, they might vary a little from year to year according to the weather, the prices and even to farming practices, but Goyder's line and its equivalent in Eyre Peninsula and the Murray Mallee was an inescapable fact around which there seemed to be no way.

The recognition that the state had run out of suitable land was a catalyst to changes and processes, and carried a number of implications. First, the rural population had very nearly reached its peak and any future expansion of the population was bound to be accompanied by an out-migration from the rural areas to the urban areas, particularly to Adelaide where the opportunities for employment for the young and especially for women were present in ever increasing numbers. In a sense, it was the reversal of all the previous flows of people on the land. For over a century the migrants had landed at Adelaide, and although some of them always stayed at the point of their disembarkation, many fanned out over the land, first into the Central Hill Country and some down to the South-East, then into the Northern Areas, and from there to Eyre Peninsula and the Murray Mallee, and also to other wheat producing areas in Australia, particularly the Wimmera of Victoria and the eastern slopes of New South Wales. After the 1930s, not only did nearly all the new migrants stay in Adelaide, but the absence of fresh lands to colonize caused the reverse drift from country to town which has continued at an ever accelerating pace.

Secondly, the end of new land meant that there was a need to make the best of what was there by intensifying the land use practices on the existing farms by the greater application of fertilizer, greater yields with new strains of grains and grasses, arresting erosion, unlocking the trace element deficient land, and generally by the adoption of better farm management and practices. This better use of the land was basically the story of changing the soil. All other activities of change, such as survey clearing, irrigation, and draining were the outcome of techniques and methods that have been known to western man for centuries, even millenia, in some cases. Labour co-operation, and the inexorable advance of families creating new holdings were the ingredients of these landscape changes, and it is possibly true to say that they could have happened as easily a thousand years ago as they did during the last 130 years in South Australia. Admittedly, rolling, the stump-jump plough, drag-lines and water pumps all helped, but they were not essential. They merely accelerated the processes of change and made them much more thorough than they might otherwise have been. But changing the soil was different. It was the response to a new internal demand and a product of a new technology. It demanded new knowledge, other than the mechanical and the hydraulic, and it brought the pioneer farmer into the realms of biology and chemistry. On the whole he was reluctant and unable to cope with the problems posed and the answers lay increasingly with the scientists, a new set of persons with a new body of knowledge.

Thirdly, the running out of land carried another implication. Like any semi-developed economy of the present day, largely dependent on agriculture and primary produce for its prosperity, South Australia in the 1930s realized that it had to alter its economic basis and industrialize in order to stop it from slipping backwards, let alone advance. So successful has been that policy over the last 35 years that Adelaide has grown enormously to contain 67 per cent of the state's population. In doing so it has also accumulated all the problems of any large city in the western world—air pollution, water-supply deficiencies, traffic congestion, high land prices, and a whole host of other social ills that all large urban centres seem heir to. As yet, these problems are not great compared to other cities; the difference is only in degree not in kind, but undoubtedly the struggle against nature is giving way to a struggle against the urban environment made wholly by man himself. The plans for a network of urban freeways and counter plans for an expanded and better public transport system, whole new sub-centres and new towns, the creation of a Department of the Environment and enquiries into environmental quality, and expanded social services, are all signs of these changes. Earlier, (see pp. 62 and 63) it was suggested that, if one takes the long view, South Australian settlement seems to be characterized by periods of pause, re-assessment and thrust. It might be that the pause and re-assessment of the late 1930s and 1940s has already produced the thrust of initial industrialization and associated urban growth, together with scientific farming, and that another pause is upon us. Certainly the feeling is growing that there is a need to assess man's relationship with his environment, particularly his vastly expanded urban environment, and that the future requires careful thought and appraisal about the way in which man lives.

The Pace of Change

Of the activities of change dealt with in this book some have virtually ended, some are slowing down, and others are accelerating in their effect on the landscape. Surveying, draining, and irrigating are not important landscape-forming forces any more. There are no new lands to survey, only old lands to re-survey and subdivide. Farm amalgamation rarely entails re-survey as the existing sections are merely re-grouped into bigger holdings. With few exceptions, the cry of the farmers in the South-East is that the swamps have been over-drained and that the water tables have been lowered by the multitude of drains to such a point, that in some cases even when the channels are dammed in the summer, they do not retain enough water for the stock. A few isolated basins and flats need attention but other than these there seems little likelihood of any further extension of activity. Substantial areas of flood irrigation further north in the Naracoorte area, based on bore water, have put a new dimension on the water resources of the South-East, and the need is to achieve the correct balance between the conflicting demands of draining and irrigation. The ever increasing water needs of urban and industrial areas of Adelaide and such centres as Whyalla and Port Pirie, have put an end to all further irrigation alongside the River Murray, and there is even the possibility of a reduction of irrigated land there in the future.

The two other activities of purposive landscape change in the rural areas, clearing the woodland and changing the soil, are different. Undoubtedly the rate of clearing the woodland has fallen rapidly over the last decade and a half.

There are few substantial areas of rewarding woodland left. Most of those in areas of high rainfall, but deficient in trace elements in the soil, have been affected already. Those in areas with better soils but lower rainfall are economically marginal lands, and the prices for primary produce would have to be substantially higher than at present to make their clearing worth while. This relationship is borne out by the move to 'open-up' the hundreds of Hambidge and Hincks in the centre of Eyre Peninsula which reached a peak during the early 1960s. These 400-odd square miles of land had been left largely untouched on account of their inaccessibility from railways and indifferent soil in an area of only moderate rainfall. As so often happens when land is of no economic use the woodland was declared a Reserve in which the original fauna and flora could exist undisturbed. With higher prices for wheat, coinciding with the huge sales to China after 1961/2, however, an intensive campaign was launched by local farmers to clear the land and create another couple of dozen farms. The campaign was countered by conservationists who won the day, a victory which was made quite clear after the drought of 1966/67 the imposition of wheat quotas and the decline in the price of wool.

The rise of the conservation lobby in this example is a manifestation of changing attitudes to the environment as increasingly people look for evidence of a landscape that retains something of the scene before man entered it and 'stamped about'. National Parks and reserves have been declared with increasing rapidity during the last few years, ranging in size from about one square mile in the remnants of the Willunga Scrub south of Adelaide, to 212 square miles of Flinders Chase on the western extremity of Kangaroo Island and 225 square miles of the Northern Flinders Ranges, to nearly the whole of the Coorong.[2]

Such moves to preserve whole environments, or at least the remnants of them will not of course stop farmers clearing a section here and there in order to enlarge their property, particularly on the western coast of Eyre Peninsula and parts of the South-East. This is especially true when they know that the capital cost of clearing natural woodland is an allowable tax deduction. Generally speaking, this has not resulted in unnecessary clearing by *bona fide* farmers, but there is always the danger, already evident in some places, that business and professional people who have invested money in rural holdings in order to attract tax relief on their incomes may attempt to compound the relief by clearing the land caring little of the ecological consequences of their actions. It is yet another example of the growing impact of the urban area on the face of the country.

Balanced against this problematical calculation of the amount and rate of clearing of the natural woodland is the simple calculation that 350 square miles have been re-afforested. It was Goyder, that practical geographer, who suggested that because the natural timber of South Australia was poor for constructional purposes certain areas should be set aside for commercial planting. The Forest Reserves were located in the Mid and Upper North during the 1880s, and they consisted mainly of stands of better milling types of eucalypts. Their long period of maturity, however, worked against a greater expansion of forestry and it was not until the introduction in 1890 of *pinus radiata* from California which grow to maturity in a little over twenty-five years that the prospect was altered completely. Today, the major plantations are on the well-drained ground of the eastern and southern uplands of the Lower South-East, where between the townships of Penola, Millicent and Mount Gambier there are over 300 square miles of pine forests. On a journey through these forests one encounters dark, sombre walls of pines on either side of the road and it is more like a traverse through parts of Southern Germany than parts of South Australia.

The fact that most clearing during recent years has been almost an incidental accompaniment to the rectification of soils with trace element deficiencies has put the story of the changing of the soil into a far more prominent place in the contemporary landscape than clearing, or indeed than any other activity. Because of the chemical and biological basis of this activity it is reasonable to forecast that new and significant discoveries about soils will be made in the future and it is in this sphere that the greatest changes will come to the rural landscape, together with the structural re-organization of farm holdings and rural services. But that is another story that awaits careful analysis.

Enough has been said in the chapter on township creation and growth to suggest that existing sites will be sorted out mercilessly in the future a process that will lead to the extinction of the smallest centres. In a sense, here is a process of landscape change that is being put into reverse; there will be less townships in years to come as the smaller centres slip out of the urban system and a few major centres grow. Finally, of all the activities of making the landscape that have been considered, the making and growth of Adelaide is the most dynamic and far reaching. Adelaide is the apogee of the urban system and a major cause of the decline of the smaller centres. Really, it should not be considered in isolation from the surrounding arrangement and hierarchies of service centres for it is the focus of all economic, social and political life in South Australia. Because of this triumph of centralization, brought about by railway and road-construction and the deliberate policy to industrialize since the mid-1930s, the regional entities that arose when new areas of the state were colonized have been relegated to almost purely locational names as increasingly the division is not between region and region but between Adelaide and the rest of the state. Obviously physical landscape differences remain but the idea of regional identity and the flowering of a regional consciousness is all but dead, as the ever expanding tentacles of economic and social influence of Adelaide spread into the rural body.

Losses and Gains

The most obvious sign of the last century and a half of creation and change has been the emergence of a modern, industrialized, western society with one of the highest standards of living in the world. It occupies a region which, about 130 years ago, was inhabited by only a few thousand nomadic tribesmen. John Stephen's boast in 1839 that the colonists were creating 'a busy civilization' where there had previously been only 'a blank on the great map of the world' came true, not only in the literal sense that the coast of South Australia which had never been charted before the early nineteenth century was now known, but also in the sense that the region had been incorporated into the map of the European mind by becoming part of the complex and far-flung system of British commercial and settlement expansion overseas. But that achievement, undeniably real and beneficial to so many hundreds of thousands of people, has been wrought at some cost to the environment and its original occupants—human, animal and vegetable. The aborigines have been relegated to the back-blocks of the country and the back-blocks of the towns; their habitat has become the reserve or the slum. In vain does one look for the wild kangaroo and emu in the settled areas, except in patches of scrub in the west coast of Eyre Peninsula and the South-East. The wallaby, the wombat, the Mallee fowl and a host of other beasts, insects and birds, are all reduced in numbers and some are so near to extinction that special reserves must be set aside for their preservation. Original grasses are rare, but there are still plenty of native trees despite savage clearing and the importation of alien species.

Too often, progress has been seen as a crusade of extirpation, and in some eyes the pioneers were 'as fine a band of stalwart men and women as ever set out to subdue a wilderness or wrest from nature her choicest gifts'.[3] This is not to denigrate the energy and achievements of the early colonists but pride should not obscure the fact that they did alter their environment, often for better, but often for worse. When in 1864 J. P. Marsh wrote 'man is a disturbing agent' wherever he sets his foot 'the harmonies of nature are set to discords' he was merely articulating the simple truth that wherever man builds his home or makes a living he modifies and alters the landscape.

But what was the landscape like before the first colonists arrived? It takes an enormous effort of the imagination to visualize the landscape as it once was untouched by man. It is possible if one stands on the eastern edges of the Mount Lofty Ranges and looks across the Murray Plains and sees the unbroken canopy of bluish-green mallee scrub stretching away to the horizon; it is possible walking along the untrodden sand of the beach that curves south-east for over a hundred miles from the Murray mouth, conscious only of the sound of rolling surf on the one hand and the cries and flight of the pelican, cormorants and gulls in the sheltered water of the Coorong on the other hand. It is possible as one picks one's way through a deep gorge in the northern Flinders Ranges, enclosed by high rocky walls with a strip of sky above, and it is certainly possible in many places in the outback interior where sky and land meet in a hard line all around one, and silence hangs heavily like a shroud. Such scenes are timeless and are tinged with a melancholy, made up as much of the loneliness of the landscape as of the knowledge that few such places exist in South Australia, or for that matter, in the world.

One does not have to stray far from the places, however, to find the imprint of man on the land. In the settled areas, over 60,000 square miles have been covered by a network of roads, fences, railways, and telegraph and electricity poles, which divide the land into parcels, yet unite it by common features and lines of communication. The very straightness of these dividing lines indicates the subjection of nature to the levelling works of man. About half the area, or nearly 30,000 square miles, has had its appearance altered completely by the clearing of woodland, remnants of this once enveloping cover existing only on steep slopes, on the tops of sand ridges, or alongside the country roads where generous reserves for travelling stock on either side retain something of their original vegetation. Some 6500 square miles of land have had their hydrographical features altered as swamps have been drained and become dry land, new water courses dug and old ones regraded or re-orientated. At the other extreme, another 260 square miles have been criss-crossed by water channels and have been irrigated. About 25,000 square miles of all sorts of land have had their basic fertility and character changed, and in them new crops of grains and grasses, together with fallows, have converted the monotony of the plains into a variety of textures, colours and shapes. Tens of thousands of square miles have had some of their top soil removed, and most of the great gullies that score the hillsides and slopes were not there when the settlers first moved on the face of the land.

Every ten to fifteen miles across the settled areas there is one of the 500 or so townships which have left a far more obvious mark upon the landscape. The towering concrete grain silos of those towns that have been selected as gathering points, look to the traveller like beacons over the plains and give some assurance to the inhabitants that their town will have a continued existence. But for every town that succeeds there are as many that are stagnant or declining and unkempt pavements and side roads, ruins and boarded-up windows are an increasingly common sight. In between and around these townships there are many thousands of farmsteads, for the most part solid stone and brick structures, which have belts and clumps of trees around and about them—the botanic character of which often denotes the age of the farm : palm trees in the gardens of the 1860s, shady pepper trees in the gardens and yards of the 1870s and 1880s, rows of pollarded peppermint gums in the 1890s and early 1900s until thick hedges of cyprus pines became popular during the 1920s, after which the quick growing radiata pines became predominant. In the Northern Areas in particular, and increasingly in all other areas, the scatter of farmsteads is augmented by the ruins of the abandoned dwellings of the past. They stand as mute testimony to frustrated hopes on the edges of cultivation and to disappointments where holdings were too small for the support of a family in reasonable conditions.

Finally, there is the epitome of man's power to modify and change the urban area of Adelaide. It is fast approaching a million inhabitants and stretches about 30 miles from north to south on the plains between the escarpment edges of the Mount Lofty Ranges and the sea. The urban landscape of roads, houses, gardens and buildings forms a fourth layer over the landscape of the agriculturist who came before, the pastoralist who came before him, and the largely untouched landscape of the aborigine and his ancestors.

These are sights for all to see, but there are other, less obvious, changes that could easily slip by unnoticed. Every remnant of forest and scrub, every unwanted piece of ground has in some way been affected by people, plants and animals. For example, olives dot the steep slopes of the Adelaide Hills, never planted but spread by birds which fed on nearby groves. Introductions from South Africa and the Mediterranean, like Cape Tulip, Salvation Jane, and Sowersobs, invade the fields and gullies with a ferocity that is alarming and is the despair of many a farmer, and proud gardener. During the winter and early spring they turn the ground to carpets of colour, the first light brown, the second deep purple, the third yellow. Sparrows (first seen coming over the Victorian border in 1863 and still not present in Western Australia) together with blackbirds, thrushes and starlings mingle and compete with parrots, kookaburras native magpies and particularly the piping shrike with its strange cracked call, that is so distinctive to South Australia that it dominates the state badge. Cats, rats, mice and rabbits mingle and compete with lizards and snakes. These and many others are what we now regard as pests and weeds, but they were all introduced during the last 130 years and are all part of that process of creating discord in the harmonies of nature as man has made the landscape.

People and Government

If the pioneer was, in a sense, an ecologist in the way he adapted and maladapted the environment to his needs, he was no less a strategist in the way in which he organized himself in space. But in the latter capacity he was not alone because there was always some form of administration that directed, advised and shared in his actions. In the beginning it was a largely personal administration and worked through the influence of the Governor, appointed in Britain, and his local Executive Council; after 1856 it was through locally elected assemblies and the creation of an extensive administrative apparatus, which continued after 1901 when South Australia became a part of a wider federation of Australian States, now independent of British control. During each of these kinds of government in South Australia two interwoven themes emerge continuously, and they have been present throughout the story of the making of the landscape. They are the blend of theory with pragmatism, and the degree of governmental control over individual action. Both are reflected in the landscape in the works of man.

The theoretical underpinnings of South Australia have been emphasized time and again. No colonial settlement ever had so much thought and theory bestowed upon it before it was born; no colonial settlement had such a set of rules upon which to operate. Nowhere were these rules more clearly seen than in the activities of surveying the landscape and creating townships which were a nicely blended balance between the theoretical and the opportune. That settlers accepted this governmental directive stemmed from two things. Foremost they regarded land ownership as unquestionably a government concern. Aboriginal land rights were ignored and in the absence of any prior claims it seemed natural that the title should be vested in the Crown with the government as its agent, but, with the understanding that Crown land was, in effect, public land for the purchase and use of the people. The government, for its part, was never willing to allow this guardianship of the land to be swept away and for there to be a free-for-all. Wakefield's theory of systematic colonization, with its intricate links between land, labour, capital and wages, was at stake, and even when that system began to break down by the late 1850s the government added methodical land registration (the Torrens System) to its role of guardian and apportioner of land. The other strand in this acceptance of governmental control was that the settlers realized that the government alone had the money necessary to achieve many of the desired economic and social objectives of the community. Only a few mining companies and larger pastoral firms had sufficient funds and resources to initiate change themselves; in any case, this was not until the later nineteenth century.

It was against this background of acceptance and understanding that the government exercised its control. At first the government was doctrinaire and rigid and set itself up as sole arbiter in land settlement matters. The size of sections, the design of subdivisions, the direction settlement should take and the pace of its movement, were all matters upon which decisions were made. But in time, the government had to bend and compromise because of its responsibility and sensitiveness to an electorate after 1856, and because of the diversity of environments encountered and of problems the new areas posed. It had to heed the voice of the people who were doing the settling. Time and again after the early 1860s the practically minded farmers were proved right in their assessment of what should and could be done. They crossed barrier after barrier which had been regarded as marking the limits of agricultural productivity, they had invented new machinery which allowed the penetration and the use of the difficult mallee lands, they were right in their clamour for credit facilities and larger sections. Bit by bit, the government relinquished its control, often by setting aside small areas in which experiments could first be tested, such as with the Scrub Areas in 1866, the Agricultural Areas in 1869, the Experimental Farms of the late 1870s, and the experimental drainage systems in the South-East, and, at an even later date, the irrigation works alongside the River Murray. Strangely enough, however, the government took a very firm hand in the design and location of townships during the 1870s when it was leaving more and more to the settlers to decide in their mass-testing of the environment.

But with the complete abandonment of control some settlers went too far; the droughts in the Northern Areas and the floods in the South-East showed that the settlers were not always right. Yet, it is indicative of underlying attitudes that when things went badly the settlers looked to the government to get them out of trouble and the government, ultimately, accepted responsibility for them. With the exception of the application of superphosphate during the late 1890s and the discovery of legumes, changes in the landscape after the early 1880s were initiated by the directives of the government rather than by the example of individuals.

A partial explanation to all this was, simply, that the sorts of change which occurred after the 1880s needed a great deal of money, and the government was the only organization capable of providing it. Nevertheless, most governmental schemes were tempered with a caution which arose partly out of an unwillingness to spend money during a time of depression and partly out of a reluctance to offend the farming population by being too domineering. This trend was evident in the halting acceptance of irrigation in which the government did not want 'further anxiety', and in its contortions over local initiative and national priorities in the draining of the South-East. During the early years of this century the government slowly re-asserted its authority and worked towards wide-ranging developmental schemes to aid settlers of new land with railways, bores, and even the compulsory repurchasing and subdivision of estates, as well as irrigation and drainage works. In urban matters government intervention and interest increased with the rapid growth of Adelaide during the 1880s, and through its instrumentalities, it provided a system of water-supply and sewage facilities that was exemplary. However, the rest of the urban decisions were left very largely, to individuals, and the subdivision and arrangement of the urban landscape was neglected and never received the same degree of control as did the subdivision of the rural landscape. By the 1930s, government influence grew again to become paramount in urban affairs, with the provision of houses, water, power, and other attractions, all of which were offered in the move to alter the economic basis of the State.

One should not get the idea that the government was a dead hand; at times it was as much an innovator as was the individual. Equally, it would be wrong to see these events as a conflict between inventive, independent, individuals (mainly farmers) and a government that was reactionary, conservative and opposed to change. The roles were often reversed and changes flowed from the governments' high ideals, particularly when forceful personalities, like Goyder and Perkins were in charge of important departments, and the role of the individual and official policy merged in a unique way.

A pride in achievement, an independence of thought, and yet a sort of collective social conscience, all worked towards the creation of a strong central authority and its widespread acceptance. In more ways than people have realized, it was an undeclared partnership between administration and individuals. Both partners were tinged with common ideals; that order and regularity were preferable to confusion, that tolerance was preferable to dogma, and that general prosperity was preferable to poverty. Some of these ideals can be read in the works which man has made on the face of the land, at the very least, they are part of that society which wove the fabric of the landscape.

10. Notes

1. D. J. Gordon, *The Central State* (1903), 21.
2. I am indebted to Mr Colin Harris of the Department of Geography, University of Adelaide for this information from his forthcoming study of the historical geography of National Parks in South Australia.
3. D. J. Gordon, loc. cit.
4. Strictly speaking the 'piping shrike' is not a species native to South Australia; the bird on the state emblem is the white backed magpie (*Gymnorhina tibicen leuconota*).

Sources and Bibliography

Unpublished

At the South Australian Archives

Correspondence of the Colonial Secretary's Office. Inward and outward letters.

Correspondence of the Commissioner of Crown Lands and Immigration. Inward letters and outward letter books.

Correspondence of the Engineers and Architects Office. Inward letters.

Correspondence of the Surveyor-General's Office. Inward letters and outward letter books.

Legislative Council Minutes.

Map collections.

Minutes of the South-Eastern Drainage Board.

Miscellaneous accessions, Nos. 448/9A, 449/9, 1054(m), 1105, 1045.

Research notes.

At the Department of Lands

Closer Settlement Leases and books.

Credit Land Office, sales and correspondence.

Diagram Books.

Grant Books.

Pastoral Leases and Books.

Plans—withdrawn plans of hundreds and counties.

Plans—private and government townships.

Records of hundred, county and township proclamations.

Scrub Leases.

At the Mitchell Library, Sydney

Map collection.

Dispatches to the Secretary of State for the Colonies (1838–55).

At the Bureau of Census and Statistics, Adelaide

Early censuses of South Australia (Blue Books).

Tabulation books of agricultural statistics (1925–   ).

Theses

Bauer, F. H., 'The regional geography of Kangaroo Island', Ph.D., Australian National University, Canberra (1959).

Harris, C. R., 'Mantung—A study of man's impact on a landscape', B.A. Hons., Dept. of Geography, University of Adelaide (1968).

Hirst, C. R., 'G. W. Cotton and the Workingmen's Blocks', B.A. Hons., Dept. of History, University of Adelaide (1963).

Kannis, P., 'Tramways in Adelaide, 1876–1907', B.A. Hons., Dept. of History, University of Adelaide (1965).

Lelacheur, H., 'War service land settlement in South Australia', M.A., Dept. of Politics, University of Adelaide (1968).

Poynter, J. I., 'The cadastral survey of South Australia', B.A. Hons., Dept. of Geography, University of Adelaide (1965).

Smith, R. F. L., 'The Butler government in South Australia, 1933–38', M.A., Dept. of Politics, University of Adelaide (1964).

Published

Newspapers

(At the State Public Library, South Australia)

Adelaide Observer.
Border Watch.
Farm and the Garden.
Farmer's Weekly Messenger.
Garden and the Field.
Jamestown Review.
Murray Pioneer.
Northern Argus (Clare).
South Australian.
South Australian Advertiser.
South Australian Gazette and Colonial Register.
South Australian Register.
Pinnaroo and Border Times.
Pinnaroo and Country News.
Port Augusta Dispatch.

West Coast Recorder.
Yorke Peninsula Advertiser.

Official Sources

Commonwealth Bureau of Census and Statistics. *Census.*
Commonwealth Bureau of Census and Statistics. *South Australian Year Book.* 1965– .
South Australian Acts.
South Australian Government Gazette.
South Australia Parliamentary Debates.
South Australian Parliamentary Papers.
South Australian Votes and Proceedings.

Books, Pamphlets and Articles

Adelaide Magazine, Adelaide, 2 vols. (1838–39).
Angas, G. French, *Savage life and scenes in South Australia and New Zealand; being an artist's impression of countries and people at the Antipodes,* London, Vol. I (1847); Vol. II (1850).
Anonymous, *Residents of the South-East,* Adelaide (1861).
Anonymous, *South Australian handbook of information for settlers, tourists and others,* 5th Ed., Adelaide (1926).
Anonymous, *Secondary Towns Association, formed for the purchasing of one or more Special Surveys or Surveys of land in South Australia for the sites of secondary towns,* London (1838).
Anonymous, *Our inheritance in the Hills,* Reprinted from *The S. Australian Register,* Adelaide (1889).
Anonymous, *The South-Eastern District of South Australia in 1880,* Reprinted from articles in *The S. Australian Register,* Adelaide (1881).
Anonymous, *An agricultural awakening: Kybybolite experimental farm,* Reprinted from *The S. Australian Register* (20, 22, 25 and 27 July 1907).
Anonymous, *The Australasian farmer: a practical handbook for the farm and the station,* Melbourne (1885).
Australian and New Zealand Association for the Advancement of Science (formerly Australian Association for the Advancement of Science, formerly British Association for the Advancement of Science), *Handbook on (of) South Australia,* Adelaide (1924).
Australia Economic History Review, Special issue on 'Urbanization

in Australia', X (Sydney, 1970), 107–225. See also under Bate, W., McCarty, J. W., and Davison, G. below.

Baldwin, B. S. (ed.), 'Letters of Samuel Davenport, chiefly to his father, George Davenport, 1842–1849. Part I, 1842–43', *South Australiana*, VI, Part I, Adelaide (1967), 17–56.

Bate, W., 'The Urban Sprinkle: Country towns and Australian regional history', *Australian Economic History Review*, X, Sydney (1970), 204–17.

Beaney, H. L., 'Water for South Australia', *S.A. Education Gazette*, Adelaide (1 Oct. 1970), 3–12.

Bennett, J. F., *South Australian Almanac, 1841*, Adelaide (1841).

Bennett, J. F., *An historical and descriptive account of South Australia founded on the experience of three years' residence in that colony*, London (1843).

Bird, J. H., 'The foundation of Australian seaport capitals', *Economic Geography*, XXXXI, Worcester, Mass. (1965), 283–99.

Bird, J. H., *Seaport gateways of Australia*, London (1968).

Blackburn, G., 'Soils of County Grey, South Australia', *C.S.I.R.O., Australia, Soils Division, Soils and Land Use Series*, No. 33, Melbourne (1959).

Blackburn, G., 'Soils of Counties Macdonnell and Robe, South Australia', *C.S.I.R.O., Australia, Soils Division, Soils and Land Use Series*, No. 45, Melbourne (1964).

Blackburn, G., and Baker, R. M., 'Survey of soils, land use and soil erosion in the northern marginal lands, South Australia', *C.S.I.R.O., Australia, Division of Soils, Soils and Land Use Series*, No. 6, Melbourne (1952).

Blackburn, M. A., *The history of Kensington and Norwood*, Adelaide, (1954).

Blake, C. D. (ed.), *Fundamentals of modern agriculture*, Sydney (1967).

Boddy, M., 'All neat, tidy and fixated', *The Bulletin*, XCIV, Sydney (18 March 1972), 10.

Bowes, K. R., *Land settlement in South Australia, 1857–1890*, Libraries Board of S.A., Adelaide (1968).

Bowden, O., 'Our agriculture at a cross road', *S.A. Journal of Agriculture*, XLVI, Adelaide (1942–3), 351–3.

Boyd, R., *Australia's home; Its origins, builders and occupiers*, Melbourne (1952).

British Parliamentary Papers. First and second reports of the Colonization Commissioners for South Australia (1836 and 1841).

British Parliamentary Paper. Second Report of the select committee for South Australia (1841).

Brush, J. H., and Gauthier, H. L., 'Service centres and consumer trips: studies on the Philadelphia metropolitan fringe', *University of Chicago, Department of Geography, Research Paper, No. 113,* Chicago (1968).

Burgess, H. T., *The cyclopedia of South Australia: An historical and commercial review: Descriptive and biographical facts, figures, and illustrations: An epitome of progress,* Adelaide, 2 vols. (1907 and 1909).

Burroughs, P., *Britain and Australia, 1831–1855: A study in Imperial relations and Crown Lands administration,* Oxford (1967).

Butlin, N. G., *Australian domestic product, investment and foreign borrowing, 1861–1938/39,* Cambridge (1962).

Butlin, N. G., *Investment in Australian economic development, 1861–1900,* Cambridge (1964).

Butterfield, M. C., *The A.M.P. land development scheme,* The Australian Mutual Provident Society, Sydney (1958).

Buxton, G. L., *South Australian Land Acts, 1869–1885,* Libraries Board of S.A., Adelaide (1968).

Buxton, G. L., *The Riverina, 1861–1891: An Australian regional study,* Melbourne (1967).

Callaghan, A. R., 'The recovery of wheat prices and some agricultural reflections thereon', *S.A. Journal of Agriculture,* XL, Adelaide, (1936–7), 916–24.

Callaghan, A. R., and Millington, A. J., *The wheat industry in Australia,* Sydney (1956).

Cam, Helen M., *The hundred and the hundred rolls,* London (1930).

Cannon, M., *The Land-boomers,* Melbourne (1966).

Chauncy, W. S., *A guide to South Australia, being a descriptive account of the colony addressed to intending emigrants, and containing the latest authentic information,* London (1849 and 1850).

Clark, A. H., *The invasion of New Zealand by people, plants and animals, the South Island,* Rutgers, University Studies in Geography No. 1, New Brunswick (1949).

Cockburn, R., *Pastoral Pioneers of South Australia*, 2 vols., Adelaide (1925 and 1927).

Commonwealth Scientific and Industrial Research Organisation (C.S.I.R.O.), (formerly Council for Scientific and Industrial Research), *Annual Reports*, Melbourne (1926/7–).

Cook, L. J., 'The improvement of pastures', *S.A. Journal of Agriculture*, XXVI, Adelaide (1922–3), 1042–5.

Cook, J. L., 'Resumé of 12 years pasture experimental work at Kybybolite', *S.A. Journal of Agriculture*, XXXVII, Adelaide (1933–4), 248–60.

Cook, L. J., *An agricultural history of Kybybolite*, mimeographed, 12 pp., n.d. (probably *c*.1957).

Cornish, E. A., 'Yield trends in the wheat belt of South Australia during 1896–1941.' *Australian Journal of Scientific Research*, series B, Biological Sciences, II, Melbourne (1949), 83–136.

Correll, J., 'Drilling grain crops with fertilizers', Paper given at *Agricultural Bureau of S.A., Eighth Congress*, Government Printer, Adelaide (1896), 7.

Cowper, W., *The Task*, 1785, Republished in *W. Cowper, Poetry and Prose*, ed. B. Spiller, London (1968).

Darby, H. C., 'On the relations of geography and history', *Transactions of the Institute of British Geographers*, XIX, London (1953), 1–11; Reprinted in *Geography in the twentieth century*, ed. by G. Taylor, London (1957), 640–52.

Darby, H. C., 'The changing English landscape', *Geographical Journal*, CXVII, London (1951), 377–98.

Davison, G., 'Public utilities and the expansion of Melbourne in the 1880s', *Australian Economic History Review*, X, Sydney (1970), 169–89.

Department of Mines, South Australia, *North Adelaide plains: Progress information on the ground water situation, Jan. 1969*, Adelaide (1969).

Dick, E., *The lure of the land: A social history of the Public Lands from the Articles of Confederation to the New Deal*, Lincoln, Neb., (1970).

Dictionary of national biography, 63 vols., London (1885–1900), and supplements.

Donald, C. M., 'Pastures', in *Introducing South Australia*, ed. R. J. Best, Adelaide (1958), 149–155.

Donald, C. M., 'Innovation in Australian agriculture', in *Agriculture in the Australian economy*, éd. D. B. Williams, Sydney (1968), 57–86.

Donald, C. M., 'Phosphates in Australian agriculture', *Journal of the Australian Institute of Agricultural Science*, XXX, Sydney (1964), 75–105.

Donald, C. M., 'The progress of Australian agriculture and the role of pastures in environmental change', *Australian Journal of Science*, XXVII, Sydney (1965), 187–98.

Duncan, H., *The colony of South Australia*, London (1850).

Dunsdorfs, E., *The Australian wheat-growing industry, 1788–1948*, Melbourne (1956).

Dutton, F. S., *South Australia and its mines, with an historical sketch of the Colony*, London (1846).

Dyos, H. J. (ed.), *The study of urban history*, London (1968).

Education in South Australia: Report of the Committee of Enquiry into education in South Australia, 1969–70, (the Karmel Report), Adelaide (1971).

Ekwall, E., *The Oxford dictionary of English place-names*, Oxford (1935).

Faludi, A., 'Der Wiener Wald-und Wiesengürtel und der Ursprung der "green belt"-Idee', *Raumsforschung and Raumordnung*, V, Berlin (1967), 193–206.

Fenner, C., *South Australia: a geographical study*, Sydney (1931).

Finnis, H. J., 'Village settlements on the River Murray', *Proceedings, Royal Geographical Society, South Australia*, LX, Adelaide (1959), 87–106.

French, R. J., 'New facts about fallowing', *S.A. Journal of Agriculture*, LXVII, Adelaide (1963–4), 42–8 and 76–9.

French, R. J., *Soils and agriculture of the Northern and Yorke Peninsula regions of South Australia*, Department of Agriculture, South Australia, Adelaide (1968).

French, R. J., and Rudd, C. L., 'Yield increases with superphosphate', *S.A. Journal of Agriculture*, LXX, Adelaide (1966–7), 336–40.

Frome, E. C., *Instructions for the interior survey of South Australia*, Adelaide (1840).

Gates, Lillien F., *Land policies of Upper Canada*, Toronto (1968).

George, H., *Progress and Poverty*, London (1883).

Glynn, S., *Urbanization in Australian history*, Melbourne (1970).

Goheen, P. G., 'Victorian Toronto, 1850–1900: Pattern and process of growth', *University of Chicago, Department of Geography, Research Paper, No. 127*, Chicago (1970).

Goode, J. R., 'Clover leys lift wheat and wool output', *S.A. Journal of Agriculture*, LXVI, Adelaide (1962–3), 358–60.

Gooden, G. W., and Moore, T. L., *Fifty years' history of the town of Kensington and Norwood*, Adelaide (1903).

Gordon, D. J., *Handbook of South Australia: Progress and resources*, Adelaide (1908).

Gordon, D. J., and Ryan, V. H. (eds.), *Handbook of South Australia*, Published in connection with the visit of the British Association for the Advancement of Science, Australian Meeting, Adelaide (1913), Adelaide (1914).

Gordon, D. J., *The 'Nile' of Australia, nature's gateway to the Interior. A plea for the greater utilization of the Murray and its tributaries*, Adelaide (1906), 2nd edit. with amendments (1908).

Gordon, D. J., *Shall we hold the South-East? A question for electors*, Adelaide (1902). Reprinted from *The S. Australian Register*.

Gordon, D. J., *The Central State*, Adelaide (1903).

Gourlay, R. F., *Statistical account of Upper Canada*, 2 vols., Vol. I, *A general introduction to statistical accounts of Upper Canada*, London (1822).

Griffin, T. C., 'The evolution and duplication of a pattern of urban growth', *Economic Geography*, XXXXI, Worcester, Mass. (1965), 133–56.

Griffiths, R. L., 'Fallowing and cultivation methods for sandy soils', *S.A. Journal of Agriculture*, XXXIII, Adelaide (1929–30), 513–23.

Griffiths, R. L., 'Wind erosion of soils in the agricultural areas', *S.A. Journal of Agriculture*, XL, Adelaide (1936–7), 25–40.

Griffiths, R. L., 'Efficient wheat growing methods', *S.A. Journal of Agriculture*, XXXV, Adelaide (1931–2), 1086–95.

Griffiths, R. L., 'Rotation and cropping methods', *S.A. Journal of Agriculture*, XXX, Adelaide (1926–7), 1122–7.

Grigg, D. B., 'Small and large farms in England and Wales', *Geography*, XLVIII, Sheffield (1963), 268–79.

Handbook for government surveyors, Government Printer, Adelaide (1887), 4th edit. (1914).

Handlin, O., and Burchard, J. (eds.), *The historian and the city*, Cambridge, Mass. (1963).

Harcus, W. (ed.), *South Australia: Its history, resources and productions*, London (1876).

Harper, N. D., 'The rural and urban frontiers', *Historical Studies, Australia and New Zealand*, X, No. 40, Melbourne (1963), 401–21; Also published in *Australian Journal of Science*, XXV, Sydney (1963), 321–34.

Harris, C., 'Theory and synthesis in historical geography', *Canadian Geographer*, XV, Toronto (1971), 157–72.

Harrison, R., *Colonial sketches: or, five years in South Australia with hints to capitalists and emigrants*, London (1862).

Heathcote, R. L., *Back of Bourke: A study of land appraisal and settlement in semi-arid Australia*, Melbourne (1965).

Heathcote, R. L., and McCaskill, M., 'Historical Geography in Australia and New Zealand', in *Progress in Historical Geography*, ed. A. R. H. Baker, Newton Abbott, Devon (1973).

Herriot, R. I., 'Soil conservation', *S.A. Journal of Agriculture*, XLIV, Adelaide (1940–1), 686–9.

Herriot, R. I., 'Soil conservation: a community problem', *S.A. Journal of Agriculture*, XLVI, Adelaide (1942–3), 376–9.

Herriot, R. I., 'The Cinderella of agriculture', *S.A. Journal of Agriculture*, XLVII, Adelaide (1943–4), 55–7.

Herriot, R. I., 'Making best use of limited rainfall', *S.A. Journal of Agriculture*, XLVII, Adelaide (1943–4), 528–32.

Herriot, R. I., 'Soil erosion: the present position and what it means', *S.A. Journal of Agriculture*, XLVIII, Adelaide (1944–5), 331–4.

Herriot, R. I., 'Soil conservation in relation to methods of production', *S.A. Journal of Agriculture*, XLVIII, Adelaide (1944–5), 349–51.

Hodge, C. P., 'Hints to settlers starting in Mallee lands', *S.A. Journal of Agriculture*, XXV, Adelaide (1921–2), 204–11.

Hofstadter, R., *Social Darwinism in American thought*, Boston (1955).

Hope, A. D., *Poems*, London (1960).

Horton, J., *Six months in South Australia*, London (1838).

Hoskins, W. G., *The making of the English landscape*, London (1955).

Jeanes, W. H., *Glenelg: Birth place of South Australia: A centenary publication to mark the attainment of 100 years of civic administration*, Glenelg (1955).

Jeans, D. N., 'The breakdown of Australia's first rectangular grid survey', *Australian Geographical Studies*, IV, Melbourne (1966), 119–28.

Jeans, D. N., 'Territorial divisions and the location of towns in New South Wales, 1826–1842', *Australian Geographer*, X, Sydney (1967), 243–55.

Jeans, D. N., 'Town planning in New South Wales, 1829–42', *Australian Planning Institute Journal*, III, Sydney (1965), 191–5.

Jeans, D. N., 'Crown lands sales and the accommodation of the small settler in New South Wales, 1825–1842', *Historical Studies, Australia and New Zealand*, XII, Melbourne (1966), 205–12; Renamed *Historical Studies* from Vol. XIII, No. 49, (1967, onwards).

Jessop, W. H. R., *Flindersland and Sturtland, or, the Inside and the Outside of Australia*, 2 vols., London (1862).

Johnson, J. H., 'The suburban expansion of housing in London 1918–1939', in *Greater London*, ed. J. T. Coppock and H. C. Prince, London (1964), 142–66.

Johnston, R. J., 'An outline of the development of Melbourne's street pattern', *Australian Geographer*, X, Sydney (1968), 453–65.

Kelly, C. R., 'Water erosion', *S.A. Journal of Agriculture*, XLIII, Adelaide (1939–40), 451–7.

Kiddle, M. L., *Men of yesterday: A social history of the Western District of Victoria, 1834–1890*, Melbourne (1961).

Lancelott, F., *Australia as it is: Its settlement, farming and gold-fields*, 2 vols., London (1851).

Leeper, G. W. (ed.), *The Australian Environment*, 4th Ed. (1970), Commonwealth Scientific and Industrial Research Organization.

Light, W., *A brief journal of the proceedings of William Light, late Surveyor-General of the province of South Australia, with a few remarks on some of the objections that have been made to them*, Adelaide (1839).

Lobeck, A. K., Gentilli, J. and Fairbridge, R. W. *Physiographic diagram of Australia*, Geographical Press, Columbia University, New York (1951).

Lowe, F., 'Dust storms in Australia', *Commonwealth of Australia, Bureau of Meteorology, Bulletin No. 28*, Melbourne (1943).

Lowrie, W., 'The farm', *S.A. Journal of Agriculture*, I, Adelaide (1897–8), 16–19.

Lowrie, W., 'South Australian farming', Paper given at *Agricultural Bureau of S.A., Second Congress*, Government Printer, Adelaide (1890), 8.

Lowrie, W., 'The position of agricultural practice in the State', in *Handbook of South Australia*, ed. D. J. Gordon and V. H. Ryan, Adelaide (1914), 115.

McCarty, J. W., 'Australian capital cities in the nineteenth century', *Australian Economic History Review*, X, Sydney (1970), 107–140.

McIntosh, S., 'Irrigation and reclamation', *S.A. Journal of Agriculture*, XV, Adelaide (1911–12), 806–13.

Mckintosh, W. A., and Joerg, W. L. G. (eds.), *Canadian frontiers of settlement*, 9 vols., Toronto (1934–40), Vol. II, (1934).

Mann, W., *Six years' residence in the Australian provinces, ending in 1839 . . . exhibiting their capabilities of colonization . . . with an account of New Zealand*, London (1839).

Marsh, G. P., *Man and nature, or, physical geography as modified by human action*, London (1864).

Marshall, Ann, 'The growth of subdivision in the Adelaide urban area'. *Proceedings, Royal Geographical Society, South Australia*, LXII, Adelaide (1960–61), 65–68.

Marshall, Ann, ' "Desert" becomes "Downs" : The impact of a scientific discovery', *Australian Geographer*, XII, Sydney (1972), 23–34.

Marston, H. R., Thomas, R. G., Murnane, D., Lines, E. W. L., McDonald, I. W., Moore, H. O., and Bull, L. B., 'Studies on coast disease in sheep in South Australia', *Council for Scientific and Industrial Research, Bulletin 113*, Melbourne (1938).

Martin, A. S., *Aspects of South Australian Lands*, Adelaide (1958). This first appeared as an article in *The Valuer*, April (1958), 76–108.

Maslen, T. J., (A. F. Gardiner), *The friend of Australia, or, a plan for exploring the interior, and for carrying on a survey of the whole continent of Australia*, London (1830).

Meinig, D. W., 'Goyder's line of rainfall: The role of a geographical concept in South Australian land policy and agricultural settlement', *Agricultural History*, XXXV, Urbana, Illinois (1961), 202–14.

Meinig, D. W., *On the margins of the good earth: the South Australian wheat frontier, 1869–1884*, Monograph series, 2, Association of American Geographers, Chicago (1962).

Mitchell, B. R., *Abstract of British historical statistics*, Cambridge (1962).

Mitchell, T. J., 'J. W. Wainwright: the industrialization of South Australia', *Australian Journal of Politics and History*, VIII, Melbourne (1962), 27–40.

Moon, Karen, 'Perception and appraisal of the South Australian landscape, 1836–1850', *Proceedings, Royal Geographical Society, South Australia*, LXX, Adelaide (1969), 41–64.

Morphett, G. C., *The life and letters of Sir John Morphett*, Adelaide (1936).

Northcote, K. H., *An atlas of Australian soils*, Melbourne (1960).

Oldham, W., *The land policy of South Australia from 1830 to 1842*, Adelaide (1917).

Oldham, W., 'How Adelaide was bought and sold', *Proceedings, Royal Geographical Society, South Australia*, XLV, Adelaide (1944–45), 15–23.

O'Driscoll, E. P. D., 'The hydrology of the Murray Basin province in South Australia', *Geological Survey of South Australia, Bulletin No. 35*, 2 vols., Adelaide (1960).

Osborn, F. J., *Green-Belt cities: The British contribution*, London (1946).

Owen, R., *A new view of society . . .: Mr. Owen's report to the Committee of the Association for the Relief of the Manufacturing and Labouring Poor*, London, 3rd Ed. (1817).

Owen, R., *Report to the county of Lanark for a plan for relieving public distress . . .*, Glasgow (1821).

Pascoe, J. J. (ed.), *History of Adelaide and vicinity with a general sketch of the Province of South Australia and biographies of representative men*, Adelaide (1901).

Pascoe, T., 'Dry farming: Professor Campbells' system of soil culture', *S.A. Journal of Agriculture*, IX, Adelaide (1905–6), 766–71.

Pattinson, W. D., 'Beginnings of the American rectangular survey system, 1784–1800', *University of Chicago, Department of Geography, Research Paper, No. 50*, Chicago (1957).

Penn, W., *Some fruits of solitude, in Reflections and maxims relating to the conduct of human life*, Philadelphia (1663).

Perkins, A. J., 'Irrigation on the Murray: Utilization of the swamp lands', *S.A. Journal of Agriculture*, VI, Adelaide (1902–3), 489–90; 532–6; 592–5; 659–64.

Perkins, A. J., *An inquiry into South-Eastern conditions*, Adelaide (1904).

Perkins, A. J., 'Possibilities of increased production in our rural industries', *S.A. Journal of Agriculture*, XIII, Adelaide (1919–20), 396–421.

Perkins, A. J., 'Is rural production on the decline in South Australia and if so what are the factors contributing thereto?', *S.A. Journal of Agriculture*, XXIX, Adelaide (1925–6), 103–43.

Perkins, A. J., 'Ten years' progress in wheat growing', *S.A. Journal of Agriculture*, XXXI, Adelaide (1927–8), 240–53.

Perkins, A. J., 'The rise and progress of the South Australian fruit-growing areas on the River Murray', *S.A. Journal of Agriculture*, XXV, Adelaide (1921–2), 488–97.

Perkins, A. J., 'Financial results of two years farming on a Murray Mallee farm', *S.A. Journal of Agriculture*, XXXV, Adelaide (1931–2), 728–40; 1066–85; 1168–76; 1316–39.

Perkins, A. J., 'Mallee farm costing', *S.A. Journal of Agriculture* XXXVII, Adelaide (1933–4), 635–48; 768–91; 929–58.

Perkins, A. J., 'Some parting reflections on wheat growing in South Australia', *S.A. Journal of Agriculture*, XXXVIII, Adelaide (1934–5), 696–717.

Perkins, A. J., 'Goyder's Line of Rainfall', *S.A. Journal of Agriculture*, XXXIX, Adelaide (1935–6), 78–84.

Perkins, A. J., 'Our wheat growing areas profitable and unprofitable', *S.A. Journal of Agriculture*, XXXIX, Adelaide (1935–6), 1199–222.

Perry, T. M., *Australia's first frontier: The spread of settlement in New South Wales, 1788–1829*, Melbourne (1963).

Pike, D., *Paradise of dissent: South Australia, 1829–1857*, Melbourne (1957).

Pike, D., 'The utopian dreams of Adelaide's founders', *Proceedings, Royal Geographical Society, South Australia*, LIII, Adelaide (1951–2), 65–77.

Podmore, F., *Robert Owen: a biography*, London (1923).

Powell, J. M., *The public lands of Australia Felix: Settlement and land appraisal in Victoria, 1834–91, with special reference to the Western Plains*, Melbourne (1970).

Pred, A., 'Industrialization, initial advantage, and American metropolitan growth', *Geographical Review*, LV, New York (1965), 158–85.

Price, A. G., *The foundation and settlement of South Australia, 1829–1845*, Adelaide (1924).

Prince, H. C., 'North-west London, 1814–1863' and '1864–1914', in *Greater London*, ed. J. T. Coppock, and H. C. Prince, London (1964), 80–141.

Prince, H. C., 'The real, imagined, and abstract worlds of the past', in *Progress in Geography* No. 3, London (1972), 3–86.

Province of Ontario, Department of Archives, *Annual Reports*, Toronto (1903–).

Rasmussen, W. D. (ed.), *Readings in the history of American agriculture*, Urbana, Illinois (1960).

Ratcliffe, F. N., 'Soil drift in the arid pastoral areas of South Australia', *Council for Scientific and Industrial Research, Pamphlet No. 64*. Melbourne (1936).

Reeder, D. A., 'A theatre of suburbs: Some patterns of development in west London, 1801–1911', in *The study of urban history*, ed. H. J. Dyos, London (1968), 142–66.

Reeves, W. P., *State experiments in Australia and New Zealand*, 2 vols., London (1908). Re-issued in Melbourne, 1969, with an introduction by J. Child.

Report of the First Interstate Dry Farming Conference, Adelaide 1911, March 6–8th, Government Printer, Adelaide (1911).

Reps, J. W., 'The green belt concept', *Town and Country Planning*, XXVIII, London (1960), 246–50.

Reps, J. W., 'Town planning in colonial Georgia', *Town Planning Review*, XXX, Liverpool (1959–60), 273–85.

Reps, J. W., *The making of urban America: A history of city planning in the United States*, Princetown, N.J. (1965).

Richardson, A. E. V., and Gurney, H. C., 'Nitrogen in relation to cereal culture', *S.A. Journal of Agriculture*, XXXVIII, Adelaide (1934–5), 954–71.

Riceman, D. S., 'Mineral deficiency and pasture establishment in the Coonalpyn Downs, South Australia', *S.A. Journal of Agriculture*, LIV, Adelaide (1950–1), 132–40.

Riceman, D. S., and Donald, C. M., 'Copper response on "coasty" calcareous soils in South Australia', *S.A. Journal of Agriculture*, XLII, Adelaide (1938–9), 959–64.

Riceman, D. S., Donald, C. M., and Piper, C. S., 'A copper deficiency in plants at Robe, South Australia', *Council for Scientific and Industrial Research, Pamphlet No. 78*, Melbourne (1938).

Roberts, S. H., *The history of Australian land settlement, 1788–1920*, Melbourne (1924).

Roberts, S. H., 'The history of the pioneer fringes in Australia', in 392–404. *Pioneer Settlement*, ed. J. L. G. Joerg, American Geographical Society, Special Publication No. 14, New York (1932).

Robinson, A. H., 'Stomach worms in sheep', *S.A. Journal of Agriculture*, XXIX, Adelaide (1925–6), 640–9.

Roediger, W. V., 'Erosion of farm lands—cause and control', *S.A. Journal of Agriculture*, XLVI, Adelaide (1942–3), 102–3.

Ross, R. D., 'Scrubland cultivation in South Australia', *Proceedings, Royal Agricultural and Horticultural Society, South Australia*, Adelaide (1881–2), 29–40.

Russel, A., *William James Farrer, a biography*, Melbourne (1949).

Russel, A., *A tour through the Australian colonies in 1839*, Glasgow (1840).

Rutherford, J., 'Interplay of American and Australian ideas for the development of water projects in Northern Victoria', *Annals of the Association of American Geographers*, LIV, Lawrence, Kansas, (1964), 88–106.

Saunders, D. A. L., 'Three factors behind the form of Melbourne's nineteenth-century suburbs', in *Urban re-development in Australia*, ed. P. N. Troy, 1–18; Papers presented to an urban seminar held at Australian National University, (Oct. and Dec., 1966), Research School of Social Sciences, Canberra (1966).

Scott, H. J., *South Australia in 1887: A handbook for the Adelaide Jubilee International Exhibition*, Adelaide, 1887. Another edition, *South Australia in 1887–8*, was published in 1888 for the Centennial International Exhibition, Melbourne (1888).

Shann, E. O. G., *An economic history of Australia*, Cambridge (1930).

Sharp, G., *A general plan for laying out towns and townships of the new-acquired lands in the East Indies, America, or elsewhere*, (?) London (1794 and 1804).

Sharp, G., *Account of the ancient division of the English nation into hundreds and tythings*, London (1794).

Shepard, P., 'English reaction to the New Zealand landscape before 1850', *Pacific Viewpoint Monograph*, IV, Wellington (1971).

Shepard, R. G., 'The hydrology of the northern Adelaide Plains basin', *Mining Review*, Department of Mines, No. 125, Adelaide (1966).

Sidney, S., *The three colonies of Australia: New South Wales, Victoria, South Australia: Their pastures, copper mines, and gold fields*, London (1852 and 1853).

Sinnett, F., *An account of the Colony of South Australia*, prepared for distribution at the International Exhibition of 1862 London, London (1862).

Smailes, P. J., 'Some aspects of the South Australian urban system', *Australian Geographer*, XI, Sydney (1969), 29–51.

Smillie, W., *The Great South Land: our articles on emigration, designed to exhibit the principles and progress of the new colony of South Australia*, Stirling (1838).

Smith, B., *The European vision and the South Pacific, 1768–1850*, Oxford (1960).

Smith, D. L., 'Market gardening at Adelaide's urban fringe', *Economic Geography*, XLII, Worcester, Mass. (1966), 19–36.

Smith, H. Nash, *The virgin land: The American West as symbol and myth*, New York (1950).

Society for the diffusion of useful knowledge, *British Husbandry*, 2 vols., London (1833 and 1837).

South Australian Government, *Report on the metropolitan area of Adelaide proposed by the town-planning committee*, Government Printer, Adelaide (1962).

South Australian Government, Land Development Executive, Department of Lands, *Progress in land development (non-irrigation)*, Adelaide (1946–62).

South Australian Land Company, *Proposal to His Majesty's government for founding a colony on the southern coast of Australia*, London (1831).

Spafford, W. J., 'Some necessary improvements in our farming practice', *S.A. Journal of Agriculture*, XXIV, Adelaide (1920–1), 815–20.

Spafford, W. J., 'South Australian agriculture and its requirements from science', *S.A. Journal of Agriculture*, XXVI, Adelaide (1922–3), 17–40.

Spafford, W. J., 'The control of drifting sand', *S.A. Journal of Agriculture*, XXXII, Adelaide (1928–9), 700–9.

Spence, Catherine A., *Autobiography*, Adelaide (1910).

Sprigg, R., 'The geology of the South-East Province, South Australia, with special reference to Quaternary coastline migrations and modern beach developments', *Geological Survey of South Australia, Bulletin, No. 29*, Adelaide (1952).

Stanislawski, D., 'The origin and spread of the grid-iron town', *Geographical Review*, XXXVI, New York (1946), 105–20.

Stephens, C. G., Herriot, R. I., Downes, R. G., Langford-Smith, T. and Acock, A. M., 'A soil, land use, and erosion survey of part of County Victoria, South Australia.' *C.S.I.R., Australia, Bulletin, No. 188*, Melbourne (1945).

Stephens, J., *The land of promise: Being an authentic and impartial history of the rise and progress of the new British province of South Australia*, London (1839). Later in the same year issued as *The history of the rise and progress of the new British province of South Australia*.

Stevenson, G., 'Three letters on agriculture and gardening in South Australia', delivered to the Adelaide Mechanics Institute during late 1839, *South Australian Magazine*, Adelaide (1840), 21–56.

Stow, J. P., *South Australia: Its history, productions, and natural resources*. Written for the Calcutta Exhibition, Adelaide (1884).

Stretton, H., *Ideas for Australian cities*, Adelaide (1970).

Summers, W. L., 'Fallowing in South Australia', *S.A. Journal of Agriculture*, VIII, Adelaide (1904–5), 141–3.

Summers, W. L., 'Fallowing', *S.A. Journal of Agriculture*, XI, Adelaide (1907–8), 56–60.

Summers, W. L., *Notes on agriculture in South Australia*, Agricultural Bureau pamphlet, Adelaide (1908).

Symon, D. E., *A bibliography of Subterranean Clovers together with a descriptive introduction*, Mimeographed Publication No. 1, Commonwealth Bureau of Pastures and Field Crops, Commonwealth Agricultural Bureau, Hurley, Berkshire (1961).

Thernstrom, S., and Sinnett, R. (eds.), *Nineteenth-century cities: Essays in the new urban history*, New Haven (1969).

Thomas, D., *London's Green Belt*, London (1970).

Thomas, W. L., Jr. (ed. with the collaboration of Carl O. Sauer, Marston Bates and Lewis Mumford), *Man's Role in changing the face of the earth*, Chicago (1956).

Thomson, K. W., 'Urban settlement and the wheat frontier in the Flinders Ranges, South Australia', *Proceedings, Royal Geographical Society, South Australia*, LX, Adelaide (1958–9), 25–37.

Thrower, N. J., *Original survey and land subdivision: A comparative study of the form and effect of contrasting cadastral surveys*, Monograph Series, No. 4, Association of American Geographers, Chicago (1966).

Tiver, N. S., 'Deficiencies in South Australian soils', *S.A. Journal of Agriculture*, LIX, Adelaide (1955–6), 100–13.

Tiver, N. S., 'Scrub to pasture in the South-East', *S.A. Journal of Agriculture*, LXII, Adelaide (1958–9), 117–34.

Trollope, A., *Australia and New Zealand*, Melbourne, 1873; and London, 1876, Reprinted as *Australia by Anthony Trollope*, ed. by P. D. Edwards and R. B. Joyce, Brisbane (1967).

Trollope, A., *An Autobiography*, London, 2 vols. (1883).

Vowles, T. H., 'Costs of production and land values in the Mallee areas over 20 years', *S.A. Journal of Agriculture*, XL, Adelaide (1936–7), 354–6.

Wakefield, E. G., *Plan of a company to be established for the purpose of founding a colony in South Australia. Purchasing land therein and preparing the land so purchased for the reception of emmigrants*, London (1832).

Wallace, A. R., *Land nationalisation, its necessity and its aims*, London (1882).

Ward, D., 'The pre-urban cadaster and the urban pattern of Leeds', *Annals of the Association of American Geographers*, LII, Lawrence, Kansas (1962), 152–66.

Ward, D., *Cities and immigrants: A geography of change in Nineteenth-Century cities*, New York (1971).

Ward, E., *The South-Eastern district of South Australia*, Adelaide (1869).

Ward, L. K., 'The underground water resources of the South-Eastern portions of South Australia', *South Australian Department of Mines, Bulletin, No.* 19, Adelaide (1941).

Ward, R., *The Australian legend*, Melbourne (1958).

Warner, S. B., *Streetcar suburbs: The process of growth in Boston, 1870–1900*, Cambridge, Mass. (1962).

Waterson, D. B., *Squatter, selector and store-keeper: A history of the Darling Downs, 1859–1893*, Sydney (1968).

Watson, J. A. S., *The history of the Royal Agricultural Society of England, 1839–1939*, London (1939).

Webb, S. J., and B., *English local government: Statutory authorities for special purposes*, 8 vols. (1906–1929), Vol. I, *The parish and the county*, London (1906).

Webber, G. D., 'Clovers will lift soil fertility and production', *S.A. Journal of Agriculture*, LXVII. Adelaide (1963–64), 354–60.

Whitworth, R. P., *Bailliere's South Australian Gazetteer and Road Guide*, Adelaide (1866).

Wilkinson, G. B., *The working man's handbook to South Australia*, London (1849).

Williams, M., 'Delimiting the spread of settlement: An examination of evidence in South Australia', *Economic Geography*, XLII, Worcester, Mass. (1966), 336–55.

Williams, M., 'Early morphological maps of Australian towns', *Geographical Journal*, CXXX, London (1964), 309–10.

Williams, M., *Adelaide: Longmans Australian Geographies, No. 26.* Melbourne (1966).

Williams, M., 'Early town plans in South Australia', *Australian Planning Institute Journal*, IV, Sydney (1966), 45–51.

Williams, M. (ed.), *South Australia from the air*, Printed for the meeting of the Australian and New Zealand Association for the Advancement of Science, Adelaide (1969).

Williams, M., 'The spread of settlement in South Australia', in *Settlement and Encounter: essays presented to Sir Grenfell Price*, ed. F. Gale and G. H. Lawton, Melbourne (1969), 1–51.

Williams, M., 'Gawler: The changing geography of a South Australian country town', *Australian Geographer*, IX, Sydney (1964), 195–206.

Williams, M., 'Two studies in the historical geography of South Australia', in *Studies in Australian Geography*, ed. G. H. Dury, and M. I. Logan, Melbourne (1968), 71–98.

Williams, M., 'The parkland towns of Australia and New Zealand', *Geographical Review*, LVI, New York (1966), 67–89.

Williams, M., 'Periods, places and themes, a review and prospect of Australian historical geography', *Australian Geographer*, IV, Sydney (1971), 403–16.

Williams, M., 'Simplicity and stability in rural areas: The example of the Pinnaroo district of South Australia', *Geografiska Annaler*, LIV Series B, Stockholm (1972), 117–35.

Williams, R. T., 'Vegetation regions', *Atlas of Australian Resources*, Department of National Development, Canberra (1955).

Wittfogel, K. A., 'The hydraulic civilizations', in *Man's role in changing the face of the earth*, ed. W. L. Thomas, Jr., Chicago (1956), 152–64.

Wood, J. G., 'The floristics and ecology of the Mallee', *Transactions, Royal Society of South Australia*, LIII, Adelaide (1929), 359– .

Wood, J. G., *The vegetation of South Australia*, Adelaide (1937).

Worsnop, T., *History of the City of Adelaide: From the foundation of the province of South Australia in 1836, to the end of the Municipal year, 1877*, Adelaide (1878).

Yi-Fu Tuan, 'Man and nature', *Landscape*, XV, San Francisco (1966), 30–6.

Index

The chapter headings and sub-headings in the Contents pages give a good guide to the topical content of this book, where topics straddle several chapters, however, they are indexed. Only the main or important counties, hundreds, townships, and streets and suburbs of Adelaide are indexed below, and they are listed under those headings.

74-1847

919.42
W67

Williams, Michael.
The making of the South Australian
landscape.

Mount Mary College

Library

Milwaukee, Wisconsin 53222

DEMCO